ALEC ISSIGONIS
THE MAN WHO MADE THE MINI

ALEC ISSIGONIS
THE MAN WHO MADE THE MINI

Jonathan Wood

DB PUBLISHING

First published in Great Britain in 2005 byThe Breedon Books Publishing Company Limited, 3 The Parker Centre, Derby, DE21 4SZ. ISBN 1 85983 449 3

This edition published in Great Britain in 2012 by The Derby Books Publishing Company Limited, 3 The Parker Centre, Derby, DE21 4SZ.

ISBN 978-1-78091-097-0

Printed and bound by Copytech (UK) Limited, Peterborough.

CONTENTS

FOREWORD

by Karl Ludvigsen

'The cutest girls drive Minis.' This was my observation when I first took up residency in London in 1980. Whizzing hither and yon, from Islington to Chelsea, great-looking ladies clearly preferred Minis. Indeed, I met and married a former Mini driver – although by then she'd graduated to a Renault 4, which I learned from Jonathan Wood was among the very few designs by other engineers that Alec Issigonis respected.

I introduced the BMC Mini and its creator to America in the June 1960 issue of *Sports Cars Illustrated*. About the car I said, 'This little automobile is so satisfying and delivers so much fun per cubic foot that it makes you wonder why cars have to be any bigger.' The inimitable Dennis May penned our profile of Issigonis, saying that 'he smokes cigarettes fast and much, talks in staccato rushes but quietly and with invariable courtesy, has a love of paradox and can be epigrammatical without having to reach for his shafts.'

May it was who met my flight at Heathrow on a 1961 visit. We piled into his Mini, which he commenced to fling along highways and byways, carving Mini-sized third lanes wherever possible – and impossible. I leaned over to Dennis and shouted, 'Is this legal?!' It was obvious that the appearance of the Mini on Britain's roads had created a whole new style of motoring.

My 1980 arrival in Britain was to take up a vice-presidency at Ford of Europe. We were preparing the Escort Mark III for launch, and I soon discovered deep concern on the part of Ford of Britain. Ford's UK unit was acknowledged as master of fleet-car sales. Fleets accounted for a substantial chunk of its business, so it was essential that our new Escort find favour with hard-bitten British fleet buyers. Such purchasers, I soon learned, were ultra-wary about the Mark III because it had dreaded front-wheel drive, an amenity they'd come to loathe as a result of their servicing and reliability experiences with front-wheel drive BMC-style. Somehow we convinced them that we were doing it differently.

In a previous Big Three career, with General Motors in the 1960s, I found the ideas of Alec Issigonis being treated with more respect. On a European visit GM's chairman, James Roche, was intrigued by the newly launched Austin 1800. Here was a car, thought Roche, that packaged an amazing amount of space in a vehicle of modest dimensions. On his return he asked styling chief Bill Mitchell to see what kind of car he could conjure up with similar packaging. Bill never received an assignment he liked less; this wasn't his kind of automobile at all. He let the idea quietly expire.

As a Yank I'm disinclined to treat the Mini with quite the reverence that it commands in the UK. Yes, it certainly inspired other designers to look at front-wheel drive in a new way, but – as Jonathan fairly relates – the configuration that everyone copied originated at Turin, not Cowley or Longbridge. So when I'm told that the Mini is the 'most technically significant car in the history of the British motor industry,' my scepticism kicks in.

I'm a huge fan of an earlier Issigonis design, the Morris Minor. It's one of the British motor industry's great tragedies that between Nuffield management's dislike for the Minor and its creator's lack of interest in improving this superb little car it suffered from a serious lack of TLC. The same could be said of the Austin/Morris 1100, an excellent small car that found transatlantic friends as the automatic-transmission Austin America. Packed with positive attributes, the 1100's many virtues would have flourished had its few faults been dealt with.

In fact the author makes a good case for the original Austin Seven as Britain's 'most technically significant car'. Such was its novelty and efficiency that it acquired license builders in America, France and Germany and inspired car makers in Japan. Though it was introduced in 1922, we learn that the Seven was considered by Austins for production after World War Two. Interestingly, Dennis May reported that Issigonis felt that car designers had given up too soon on the solid front axle! As Wood relates, he made good use of it in his much-modified Austin Seven racers.

Fascinatingly portrayed in this biography are the interlinked relationships among Britain's auto makers, component producers and their personnel, relationships that somehow allowed cars to be produced in spite of the pusillanimous posturing of many senior managers. Wood introduces us to these managers as well, men like the decisive Leonard Lord, the indecisive George Harriman and ex-journalist Miles Thomas, well-defined by Wood as the best chief executive the British motor industry never had.

I enjoyed meeting the industry's many characters, such as the car tuner whose 'formidable wife' produced his correspondence on a 1927 Imperial typewriter and the engineer who erected a tent in his sitting room. The latter was a guiding sprit at SU, who in the event of problems with an early version of his firm's electric fuel pump suggested that one should 'tap the pump smartly, though not too vindictively, say, with a spanner'. As the former owner of an MG TC I'm only too familiar with this measure and relieved to learn that the remedy had an official character.

At the heart of this engrossing story is, of course, the most fascinating of all these personalities. Another individual in the story of Alec Issigonis is portrayed as having an 'inverted inferiority complex'; this might have been descriptive of the great man himself. His genius as an innovator was beyond question, and if he had the faculty of convincing others of the applicability of that genius to automobiles large as well as small, that was their problem, not his.

Most compelling was the young Issigonis's determination to forge a career in engineering. He let nothing stand in the way of this objective, least of all his abhorrence of mathematics and his peripatetic secondary education. This focus and drive were with him all his life, as Dennis May wrote: 'Perhaps incapable of true relaxation, Issigonis seemingly isn't happy unless he's as busy as a valve spring. He is an habitual worrier and practically never gets BMC business off his mind.' Here was the secret of the engineer's success: a steadfast commitment to the achievement of his goals in his manner, untrammelled by peripheral considerations. No conventional manager could aspire to be his equal.

Although its subject is the offspring of a Greek father and German mother, this is a very British story. Like the author's superb work, *Wheels of Misfortune*, it illuminates afresh the victories and defeats of a great national motor industry in a manner that should be of profound interest to all in the UK and many abroad. I found it so, and if among my reasons for accepting the invitation to write this foreword was that I'd be one of the first to read Jonathan's latest book, can you blame me? Now it's your turn.

INTRODUCTION AND ACKNOWLEDGEMENTS

OR THE past few years my office wall has been graced by a framed pencil drawing of an engine. To British eyes the power unit is unconventional, a horizontally opposed so-called 'flat' configuration, and is one of a series of sketches executed by Alec Issigonis just prior to the outbreak of World War Two. It was intended for what eventually appeared, in 1948, as the Morris Minor, although by then its creator's bespoke engine had been replaced by the company's existing, more prosaic but reliable, eight horsepower unit.

The drawing is wholly assured in execution but part of its appeal is that the perspective is not quite correct; the pair of offside cylinders do not seem to relate to those on the opposing side. It is a reflection of the fact that Issigonis never received any drawing lessons; his was a natural artistic talent which flowered untainted by practical instruction.

Alec Issigonis was a man, more architect than engineer, of astonishing creativity and influence, so his life is one of particular fascination. In setting it down I have not only told the story in his own words, but also drawn on the recollections of many of his friends and colleagues. The result, I hope, is a portrait where the highs of a career are tempered by lows, and the public face is balanced by insights into how Issigonis spent his leisure hours, both at home and abroad.

First and foremost my thanks should go to Christopher Dowson. As the son of George Dowson, who with Issigonis had built the Lightweight Special in the 1930s, he knew Alec as a youngster and the man who made the Mini was his unofficial godfather, forging a friendship that endured until Issigonis's final days. His recollections of the private face of the subject are at odds with the stridency and intolerance Issigonis often displayed in his professional life. Christopher had committed his own thoughts to paper, which he kindly put at my disposal, and I was able to supplement this account with interviews and correspondence.

Ronald 'Steady' Barker knew Alec Issigonis both professionally, as a motoring journalist on *Autocar* magazine, and as a friend of some 25 years standing. He offered me every assistance, his contributions enlivened by the perception and wit which so invigorate his prose. Dr Alex Moulton, whose professional alliance and friendship with Issigonis found expression in both the Mini and Morris 1100, was similarly generous with his time and his memories. Lord Snowdon recounted some memorable highlights of an enduring friendship and his son, Viscount Linley, a classic car enthusiast, contributed his recollections of his meeting with the creator of the Morris Minor. Fascinating insights into Alec Issigonis's leisure hours during his Oxford years came from Jennifer Gilman and Malcolm Axtell, whose memories began in their respective childhoods and continued until Alec Issigonis left the city in 1963 to live in Birmingham.

No account of Issigonis's career would be complete without a contribution from the late Jack Daniels and I spent an enjoyable day with him when he recounted his many years with 'Issy', as he always referred to him, as his right-hand man and draughtsman. John Sheppard is the sole surviving member of the inner circle of Longbridge-based engineers who created the Mini, and his recollections were marked by their precision and good humour.

Geoffrey Rose's long association with Alec Issigonis spanned his Morris Minor to British Leyland years and his memories were both enlightened and fair minded. Ron Lucas, also now deceased, provided a shrewd assessment of Issigonis's BMC career which he underpinned with candid behind-the-scenes recollections of the Longbridge boardroom.

The view from Cowley was recalled with great clarity by Peter Tothill. Eric Moore's recollections of the Morris experimental department were invaluable, as were the memories of Doreen Schreier. She was Morris's first female engineering apprentice, and in her later years she became Sir Alec's unofficial secretary. She was able to provide revealing insights into the years in which she knew him.

Spen King's recollections began with the view from Rover and he later, as British Leyland's technical supremo, had professional contact with Alec Issigonis. His contribution, as might be expected from the creator of the Range Rover, was infused with depth and relevance.

While John Bilton and Peter Stubbs worked with Alec Issigonis on the Gearless Mini, his last project, their vivid memories of him were coupled with engineering and corporate insights. Charles Bulmer provided an incisive two-faceted view of a man he knew from his time as technical editor and editor of *Motor*, and then from the standpoint of a British Leyland executive.

I obtained a vivid first-hand account of the birth of the Mini-Cooper from the late John Cooper, while Stuart Turner, as BMC's competitions manager, made a characteristically forthright contribution, laced with the humour and pertinence for which he is renowned. And Paddy Hopkirk, who co-drove a Mini-Cooper to provide BMC with its first Monte Carlo Rally victory in 1964, contributed a pithy driver's-eye view of the car's creator. Dr Bernd Pischetsrieder, despite the demands on his time as chairman of Volkswagen, readily answered my questions, both as a relative of Issigonis and as initiator of the new MINI.

I owe particular thanks to former BMC apprentice and BL executive Peter Seymour, whose researches into the histories of the Morris companies and the Corporation have, over the years, greatly expanded my knowledge of both businesses. I am indebted to him for the work he undertook into the life of Leonard Lord, who played such a pivotal role in the career of Alec Issigonis. My researches into his life reach back some 30 years and in that context I should acknowledge contributions from John Barber, Sir Terence Beckett, Ian Duncan, Alan Lamburn, Hamish Orr-Ewing, Lord Stokes of Leyland, John Thornley and Harry Webster.

The task of recording the details of Alec Issigonis's brief career at Alvis was made all the easier by the material generously supplied by Julian Collins, Singapore-based editor of *The Bulletin*, the Alvis Owners' Club's magazine. I also much appreciate the assistance of Rob Golding, author of the definitive *Mini*, for making available hitherto unpublished material supplied to him by BL Cars's public affairs department.

I should also record my grateful thanks to the following in the preparation of this book: Christopher Balfour, Robin Barraclough, Stuart Bladon, Malcolm Bobbitt, Paul Buckett (head of Press and PR Volkswagen), John Burnett (Burlen Fuel Services), Lionel Burrell, Iain Cheyne (Lightweight Special), Tony Clark, Steve Cropley (Editor-in-Chief, *Autocar*), Neville Daniel, Dave Daniels, Jeff Daniels, Lisa Davies and Fenella Whittaker (Institution of Mechanical Engineers), Paul Davies, Harry Edwards (Morris Register), Ian Elliott, Martin Eyre, Chris Gould, Tim Graham, Philip Hall, Anne Hope, Malcolm Jeal, Peter Knight, Peter Lane (Lane Lister Associates), Bob Light (Bugatti Owners' Club) Bob Maher (the Trout, Godstow), Andrew Marfel, Eleanor and Robert McLoughlin, Professor Ian Milburn, Liz Morgan-Lewis and Maureen Shettle (University of Surrey), Brian Moylan, Norman Painting, Philip Porter, John Reynolds, Graham Robson, Gurmail Sidhu (12, Westbourne Gardens), Paul Skilleter, Rogers Sogaard, Marc Stretton (*Mini Magazine*), Michael Walden and Lyn Kilpatrick (9, Overhill Road), Allan Webb, Mick Woollett and Michael Worthington-Williams.

My thanks to the staffs of the following libraries and institutions: Abingdon Library, Birmingham Central Library, Birkenhead Library, Kenilworth Library, Croydon Library, National Motor Museum Library, The National Archives, Kew, Liverpool Record Office, Oxford Library, and the libraries of the Royal Society, the Royal Society of Arts and the Vintage Sports-Car Club.

I gratefully acknowledge the assistance of Haymarket Magazines, publishers of *Autocar*, for permission to reproduce engineering drawings from its past issues. Where would we historians be without this marvellous reference source? Details of the current magazine are to be found at www.autocar.co.uk

I should record my appreciation to Karl Ludvigsen for contributing the Foreword to this book. An internationally acclaimed award-winning motoring historian, his works draw on the unique perspective of one who has also held high office in the motor industries on both sides of the Atlantic.

My researches into the life and career of Alec Issigonis date from 1974 when, as a founder member of the staff of *Classic Car* magazine, I contributed a profile of him for our 'Men and Machines' feature, which was complemented by a portrait, the work of acclaimed motoring artist Michael Turner. It is wholly appropriate, therefore, that it has been used for the front cover of this book. Indeed, Sir Alec told me in a letter that he was a reader of *Classic Car* and Michael recalls that when that year he held his first exhibition at The Mall Gallery in London, Issigonis attended and expressed an interest in acquiring the original. This was provided that Turner deleted his likeness: 'I don't want me in it,' he said, which just left the cars! Not surprisingly, Michael was unable to comply.

As far as the content of this book is concerned, I have quite deliberately not recorded the gestation and evolution of Alec Issigonis's production models in very great detail because these have been ably chronicled by others.* But I have sought to identify the influences, both animate and inanimate, that shaped his thinking. This has been a challenging exercise as he was invariably reluctant to acknowledge them, preferring to present his cars as having emerged *in toto* from the recesses of his remarkable mind in much the same way that the goddess Athena sprang fully-armoured from the head of Zeus.

I would welcome comments, great or small, on this book at jonathanwood@eludlow.co.uk and I will be pleased to supply details of the lecture, *Alec Issigonis – The Man Who Made the Mini*, that I have prepared which is based on this work.

I trust that the reader will enjoy what for me was the most demanding but invigorating of commissions.

Jonathan Wood,
Ludlow, Shropshire, April 2005

* *The Mini Story* by Laurence Pomeroy, *The Morris Minor* by Paul Skilleter and *Men and Motors of 'The Austin'* by Barney Sharratt.

Chapter One

WEALTH, A WARSHIP
AND WILLESDEN

'As a small child he was very clever and his father of course was a brilliant man and his grandfather too.'[1]

Hulda Issigonis

TODAY SOME 70 motor manufacturers produce about 41 million cars worldwide. Of these vehicles, an overwhelming 80 percent are driven by their front wheels from engines that are mounted transversely under their bonnets. Yet back in 1959 a mere 25 car makers built some 10.3 million automobiles, of which the vast majority were pushed along by their rear wheels, driven by front-mounted inline engines in a manner laid down in 1891 by the French engineer Emile Levassor. Of this 1959 total, a mere 220,000 or so were front-wheel drive cars and even then most of these retained orthodox north/south located power units.

The vehicle that brought about this radical change to the way in which the world designs its motor cars was the British Motor Corporation's Mini, introduced in 1959. And unlike practically all of its contemporaries this vehicle was the product of a single individual's extraordinary creativity. The Mini, which also bequeathed its name to the language, represented the apogee of Alec Issigonis's career and it also stands out as the most technically significant car in the history of the British motor industry. By virtue of that accolade its creator's reputation as his adopted country's most influential automobile engineer remains unsullied.

There was, however, a downside to this extraordinary achievement. In 1959, the year of the Mini's arrival, the BMC built some 430,000 cars and was the world's fifth-largest motor manufacturer, outside the American Big Three of General Motors, Ford and Chrysler. In Europe only Volkswagen produced more motor vehicles. Thanks to the Mini and its 1100 derivative, output would soar to some 730,000 in 1964. But its descendant, MG Rover, which occupied the site in Longbridge, Birmingham, where the Mini was created, built a little over 105,000 cars in 2004, its last year of production, before calling in the receiver in 2005.

The reasons for the collapse of Britain's last volume car manufacturer are multifarious but they are deep rooted. One unpalatable truth is that in the 1960s the flair and ingenuity for which the Mini is so rightly famous were not apparent in subsequent larger models. This is because Issigonis's formidable creative ability could only express itself in the design of small cars. Intuitively committed to the need to save weight, he was a minimalist before the word became current. This goes some way to explaining why the Mini's larger-engined successors failed to sell in the expected numbers and was one of the reasons for the BMC tumbling into decline and deficit. As corporate technical director Alec Issigonis, an uncontrolled force who was given a free reign by a weak and vacillating chairman, must share some responsibility for its demise.

While the Mini represents the pinnacle of his career, it was his second significant design. The first, the Morris Minor, was the first British car to sell a million examples. Although not as innovative as the BMC baby, it was more successful, if the criterion of financial return is taken into account. The Minor produced significant profits for its manufacturer while the Mini lost money for much of its production life.

Alec Issigonis's origins were cosmopolitan. Turkish-born of Greek/Bavarian parentage, he was a fairly tall, slightly stooping figure with an aquiline nose and intensely blue twinkling eyes that were alive with creativity and humour. He was a man of contradictions: had it not been for his name, his voice and dress were suggestive of the English upper middle classes, yet this donnish figure designed cars for the masses. He was, by his own admission, arrogant – he readily described himself as 'Arro-gonis' – but he self-deprecatingly considered himself to be 'a mere ironmonger.' Intensely proud of Britain and devoted to its royal family, he venerated the Establishment and also possessed, as one of his friends diplomatically expressed it, 'strong views on certain foreign countries and nationalities.'[2] Roughly translated he was, despite being half Bavarian, stridently anti-German, an ardent Francophile and dismissive of Americans. He also held trenchant views on Britain's coloured immigrant population.

Alec Issigonis thus presents the figure of an automotive Janus. One face is represented by a creative force that changed the course of car design throughout the world. His drawings, which he could produce with astonishing rapidity, delighted the public, who viewed him as a sort of latter-day Leonardo da Vinci. He was disarmingly shy, humorous, charming and excellent company, and he maintained lifelong friendships outside his workplace.

However, his other face reflects a more bigoted, narrow and introspective personality. Throughout much of his motor industry career he could be domineering and dismissive of the opinions of others and he was incapable of according praise or credit to any of his colleagues. The only exception was if the individual in question was of such a lowly order that the approbation was manifestly insincere.

Yet, more positively, an oft-overlooked characteristic is that Alec Issigonis was an intensely practical man who knew how to use tools and did so with remarkable dexterity. His hands, 'big with knobbly knuckles,'[3] as one of his contemporaries described them, were those of the artist-craftsman.

It comes as no surprise to find that his childhood was as unconventional, certainly from a British standpoint, as the cars he produced, and, indeed, goes some way to explaining why he designed them as he did. He was born in Smyrna, Turkey, into the final, flickering years of the Ottoman Empire, the only child of a Greek father and Bavarian mother. His birthplace in Asia Minor was in some respects predictable, because when, in 1425, Smyrna was annexed by the Ottomans, it had been a Greek settlement for some 2,500 years. By the early 20th century about half the city's population was Greek, with only a quarter Turkish and much of the balance made up by Armenians and Jews.

Despite being damaged by earthquakes in the 17th and 18th century, Smyrna, the second city of Turkey, remained an important and prosperous port. This was thanks to its geographical location at the head of a sheltered gulf which protected shipping from the uncertainties of the Aegean Sea. A long established and busy harbour played host to maritime businesses of many kinds and, at some time during the first half of the 19th century, W. Issigonis arrived from his native Greece and established a firm that specialised in the manufacture of manually operated pumps for ships. His business thrived and by 1896 it had expanded to employ '150 to 200 workmen in making and repairing engines, boilers etc.'[4]

These were the years when the British Empire dominated the world, underpinned to a great extent by its shipping and engineering. In 1887 W's eldest son, George Demos Issigonis, the as yet unborn Alec's uncle, who was in his 24th year, became the first of at least three members of the family to expand their horizons and further their education, from a theoretical, practical and social standpoint, in England.

In 1880 George had been apprenticed at his father's works and had also attended the English Commerce School in Smyrna. On arrival in England, he initially took 'private lessons' in engineering subjects,[5] following this, in 1890, by becoming a draughtsman with Taylors Britannia Engine Works in Birkenhead, where he remained until 1890. Nearby Liverpool was at that time Britain's second port after London and its Waterloo district was also the home of a cousin, Constantine Issigonis, who was a book keeper. In 1888 George's father had established a business contact with John Titley, a Liverpool metal broker. Trading from 11, Rumford Place, his home at 85 Newsome Drive was a three-storey semi-detached house which overlooked Newsome Park and just the type of residence to be occupied by a well-to-do Victorian businessman.

Thereafter, from 1890 until 1892, George Issigonis acted as the firm's English representative and continued with his private tutorials. At the end of 1892 he returned to Smyrna to take over as works manager of The W. Issigonis Works and, on the death of his father in December 1893, he became the head of the firm. However, he maintained his contacts with Britain and in June 1896 he was elected an Associate Member of the Institution of Mechanical Engineers.[6]

While George was in England he had been joined there by his 19-year-old nephew, Constantine Demostenes Issigonis, who, in due course, would become Alec's father. He had been born on 1 March 1872, the son of Demostenes and Irene Issigonis who, despite living in Smyrna, were 'both subjects of the Kingdom of Greece.'[7]

Constantine arrived in London in June 1891 and took up residence at 12 Winchester Road, Hampstead. He moved to 12, Porchester Gardens in 1893/94 and later in 1894 his address was recorded as 20, Upper Westbourne Terrace. He may have stayed there for the remainder of his time in the British capital. In 1896 he was to describe himself as an 'engineering student' in pursuit of a career in mechanical engineering. It is not known if he attended a technical college or similar institution or whether, as seems more likely, the instruction was given privately on a tutorial basis, following the precedent established by his uncle.

Some four months after Constantine arrived in England he was joined by his younger brother, Miltiades Demostenes Issigonis. He had also been born in 1872, his birthday being 14 November, so Irene must have become pregnant very soon after Constantine's birth. John Titley in Liverpool, as far as geography would allow, kept a metaphorical and occasional physical eye on both brothers and Miltiades received an allowance from his father which was conveyed to him by the metal broker. Indeed Constantine may well have benefited in a similar way although this is not stated in the surviving documents.

In 1896 both brothers applied for British nationality. It may be that they were following the example of their cousin, the Liverpool-based Constantine, who in 1893 had applied for and been granted this status. Twenty-four-year-old Constantine Demostenes applied to the Home Office in July 1896 but the Certificate of Naturalization was not granted until 28 June 1897.[8] This hiatus was mainly caused by the fact that he had decided to return to Smyrna for two or three months in the summer of 1896, although he may have been away for longer than he intended. His referees were John Titley and James Potter, a civil engineer, Norman Dallas Forbes, William Alfred Malony and Henry Cornelius Usher, a schoolmaster. All, with the exception of Titley, lived in London.[9]

In the meantime Demostenes had also applied and his British nationality was confirmed on 12 December 1896.[10] Some 26 years later, in 1922, both brothers and their descendants would be eternally grateful for their decision to become subjects of Queen Victoria. Throughout the remainder of his life Constantine remained devoted to Britain and its monarchy, a commitment to royalty his son was destined to inherit. Indeed, in later years he recalled that when there was an earthquake in Smyrna, a not infrequent occurrence, his father, looking out of the window and seeing the chimney pots shaking, would invariably exclaim: 'God bless the Queen!'[11]

According to Alec Issigonis,[12] his father returned to Smyrna in 1900, which would have made him 28. There he joined his brother and uncle at the family works and, five years later, in 1905, he married Hulda Josephine Henriette Prokopp, the strong-minded daughter of a Bavarian couple who were family friends. She was aged 19, and was thus some 14 years his junior. Her wealthy father had the distinction of having built Smyrna's first brewery.

Constantine and Hulda's only child was born on 18 November 1906 and christened Alexander Arnold Constantine, names that accurately mirrored his Greek ancestry and the high regard that his father felt for Britain. Known throughout his adult life as Alec, his memories of the family home were of it being 'so large that not only did it have *two* verandas,'[13] there were some parts of it, the servants' quarters for instance, that he never saw. Whenever he went into the town he was accompanied by a *kavass*, a personal servant who doubled as a bodyguard. Then there were family picnics that were 'grand affairs with tables under the trees and servants in attendance.'[14] The party invariably included Hulda's cousin, Hetty Walker, and her children Gerald, May and Tony, who were to share Alec's lessons.

In 1911, when as a five-year-old he might have begun to attend school, perhaps reflecting the family's social standing and wealth, an elderly English governess was recruited to instil in him the essentials of the three R's. While reading can be taken as read, in later years he confessed to finding writing 'a disagreeable occupation'[15] and 'rithmetic even more so. Even though he was coached in the subject by an Irish tutor, he had the greatest difficulty in mastering its most basic essentials and subsequently declared with characteristic disdain: 'All creative people hate mathematics. It's the most uncreative subject you can study, unless you become an Einstein and study it in an abstract, philosophical sense, as to why numbers and things exist.'[16]

This lack of a conventional education would have a profound influence on Issigonis's subsequent career in the British motor industry. Without academic influences to distract him, what might be described as his natural talent was free to flourish. There are parallels here with the life of the Italian-born, French-domiciled artist engineer Ettore Bugatti, whose lack of a technical education allowed his precocious sensibilities to flower unchecked. Like Issigonis he did not appear to lack confidence in his own abilities and one of his more memorable statements, 'I shall never starve because I can do everything'[17] displays sentiments worthy of the creator of the Mini himself. Unlike Issigonis, who would dedicate himself to designing cars for the mass market, Bugatti is forever identified with the expensive and visually exquisite Type 35 racing car of 1924. But the parallels between the two are inescapable and in the 1970s Alec would immodestly but perceptively describe himself as 'the last of the Bugattis.'[18]

There was one discipline in which he displayed a precocious talent and that was drawing, a gift he inherited from Constantine Issigonis. 'My father always had a drawing board in his dressing room,' he remembered. 'As a little boy I used to go and watch him drawing, and when I was quite, quite small I was determined to become an engineer.'[19]

Alec delighted in visiting the family's works. There he encountered the large steam engine that drove machinery throughout the factory and he immediately responded to its leisurely hiss and the scent it generated: a heady combination of hot oil and cotton waste. And then there was the railway. Turkey's system expanded considerably from the late 19th century following a visit to Constantinople in 1898 by the German Kaiser. He financed an extension of the track that had previously stopped at Izmit and then ran on to Konya. This permitted the construction of a spur line from the town of Afyonksrahisar to Smyrna and many of Constantine and Hulda's friends were connected with this work.

It was through their good offices that young Alec was able to secure a number of distinctly unofficial rides on the footplates of locomotives until the escapades were discovered. He paid for his enthusiasm with a severe chastisement, although his fascination with steam remained with him throughout his life. His interest found expression in a miniature railway he built in the garden of his Edgbaston home and for a few years he even toyed with the concept of a steam-powered Mini.

Aeroplanes were another agreeable diversion and aviation and aeronautical matters were an ongoing interest. He was only in his fifth year when, in 1912, his father took him to see the French aviator, Adolphe Pégoud, at the controls of his Blériot monoplane. Pégoud took off at the Paradise racecourse in the hills behind Smyrna and Alec saw him land safely after making a circuit.

This was a period of his life that Issigonis would look back on as being a happy time, although his press officer and friend Tony Dawson[20] believed that 'this semi-secluded upbringing may to some extent account for his apparent shyness and diffidence when meeting strangers.'[21] In fact Issigonis did have playmates. In addition to the Walker children there was another cousin, Peter Giudici, who also lived in the house with his parents. Hulda's sister had married Julielmo Giudici, an Italian living in Smyrna, and her grandson is Dr Bernd Pischetsrieder, today the chairman of Volkswagen. He recalls that both boys were 'excited about motor cars and any other kind of vehicle. They apparently "designed" and assembled all sorts of vehicles as children.'[22]

Alec was seven years old in 1914 when World War One broke out and although the conflict would initially have little impact on the Issigonis family, in retrospect it can be seen as bringing an end to an idyllic but sheltered lifestyle which combined Edwardian opulence within a structured social order in an agreeable Mediterranean climate. In later years one of Alec Issigonis's relatively few indulgences was relaxing with friends at the luxurious Hotel L'Hermitage in Monte Carlo, perhaps echoing those balmy carefree days of his childhood.

Britain declared war on Germany on 4 August 1914 and the Ottoman Empire threw its lot in with the Kaiser. As British subjects the Issigonis family found themselves on the opposing side, although initially the only indication of war was the presence of a French Farman biplane, flown by a British crew, which was seen over Smyrna at about six o'clock every morning. The observer would throw a bomb or two over the side but the only casualties were the occasional donkey or goat that happened to be in the wrong place at the wrong time. One day the Farman did not return to its base on the island of Mytilene, today known as Lesbos, the Germans having dispatched a squadron of Fokkers to bring the lone British aircraft down. Alec's *kavass* took him to see the smouldering remains of the Farman. The crew, who survived, set fire to their craft on the ground.

Initially the Turks treated the Issigonis family with respect and sensitivity. They were escorted to church for Sunday worship and Alec was even taken to the nearby German base, where friendly air staff lifted him into a Fokker's cockpit to sit at the controls. However, when the German army arrived the British community, of which the Issigonis family were prominent but adopted members, conditions grew progressively harsher. Apparently Constantine Issigonis refused to allow his works to be used for the repair of German U-boats and, as a result, the family was interned. These experiences as a small boy may well have coloured Alec's view of Germany, an opinion probably reinforced by World War Two, because a dislike of the country and its people were certainly apparent in his character in the 1950s and maybe before then.

The family no doubt viewed with dismay the calamitous outcome of the

Gallipoli landings of 1915, when British and Australasian troops failed to establish a bridgehead on the Black Sea peninsula and so find a back door into Germany. The Allies finally withdrew early in 1916 after suffering heavy casualties, and it would not be until September 1918 that General Allenby, having taken Jerusalem, pushed the Turkish army back through Syria. This led to the Ottoman surrender being signed on 30 October 1918, 12 days before the ending of the war in Europe.

This Armistice of Mudros brought only a short-lived peace. In an attempt to bring Greece into the war, in 1915 the British government had offered its prime minister, Eleutherios Venizelos, 'important territorial concessions on the coast of Asia Minor'[23] which could only mean Turkey. Yet despite his wish to join the Allies, for domestic reasons Venizelos was not able to do so until 1917.

Just seven months after the Ottoman defeat, on 15 May 1919, Venizelos's troops entered Smyrna, to the delight of the Greek population and the blessing of the city's Metropolitan, who was a high-ranking official in the Greek church, above the status of an archbishop. But the centuries-old enmity between the two nations spilled over and the Greeks then embarked on a systematic programme of massacring many members of the city's Turkish population and its adjoining province. The world stood by aghast but there was little that could be done. Once the Allies had enticed Greece into the war, the price they paid was the tragedy of Smyrna.

Alec Issigonis would, in later years, recall the arrival of the Greek air force, complete with Sopwiths, SPAD fighters and Breuget bombers. Yet, more significantly in the light of his own career, this period also marked his first encounter with motor cars. Then, as now, Turkey had no indigenous motor industry, so all automobiles were imported and these were mostly of American origin. Alec could not remember exactly how old he was when he first saw a motor vehicle: 'When I was eight, or ten. It was either a Willys-Overland or Model T Ford.'[24] This would place it at some time during the war, between 1914 and 1917.

During the Greek occupation of the city, which began in 1919 when Alec was 13 and lasted until 1922, when he was 15, he saw a car that was destined to make a deep impression on him. It was an example of a Cadillac V8 which belonged to a Mr Smith, an employee of the Standard Oil Company of New Jersey. Young Alec became friends with the chauffeur, who would take him for short, subversive rides. 'This car ran with no noise at all; he used to drive it with the tyres running on the tram lines, which were just the right gauge to avoid the rough cobbles. It was then perfection – not a sound,' he remembered. 'In those days I was not even aware of the existence of the Rolls-Royce.'[25]

Such happy excursions were soon overtaken by international events. The

Greek invasion of Smyrna had been formalised on 10 August 1920 by the signing of the Treaty of Sèvres, when the victorious Allies made a peace settlement with Ottoman Turkey. The most significant condition, as far as this narrative is concerned, was that Greece was to acquire Thrace and Turkish islands in the Aegean, together with a five-year administration of Smyrna, pending a plebiscite. As a result of these and other conditions Turkey was restricted to a small area around Constantinople and was allowed to retain Anatolia.

The harsh conditions demanded by the Sèvres agreement, in particular the concessions made to Greece, caused widespread resentment throughout the country. Under the leadership of Mustafa Kemal, victor of Gallipoli, an uprising against the Greek occupation began in January 1921. An armistice between the two sides was proposed in March 1922 but rejected by the Turks. On 26 August the Greek army was subjected to an intense artillery barrage, soon scattered and fell back on Smyrna where ships were waiting.

It was soon over. On 9 September Mustapha Kemal rode into the city, followed by more Turkish troops who wasted little time in avenging the Greek atrocities of three years before. The Metropolitan was assassinated and many members of the Greek population massacred. Then fire broke out in their quarter, which was to destroy about half the metropolis, leaving a visual scar on Smyrna that was still apparent in the 1960s. Then the French travel writer, André Falk, dismissed the city in a few forceful words: 'Since the fire of 1922, after the wind from the sea had dispersed the stench of burned flesh in the ruins of the Greek quarter, there is not a stone left on stone worth looking at...'[26] Today no trace of the Issigonis's property remains and even the road on which it was located has disappeared.

In 1914 Smyrna had had a population of 260,000; by 1926 it stood at a mere 70,000, the result of forced migration and massacre. It was one of four Turkish cities in 1930 which still possessed a Greek name and this was later changed to Izmir, at the same time, incidentally, that Constantinople became Istanbul. By then the Turkish Republic was well established, it having come into being on 29 October 1923 with Kemal at its head.

In such mayhem the Issigonis family had been lucky to escape with their lives, although they left behind a factory destroyed in the carnage. We can get a picture of the urban chaos that they would have experienced from a first-hand account set down in October 1922,[27] a month after the event, by the Revd Charles Dobson, a young New Zealander who had been British sub-chaplain to the English Church in Smyrna.

By the time of Kemal's arrival in the city on 10 September, which was a Saturday, Dobson witnessed the roads 'congested by about 100,000 refugees who had been pouring into the city in the previous day.'[28] However, the Turkish troops had been preceded by some of their forces, 'telling the people to have no fear.' But during the night of the following day 'there was sporadic firing and screaming...' and, by Wednesday the 13th, the situation had deteriorated to such an extent that the word went out that 'all British subjects... must now leave the city.'[29]

The populace descended on the harbour, although Charles Dobson recorded that 'down the side streets there was much shooting and terrified screaming and some of the narrower streets were choked by running masses of people carrying their children in their arms. In one of the streets a man was dragging himself across the road on his elbows. He was shot through both thighs.

'Most of the people escaped only with their clothes and such valuables as they were able to carry. Many on their way to the ships were robbed even of their boots. In the harbour were floating the bodies of people who had been killed or had been drowned in desperate attempts to reach the ships.

'Throughout the night boatloads of exhausted and terror-stricken people were being taken off. Nothing, no words can describe the awful effect of the city, one appalling mass of flames, the water front covered with dark masses of despairing humanity, from whom we in the ships could hear the dull cries of anguished despair.'[30]

Dobson also recorded that it was 'impossible' for the British population to take their Greek servants with them. Many suffered 'an awful fate,'[31] and this may well have applied to the domestic staff who served the Issigonis family. They were roused in the night and told to take only blankets with them. The fact that Constantine was aged only 50, and that he was to die within months of his evacuation, suggests that he may well have been injured during the exodus.

The British government had dispatched a fleet of warships from its naval base in Malta to evacuate British nationals and subjects from the city. These included HMS *Cardiff, Curacoa* and *Bavarian,* although the Issigonis family escaped on the eight-year-old dreadnought *Iron Duke* which arrived on 15 September. Constantine's decision, taken in 1896, to apply for British nationality had probably saved his life and those of his wife and only child. Having said that, thousands of Greeks were saved from the burning city, but even then the family would probably have ended up in Greece. With no motor industry, Alec Issigonis might well have joined a maritime engineering company, and there would never have been a Morris Minor and certainly no Mini.

The family's rescue by the Royal Navy would underpin in the young Issigonis the esteem in which he already held British institutions: 'There was a deep, deep gratitude built into him and a respect for the British upper class, of the Navy and all the trappings of the Establishment,' says Alex Moulton,[32] for some 15 years Issigonis's friend and collaborator.

The evacuation from Smyrna was soon completed. On 29 September 1922, acting British Vice-Consul in Smyrna, R.W. Urquhart, reported to Sir Horace

Rumbold, British High Commissioner in Constantinople, that the last British family requesting evacuation had been taken on board ship that day. A total of 180,000 people had been saved, which included a significant number of Greeks, although there were still many awaiting deportation.[33]

By this time the Issigonis and Walker families were well on their way to Malta, where they were housed, together with the many other refugees, in a hastily erected tented village. The evacuation would have been the most traumatic event in Alec's until then carefree but cloistered life. He celebrated his 16th birthday in November 1922. Some months later came a further shock when his father died on the island. Thirty-seven-year-old Hulda and Alec then continued their journey to Britain, arriving in the summer of 1923.

Thereafter mother and son would remain together. Alec never married, and, apart from occasional absences, he would share a home with his formidable mother until her death in her 86th year in 1972. He then lived alone, although looked after by a married couple, for a further 16 years until he died in 1988.

In such domestic circumstances there was a widely held view within the British Motor Corporation, and indeed the motor industry, that Alec Issigonis was a homosexual. It should be said that this supposition was fuelled to some extent by his habit of peppering his speech with 'my dear,' an affectation he probably acquired from his friend, the unquestionably heterosexual Laurence Pomeroy, which was coupled with what can best be described as a theatrical delivery.

So was Issigonis gay? 'Probably, but non-practising,' believes former *Autocar* journalist Ronald 'Steady' Barker, who knew him professionally in the early 1960s, from which acquaintance sprang an enduring friendship. 'Oedipus, attached to his mother. She was a millstone but I think he was devoted to her. I never saw any inkling of his sexuality.'[34]

Having said that, neither did Barker 'ever see him show affection to another man and he may have been sexually neutral. Issigonis used to have a birthday party every year at Edgbaston. I was invited and Tony Dawson, his press officer, was present but there were no other journalists. He used to have these individuals, artisans whom he was obviously very fond of and he remained totally devoted and loyal to them because of the way they worked all hours to create his masterpiece. I had the feeling that he'd have loved to have had one of them at least as a son. There was real affection there without it being sexual.'

Christopher Dowson is the son of George Dowson, with whom Issigonis built the Lightweight Special hillclimb car in the 1930s. The Dowson farm near Pershore in Worcestershire was a bolt hole for Alec, and he was a welcome and regular visitor over a period of 50 or so years. There he was able to enjoy some of the trappings of family life. Christopher knew Issigonis from his childhood, viewing Alec as a sort of unofficial godfather (his sister Penny was Issigonis's actual godchild), and he spent a considerable amount of time with him until his death. Christopher 'never had any indication or suspicion' that Alec Issigonis was gay. 'He lived for his engineering, his mother, his hobbies and, of course, his Dry Martinis and Yellow Perils, his name for the Gold Flake cigarettes he smoked.'[35]

Without the presence of a wife and family, Issigonis was able to concentrate his formidable talents on car design, unencumbered by domestic distractions. 'How else could I get my work done?' he would say.[36] That this produced such outstanding vehicles as the Morris Minor and Mini is indisputable. But it also meant that his more extreme opinions went unchecked. Some of his pronouncements in the 1960s, such as, 'I never wear a seat belt. It's much easier to drive without having an accident,' and 'I never have a radio in the car, I need to concentrate on the job of driving,'[37] were at best controversial and, less charitably, plain dotty. He had clearly never been challenged by a wife or the questioning and occasional undisputed logic of a child.

Circumstance, prompted by his father's untimely death in 1923, may have dealt Issigonis a cruel hand, and there was, of course, one woman in his life. Hulda dedicated herself to her son's well-being and career. Mother and son arrived in Britain as refugees and made their home in South London, having friends there that they had made in happier pre-war days. Lodgings were found and, in due course, Hulda returned to Smyrna to salvage what she could of the family assets. In December 1922 Miltiades Issigonis had issued an action for damages against the Turkish government and it may be that this was wholly or partially successful. In any event Hulda came back to London with some funds, and as a result mother and son were to enjoy a comfortable, although not lavish, lifestyle during the 11 years they spent in the British capital.

On their arrival the question of 16-year-old Alec's education had to be addressed. There was talk of him attending Oundle public school,[38] possibly because it enjoyed an engineering tradition, but financial circumstances ruled this out. Because of her son's artistic abilities, Hulda was advised by her friends to send him to art school, but he was determined to pursue his long-cherished ambition to become an engineer. Had he attended a British public school, a natural habitat for a boy of his background, he would probably have made the natural progression to university. But his upbringing in Smyrna meant that he was effectively uneducated, which presented Mrs Issigonis with a dilemma.

'I wanted him to go to University, but never could he pass the matriculation,' she remembered.[39] This suggests that he tried and failed, and in one interview Issigonis did reveal that he 'studied at London University but I did not take a degree.'[40] That institution told the author that, in such circumstances, it would have no record of his attendance, but there is no reason to doubt Issigonis's word.

So not for him the Regent Street Polytechnic, the institution attended by some of his contemporaries.[41] Instead he enrolled as a student at unfashionable Battersea, which served the district in which he and his mother then lived, which provided him with the only technical instruction he ever received.

Passing the entrance examination produced its own problems and Issigonis recalled: 'I tried to matriculate for three years, and failed each time – which was then a disappointment to me because I wanted to get a BSc in engineering, despite taking them on three occasions.'[42] Battersea had offered this University of London degree since 1896. To again quote Hulda: 'So I go to the [Battersea] Polytechnic and say "what is going to happen?" This is the third time he tries. And the man say to me, "Never have I met such a brilliant young child [sic!]. He draws like a grown up."'

Hulda's persistence finally paid off. Was 'the man' the Principal, Dr Robert Pickard FRS, and if so had he any idea that he was admitting a future Fellow of the Royal Society? Whoever it was, he appears, to his credit, to have recognised Issigonis's worth, and in the autumn of 1925 Alec, by then nearly 19, was duly enrolled for a higher full course diploma in mechanical engineering. It was, as he later put it, 'almost the same qualification [as a BSc] but without the status.'[43] As far as his fees were concerned, he recalled obtaining a 'wonderful training at Battersea… for £3 a term.'[44] In the 1960s the Polytechnic evolved into the University of Surrey and its records reveal that Issigonis also took a second subject, engineering economics, in 1927/28, an unlikely choice bearing in mind his avowed dislike of mathematics. Not surprisingly the record cryptically states: 'no course marks entered'.

Battersea Polytechnic was one of nine similar institutions established across London in the 1890s. They sprang from a need, belatedly recognised in the latter part of the 19th century, for Britain to respond to the overseas challenge to its industrial supremacy. Technical education, as practised in particular by Germany, provided an example to emulate.

The Polytechnic opened in 1894, and the intention of its architect, E.W. Mountford, was to produce 'a kind of oasis in the desolate bricks and mortar, speculating builders' houses of the worst kind, laundries, hideous factories and dreary railway arches, of which this part of Battersea principally consists.'[45]

Built on Battersea Park Road for the residents of Battersea, Clapham and Wandsworth, of the 2,046 students who registered for the Polytechnic, more than half came from 'the poorer and artisan classes.'[46] Interestingly, in the light of future events, the first Principal was Sidney Wells, 'an unqualified engineer,'[47] who was appointed because it was believed that he possessed 'all the engineer's genius for overcoming difficulties.' One of his successors, Dr Pickard, who was also a consultant to the cotton and leather industries, did not arrive until 1920 and he appears to have done a sound job. The Board of Education's Inspectors said as much following a visit to the Polytechnic in 1924, 'despite the dinginess of its corridors and some of its rooms.'[48]

By the time of Alec Issigonis's enrolment, Battersea had about 3,000 students, but most of these attended evening classes. The largest group, 21 percent, were clerks, with engineers accounting for 18 percent and chemists and physicians 7 percent. Only 19 percent of the total, just 570 individuals, were classed as 'students only', like Alec, for according to Surrey's student records, he enrolled at the Day Technical College, which provided 'a thorough scientific training extended over three or four years for students intending to enter one of the various branches of Engineering, Chemical or allied Professions. Full courses... are provided in the Faculties of Science and Engineering.'[49]

During his time at Battersea, Issigonis was separated from his mother and in 1971 recalled that he lived 'in digs in – dare I say it – Clapham Common. It used to be quite respectable in those days'.[50] This was a reference to the area's latter-day reputation as a place for sexual encounters. Hulda's improved financial situation was reflected by the fact that she provided him with 10 shillings a week pocket money, the equivalent of £13 today. 'It was a lot in those days,' Issigonis remembered. 'I used to go once a week to Lyons Corner House and have a real slap-up meal.'[51]

As all academic records relating to this period are no longer extant, we can only speculate on how Alec fared. He probably excelled at draughtsmanship and any practical aspects that the course may have offered. But mathematics would have provided a significant hurdle that he would have been unable to overcome.

However, some records of his extra-curricular activities do survive. He appears in a photograph (see page 68) of a tug-of-war competition taken at the Polytechnic's sports day, held at its grounds at Merton Abbey on 11 June 1927. It is captioned in *The Battersea Polytechnic Magazine* of July as 'The Second Year's Work – A Record!'. Alec also joined the Polytechnic's Engineering Society and he may well have contributed to a discussion, held on 24 November 1927, on the subject of 'The Relative Merits of the Internal and External Combustion Engine.' And did he attend the meeting of 25 October? Then a paper entitled 'Some Applications of the Indicator Diagram' by R.W.T. Pryer was read by Brian Robbins, MSc, who was teaching and undertaking research at Imperial College. Robbins was destined to play a crucial, catalytic role in Alec's future career. In his final year at Battersea, Issigonis raised his own profile within the Engineering Society and in the spring of 1928 he presented a paper to its members. It was not, as might be expected, on an automotive subject, but was entitled: 'The Development of Commercial Aviation.'[52] This fascination with aircraft would remain with Issigonis throughout his life and many years later, in 1967, Jeff

Daniels, then at *Car* magazine, got into conversation with him at a Birmingham dinner. 'I imagined motor cars would dominate the discussion. But when he knew that I had a background in the aircraft industry all he wanted to talk about was aeroplanes. The conversation was only cut short because "the girl who sits with my mother has to be home by 11 o'clock."'[53]

Back in 1926 Issigonis would have had plenty of opportunities to study aircraft at first hand because in that year he and his mother moved to a new home at Purley, Surrey, which was located on the fringes of Croydon Airport, then London's only civil airfield. The move had been prompted by the family's new financial security, which was reflected by Hulda's purchase, in 1925, of a car. And it was a new one, an example of Singer's recently introduced 10hp model that the factory offered with an upright, boxy but light Weymann saloon body. Not particularly cheap, it was priced at £280, the equivalent of about £7,200 at today's prices.

Alec wasted little time in taking the Singer to Brooklands, where he entered this distinctly non-sporting vehicle in the Junior Car Club's High Speed Trial, held on Saturday 1 May 1925. He was probably participating in his first-ever competitive event. Eighteen-year-old Issigonis ran in Class A, for which entrants were required to average 33mph. Although he made a slow start and fell back eight places in the first lap, he soon settled down at a steady pace but was disqualified for overtaking in the eighth lap.[54]

The following year Mrs Issigonis and Alec moved into their new home. Then, as now, Overhill Road was a discreet gravelled cul-de-sac with a Purley address, although it is actually in the London Borough of Sutton. Allied to nearby Coulsdon and Sanderstead, this quiet corner of suburbia offered, as the Official Guide to the district in the interwar years proclaimed: 'Garden Homes Set Amidst the Surrey Hills.' Mother and son moved there early in 1926, when number nine was a newly-built pebble-dashed chalet bungalow, completed in 1920. The last secluded property on the east side of a road which contained only four houses, it had been acquired by one Roger Davies Marshal, who was probably responsible for giving it the name of 'Barton', which was attached to the paling of the front gate. Marshal continued to own it until his death in 1947 and Mrs Issigonis therefore rented the property from him.

Today[55] its layout remains essentially the same as it did in the 1920s. To the right of the centrally positioned hall are two reception rooms, for dining and sitting, which run the depth of the property. To the left of the front door was a bedroom with the bathroom behind it, while the kitchen partially occupies a shallow extension at the rear. Steep stairs lead to a single bedroom in the roof space, which Alec probably occupied, leaving his mother with the larger and more convenient ground floor room.

There were visits from the Walker family and friends who could have been entertained on a small terrace at the rear. Access was gained from french doors, which led into the back reception room, and it was sheltered on its north side by the kitchen wall. The view was of a pleasant and secluded garden. We can imagine the scene: Alec, shy and intense, clad in a fashionable Fair Isle pullover, pausing perhaps to cast his eyes upwards to view one of the Handley Page biplanes of Imperial Airways that had just taken off from Croydon Airport, the suburban silence being broken only by the roar of its Rolls-Royce Condor engines. Barton's boundary was located below and beyond its southern perimeter and was then clearly visible. Today a thicket of trees masks the view.

His mother could have been reading and there was a table with folding and wicker chairs on the terrace. There are inescapable echoes here of Smyrna and although Purley did not begin to resemble the grandeur of the family's home in Turkey, after the traumatic events of the previous four years Overhill Road must have represented a period of stability and consolidation for mother and son.

As Alec was then attending Battersea Polytechnic and was in digs in Clapham, he may well have only returned to Purley at weekends and during the holidays. There were probably days out in the Singer, for there was room to park the car in the small drive at the front of the property on its southern side.

Following the completion of his time at Battersea in the summer of 1928, when he received a Diploma (Mechanical Engineering) First Class, Hulda suggested a Grand Tour of Europe. Accompanied by Alec's cousin, Gerald Walker, they all set off for France in the by then three-year-old saloon. Unfortunately the car ran its big ends at Versailles and Alec's practical abilities came to the fore when he helped a garage mechanic rectify the problem. From there they set off for the Riviera, and drove down the coast via the principal resorts to Monte Carlo. It was to give Issigonis a liking for the Principality of Monaco. He went to the Grand Prix there in 1937, and would thereafter regularly attend the fixture into the post-war years. Elements of the Mini's design took shape during brief working holidays in the sunshine of the Mediterranean coast.

The return journey was made via Switzerland, whereupon the tyres succumbed, probably on account of the poor roads. The more practically-minded occupants of the Singer were forced to stuff the covers with grass while getting from one village to another. This cut short the tour, which had already taken some three months to complete, and the faithful saloon was destined to provide Alec with a further 80,000 miles or so of motoring.

On his return from Europe, 21-year-old Issigonis was faced with having to earn a living. His mother told him that 'it was now his duty to become a wage earner and the family's provider,'[56] and he went on to seek 'advice from every quarter,'[57] a trait that would be notably absent in his later years! He had joined the Institution of Automobile Engineers as a student member and on 26 March 1928 became a graduate. Although he attended its lectures, he never played any part in its discussions and may have allowed his membership to lapse, particularly following the IAE's absorption in 1946 by the larger Institution of Mechanical Engineers, which has no record of Alec Issigonis on its albeit incomplete files.

One day in 1928, while in the Institution's office at Watergate House, York Buildings at the Adelphi, off the Strand, Issigonis asked the newly appointed assistant secretary Brian Robbins if he knew of any vacancies. This was the same Robbins who had spoken at Battersea's Engineering Society meeting during the previous year. He was in luck. Robbins 'pulled out a card index, produced the name of Edward Gillett... who was developing a mechanism for automatic clutch control... '58 Issigonis applied and was accepted as the senior and, in truth, the only draughtsman at Gillett's company, Reduction Gears Ltd, beginning work late in 1928.

It had been about 10 years since his first encounter with the automobile in Smyrna and he had achieved his ambition of becoming an engineer. More significantly, the appointment paved the way for him to join the motor industry. In later years, whenever he passed Gillett's one-time Westminster office in Victoria Street, SW1, he always made a point of taking 'my hat off at number 66.'59

Edward Henry Gillett, 52 years old in 1928, had, up to this point in his life, enjoyed a distinctly chequered engineering career. The product of a full-time course at Finsbury Technical College, from where he went on to become an articled pupil with Thomas Middleton and Co. of Southwark, his career proper began in the late 1890s with five years as managing director of the Motor Omnibus Syndicate. Backed by the financial shyster, H.J. Lawson, it espoused the by then outdated concept of a steam bus. Gillett then worked on his own account, although after the war he joined British Ensign Motors of Hawthorne Road, Willesden Green, as its managing director and engineer.60

The firm had begun building cars and commercial vehicles in 1913 but Gillett was responsible for the design of the EP6, a wholly new model that was sold under the name of Ensign. Visually impressive and dominated by a Bentley-style radiator, it was powered by a 6.8-litre six-cylinder overhead camshaft engine which had much in common with the Hispano-Suiza H6 aero unit that had been made under licence in Britain during the war. With a chassis price of an astronomical £1,700, there were few takers and only about six examples were built. Gillett fared little better with a smaller Meadows-engined 11.9hp model for the 1923 season. The Ensign Twelve was expensive at £415, and only 37 were completed before both car and truck production ceased at the end of the year.

Edward Gillett then undertook a marketing somersault but miscalculated yet again when he launched his 'All-British £100 car' at the 1926 Motor Show. This open two-seater was powered by an 8hp four-cylinder overhead valve proprietary engine and, while British Ensign was named as its manufacturer, it soon distanced itself from the project. Its inventor was clearly looking for another car company to take the idea up but, it appears, there was no response and nothing thereafter was heard of the Gillett.

Apparently undeterred, Gillett then turned his attention from motor manufacture to simplifying the gear changing process on cars and Reduction Gears was established to this end. At this time moving from one gear to another demanded both skill and practice, requiring a driver to double-declutch when changing both up and down the box. If this was not achieved, the action resulted in a noisy clash of straight-cut gears.

Gillett was not alone in his pursuit. In 1926 Riley had introduced its 'twin top' constant mesh gearbox, which greatly eased the change from third to top gear and vice versa. At the end of 1927 Vauxhall had concluded its experiments with the expensive, complex but effective Wilson pre-selector gearbox, a semi-automatic transmission in which the driver selected a gear and then engaged it by depressing the 'clutch' pedal, a relatively silent operation. The device was taken up by Armstrong Siddeley in 1929 and the Wilson was widely used on more expensive British cars throughout the 1930s. However, across the Atlantic in America Earl A. Thompson, a talented hydraulics engineer, was at work at Cadillac perfecting his Synchro-Mesh, as his invention was originally rendered. It worked in a constant-mesh box by synchronising the cogs of the respective gears so that they engaged when rotating at the same speeds. This transformed gear changing into a straightforward and relatively quiet operation and removed the ever-present element of uncertainty from the process.

Gillett's invention was far less radical. It retained the car's existing mechanicals but eliminated the clutch pedal and so reduced the number of pedals from three to two. When the driver depressed the accelerator, a small hydraulic pump mounted at the front of the engine was activated, which mechanically withdrew the clutch. The driver then selected gear in the usual way.

What Gillett needed was a draughtsman to interpret this raw idea and transform his gadget into a workable device and Alec Issigonis was required to undertake this role. But he also had a secondary function. Once the concept had been perfected as far as was possible, he would be required to drive an appropriately modified car to the Midlands. Most of the businesses that constituted the British motor industry were located in and around the cities of Coventry and Birmingham. Such was the potential importance of the area that arrangements were put in hand with Coventry Climax to use part of its premises in Friars Road as a local headquarters.

It was this impending requirement that probably prompted a move for Alec and his mother across London from the semi-rural tranquility of Purley to the bustle of a North London suburb. In 1929 and probably at Gillett's request (he, in any event, knew the area well), they moved to 5 Grove Road, Willesden Green, NW10, a quiet thoroughfare, flanked by three-storey late Victorian semi-detached houses with bay windows lighting the front rooms of their first two floors. These are large houses and were built in the days when the occupants were attended by domestic servants, but they had probably been divided into flats by the time the Issigonises lived there. Although there was on-street parking, number five now possesses a small drive which could accommodate a car, a facility that may well have been available in the 1920s.

Unlike suburban Purley, beyond its main streets Willesden possessed factories aplenty. British Ensign was typical of the type of businesses to be found throughout the borough. Indeed, by 1933 the area of Park Royal and Perivale, with adjacent parts of Wembley and Willesden, had the greatest concentration of manufacturing industry in southern England.[61] S. Smith and Sons, which produced car instruments and electrical equipment, arrived at nearby Cricklewood during World War One, and in nearby Oxgate Lane were the premises of Bentley Motors.

The big green cars had won the Le Mans 24-hour race for the third time in 1928, and Alec, with his passion for motoring and motor sport, who now lived only about a mile and a half away, may have availed himself of its factory. On the face of it, had the funds been available, he might have appeared a likely candidate for a Bentley, or indeed a 30/98 Vauxhall, which was a sports car of much the same stripe. But in his later years he told Ronald Barker that he was 'not much interested in large cars,' which clearly reflected a lifelong preoccupation. He added a sentence that encapsulates the very core of his design philosophy: '*A small one sets a tremendous design challenge non existent with a large one.* [author's italics] Mr Royce had nothing to do.'[62]

Enlarging on this theme, Barker recalls a conversation he had with W.O. Bentley on this very subject. 'I got to know him pretty well and he told me that in the days of Bentley Motors all his directors wanted were bigger and bigger cars. What he would have liked was the challenge of designing a small car, like the Mini. On one occasion I had picked him up for a Bentley Drivers' Club dinner in a Renault 4 and his wife later told me that "he hasn't stopped talking about the little car."'[63] In such circumstances it comes as no surprise to find that Bentley had run a succession of Morris Minors, which he considered 'near-perfect small motor cars for British roads.'[64]

If it is not known for certain whether Alec Issigonis ever visited Bentley Motors at Oxgate Lane, we are on far firmer ground in stating that he was a regular visitor to a modest garage in West End Lane, West Hampstead. This was almost the same distance as the Bentley works from his new home, but in an easterly direction. The premises were run by R.L. 'Jack' Duller, who not only sold Austin Sevens, but was also a Brooklands habitué who raced and tuned them.

Duller also sold new Sevens and mechanic 'Wilkie' Wilkinson, who in the post-war years was best known for tending the Ecurie Ecosse racing team, had, recalls a contemporary, 'an infallible quick tune' for such cars 'which were slightly off colour when new. This was to drive them flat out in top gear down the one-in-four gradient of Netherhall Gardens, after which they were never the same again.'[65]

This peccadillo apart, and there were others, here was a car to which Alec Issigonis's soul could instantly respond. The Singer was replaced by a Gordon England-bodied two-seater Cup model Austin Seven. This desirable variant sprang from the production family tourer, a car that was just 8ft 8in long, and weighed a mere 6.5cwt. As a concept this diminutive Austin had an overriding influence on Issigonis's future motor industry career. Some 30 years later not only would the Mini incorporate a number of Seven-inspired features, but the Austin version was also, for the first three years of its life, endowed with the 'Austin Se7en' name.

The original Seven was an unplanned baby, born in 1922 at a time when the Austin Motor Company was operating in receivership. In 1919 Sir Herbert had launched his gargantuan and unsuitable Model T Ford-inspired 3.6-litre Twenty for the British market. But in 1921 the government introduced its so-called 'horsepower tax', which geared the RAC rating of a car's engine, at the rate of £1 per unit of horsepower, to its road fund licence, which was an incentive for a manufacturer to stress the figure in a model's name. The owner of a Twenty, which was actually rated at 22.4hp, would therefore pay £23 a year to tax the car, whereas his next-door neighbour, with one of William Morris's increasingly popular 11.9hp 'Bullnoses' in his garage, would spend only £12.

Demand for the big Austin plummeted, which coincided with the sudden collapse of the post-war boom in 1921 and toppled the business into deficit. Its proprietor instantly responded by scaling down the Twenty and producing the durable and enduring 1.6-litre Twelve. Although the economy was beginning to pick up Sir Herbert decided he needed an even smaller car – how Issigonis would have approved – and the outcome was the Seven. It was to provide Austin with its salvation and was destined to be one of the British motor industry's truly great designs.

Perversely, its revolutionary specification evolved almost by chance. Austin had been unable to secure the agreement of his co-directors to proceed with his idea for 'a 6hp cyclecar,' but despite their opposition he nevertheless pressed ahead with the design at Lickey Grange, his Bromsgrove home. However, he needed a draughtsman to interpret his sketches and recruited 18-year-old Stanley Edge from his Longbridge drawing office. But Stan, a blunt and informed Black Country man, had the temerity to reject his chairman's ideas. Then British cars of less than 1 litre capacity were powered by rough running two-cylinder engines and Sir Herbert wanted to produce a car in the mould of the popular air cooled Rover Eight.

As Edge subsequently wrote,[66] 'if I was responsible for anything it was sticking to the view that a small four-cylinder engine could be built more cheaply than one with two or more cylinders.' Inspired by the FN motorcycle unit, the Seven was the smallest capacity four-cylinder British car of its day. The heart of the Longbridge baby's appeal was Edge's diminutive 696cc engine, soon enlarged to 748cc, making the Seven effectively a large car in miniature. In consequence it was the company's best-selling model between 1926 and 1936 and remained in production until 1939. Austin's position as second only to market leader William Morris was assured.

It was, of course, a four-seater. But Austin's son-in-law, the Australian, Captain Arthur 'Skipper' Waite, recognised that its qualities of reliability and low weight were sufficient to overcome the Seven's twin deficiencies of poor road-holding and questionable braking. As such it was an ideal candidate for a competition car and the miniature Austin proved itself to be a versatile performer in road and track racing, hillclimbs and record breaking. In 1925 Waite began supercharging the Seven's engine, which led to the factory's E Super Sports of 1927/8 of which, literally, a handful were built. A team of four ran in the 1929 Tourist Trophy race, held in the Ards district of Belfast, and put up an excellent showing, coming in third, fourth, 16th and 19th.

As a result Austin decided to offer the car as a production model and what was to be informally named the Ulster went on sale in February 1930. It was available with a choice of engines; there was the 24bhp Sports, while the Super Sports was powered by a 33bhp version, its performance enhanced by the fitment of a Cozette supercharger. These mechanicals were cloaked in a purposeful open two-seater body with a pointed tail and external fishtail exhaust. The blown car cost £225, was accordingly £95 more than the mainstream Seven touring two-seater, and was a bid by Austin to challenge the success of William Morris's new M-type MG.

A mere 200 examples of this delightful sports racer for the road were sold over a two-year period and one lucky customer was Alec Issigonis, who in 1930 took delivery of his second Seven, a blown Super Sports. There were only 50 or so of these, his was finished in a striking yellow hue and registered GH 1645. While the commodious Singer saloon had clearly been his mother's choice, the Ulster represented a tangible expression of his ideals, although Hulda paid by selling a precious solitaire ring. 'It was my first hot car,' Alec remembered, 'but I was mad, for I lived on bread and cheese to be able to have the beastly thing.'[67] He now possessed a car specifically designed for competition and wasted little time in campaigning the Austin in trials and hillclimbs.

One such event was the Surbiton Motor Club's annual London to Barnstaple Trial, held on 1/2 August 1930, and a surviving report not only underlines the distance Alec was prepared to travel to participate in such events, but also demonstrates his abilities as a driver. *The Light Car and Cyclecar* noted that the Devon course was 'in a very bad state following torrential rain.' But at Grabhurst hill, despite the atrocious conditions, 'A. Issigonis (supercharged Austin) was one of three entrants to have made outstandingly good climbs. Issigonis was almost baulked on his ascent and cleverly avoided the [unnamed] obstruction, continuing to the top of the hill at speed – a fine piece of driving.'[68] He was awarded a bronze medal and third class award for his efforts.

Alec would have delighted in showing off his purchase to the denizens of Jack Duller's garage and it was there that he made the first of a number of lifelong friendships. Laurence Evelyn Wood Pomeroy was a year younger than Issigonis and the son of Laurence Henry Pomeroy, one of Britain's outstanding automobile engineers of the interwar years. Responsible for the design of the Prince Henry and 30/98 Vauxhalls, by this time he was chief engineer of the prestigious but profitless Daimler company.

In 1963 Issigonis would write: 'I have known Pomeroy almost as long as I can remember'[69] and 'Pom' was able to recall that they had met in 1931 'at the Sunday morning meetings at R.L. Duller's garage.'[70] His observations on Wilkinson's treatment for recalcitrant Austin Sevens have already been recorded. Pomeroy had failed the entrance exams for Cambridge, so learnt his engineering from his famous father, working in London for one E.T. White in 1929. White possessed the manufacturing rights to the German Zoller supercharger in Britain, which Pomeroy was later to implement. This larger than life *bon vivant*, an ultimately portly and monocled Edwardian figure, would remain a friend of Issigonis's until his premature death in 1966.

However, we should not lose track of the fact that the reason for the accessibility of Duller's garage was, of course, the move to North London. While Alec was enjoying his Sundays in Pom's convivial company, during the week he was working for Edward Gillett. Grove Road also had the virtue of being very close to Willesden Green station so his employer's Victoria Street office was easily accessible, if the need arose, by the Metropolitan Underground railway.

Above all the new address was well positioned for access to the Midlands. From Willesden it was just a matter of Issigonis joining the nearby Edgware

Road, which soon transformed into the A5, and remaining on it until branching off on to the A45 just to the south of Daventry. From there the road went direct to Britain's Motor City of Coventry.

So much for the future. Alec's contribution to refining Gillett's somewhat crude two-pedal concept was to introduce a second valve, controlled by a centrifugal engine-driven governor. As a result, when the driver slightly depressed the accelerator, 'a controlled degree of slip in the clutch, and creep in the car, could be generated for manoeuvring at slow speeds.'[71]

When this work was completed at least one vehicle, a 'Flatnose' 15.9hp Morris Oxford, was adapted to incorporate the device. In view of the choice of vehicle it would have been surprising if Gillett had not tried to interest Morris Motors, as Britain's largest car maker, in the conversion, but his approach was not a success. By all accounts Chrysler was more impressed, although whether this was the company's Detroit business or its Kew-based British operation is unclear.

It was Issigonis's unenviable task to try and obtain positive responses from Britain's car makers. As an assignment it was made all the more difficult by the onset, in the autumn of 1929, of the Depression that reached its nadir in 1931. Nevertheless, there were key employees at two Coventry-based motor manufacturers that Alec met in the course of his work for Gillett and they were to have a profound impact on his future.

The Rover Motor Company of Helen Street was in the process of being rescued from near bankruptcy by Spencer Wilks and his younger brother Maurice. The latter shared design responsibility with the capable Robert Boyle and he and Issigonis were destined to become long-standing friends. The other was a talented Scot, 'Jock' Wishart, who was technical engineer of the respected Humber company based in the Stoke district of the city. Like Rover, the business was being restructured, in this instance under the dynamic direction of the Rootes brothers.

Despite establishing contact with such influential figures, and there were no doubt others, Issigonis was unable to transform these rapprochements into firm orders. It was probably after numerous rebuffs that Edward Gillett decided to go public with his invention. The results were published by *The Autocar* in its issue of 21 November 1930, perhaps in the hope that Reduction Gears would find a car maker which might adopt the device.

The magazine's representative took the modified Morris to Brooklands, where it underwent 'drastic experiments'. He reported that driving the car was 'absurdly simple,' and after moving off from rest, 'to change gear, either up or down, one merely lets the accelerator pedal come fully up, slides the gear lever to the desired position, and once more depresses the accelerator pedal. In order to stop, the accelerator pedal is released...'

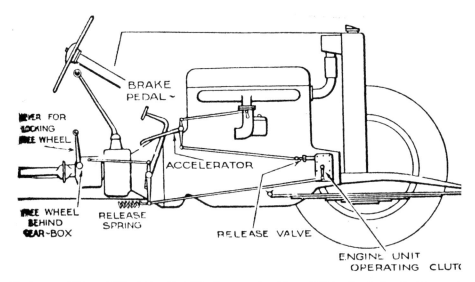

The layout of Edward Gillett's Two-Pedal Device, as refined from 1928 by Alec Issigonis. (*Autocar*)

However, *Autocar* did voice two criticisms of what it dubbed the 'Gillett Two-pedal Device'. One was that 'even when the engine was not driving it cannot be used as a brake.' The scribe also cautioned that, when the clutch was automatically disengaged, it would place 'a heavy stress upon the clutch withdrawal race.'

Alas! Such shortcomings were, by this time, academic. In America, Thompson's Synchro-Mesh experiments had borne fruit and General Motors introduced the device on its Cadillac and new La Salle marque for the 1929 season. It rapidly spread throughout the American motor industry and by 1932 had reached Britain. Ford and Vauxhall, both subsidiaries of US companies, together with indigenous Rolls-Royce, all introduced this clashless gearchange for the 1933 model year.

This effectively meant the end of Gillett's dream and he was in any event to die a few years later in July 1936 at the relatively early age of 60. But Alec Issigonis's Coventry contacts had found practical expression and in 1934 Jock Wishart recruited him to the Humber drawing office as a draughtsman. At the age of 27 his motor industry career could now begin in earnest.

Notes

1. Judith Jackson, 'The Minor Revolutionary', *Sunday Times Magazine*, 14 November 1971.
2. Laurence Pomeroy, *The Mini Story*, 1964.
3. Spen King, interview with author, 2004.
4. Institution of Mechanical Engineers, Proposal of Member, 5 March 1896.
5. Ibid.
6. Ibid.
7. The National Archives (TNA): Public Record Office (PRO) HO 144/401
8. TNA: PRO HO 334 26
9. TNA: PRO H144 *op cit.*
10. TNA: PRO HO 144/397
11. Ronald Barker, interview with author, 2002.
12. Ronald Barker, Alec Issigonis in *Automobile Design: Great Designers and their Work*, 1970.
13. Tony Dawson, 'Father of the Mini', *Classic and Sportscar*, January 1985.
14. Ibid.
15. Pomeroy, *op cit.*
16. Barker, *op cit.*
17. Quoted in Jonathan Wood, *Bugatti the Man and Marque*, 1991.
18. Barker, *op cit.*
19. Alec Issigonis, *The Ironmonger*, BBC Radio 4, 18 November 1986.
20. Anthony Lawrence Hawkins Dawson, Assistant Press Officer, Nuffield Organisation 1957–61, Press Officer 1961–1964, Executive Press Officer, the British Motor Corporation 1964–1969, Public Relations Officer, British Leyland Motor Corporation 1969–77.
21. Dawson, *op cit.*
22. Bernd Pischetsrieder, interview with author, 2004.
23. Letter from Sir Edward Grey, British Foreign Secretary, quoted in Pomeroy, *op cit.*
24. Kenneth Ullyett, *The Book of the Mini*, 1964.
25. Barker, *op cit.*
26. André Falk, *Turkey*, 1963.
27. TNA: PRO/E12182. Dobson's account, compiled in Malta, followed a meeting held at the Lieutenant Governor's house with five prominent citizens of Smyrna. It was forwarded to Lord Curzon, the British Foreign Secretary, on 2 November 1922 by the British Embassy in Rome, the Ambassador, Sir Ronald Graham, being 'impressed by Mr Dobson's moderation and good faith.'
28. Ibid.
29. Ibid.
30. Ibid.
31. Ibid.
32. Alex Moulton, interview with author, 2003.
33. TNA: PRO E10895/9024/44
34. Ronald Barker, interview, 2002.
35. Christopher Dowson, interview with author, 2002.
36. David Peters, 'With Camera and Pen', *The Oxford Times*, 2 February 1962.
37. Quoted in Gillian Bardsley, *Alec Issigonis as Designer*, British Motor Industry Heritage Trust, 1997.
38. Dawson, *op cit.*

39. Jackson, *op cit.*

40. Ullyett, *op cit.*

41. Regent Polytechnic graduates who entered the motor industry included George Smith-Clarke, chief engineer of Alvis 1922–50 and Tom Murray Jamieson, who joined Austin as a racing car designer in 1932, and knew Issigonis, although he sadly died at an accident at Brooklands in 1938. His colleagues at Cowley, Morris's chief body engineer, Leslie Hall, and Gerald Palmer, had both attended 'The Poly.'

42. Jackson, *op cit.*

43. Barker, *op cit.*

44. Anne Hope, 'The genius today', *Autocar*, 25 August 1979.

45. Christopher Pick, *Understanding the Real World: A visual history of the University of Surrey*, 2002.

46. Pick, *op cit.*

47. Pick, *op cit.*

48. H. Arrowsmith, *Pioneering in Education for the Technologies. The Story of the Battersea College of Technology*, 1966.

49. *Battersea Polytechnic*, Session 1927–28.

50. Jackson, *op cit.*

51. Ibid.

52. *The Battersea Polytechnic Magazine*, Volume 20, June 1928.

53. Jeff Daniels, conversation with author, 2005.

54. Kevin Atkinson, *The Singer Story*, 1996.

55. Visit by author, 18 March 2004.

56. Pomeroy, *op cit.*

57. Ibid.

58. Ibid.

59. Barker, Alec Issigonis, *op cit.*

60. The Institution of Automobile Engineers, *Proceedings*, Volume 31, Session 1936–37, Obituary, Edward Henry Gillett.

61. Len Snow, *Willesden Past*, 1994.

62. Barker, *op cit.*

63. Barker, interview, *op cit.*

64. W.O. Bentley, *The Cars in my Life*, 1961.

65. Pomeroy, *op cit.*

66. Quoted in Jonathan Wood, *The Austin Seven*, 2002.

67. Peters, *op cit.*

68. *The Light Car and Cyclecar*, 8 August 1930.

69. Pomeroy, *op cit.*

70. Ibid.

71. Ibid.

Chapter Two

LIGHTWEIGHT
VERY SPECIAL

'George Dowson and I... designed and built the Lightweight Special. Being young we tended to copy prevailing design trends of the day...'[1]

Alec Issigonis

W ITH HIS move to the Midlands in 1934, Alec Issigonis was fortunate to be able to concentrate his talents on his developing interest, that of suspension design. It was a discipline which was being simultaneously addressed by some of the world's leading automobile engineers.

Many of his ideas found practical expression in the design and construction of the Lightweight Special, the most advanced British hillclimb and sprint car of its day. This sprang from his recognition that 'it was no use designing and studying one part of a car. Everything was too tightly integrated for that. The influence of one part on another is far greater than people think, so before I knew where I was I had become interested in all the other parts outside my specialism and was soon building complete experimental cars in my spare time.'[2]

The Lightweight took an agonising four years to complete and the single-seater, which happily survives, remains as a testament to its creator's growing intellectual abilities and his strong practical bent. Above all he was able to demonstrate that he could create a complete car, a discipline he would apply first to the Morris Minor and then the Mini. Some automobile engineers concentrated their talents on a vehicle's mechanicals; others are accomplished stylists. Some, and here artist-engineer Ettore Bugatti immediately springs to mind, could do both.

It will be recalled that, during his visits to Coventry, Issigonis had established contact with Jock Wishart of Humber. It was thanks to his good offices that he joined that company's drawing office and by the time he left in 1936 he would be earning £90 7s a year. But first he and his mother needed somewhere to live. They chose the small town of Kenilworth, just five miles south-west of Coventry, and were thus well placed for access to the Humber factory, which was located on the southern side of the city. 'Although formerly a market town,' observed the local *Kelly's Directory* of 1936, 'the Kenilworth of modern days has every appearance of a rural village.' At the time of the Issigonises arrival it had a population of some 7,500.

Alec was also in good company because the town had long provided a sanctuary for representatives of the city's motor industry from the grime of Coventry. Its better-known residents, who owned large, imposing houses in and around Kenilworth, were John Davenport Siddeley, managing director of Armstrong Siddeley, Dudley Docker, who was chairman of BSA (the company which owned Daimler), its chief engineer Percy Martin and machine tool magnate Sir Alfred Herbert. T.G. John, who had founded Alvis in Coventry in 1919, in his later years lived in some comfort in the commodious surroundings of Rouncil Towers, set in impressive grounds which were often used for local garden fêtes.

John's house was situated off Rouncil Lane, only developed in 1932, on the southern outskirts of Kenilworth. Then, as now, it was a quiet highway which adjoined the Warwick Road. In those days it was only developed on its north side, so the houses overlooked greenery and scattered woodland. Fortunately number 12, the eastern half of a modest but comfortable newly completed two-storey semi-detached house, had been vacated by its tenant, James Robinson, earlier in 1934, so mother and son were able to move in straight away. Alec had no doubt observed with pleasure that there was a wooden garage in the garden which would also serve as a workshop.

Coventry was to boom in the 1930s, thanks principally to the growth of its motor industry. It was a community with a long industrial heritage that had progressed from wool and cloth in the Middle Ages to weaving and watchmaking and, in the 1860s, to bicycle production. Not only would bicycles provide British citizens with their first taste of mobility, but they were also exported throughout the world. But when, in the late 1890s, the industry was successfully challenged by cheaper, mass-produced two-wheelers from America, many bicycle businesses, such as Hillman, Lea-Francis, Rover, Riley, Singer and Triumph, switched to the manufacture of motor cars. This followed Benz and Daimler's invention in Germany in 1886 of the horseless carriage.

Coventry had the distinction of being the birthplace of the British motor industry, which dated from 1896, when English Daimler began the production of cars in an empty cotton mill in Sandy Lane. The early post-World War One years had seen its ranks swelled by the likes of Alvis and Armstrong Siddeley, but of even greater significance was the arrival from Blackpool, in 1928, of 28-year-old William Lyons, who took over an empty shell-filling factory in the Foleshill district to manufacture his Austin Swallow. This was a special-bodied version of the famous Seven, an initiative that evolved into the SS marque of 1931, from which sprang the world-famous Jaguar line.

Morris, as Britain's largest car maker of the 1920s, built its engines in Coventry and also made many of its bodies there. A daily procession of Scammell lorries, many of them pulling trailers, en route to Morris's assembly plant at Cowley, became a familiar part of Coventry's civic scene. Little wonder then that it was Britain's fastest growing city of the interwar years, with a population that leapt from 167,083 in 1931 to 224,267 in 1939. During this period some 40,000 migrants entered Coventry, mainly thanks to its booming motor industry.

The Rootes brothers were in the vanguard of this movement and the Humber company, like so many of its contemporaries, had in 1898 followed the familiar route from bicycle maker to automobile manufacturer. By the 1920s it was producing finely engineered cars which attracted the more discriminating, affluent middle-class buyers, who would never have contemplated acquiring a Morris or even an Austin.

The business was chaired by Lt-Col John Cole, OBE, 'a dear old boy who had the wonderful knack of making a sonorous speech that was both impressive and carried very well.'[3] But he was also deeply conservative and distrustful of change. In 1927 Humber was still using splash-lubricated, rather than pump-pressurised, engines and cone clutches, dated features which harked back to the Edwardian era. Cole was similarly wary of front-wheel brakes and waited until 1925 to adopt them, two years after the rest of the industry. The quality of Humber's engineering was not in doubt, but from 3,158 cars built in 1926, production tumbled to a mere 1,916 in 1928. Profits fell and no dividend was paid that year.

The company was ripe for a takeover and it effectively came in December 1928 from the dynamic Rootes duo, William (Billy) and Reginald, who had built up their Kent-based car distribution business to become, by 1926, the largest in the country. In 1919 Billy had made the first of many visits to America – indeed his voice betrayed a distinctive transatlantic twang – and he was impressed by

General Motors, with its bevy of makes which were soon to challenge the supremacy of Henry Ford's Model T.

The brothers had decided to expand into car manufacture and Humber, in which they took an initial financial interest in 1928 that was consolidated by a complete takeover, was their first prize. Then, in 1929, Hillman, which had unsuccessfully attempted to challenge Austin, and Humber's next-door neighbour in the appropriately named Humber Road, was annexed.

In 1931 Rootes spearheaded the replacement of the mass-produced indigenous 12hp family saloon of the 1920s, encapsulated by Morris's famous Bullnose Cowley, with a 10hp car in the shape of the Hillman Minx. It was the success of this model that elevated Rootes to its position as a leading player within the British motor industry.

Billy and Reginald Rootes retained Lt-Col Cole's services because they had a regard for his diplomatic abilities and wished to build on Humber's existing clientele. But they reduced manufacturing costs by rationalising, updating and simplifying the cars' components and applying them to both marques. In consequence, the Hillman and Humber drawing offices were combined.

The implementation of much of this strategy fell on the capable shoulders of Norman Macdermid Wishart, who had received his technical education at Heriot-Watt Technical College, and this was followed by an apprenticeship with the Arrol-Johnson concern. Wishart then moved to Coventry, where he joined Humber as a draughtsman, and subsequently went to Armstrong Siddeley where his qualities were reflected by promotion to section leader. He returned to Humber, first as chief draughtsman and, with Rootes reinvigorating the business, he was again promoted, this time to the post of technical engineer.

One of Humber's draughtsmen who had a considerable regard for Jock Wishart's abilities was William Heynes, who had joined the company as an apprentice in 1923. In his later years he would enjoy a distinguished career as chief engineer of SS and Jaguar Cars. Heynes acquired a taste for design from the able Scot and he readily absorbed Wishart's maxim of 'if it looks wrong, it cannot be right.' In his later years Heynes conceded 'it wasn't infallible but I've found it remarkably consistent!'[4]

Alec Issigonis was fortunate to have been recruited by such an able engineer as Wishart. Indeed he was lucky, in his formative years in the British motor industry, to find superiors who appreciated his considerable talents. There were some, it should be said, who were less enamoured of his personality, his relentless quest for knowledge and his uncompromising standpoint on a range of engineering issues.

By this time Issigonis had already interested himself in suspension and, while Heynes was already running his own small department, Alec was in the main drawing office. As it happened, at the time of his arrival in 1934, internationally the most significant changes were being made to the suspension of the motor car since its birth some 50 years before. It is necessary for us to briefly pause and examine these developments because they were to preoccupy our subject during most of his waking hours in these all-important interwar years.

When motor cars, or horseless carriages as they were originally named, first appeared, their suspension was inherited by their predecessors and was accordingly described as cart springing. This took the form of leaf springs front and rear, which by the 1920s were invariably of the half elliptic variety. There were, of course, exceptions, such as Morgan's three-wheeler Runabout of 1910 and Lancia's Lambda of 1922, both of which featured independent front suspension (ifs). But, in the main, the 19th-century inheritance ruled supreme.

Although cheap and relatively easy to manufacture, cart springs did have considerable drawbacks, which became apparent when a driver encountered an uneven road surface. When one of the car's front wheels made contact with such an undulation, this produced wheel wobble or shimmy in the opposing wheel and the resulting vibration was then felt throughout the vehicle.

In the early 1930s these limitations began to be addressed, not so much in Britain but by the motor manufacturers of continental Europe. As Douglas Clease, technical editor of *The Autocar*, pointed out in September 1933: 'On the Continent... it seems that much less attention has been paid to... transmission problems [addressed, for one, by Edward Gillett] and very much more to the question of suspension, the result being independent suspension of the front wheels, the rear wheels, or of all four wheels is now a feature of many designs.'

The fact that the surfaces of many European roads were inferior to Britain's was a factor in the continental pioneering of such innovations. But the principal reason for this innovative climate was that Europe's car makers tended to recruit their engineers and designers from technical universities and polytechnics. The latter had been created in the 19th century to challenge Britain's industrial supremacy and offered structured, wide-ranging syllabi which by their nature pushed forward the frontiers of engineering research and knowledge.

With a few notable exceptions such institutions were anathema to Britain's motor manufacturers, which invariably relied on the well-established practice of engineering apprenticeships, which, historically, placed a strong emphasis on practical experience. An exception was provided by Morris, which had no proper apprenticeship scheme until World War Two, when one was established by Sir Miles Thomas, its vice chairman, because its founder came to cars via the motor trade, not a traditional engineering business. Wolseley, which he acquired in 1927, did, however, and many of the corporate executives in the BMC era had served apprenticeships with that business.

Such practical instruction was fine as far as it went and, underpinned by theory, tended to result in sound, reliable, inexpensive but unadventurous designs. This in turn produced an introspective corporate self-propagating orthodoxy that generated in its wake a resistance to change. Sir Roy Fedden, between 1920 and 1942 the Bristol Aeroplane Company's dynamic chief engineer, had begun his professional life in the motor industry and found that university graduates who did attempt to pursue such a career invariably 'became disillusioned and turned to other professions, chiefly because those who had come up the hard way mistrusted what they called "mere theory" and were afraid of them.'[5]

Alec Issigonis, because of his unconventional education and cosmopolitan background, had bypassed this particular hazard. His intellectual curiosity and learning knew no geographical boundaries and continued throughout much of his professional life. But because of his own considerable manual abilities, he also had a high regard for practical experience as part of an engineer's training and his own lack of academic success meant he disregarded the benefits of a university education. It was a theme which chimed precisely with that of the British motor industry's first generation leaders, who, in many instances, had built their first cars with their own hands.

This creed was readily apparent at Morris and Austin, the market leaders, and was summarised by Issigonis's friend, Laurence Pomeroy, for 20 years the technical editor of *The Motor* magazine. In 1964 he wrote that both companies had 'made their reputations... by the construction of sound, reliable cars... designed by successive generations of engineers who must have had a common sympathy with the sentiments expressed by the Duke of Cambridge: "All change, at any time, and for any purpose is utterly to be deprecated."'[6]

For these reasons British car makers lagged behind their European counterparts in the adoption of independent front suspension. In December 1937, Maurice Platt, by then a member of the engineering department at Vauxhall, which in 1926 had been acquired by General Motors, reminded his fellow automobile engineers: 'ifs has been very slowly adopted by British manufacturers in contrast with the rapid progress made on the Continent and in America.'[7] Even by 1939 no Morris, Austin nor Dagenham-built Ford was so enhanced. It was not until the 1948 Motor Show that *The Autocar* could report that 'there are few new cars which are not fitted with ifs'[8] and many of these models used the wishbone and coil spring system which is still current today.

Its origins are to be found rooted in the year of 1933, no less than 15 years before, at the Berlin and New York Motor Shows. *The Autocar* headed its report of the German event: 'Independent Springing an Outstanding Feature', which was applied to the entire spectrum of cars from the cheap front-wheel drive DKW to the more exclusive models from Mercedes-Benz. The latter company introduced no fewer than three different types of ifs to complement a swing rear axle introduced in the previous year.

One version, fitted to its supercharged 3.8-litre 380 model, employed what the magazine's correspondent, Edwin P.A. Heinze, described as 'entirely new and exceedingly simple...' 'The front wheels,' he wrote, 'are held between the ends of two triangles hinged on the frame.'[9] These are what today we call wishbones. Although initially two coil springs were employed as the suspension medium, this was subsequently reduced to the more familiar one.

Paradoxically, Mercedes-Benz's innovative design had relatively little impact on the British motor industry, probably because the 380 was only produced in relatively small numbers. Although it went on sale in Britain in 1934 it was an expensive model, selling for £1,535.

It is apparent from his writing on the subject that Alec Issigonis was unaware of the 380's existence, but he was all too familiar with the innovations that were being adopted on the other side of the Atlantic. For at the New York Motor Show, held in November 1933, General Motors, America's, and indeed the world's, leading motor manufacturer, unveiled its own coil and wishbone system on its Cadillac, Oldsmobile and Buick marques. Like Mercedes, GM hedged its bets and introduced an alternative design, and its cheaper Chevrolet and Pontiac lines perversely used a more expensive layout financed by the Frenchman André Dubonnet. But the coil and wishbones held sway and by 1939 had been extended to the entire GM family.

Throughout his entire motor industry career Alec Issigonis rarely acknowledged a debt to any of his engineering contemporaries, but he made an exception in the case of the creator of GM's coil and wishbone layout, who remained a lifelong 'professional hero.'[10] He was not American but an Englishman of Huguenot descent and his name was Maurice Olley.

Born in Scarborough in 1889, Olley matriculated at Victoria University, Manchester in 1905, although an honours engineering course was cut short by illness and he spent a year working on a farm, living and sleeping in the open air. Apprenticed with Birmingham machine tool manufacturer H.W. Ward, in 1912 he moved to Rolls-Royce. In 1913 he was aged only 24 and it says much for his abilities that he was working for Henry Royce as one of his two designers at Le Canadel, the latter's wintertime drawing office on the French Riviera. Accorded the abbreviation of Oy in Rolls-Royce corporate parlance, Olley's colleague was Albert Elliott (E) and, as Royce's biographer Donald Bastow has pointed out, 'E relied heavily on his practised eye, Oy much more on his abilities to analyse and calculate. It is surprising how quickly such a combination can work.'[11]

In 1917 Olley went to America on behalf of Rolls-Royce, to discuss Eagle and

Falcon aero engine production there. This was to culminate in him becoming, in 1919, chief engineer of Rolls-Royce of America Inc., the ill-fated corporate enterprise that established a branch in Springfield, Massachusetts, but closed in 1933. Left-hand drive versions of the Silver Ghost and Phantom I were produced there, but Olley was troubled to find that both models behaved differently from their British-sold counterparts. He observed that the US-built cars suffered from pitching, on account of the poor road surfaces prevalent in America, and, recalled Olley, for 'several years, we had been engaged in a concentrated drive on riding quality.'[12]

Olley took this work, begun at Springfield, with him when he joined General Motors in November 1930, being allocated to its prestigious Cadillac division. A little over a year later, early in 1932, Olley and his team built what he described as a K2 rig[13] and 'we began to feel the urge towards independent suspension... it was telling us, in no uncertain terms, that a flat ride, which was an entirely new experience, *was possible if we used front springs which were softer than the rear* [author's italics].'[14] This was a revolutionary concept at the time, being the reverse of the conventional wisdom being applied to the half elliptic springs, hitherto used throughout the motor industry.

The next step was a costly exercise, and Lawrence P. Fisher, Cadillac's general manager, accused Olley 'of being the first man in GM to spend a quarter of million dollars in building two experimental cars!'[15] One was equipped with what was internally described as an SLA system, for Short and Long Arm, which reflected the fact that the upper wishbone was shorter than the lower one. The Mercedes-Benz concept, by contrast, had near parallel arms. So was Olley influenced by the German system? Apparently not. 'I cannot recall having actually seen the Mercedes suspension,'[16] he said, an instance no doubt of two design teams working independently, as it were, of the other. The second GM experimental vehicle was fitted with the Dubonnet system.

After the corporation's president, Alfred Sloan, travelled in both cars he recognised that ifs should be adopted, even though the year of 1933 represented the nadir of the Depression. His view was supported by Dick Grant, GM's vice president of sales, who declared: 'if I could have a ride like you've shown us, for a matter of fifteen bucks, I'd find the money somehow.'[17]

Maurice Olley readily shared the results of his pioneering research with fellow engineers on both sides of the Atlantic in papers that sparkle with clarity and humour. He also possessed another attribute that would not be wasted on Alec Issigonis. In 1932, William (Roy) Robotham, head of Rolls-Royce's experimental department, visited Olley in America and remembered him as 'a brilliant technician... [who] could produce lightning and lifelike sketches of a piece of mechanism – or anything else – at a moment's notice.'[18]

The fact that General Motors had adopted the device, and was mass producing it, was to have an influence in the drawing offices, if not on all the managers, of Britain's motor industry. At Rootes the progressive Jock Wishart sanctioned some experimental designs and William Heynes recalled that a 'considerable time was spent... on designing ifs, both leaf and coil springs.'[19] He was responsible for an experimental Hillman Minx 'with a leaf spring carried on an overhung pin at the lower end of the stub axle' and although the design 'looked precarious,' it 'became one of the most popular cars on the experimental fleet.'

This was a properly sanctioned project. In the meantime, Alec Issigonis was undertaking a similar but distinctly unofficial exercise. His enthusiasm for Maurice Olley's thinking was shared with a fellow Humber draughtsman named Clapham. Together they designed an experimental ifs system for the wholly orthodox, cart sprung Hillman Minx.

Drawings of what probably closely followed GM's unequal wishbone and coil spring layout were illicitly prepared, parts made and a car accordingly enhanced in the corporate experimental shop. In their youthful enthusiasm Issigonis and Clapham found the steering had been reversed, owing to the thread of the steering worm being wrong-handed. As a result the head of the experimental department refused to let the Minx out of the building, even to be driven down the works drive.

Despite remedying the problem, the pair discovered too late that Rootes had a leaf spring manufacturer in their corporate portfolio and all of its products would have to incorporate that component, be it independent or no. For the record the production Minx retained its semi-elliptic front leaf springs until the arrival for the 1949 season of the Mark III version, which featured coil and wishbone ifs, a good 14 years after Issigonis's experiments.

Internationally, Maurice Olley's wishbones and coil springs did not go unchallenged. In May 1934, just six months after the announcement of General Motors' ifs, yet another medium, that of the torsion bar, featured on a car that its manufacturer, André Citroën, hailed as a 'new concept in motoring.' This was his Traction Avant saloon, the world's first mass-produced front-wheel drive car. One of the truly great designs of motoring history, it rendered the opposition technologically obsolete overnight and while none of its key mechanical components were new, they were united to create a harmonious automotive *tour de force*. This was at a time when the conventional car, driven by its rear wheels, was universally espoused by American motor manufacturers and widely imitated by their British counterparts.

The torsion bar, patented in 1931 by Ferdinand Porsche, a simple and ingenious invention, was, in effect, a coil spring unrolled in the form of a bar. In the new Citroën, it provided the suspension medium for the wishbone ifs in the form of longitudinally located bars which were attached to the lower suspension arm at one end and anchored to the body substructure at the other. There was a different arrangement at the rear where they were mounted transversely to support the undriven 'dead' back axle.

Front-wheel drive not only imbued the new Citroën with outstanding road holding, but the configuration, with its absence of propeller shaft, also made for a roomier passenger compartment, and allowed André Lefebvre, the former Voisin engineer who masterminded the project, to adopt the low, graceful lines of the saloon body styled by Flaminio Bertoni. Aerodynamically honed, another continental preoccupation, it was endowed with a sense of movement, even when stationary.

Of even greater significance, the Citroën was built to unitary construction principles, thereby avoiding the use of a chassis frame, which resulted in a light though strong, if rust-prone, body structure. However, this was achieved at the expense of higher initial tooling costs. The advanced mechanicals were extended to the engine, which was a robust overhead valve wet liner unit, while hydraulic brakes completed the impressive mechanical specification.

Citroën claimed, with extraordinary understatement, that the Traction Avant was 'two years ahead of the opposition.' In reality, so advanced was the concept that it was destined to survive for 23 years, lasting until 1957. Alas, André Citroën, an inveterate gambler, had hopelessly overreached himself financially with the car's creation. Already ailing, he died of stomach cancer on 3 July 1935 at the age of 57 and four weeks later, on 31 July, his business was taken over by Michelin, his largest creditor. It wasted little time in radically reengineering the model, without diluting the innovative essentials of the car, which, in truth, had been rushed into production. By the end of 1935 the suspension and transmission were redesigned, the body substantially reworked and strengthened and, most significantly, its handling was transformed by the arrival, in May 1936, of rack and pinion steering. By the time that production ceased, some 759,000 Traction Avants had been completed.

Citroën's new owners, the brothers Edouard and Pierre Michelin, gave the Traction Avant's creator a free hand to pursue his ideas and André Lefebvre was able to continue his advanced thinking, unfettered by his corporate masters. He was the 'archetypical artist-engineer, worshipping novelty for its own sake and taking a perverse delight in doing things differently, refusing to copy proven techniques successfully used elsewhere.'[20] Sounds familiar? As such Lefebvre became the European motor industry's most idiosyncratic engineering supremo, until Alec Issigonis became BMC's technical director in 1961.

Although popular in France – the Traction Avant's strong sales allowed Michelin to pay off all Citroën's debts and liabilities by 1937 – this positive reception was not repeated in Britain. As motor industry veteran Dudley Noble, who, coincidentally, worked for Rootes during the time that Alec Issigonis was employed at Humber, observed during the 1930s: 'the general public fought shy of a car that was pulled by its front wheels.'[21] This was mainly on account of the bad press front-wheel drive had received, a prejudice that was buttressed by the conservatism of the British buyer. It had little to do with the virtues of an outstanding car.

At the cheap end of the market BSA had, in 1929, introduced a front-wheel drive three-wheeler that was not highly regarded. But opposition existed largely on account of the fact that in 1928 Alvis offered a front-wheel drive model, a concept inherited from its unsuccessful 1925 Grand Prix car. The company prefaced its announcement with the statement that it considered 'purchasers should be experienced folk [sic] as the cars will be very fast...'[22] Quite how such a prerequisite would be policed is unclear.

Designed by William Dunn, the front-wheel drive Alvis, based on a conventional rear-drive chassis, was capable of a respectable 85mph. It did not use constant velocity joints which, ideally, are required to transmit the combined steering and driving forces to the front wheels. (Neither for that matter did the Citroën, which relied instead on conventional Hardy Spicer universals mounted back to back). Such a bespoke joint did exist, however. This was the Tracta, invented in 1926 by the Frenchman Jean-Albert Gregoire, which had been incorporated in his front-wheel drive Tracta, produced in small numbers between 1926 and 1934.

From a European perspective Gregoire dismissed the Alvis as 'a tentative effort... and the transmission was by a simple cardan joint and ball joints, a costly and complicated system... This model was quite reliable but being a sports machine with very hard suspension and a noisy drive train it did not endear itself to the British public.'[23]

This view was shared by respected British vintagents Cecil Clutton and John Stanford, who in 1954 wrote that the model's 'long wheelbase and low centre of gravity... rendered it rather difficult to hold; and this, combined with a high fuel consumption and complexity of the front/suspension drive unit prevented it from becoming a very popular car.'[24] Stanford subsequently opined that the Alvis's: '...odd weight distribution and heavy steering led to decidedly unusual handling qualities, wheel spin being common on wet surfaces, and a complete *volte-face* readily obtainable.'[25]

Ironically this Alvis was only available for two years and a mere 150 or so examples found buyers. But the car's reputation for unpredictable handling, true or otherwise, cast a long shadow. Insurance companies penalised owners of front-wheel drive cars with high premiums and this entrenched prejudice continued until the arrival, in 1959, of Alec Issigonis's Mini.

So when Citroën introduced its front-wheel drive model, a vehicle that had been designed from the outset to reap the advantages of the configuration, there were relatively few British customers. A mere 3,000 or so right-hand drive examples, enhanced with wooden dashboards, leather upholstery, and six rather than 12 volt electrics, left Citroën's Slough factory. They were sold in Britain as the Super Model 12 and Light 15 in the five years between 1935 and 1939. Nonetheless, the model soon generated a small but dedicated British clientele who responded to the car's technical credentials, impressive stability and outstanding road holding, even if its universal joints required lubrication every 600 miles! *The Motor* for one was much impressed; 'a car we could not overturn' it enthused in its road test published in 1934. Although well chronicled by the weekly motoring press, the influential new Citroën was all but ignored by the heavyweight *Automobile Engineer*.

Among the ranks of Traction Avant owners was Tim Carson, secretary of the Vintage Sports-Car Club (VSCC), established in 1934 for owners of pre-1930 vehicles, and there were other like-minded influential members. It was for this reason that the Citroën was added to the list of Post Vintage Thoroughbreds set down by the Club in 1945 – quite an achievement for a mass-produced saloon.

There was no greater enthusiast for this revolutionary front-wheel drive car than VSCC member John Morris, a talented if eccentric engineer whom Alec Issigonis met, probably in the early 1930s, and who was to remain a lifelong friend. Indeed, it was Morris's passion for the Traction Avant – he was also an ardent francophile – that introduced Issigonis to the advantages of front-wheel drive. For this reason some mechanical elements of this revolutionary French car would find their way into the conventionally driven Morris Minor.

A further factor in the Citroën's extraordinary stability was that its wheels were placed at each corner of the car in the manner of vehicles of the previous decade, and this was to become a key tenet of Issigonis's design philosophy. The French car's small boot, a downside of layout, was a less desirable inheritance. It should be said that Alec was not alone in his regard for this revolutionary Citroën and many of Britain's automobile engineers, from W.O. Bentley to William Heynes, held the car in similarly high esteem.

John Morris's influence runs like a consistent thread throughout Issigonis's career, which reached its climax with the creation of the Mini, a car that was destined to bring the concept of front-wheel drive to an international rather than a European public. Yet today the name of John Neville Morris is barely known, although he was an informed, versatile, theoretical and practical engineer of precocious talent and progressive thinking. For many years chief engineer of the SU Carburettor Company, the tall and bespectacled 'Johnnie' Morris is remembered by Norman Painting, who worked with him at SU's Birmingham factory in the 1960s, as being 'on the knife-edge of brilliance and insanity. It was also rather difficult to understand what he was saying because he mumbled a lot.'[26]

John Morris's career was punctuated by what might be regarded as an unnecessary element of derring-do which, on various occasions, threatened his life. As will emerge, the circumstances of his death in 1976 were bizarre and wholly in accord with his shadowy but immensely influential personality.

Morris was born in Harrow, Middlesex, on 23 December 1900, into a comfortable middle-class home, Fairview, in a then tree-lined Pinner Road. His father, Charles Neville Morris, a silk merchant, was sufficiently prosperous to employ two servants at the time of John's birth. His mother, Minnie Helene, although born in Tottenham had the maiden name of André, which suggests a French connection. This may have been the source of Morris's ardent francophilia, which also expressed itself in his love for such illustrious Gallic makes as Bugatti and Delage, or anything similarly grand.

At the age of 11 John was sent away to prep school at Clacton College, Clacton-on-Sea, prior to attending, in 1913, Highgate public school, where he remained until July 1917. There is evidence to suggest that he possessed an early enthusiasm for motor cars because, soon after leaving school between April and September 1918, he served an apprenticeship with Humber at the same Coventry works that Alec Issigonis was to join as a draughtsman 18 years later. Such instruction was then regarded as being the best available in the industry. Morris returned to Humber on two subsequent occasions, between April and October 1921 and during the same months in 1922.[27]

Morris's time in Coventry represented part of his training because in 1920 he entered London University where he undertook a four-year civil and mechanical engineering BSc degree course. He passed the intermediate stages on engineering, pure and applied maths, engineering drawing and sound and optics and attained his BSc (Eng) in July 1924.

Three months previously, in April, Morris had applied for his first patent, for a cine projector, the application being made jointly with Raphael's Ltd of Hatton Garden, who were manufacturing opticians and specialised in lenses, eye and opera glasses and telescopes. It seems likely that Raphael's was John Morris's first employer.

At this time he was living in a rented apartment at a fashionable address: 55 Cambridge Terrace, Hyde Park. But his passion for motor cars once again surfaced because his next patent, for which he applied in April 1928, it being granted a year later, was a device intended to ease gear changing, a subject that was already exercising Alec Issigonis's talents at about the same time not far away in Victoria Street. In such circumstances it is possible that they could have met, although nothing is known of any encounter. Unlike Edward Gillett's crude mechanism, Morris's was a much more sophisticated device, but it was unrealistically expensive as it relied on an electrically actuated small auxiliary gearbox to effect a silent change. At that time Morris was living at the family home at 5 Redcliffe Square, South Kensington.

Two further patentees were listed with the application: Cyril Cornelius Bone and Murray Duncan Scott. The latter cooperated with Morris again to produce a further invention, the patent for which was applied for in July 1929 and accepted in January 1931. Once again aimed at the motor industry, it was for an electrical petrol pump. This was a much more viable proposition and was taken up by the SU Carburettor Company. And, it seems, this was how John Morris came to join the business to see his invention into production. It should be said that he shrewdly had a royalty agreement written into his contract and while the Petrolift was destined for a relatively short life, his other designs for SU were to be much more enduring and would produce substantial revenues over the years, permitting Morris to live in a manner to which he had already become accustomed.

Originally based in North London, SU was established by the brothers Herbert and Carl Skinner in 1910. Theirs, they jocularly decided, was a true Skinners' Union and the invention was duly accorded those initials. But by 1926 their business was in financial difficulties, which did not reflect on the worth of the ingenious constant vacuum carburettor, and in December of that year SU was acquired by William Morris for £100,000. Soon afterwards, at the beginning of 1927, Morris also purchased Wolseley with two Birmingham factories, one at Ward End and the other at Adderley Park.

Car production was concentrated on the former facility and Morris moved SU from its premises in Prince of Wales Road, Kentish Town, to be part of the much larger East Works at Adderley Park, which it shared from 1930 with Morris's commercial vehicle manufacturing facility. With £17,000 of investment for new plant and Carl Skinner as manager, SU was on its way. From 1927 Morris fitted the carburettor to his Flatnose model, which was Britain's best-selling car, selling at least 1,000 units a week. By 1939 production was running at over 4,000. SUs thereafter featured on all successive Morrises, and later practically all BMC's models, right up until carburettor production ceased in 1994. Morris's ownership did not prevent the company selling its products to other manufacturers and they also appeared on a wide variety of British cars. Bentley, Jaguar and Rover were just some of the customers.

The original rendering of John Morris's pump, which reflected its principal patentees, was the Morriscott Petrolift. Not only was it complementary to SU's carburettor manufacture, it was also well timed because it came when rear located petrol tanks were replacing scuttle mounted gravity fed ones. Otherwise the fuel was invariably supplied to the carburettor by Autovac, which relied on the vacuum produced by the engine to draw petrol from the tank to a smaller scuttle-mounted one. Thereafter gravity took over.

The Petrolift also delivered its supply by gravity, but the fuel was drawn into the unit by an electric pump. It should be said that the device was not wholly reliable and John Morris did subsequently concede that it was susceptible to blockage by small particles of grit which emanated from the tank. In such circumstances his remedy was to 'tap the pump smartly, though not too vindictively, say, with a spanner.'[28]

Morris's next contribution to SU was as an employee and was destined to be much more enduring. In 1933 it announced its L-type (for low pressure) electrically operated diaphragm petrol pump, which he had designed in the previous year in collaboration with Leslie Kent. Destined to almost immediately supersede the Petrolift, it was to be made by the million and remains in production to this day (2005), being produced by the Salisbury-based Burlen Fuel Systems. Not all of Morris's ideas were so successful and he devoted much of the 1950s to developing a self-feeding carburettor in which the unit was combined with a fuel pump.

By 1933 John Morris was living in the fashionable Edgbaston district of Birmingham, and indeed he was destined to spend the rest of his life in the area. His first address was 63B Elkington Row, where he remained until 1936. He married and the couple had a daughter, Anna Victoria, but the union ended in divorce. He then moved nearby to Francis Road and in 1943 changed his home for the third and final time to leafy Carpenter Road, which was to be his home for the next 32 years. Number 38 is a fine Georgian-style residence, enhanced by light-giving bay windows in the Victorian era. An adjoining double coach house provided excellent garaging for the succession of Citroëns that SU's chief engineer was to own.

It seems likely that Morris and Alec Issigonis met following Morris's move to the Midlands, although they might have been consolidating a friendship made in the British capital. According to Alex Moulton,[29] who knew both parties, Issigonis and Morris cooperated in the design of a car with all independent interconnected suspension, in retrospect an advanced but overly complicated concept.

The patent application of 1934 for an 'improved anti roll device,' only appears in John Morris's name, perhaps because Issigonis was then working for Rootes, which would have had rights to all his work. There are wishbones front and rear, in the Maurice Olley idiom, which suggests Issigonis, but the suspension medium is longitudinal 'torsion rods' [bars] in the manner of the Traction Avant Citroën, which points to Morris. There is a minor mystery because the application is dated

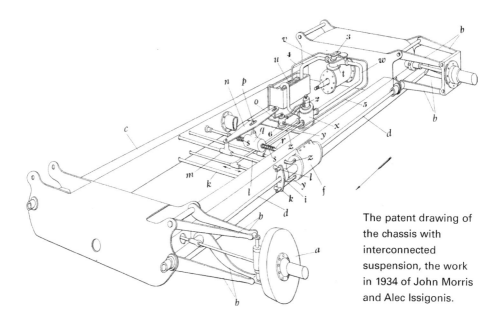

The patent drawing of the chassis with interconnected suspension, the work in 1934 of John Morris and Alec Issigonis.

10 May and news of this revolutionary French car had only reached the press in April. If Morris was so influenced he would have had to have acted very promptly or have had prior knowledge of the design.

The idea was to prevent cars rolling on corners. The front and rear bars met in a cylinder – there was one on either side of the chassis – the interconnection medium being 'fluid or gas' by a pump that was activated by a movement of the road wheels. It seems likely that this was a private venture and it must be doubted whether the design ever progressed beyond the paper stage. In truth it represented something of a distraction from another far better known Issigonis project. This was the Lightweight Special, a purpose-designed car for hillclimbs and sprints, events in which the driver has to compete against the clock rather than the instantaneous rivalry of other cars.

Alec's superior at Rootes, Jock Wishart, regularly caught him undertaking some subversive draughtsmanship on this Special during the year of 1934. It has been described by that arch exponent of the genre, John Bolster, as 'one of the most amazing specials (or should I say *the* most amazing special?) ever constructed.'[30]

To chronicle the Lightweight's origins it is necessary to retrace our steps to 1930 when Alec acquired his Austin Seven Ulster. He competed in this in weekend sprints and hillclimbs, which included such fixtures as the Lewes Speed Trials and Shelsley Walsh hillclimb. There was a strong social element to these events, with competitors invariably gathering at a pub afterwards to discuss the day's proceedings and talk motor cars. It was over a glass or two of beer that the shy, diffident Alec would widen his circle of acquaintances and forge enduring friendships.

He continued with his hillclimb activities following his move to the Midlands and it was then that Issigonis met John Miller Pendlebury Dowson (1908–79), whom he called 'George,' or 'Geordie'. Educated at Uppingham, Dowson had read engineering at Pembroke College, Cambridge, and, after graduation, obtained employment with English Electric at Rugby where he was assigned to work on 1500hp Fullager diesel engines. A keen motorist, Dowson had acquired a Morgan three-wheeler while at university, which he retained to commute to work from The Poplars, the comfortable and elegant Georgian house near Pershore in Worcestershire from where his father farmed a 460-acre estate.

George Dowson had a friend named Rupert Instone, whom he met when they both attended Dunchurch Hall prep school near Rugby. Instone's father Ernest was a one-time managing director of Daimler who, in 1921, had established, with the company's London manager, the respected retail outlet of Stratton-Instone. The young Instone was a regular competitor at Shelsley Walsh, where he ran a special named the GN Martyr, and he already knew Issigonis. The introductions were made at the Queen and Castle Inn in Kenilworth, just a mile away from Alec's Rouncil Lane home and within a bow shot of the walls of the ruins of Kenilworth Castle. 'I understand that this was after a Shelsley meeting, John Bolster was there and they all got thrown out after he poured some tomato ketchup into a piano!' recalls George's son, Christopher.[31]

As a result of this meeting, George Dowson would tow Issigonis's Austin Ulster to race meetings behind the 3-litre Bentley he subsequently acquired. By this time the car had undergone a considerable amount of modification because the more Alec used it, as his knowledge increased, the more he began to recognise its limitations. It was after all based on a passenger model that had been designed in 1922.

Evolving into a Seven-based special which Issigonis christened Susie, the flexible chassis was considerably stiffened at the front by stressing the bonnet sides and the radiator. It was now a single-seater with the passenger's compartment covered with a protective cowl. Issigonis also addressed the all-important matter of suspension and cut the axle in half, widening the track by 4.5in, to produce a crude ifs system. These changes required new radius arms and its creator made temporary wooden mock-ups from broom handles that were cut to the required length.

On the Ulster the supercharger occupied a space on the nearside of the engine but if the drive was reversed it was possible to mount it in front of the power unit. Issigonis introduced this modification and replaced the original Cozette blower with a Zoller, supplied no doubt by his friend Laurence Pomeroy, but this meant moving the engine back in the chassis to accommodate it. This in turn necessitated altering the position of the seat and this requirement meant extending the frame so that the car had a longer wheelbase than the original. Special builders often used the Seven's post-1932 chassis to these ends. Like so many baby Austin-based specials, Issigonis's suffered its fair share of broken crankshafts, which succumbed to the limitation of two main bearings.

The car, says Bolster, suffered the fate of many a tuned Ulster and 'blew up in a big way'.[32] Issigonis said that 'the Ulster was devoured piecemeal by the Lightweight,'[33] presumably after he ran it at Shelsley Walsh in June 1934. But the fact that it reappeared in different hands and in a wholly recognisable form in 1939 suggests that he owned *two* Seven specials. Alec still required a road car and, whether by accident or design, remained loyal to the marque and acquired an example of Austin's soundly engineered, robust but pedestrian 12/4. It was, he enthused in later years, 'one of the best cars I ever owned.'[34]

It soon became apparent that if he was to achieve the performance and road holding that he required he would have to begin with a completely clean sheet of paper. The ensuing car was the Lightweight Special, although it would not be so named until 1939, having hitherto been described as an Austin Seven Special. Work began in earnest in 1934 and would absorb Issigonis's energies, and those of George Dowson, for the next four years. One factor in this protracted gestation was that neither party possessed power tools, only manually operated drills. The Lightweight was wholly hand-crafted. 'Alec valued my father's hands because he was very good practically,' says Christopher Dowson. 'But he told me that George irritated him throughout the Lightweight's construction because he wasn't good enough with a hacksaw! "Push it along George" he used to say, "not straight down". Basically my father was the rich man and Alec was the pauper.'[35]

In later life Issigonis repeatedly claimed to have designed the Lightweight in 1933[36] and the concept of its advanced unitary construction and use of ifs, in general rather than specific terms, may indeed date from that year. What he was aware of, as he later wrote, was in that year, 'or thereabouts, almost anyone with slight technical knowledge, had some idea that reduced unsprung weight, which independent suspension made possible, would lead to better wheel adhesion.'[37]

But the Lightweight's visual similarity, both above and below the bodywork, to the Mercedes-Benz's Grand Prix W.25, which was not seen in public until the Eifelrennen race, held on 3 June 1934, is inescapable. Indeed John Bolster was to reflect that 'many people describe it as a scaled-down Mercedes,' adding with characteristic nationalism, 'I would rather describe the Mercedes a "scaled up" Lightweight.'[38] These are sentiments that sprang directly from Alec himself!

Having said that, Issigonis always insisted that when the Lightweight was running the competition number be applied in red, just like the Mercedes-Benz team. It was a tradition maintained by Christopher Dowson, who drove the car in the 1970s, and he recalls that 'Alec always required that I use red when painting on the figures.'[39]

The mechanicals of the Mercedes-Benzes and, indeed, the rival Auto Union team, were extensively drilled for lightness because both cars had been designed in accordance with a new racing formula, which came into force in 1934 and limited participants to a weight of 750kg, less fuel, oil, water and tyres. However, on their public debut the W.25s were found to be 1kg (2.2lbs) overweight and team manager Alfred Neubauer ordered that the paint be scraped off the monoposto bodywork to reveal the bare aluminium. The legend of the Silver Arrows was born.

The new German cars were not exposed to the full glare of the world's motoring press until the French Grand Prix, held at Montlhéry on 1 July 1934, so Issigonis cannot have begun detailed design work on his special until mid-1934 at the very earliest. There the German racing teams, backed by Hitler's Third Reich, ushered in a new era of scientific racing car design. Mercedes-Benz perpetuated the conventional front engine/rear drive configuration, but unorthodoxy was given its full reign with Ferdinand Porsche's mid-engined P-Wagen Auto Union.

Both cars reflected German prowess in the field of all independent suspension, Porsche's employing his own torsion bar system. But Hans Nibel and Max Wagner's W.25 Mercedes-Benz incorporated the 'prevailing design trend' Issigonis referred to in the introductory quotation to this chapter. Again the Germans had kept its mechanicals secret and, as Karl Ludvigsen has pointed out, 'Not until the first check-in to check the maximum weights would observers be actually able to see that the new cars had independent suspension.'[40]

In due course details did become available in the motoring press and they are, of course, widely known today. At the front the W.25 featured a variation of the wishbone and coil system introduced on the 380 passenger car of the previous year. On the Grand Prix car there were short wishbones of approximately equal length, while the compact coil springs were located horizontally within the front cross member. They were connected to the bottom wishbones through a bell crank, which is a bent lever with two arms at an angle to one other, which pivots at the point where they join. Vertical travel was limited to just 1.8in. As Laurence Pomeroy has observed, this design was 'far from offering the soft low-rate suspension which later proved highly beneficial.'[41] At the rear the independent swing axle was suspended on stubby transverse quarter elliptic leaf springs.

As it happened, both German cars failed to find their form at Montlhéry and the race was won by a cart sprung Alfa Romeo. But in 1935 the German teams moved ahead to dominate the racing season and from 1936 could be regarded as supreme on the racing circuits of Europe until the outbreak of World War Two.

Alec Issigonis's interest in the Mercedes-Benz led him to want to witness its performance at first hand. Therefore in 1935 he and George Dowson, in the latter's Riley Nine saloon, decided on a European tour which took in the Grossglockner Pass in Austria. But their principal destination was that year's German Grand Prix, which was to be held at the Nürburgring on 28 July. Inevitably the Germans dominated the entry with nine of the 20 cars and, of these, six were W.25s. The only real challenge came from Italy with eight cars, Alfa Romeo and Maserati entering four apiece. Britain was represented by a lone ERA.

Fortunately Issigonis and Dowson arrived in time for practice and Alec was able to closely observe the Mercedes-Benz's performance and pinpoint the limitations of their 'hard' independent suspension. He subsequently recalled that 'it was quite apparent that the riding of the cars was little or no better than that of the much older Alfa Romeos and Maserati designs using the cherished cart spring suspension [In fact the P3s were fitted with Dubonnet ifs]. The German cars were faster because they were fitted with much more powerful engines.'[42] He went on 'What was wrong with these early cars was that they were being run backwards. By this it meant the pair of wheels that were softly sprung were at the wrong end of the vehicle. A car will not ride flat unless the front suspension has a lower period than the apparatus that is following closely behind.'

The visitors from the English Midlands could not have watched a better race – the event was destined to be one of the great German GPs of the interwar years. Although Mercedes-Benz dominated the event, the great Tazio Nuvolari, at the wheel of a dated P3, pressed von Brauschitsch in his W.25 so hard that he burst a tyre only seven kilometres from the end, leaving 'the Flying Mantuan' to take the chequered flag. This represented Alfa Romeo's last major success in a Grand Prix event and German cars won at the Nürburgring every year until the lights went out in 1939.

Bearing in mind that the design of the Lightweight Special was by then underway, Issigonis was also critical of the fact that Mercedes-Benz had not chosen to contribute to the cars' structural rigidity or weight-saving by the adoption of a stressed-skin body. Instead the Unterturkheim engineers relied, like all of their contemporaries, on a conventional chassis, in this instance a box section welded structure. It was not until 1962, no less than 27 years after Issigonis's German visit, that Colin Chapman would revolutionise racing car design with the introduction of the Lotus 25, which was the world's first significant stressed-skin Formula 1 car.

Back in 1934 the Lightweight began to take shape and although he relied on his notebooks, which were filled with his own distinctive drawings, Issigonis also took a leaf out of coachbuilding practice and drew large scale plan views of the car on the walls of his small garage in Rouncil Lane, Kenilworth. (There they remained until the 1980s when Mr Goodman, the then owner of the house, unaware of Issigonis's occupancy in the 1930s, removed the shed and disposed of it to make way for his present larger garage).

The project was seen at Kenilworth by special builder *par excellence* John Bolster, better known for the creation of the fearsome wooden-chassied Bloody Mary, who like Issigonis had also begun his motoring career at the wheel of an Austin Seven, a car which he held in high esteem and great affection. Writing in 1949 Bolster recalled that he used to visit Issigonis at Kenilworth 'and argue about his modern theories. The discussions became quite heated, because I was of the brute force and adjectival ignorance school.'[43] There were no hard feelings on either side and Issigonis was 'usually a member of the party when the Bolsters went a'motoring.'[44]

From the very outset Alec's intention was to reap the full advantages of all-independent suspension by adopting a stressed-skin body structure. This combined great rigidity with light weight, an approach he had begun to introduce to his much-modified Ulster. To these ends, instead of retaining a conventional chassis frame, he used two boards of five-ply wood that was then faced in 28 gauge aluminium sheet. It seems he was inspired by the trio of cars that Gabriel Voisin entered for the 1923 French Grand Prix, but these were semi-monocoques, with aluminium-faced plywood chassis. Interestingly they were the work of André Lefebvre, who drove an example into fifth place and was later to mastermind Citroën's groundbreaking Traction Avant saloon. On the Lightweight these two wooden members represented, in effect, two sides of a very light box section girder with the other load-bearing constituents comprising the projected blower casing, engine, differential, seat pan and undershield, together with the bulkhead and cross tubes. Its wheelbase was 7ft 2in, some 11in greater than the Austin Seven's, and the track 4ft 2in.

The suspension of the Lightweight, both front and rear, was clearly inspired in the manner of the W.25. The former took shape on the Rouncil Lane dining room table, the marks it made remaining there for many years afterwards, and consisted of two very short fabricated A arms, the lower being slightly larger between the centres than the upper one. And while the Mercedes-Benz had used coil springs, adventurously Issigonis opted for rubber as the suspension medium. This took the form of a series of rubber rings contained within a 16 gauge chrome molybdenum steel tube cross member which united both the assemblies.

These were located within a pair of load-bearing spats which projected each side of the radiator, and absorbed bending and brake torsion loads. The offside one housed the single SU carburettor that was attached to the supercharger driven

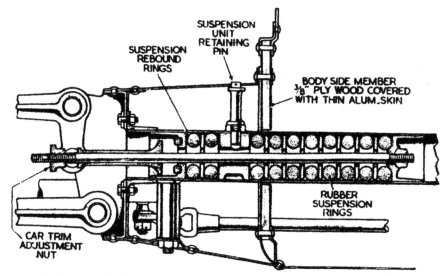

How the Lightweight Special's independent front suspension worked. (*Autocar*)

off the front of the engine. Its dash pot projected through the alloy, the air being drawn through a grilled duct at its forward end.

Although more expensive than steel, Issigonis was no doubt attracted by the rubber's lightness, its space saving attributes and variable rate characteristics. Although Dr Fred Lanchester had presented a paper to the Institution of Automobile Engineers in 1928 on the use of rubber for suspension, this was as an auxiliary to steel half elliptics. Rubber blocks were often used to prevent a vehicle from 'bottoming', to act as a buffer between the frame and spring. But in 1927 the French De Levaud car used a column of rubber discs in a vertical tubular housing at each end of the rear axle and within each steering pivot of the front

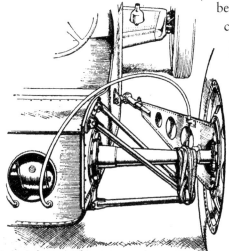

beam axle. Rubber was similarly used in compression in the Harris-Leon Laisne of 1929, which took the form of rubber blocks within the tubular side members.

It is possible that Issigonis's attention was drawn to the use of rubber as a medium when it was crudely applied to the independent rear suspension of the Rover Scarab, a small economy car powered by a rear-

Removal of the Lightweight's tail and rear fairing reveals the swing axle rear suspension with rubber bands used as the medium. (*Autocar*) located air-cooled V-twin engine in which his friend Robert Boyle had a hand. Attracting great interest at the 1931 Motor Show with its projected selling price of £89, happily Rover decided not to put it into production.

Even more adventurous and far more likely to have influenced the designer of the Lightweight Special was the small, very light but unconventional Imperia of 1935. This German car, a sleek aerodynamic sports coupé, was powered by a mid-located three-cylinder radial two-stroke engine, and was the product of the motorcycle manufacturer of the same name. Appearing at the 1935 German motor show, it used a simple all independent suspension which, reported *The Autocar*, was 'by means of rubber bands,' and it also published an illustration of the same.[45] The device had been conceived in accordance with Neimann's patents. Like the Scarab, it was stillborn and, indeed, precipitated Imperia's collapse. But Alec Issigonis was to use the same medium on the rear swing axle suspension of his special.

This took the form of what Bolster aptly described as 'catapult elastic,' rubber loops in tension, made from old tyre inner tubes, in place of the W.25's far heavier steel quarter elliptic springs. Issigonis opted for upper wishbones with a single lower strut, a combination which bore some resemblance to the Traction Avant's front suspension, with a radius arm effectively contributing the secondary lower wishbone.

As the car was only intended for short runs, the six-spoked Bugatti-inspired wheels were fixed and, like its celebrated Type 35 racer, the Austin Ulster brake drums were integral. Although outwardly impressive, in later years Issigonis pondered whether they were actually round... The wheel centres were cast Elektron subversively supplied by Dunlop with Duralumin rims. Brakes, perhaps the weakest feature of the car, were cable-operated, and in later years Issigonis conceded 'we never had any brakes,' to which Dowson added 'we never knew which wheel the brakes would work on.'[46] Matters were not helped by the fact that when they got hot the Elektron rims expanded to detach themselves from the drums. Tyres were 5.25 x 16in covers.

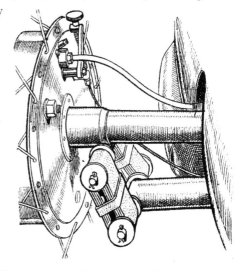

The original caption read: 'rear independent suspension of the Imperia by means of rubber bands.' Was this the inspiration for the Lightweight's rear suspension? (*Autocar*)

Word of the Issigonis/Dowson special soon spread beyond the the bounds of the Rootes drawing office. Just a mile or so away from its Stoke factory at the Holyhead Road premises of Alvis, John Cooper, later sports editor of *The Autocar*, who in 1935 was serving an apprenticeship there, later recalled that 'persistent rumours reached my ears of an extraordinary light sprint car based on an Austin Seven power unit.'[47]

As will have been apparent, Alec had intended to use the Ulster's supercharged engine to power the Lightweight. But then he received a visit from the talented, bespectacled Murray Jamieson, who was a year younger than Issigonis and, by all accounts, an equally single-minded engineer! In 1932 Jamieson had joined Austin, which had been jockeying for dominance in the 750cc racing with MG, the product of the rival Morris Motors, that was powered by a new and more efficient single overhead camshaft engine.

A supercharger expert then employed by Amherst Villiers, Jamieson first imbued greater reliability to Rubber Duck, a racing Seven, and then went on to produce, in 1933, a single-seater and two further cars. Ultimately Jamieson was responsible for the design of a trio of single-seater racers, powered by an unrelated small but potent 744cc supercharged twin overhead camshaft engine. Like Issigonis, Jamieson's visual inspiration had been the W.25 Mercedes-Benz, although he had been constrained by the use of the Seven-inspired cart sprung suspension. The twin-cam Austins appeared in 1936 and the programme had personally cost Sir Herbert Austin the considerable sum of £50,000, although MG had withdrawn from racing in 1935...

The orthodox specification was in accordance with Austin's requirements but Jamieson's original concept had been, like the Lightweight, a monocoque single-seater. This would have been powered by a mid-located engine, à la Auto Union, with surface radiators in the manner of the Supermarine's S6B Schneider Trophy seaplane and a potential top speed of 155–160 mph. But the ultra-conservative Austin chairman vetoed this adventurous concept, maintaining that it was a lethal device for winning races and not a motor car.[48]

Despite this rebuff Jamieson was no doubt impressed to see that he and Issigonis were thinking along similarly advanced lines as far as monocoque construction was concerned. He therefore arranged for Austin to supply him with 'all the necessary parts' to convert an Ulster engine to a works specification. According to George Dowson,[49] this was in exchange for a counterbalanced crankshaft with bolt-on weights that Issigonis had designed for his Ulster, and Jamieson received Alec's drawing of the same. In return Austin provided him and special builder Rod Turner with the latest works components, although Turner's had a conventional crank! The cylinder head was aluminium, there were two plugs per cylinder, one ignited by magneto and the other by coil, and although Issigonis may have been concerned by the additional weight this represented it was offset by the extra power the engine developed. Because the Roots type

Jamieson supercharger blew at 22psi, the cylinder head was held in place by no fewer than 32 studs. Power output was put at 70bhp at 7,000rpm. As Jamieson left Longbridge early in 1937, Issigonis probably received an 'Ulster-based engine with Jamieson additions'[50] in 1936 and also had a second.

It was mounted as low as was practicable and drove through a Seven gearbox with a stubby lever operating in a centrally positioned gate. Thereafter the propeller shaft drove the chassis-mounted differential via a pair of straight-toothed pinions mounted just ahead of the diff. The design was adopted to permit low seating to be introduced and so avoid the weight and complication of an offset transmission, as used by Austin's works Sevens. Because the Lightweight was only to be used for runs of short duration, a small aluminium fuel tank occupied the space directly above the supercharger in front of the radiator. The steering gear was simple and direct, the heads pivoting to the ends of swinging links set transversely to the frame. It had taken George Dowson six months to cut the steering wheel from a sheet of unyielding Vickers Vitrax spring steel. On completion it weighed only 3lb.

Some of the material Issigonis needed for the Lightweight's construction had been acquired from Rootes. One surviving invoice, dated 31 January 1936, is made out to 'Mr Issigonis. Drawing Office' for a sheet of Duralumin for 5s 3d. Unfortunately Alec's time at Humber was overshadowed to some extent by the sudden death, on 23 January 1935 at the age of only 35, of Jock Wishart, who had turned such an acceptable 'blind eye' to his draughtsman's extracurricular activities. Wishart's death was to have a profound influence on at least two of his staff and it is not too much of an exaggeration to state that, had he lived, there would probably never have been the Jaguar XK engine as we know it, or indeed the Morris Minor.

As has already been noted, Heynes, by then head of the stress office in the design department, had a high regard for Wishart, but following the latter's death he was soon being courted by William Lyons, whose SS marque, established a little over four years before, was beginning to make its presence felt. This was a new and untried company, but it needed a chief engineer. It seems unlikely that Heynes would have accepted Lyons's offer – he began work for SS in April 1935 – had it not been for Wishart's demise some three months before. Destined to become the most influential man in the company after Lyons, it was Heynes's advocacy of twin overhead camshafts that lead to the XK unit being so enhanced. He and Alec Issigonis were destined to meet again professionally some 30 years later, although, as will emerge, their meeting was to be far from memorable.

It will be recalled that, prior to his death, Jock Wishart had initiated a programme of independent front suspension for Rootes's larger cars. The 1935 Motor Show saw the launch of the Humber Snipe and Hillman Hawk, enhanced with what was named the Evenkeel system for the 1936 season, a feature that was destined to survive until 1947. As might be expected, and bearing in mind the Rootes corporate commitment, this incorporated a single traverse leaf spring at its lower extremity with a yoke which carried the stub axles for the steering. It connected at its upper ends with a transverse radius rod in the form of a wishbone. Damping was supplied by a large Luvax hydraulic shock absorber located directly above and attached to the upper wishbone by a linking rod. It should be said that the essentials of the design had not originated in the Humber drawing office. Billy Rootes had been influenced by his friend, Studebaker designer Barney Roos, who had been responsible for the ifs system introduced on its President model of 1935.

During development work at Coventry it was found that the spring was set too hard. Issigonis progressively softened it until, one day during a road test, the car went into a pot hole and it bent the suspension backwards. In later years he quipped, 'Well, by the time we'd finished it was far from even!'[51]

Jock Wishart's replacement was an individual of a very different stripe. Unlike the talented Scot, who had an excellent technical education, Bernard Bradbury Winter had none. After serving as a corporal in the Royal Engineers in World War One as a despatch rider he was later promoted to the rank of captain in the Royal Army Service Corps, whereupon he left England for India to join Ford as manager of its Calcutta operations.

Returning to Britain, BB, as he was invariably known, joined Rootes in London as its chief service executive, continuing in this role with Humber-Hillman until Wishart's untimely death provided him with unexpected promotion. Little wonder that, with his paucity of technical knowledge, Winter's engineering approach was conservative in the extreme. He would never have contemplated the all-synchromesh gearbox, to which William Heynes contributed, that Wishart had introduced to the Minx for 1935 and, indeed, Winter deleted it from the 1939 season on the grounds of cost.

Having said that, with his servicing background he approached car design from a practical and cost conscious standpoint. Indeed *The Motor's* technical editor Maurice Platt found BB 'sardonic, able and quick witted.'[52] Winter was not, as far as I am aware, a direct descendant of the Duke of Cambridge. But his was an approach which chimed with that of his superiors, who had made their money from selling cars rather than designing them. It was an alien creed as far as Alec Issigonis was concerned and it could only be a matter of time before he made a move within the industry to a motor manufacturer which placed a greater emphasis on the development of an engineering philosophy.

Notes

1. Pomeroy, *op cit*.
2. Bardsley, *op cit*.
3. Maurice Platt, *An Addiction to Automobiles*, 1980.
4. Andrew Whyte, *Jaguar*, 1980.
5. Sir Roy Fedden, *Britain's Air Survival*, 1957.
6. Pomeroy, *op cit*.
7. Maurice Platt, The Effect of National Conditions on Automobile Design in Great Britain, *Proceedings, The Institution of Automobile Engineers*, Volume 32, 1937–38.
8. *The Autocar*, 5 November 1948.
9. *The Autocar*, 22 February 1935.
10. Barker, *Alec Issigonis, op cit*.
11. Donald Bastow, *Henry Royce – Mechanic*, 1989.
12. Quoted in Alfred Sloan, *My Years with General Motors*, 1963.
13. This was expressed as k2/AB.
14. Sloan, *op cit*.
15. Ibid.
16. Maurice D. Hendry, *Cadillac Standard of the World*, 1973.
17. Sloan, *op cit*.
18. William Robotham, *Silver Ghost to Silver Dawn*, 1970.
19. William Heynes, Milestones in the life of an automobile engineer, *Proceedings, The Institution of Mechanical Engineers (Automobile Division)*, 1960–1961.
20. John Reynolds, *Citroën Daring to be Different*, 2004.
21. Dudley Noble, *Milestones in a Motoring Life*, 1969.
22. Peter Hull, *The Vintage Alvis*, 1967.
23. Jean-Albert Gregoire, *Best Wheel Forward*, 1954.
24. *The Vintage Motor Car*, 1954.
25. John Stanford, *The Sports Car*, 1957.
26. Norman Painting, interview with author, 2003.
27. John Morris's proposal form, dated 18 February 1921, to join the Institution of Mechanical Engineers. He was elected a student member of the graduate section but his membership lapsed in June 1925, due to areas in 1923/24.
28. John Morris, Electric Fuel Pumps, *Proceedings, Institution of Automobile Engineers*, Volume 31, 1936–1937.
29. Alex Moulton, Hydrolastic Springing, *Automobile Engineer*, September 1962.
30. John Bolster, *Specials*, 1949.
31. Christopher Dowson, *op cit*.
32. Bolster, *op cit*.
33. Barker, *op cit*.
34. Barker, *op cit*.
35. Christopher Dowson, *op cit*.
36. Quoted in Dennis May, Beautiful Screamer, *Automobile Connoisseur 2*.
37. Alec Issigonis, A Revolutionary Discusses Racing Cars, *The Autocar*, 4 April 1947. A rare feast, an Issigonis article!
38. Bolster, *op cit*.
39. Dowson, *op cit*.
40. Karl Ludvigsen, *Classic Grand Prix Cars*, 2000.
41. Laurence Pomeroy, *The Grand Prix Car*, 1953.
42. Issigonis, *op cit*.

43. Bolster, *op cit.*
44. Bolster, *Motoring is my Business*, 1958.
45. *The Autocar*, 22 February, 1935.
46. May, *op cit.*
47. John Cooper, The Lightweight Special, *The Autocar*, 10 March 1950.
48. Charles Goodacre, Lord Austin's Murray Jamieson Twin Cam Cars, *The Bulletin*, Vintage Sports-Car Club, No.166, winter 1972.
49. I am grateful to Austin Seven historian Martin Eyre for this information and it followed a meeting he had with George Dowson. Having been given an introduction to Issigonis by Dowson, Eyre telephoned him although his response was, 'I don't remember that period. I can't remember anything.' But Dowson had the drawing and Eyre was able to make a copy.
50. Peter Moores, The Jamieson Side-Valve Austins, *The Bulletin*, *op cit.*
51. Philip Turner and Tony Curtis, The Man who Made the Mini, *Motor*, 14 October 1978.
52. Platt, *op cit.*

No. 9711

NATURALIZATION ACTS, 1870.

Certificate of Naturalization to an Alien.

HOME OFFICE, LONDON.

WHEREAS *Constantine Demosthenes Issigonis*

an Alien, now residing at *20, Upper Westbourne Terrace, London.*

has presented to me, the Right Honourable *Sir Matthew White Ridley, Ba rt.* one of Her Majesty's Principal Secretaries of State, a Memorial, praying for a Certificate of Naturalization, and alleging that he is a

subject of Greece, having been born at Smyrna and is the son of Demosthenes and Irene Issigonis, both subjects of Greece = of the age of Twenty-four years = an Engineer Student = is unmarried

The hinge of fate: first page of Constantine Issigonis's Naturalization Certificate, dated 28 June 1897. It was his decision to become a British subject that probably saved the lives of his son Alec and his wife and allowed them to make their home in Britain. (*The National Archives*)

Battersea Polytechnic, designed by E.W. Mountford, which Alec Issigonis attended in the years between 1925 and 1928. This is the east corner, photographed soon after the opening of the Great Hall on the right in 1899. (*University of Surrey*)

Team effort: Alec Issigonis, third from front, in a tug of war competition at Battersea Polytechnic's sports day held at Merton Abbey, Surrey, on 17 June 1927. His fellow students, from right to left, are Ottman, Lofts, McCarthy, Lee, Robertson, Man-Son-Hing and Velge. (*University of Surrey*)

Barton, the chalet bungalow in Overhill Road, Purley, Surrey as it is today and outwardly little changed, apart from the windows, since Alec and his mother lived there in the years between 1926 and 1928. (*Author*)

When Issigonis started work in 1928, Alec and Hulda moved to 5 Grove Road, Willesden, in London NW10, which was more accessible to the Midlands than Purley. They remained there until 1934. (*Author*)

When mother and son moved to the Midlands in 1934 they made their home at 12 Rouncil Lane, Kenilworth. It was here that Alec began work on the Lightweight Special. (*Author*).

The Austin Seven, a small car in miniature, had an overriding influence on Alec Issigonis during the interwar years and it continued throughout his life. Able to accommodate four people, this example of a Chummy tourer dates from circa 1927. He also perpetuated the Austin's wheel-at-each-corner, so typical of the day, which was made possible by the absence of a boot. (*Tim Harding*).

The title page of the instruction manual for Issigonis's supercharged Austin Seven Ulster. Quite why he has written the words 'From which the L.W. [Lightweight Special] was built!' upside down is unclear! (*Christopher Dowson*)

Issigonis's much modified yellow Austin Seven Ulster, which was owned by Monica Strain, née Whincop, just before and after World War Two. (*Christopher Dowson*)

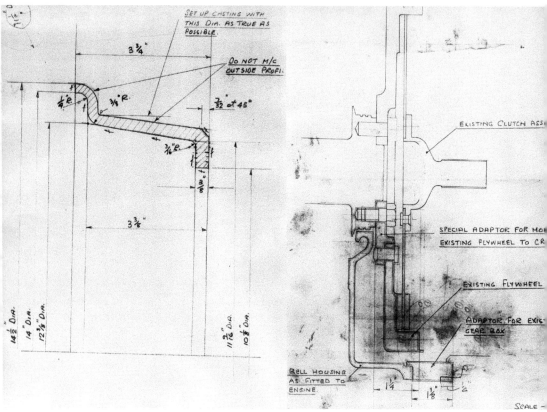

While Issigonis's sketches are now well known to a wider public, his draughtsmanship is less familiar. These two examples relate to the Lightweight Special and shows a detail of a brake drum and modifications to the flywheel of its Austin Seven engine. (*Christopher Dowson*).

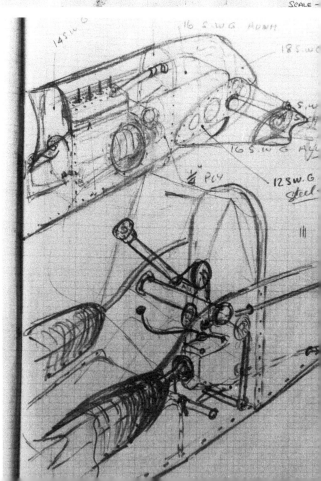

A page from Alec Issigonis's notebook showing the design of the front of the Lightweight Special. Note the amount of aluminium he specified, with steel only being used for the mounting plate for the front suspension binnacle. (*National Motor Museum*).

The quality of workmanship expended on the Lightweight Special is immediately apparent. The air intake is for the SU carburettor and its projecting dashpot can be clearly seen. This 1936 photograph, according to a note written on its reverse in Issigonis's hand, reads 'Abingdon Radley Park'. (*Christopher Dowson*).

The Lightweight Special, *sans* engine but with the Zoller supercharger in position. The car's aluminium-faced plywood cheeks taper Bugatti-like to their deepest point just behind the engine. (*Christopher Dowson*).

Citroën's famous Traction Avant model of 1934 introduced Issigonis to the benefits of front-wheel drive and, unlike many of its contemporaries, it perpetuated a wheel-at-each-corner, a layout Issigonis would also espouse. This is the 1.3 litre 7A. (*Citroën*)

Jack Daniels, an outstanding draughtsman and rarely seen without his pipe, who worked with Issigonis from 1937 until the 1970s. It was Daniels who transformed his sketches into full engineering drawings, filling in some of the detail on the way. He is pictured here at about the age of 50 in the early 1960s. (*Dave Daniels*).

Chapter Three

THE MOVE TO MORRIS

'When I was middle-aged I was doing research work at Morris and had a pretty free hand on the development of suspension and chassis problems...'[1]
Alec Issigonis

OUR SUBJECT clearly considered himself 'middle-aged' under the age of 40 because when he joined Morris Motors, then Britain's largest car maker, late in 1936, he had just celebrated his 30th birthday! No matter. By the end of the decade Issigonis could justifiably regard himself as one of Britain's foremost experts in this rapidly evolving field although, as will emerge, he still had much to learn.

It was sometime in 1936 that the second contact Alec Issigonis had made in Coventry during his spell with Edward Gillett came to fruition. Robert Boyle was at Rover when he first encountered Issigonis but he subsequently moved to Morris's Engines Branch, also in the city, and from there, in about 1935, had been elevated to the position of chief engineer of Morris Motors at its Cowley headquarters. For this appointment Boyle had to thank Leonard Lord, Morris's managing director, who had spent five years of his motor industry career at the same engine facility. Lord was destined to become the most powerful and controversial figure in the British motor industry and he was also to have a profound influence on Alec Issigonis's career, both indirectly and directly, for a period of 25 years.

Leonard Lord had built his reputation on being one of Britain's finest production engineers, although he could relate to machines in a way he never achieved with people. He was, in truth, a flawed personality, a self-made man who possessed, in excess, all the strengths and weaknesses of having had to make his own way in the world.

Bespectacled with a beaky nose, a tuft of ginger hair and with a cigarette invariably dangling from his lips, Lord was tough, impulsive, ambitious and able but suffered, according to his colleague at Morris, Miles Thomas, from an 'inverted inferiority complex'[2], whatever that might be. One consequence of this condition was that he invariably feared rather than respected ability and although he was capable of individual acts of kindness, he harboured resentment against more able colleagues which could smoulder away for years. At worst the luckless individual could find himself demoted or dismissed. Lord ruled his businesses through fear and his diction was invariably peppered with expletives to the extent that he was privately dubbed 'Lord Foulmouth' by many members of his workforce.

Throughout his motor industry career Lord rarely, if ever, gave newspaper and magazine interviews, for reasons that will become apparent, and only very occasionally spoke about his childhood to colleagues. What follows[3] is probably the first occasion that full details of his education and career up to the age of 26, which was when he joined what became Morris's Coventry engine works, have appeared in print.

Leonard Percy Lord was born in Coventry on 15 November 1896. His father, William, was the city's baths' superintendent and the Lord family lived on the premises in Priory Street. He was devoted to his mother, Emma (née Swain), although, perversely, he consistently omitted her name from his *Who's Who* entry, which only mentions his father. William Lord subsequently became landlord of the Hare and Hounds public house in Whitefriars Lane and with such a working-class background, Lord's prospects did not look promising.

But Len was a bright lad and, after attending Wheatly Street Elementary, he won a scholarship to Bablake, the city's famous public school, established in 1344, arriving in August 1906 as a day boy at the age of nine. Unfortunately in 1909 William Lord died, which would have immediately threatened young Leonard's education. Yet such was the promise he showed that the Coventry Education Committee agreed to pay his fees and Lord, by then living with his mother at 305 Foleshill Road, was destined to remain at Bablake until he left in August 1913 at the age of 16.

Cocky, outwardly self-confident and the beneficiary of an excellent education, Len Lord decided to become an engineer. He had passed the London University matriculation exam but did not take up the place, probably for financial reasons.

Instead he got a job as an apprentice draughtsman with Courtaulds, which in 1904 had opened a large factory close to his home to manufacture rayon. In the evening he studied engineering at Coventry Technical College.

One day at Courtaulds Lord found himself in his superior's office and, when he was asked by his boss what his ambitions were, Lord cheekily responded: 'I am going to sit in the chair you're sitting in now.' Later he predicted he would retire, a self-made man, when he was 40. 'Sloppy wasn't it?'[4] was his recollection of this episode in later life. After two years in the drawing office and six months in the works, he left Courtaulds in December 1915. World War One had begun 16 months previously and he immediately joined the Coventry Ordnance Works, opened in 1905 by Cammell Laird and John Brown as a rival to Vickers for the manufacture of munitions.

Lord remained there until the end of the war in 1918 and in the following year obtained his first job in the motor industry, joining Daimler but only remaining there for two months, probably because he had been offered a better job, this time as general manager, at the age of 22, of the Jig and Tool and General Engineering Company in Coventry. But in September in 1920 he was on the move again, this time to London, where he became chief designer of Holbrook and Sons in Stratford, manufacturers of precision machine tools. It was at this time, in 1921, that Lord married; his bride was Ethel Lily Horton and the couple were to have three daughters.

In April 1922 Lord returned to Coventry, having secured the post of assistant chief engineer with the Hotchkiss company at its factory in Gosford Street, which in 1919 had secured a contract to produce engines for William Morris's famous Bullnose model. He began as a draughtsman in the jig and tool office and in 1923 Morris's purchased the business and renamed it Morris Engines. (It was retitled Engines Branch in 1926, following the public flotation of Morris Motors).

When chief engineer Herbert Taylor conceived the idea of harnessing a series of transfer machines to mass-produce ready-machined engine blocks, which gave the plant a world lead in such technology,[5] the idea found a receptive ear in general manager Frank Woollard. In his turn he allocated Leonard Lord responsibility for designing the necessary machine tools, which were built in Birmingham by James Archdale. As a result the output of engines and gearboxes quadrupled from 300 a week in May 1923 to 1,200 in December 1924. Leonard Lord had made his mark.

In 1928 Morris introduced the Minor, its response to the side valve Austin Seven, which was powered by a sophisticated overhead camshaft engine. Although ideal when extended to the in-house M-type MG sports car, it proved to be wholly unsuitable for a cheap one. In consequence sales director Miles Thomas dubbed the Minor his 'troublesome baby.'[6] The engine was produced by

Wolseley and Morris promoted Lord to the post of managing director. Once there he wasted little time in introducing a simpler and cheaper side valve engine which improved the Minor's sales potential.

However, although Morris Motors had dominated the British motor market during the 1920s, the early 1930s saw the company introduce an unwieldy multiplicity of models and in 1933 and 1934 Austin, their great rival, produced more cars. Managers came and went and Sir William, as Morris became in 1929, impressed by what Lord had achieved at Wolseley and to the astonishment of the industry, elevated him at the age of 36 to the position of managing director of the entire organisation. He took up his Cowley-domiciled position in April 1933.

There the cars were still being pushed along the assembly lines by hand and Lord embarked on a radical £300,000 reinvestment programme, which transformed the facility into one of Europe's most modern car factories, capable of producing 2,000 cars a week. But his ruthless drive for efficiency made him few friends on the way. In 1934 he introduced the Morris Eight, clearly inspired by Ford's successful Model Y, which was destined to be Britain's best-selling car of the decade. Thanks to Leonard Lord's efforts, Morris was back in pole position and his achievements were soon reflected in the pre-tax profits of Morris Motors, which rose from £844,000 in 1933, the year of his arrival, to £2.1 million in 1936, albeit for a 16-month period.

In addition to the programme of reinvestment Lord had initiated at Cowley, he also turned his attention to the engineering side of the business. Prior to his arrival car design had ostensibly been vested in works director Hans Landstad, who, with William Morris, had in 1914 created the best-selling Morris Cowley.

Landstad by then was in his mid-50s and Morris Motors lacked a hands-on individual in overall technical command so Lord appointed Robert Boyle, a younger man, to the post of chief engineer. Once ensconced at Cowley, and alarmed by the amount of paperwork that landed on his desk, Boyle complained to his managing director of his workload. Lord responded by picking up the offending letters and throwing them into the wastepaper basket. 'If it's important, they'll write again,'[7] he told his new recruit.

Robert Boyle was soon despatched to America to see how General Motors designed its cars. GM had initiated a design procedure which it named 'sectionalising', as Maurice Olley later explained to his British engineering contemporaries.[8] This consisted of a dozen or so engineers who were 'presented with full responsibility for a section of the car: engine, transmission, axles, suspension steering, chassis, tinware, cooling, electric parts etc.'

Chief engineer Boyle returned to Cowley and immediately began to implement an abbreviated version of GM's sectionalising scheme at Cowley and he sought to attract new, younger blood to Morris Motors. Leslie Hall and Seddon were already chief body engineer and body draughtsman respectively, but Boyle needed an engine specialist. He recruited 29-year-old Tom Brown, a one-time employee of Wolseley, where he had been engaged on general design and prototype development, and in 1933 had joined Austin to lay out, under Murray Jamieson's direction, the twin-cam engine for his single-seater racers. Brown arrived at Cowley in 1936, as did Alec Issigonis, who had just turned 30 when he reported to Morris Motors's Cars Branch, as Cowley was titled, at the end of the year.

One R. Cordey had been assigned suspension but Issigonis, much to his disgust, was allocated rear axles. 'I said, 'not on your bloody life, I won't do a back axle – but I'll do the suspension for you if you like,'[9] he later remembered. He got his way and the luckless Cordey had to content himself with the seemingly little changing world of axle design.

By this time Leonard Lord had left Cowley, having resigned from Morris Motors on 24 August. Although this rupture was to have a wholly negative effect on the British motor industry, on a more positive front, had Lord, an engineer with his own very firm views of car design, remained running the business, there would never have been a Morris Minor. Issigonis was destined to be given a free rein by Miles Thomas, then vice chairman of Morris Motors but a marketing man. Indeed, his lack of technical knowledge was such that when Robert Boyle attended a meeting addressed by Thomas, to the amusement of the engineers present, the latter displayed a graph that, unknowingly, he had positioned upside down![10] With such a limited grasp of technicalities he would be ready to leave Issigonis to his own devices.

Back in the latter half of 1936, the seismic shocks caused by Leonard Lord's resignation only a matter of months before Alec's arrival were still being felt. Indeed *The Motor* described it as 'quite the biggest sensation in the motor industry for some years...'[11] The reason for his abrupt departure at the very height of his powers at the age of only 39 has always been thought to be related to Lord Nuffield, as Morris became in 1934, not being prepared to provide his managing director with a share of his profits. Another cause often cited is that Lord had also sided with the Air Ministry in the face of opposition from his chairman with regard to Morris Motors's involvement in the shadow factory scheme. This government initiative, which recognised that a war with Germany was inevitable, required that companies within the motor industry would manage factories built at government expense for the manufacture of Bristol aero engines.

However, recent research has revealed[12] that in the summer of 1936 it was an open secret at Cowley that Leonard Lord had blotted his copybook on a more personal level because he was found to be conducting an illicit affair with a female employee. This may well explain why, for the remainder of his life, Lord rarely gave interviews to journalists or writers and only spoke to them on an informal, non-attributable basis. It is also possible that word of the affair reached the disapproving ear of Lady Nuffield and it would have been wholly in keeping with her strictly moralistic tone if she had exercised pressure on her husband to dismiss Lord. (According to Miles Thomas,[13] Lady Nuffield was to play a similar role when, in 1941, her husband sacked Cecil Kimber, creator of the MG marque, whose domestic affairs had been in some turmoil and who was conducting a relationship with a lady whom in 1938 he married).

Nuffield, who was a generous employer, gave Lord a £50,000 'golden handshake', today the equivalent of some £2.5 million, perhaps as a disincentive for him to work for another motor manufacturer, and, outwardly at least, his former managing director bore Lord Nuffield no ill will. Soon after his departure he went on holiday to America and, on his return, on leaving the *Queen Mary*, he made his first public and uncharacteristically self-deprecating comments on the rift. 'I am pigheaded and Lord Nuffield has his opinions,' he told the waiting newsmen. 'There was no row between us. A few minutes after we had decided to break our business relations we had a gin and French together, and we laughed over the fact that we could both sit drinking, although we had taken a step that grieved us both.'[14]

Miles Thomas, who knew his former colleague better than most, thought otherwise and believed that the 'intensely sensitive' Lord was 'hurt... deeply'[15] by his abrupt dismissal, although he does not allude to the real reason for his departure. In the short term Lord, from January until December 1937, oversaw Lord Nuffield's initiative to distressed areas, for which he was paid the princely salary of £416 13s 4d per month or exactly £5,000 a year, the equivalent of about £150,000 by today's values.

The calamitous reverberations of Lord's dismissal have echoed down the years and its effects are being felt to this day. In a celebrated exchange with his colleague Miles Thomas, following the rift with Lord Nuffield, a clearly embittered Lord pledged to 'tear Cowley apart brick by bloody brick.'[16] And while it would be overly simplistic to place the decline of Britain's motor industry wholly at Leonard Lord's door, he did, nevertheless, play a commanding role in its demise. And in 1993 the bricks of Morris's one-time factory in Cowley were indeed torn apart, by building contractors, to be replaced by a science park, and although motor manufacture continues nearby, it is where BMW now produces its new MINI. Paradoxically it is the spiritual successor to the car that Lord commissioned from Alec Issigonis, but the name is now the property of, and the car is being produced by, a German company. It is a state of affairs that the fiercely nationalistic Lord and the anti-German Issigonis could never have countenanced.

In February 1938 Lord defiantly joined Morris's arch-rival Austin, as its founder's heir apparent. While this has usually been presented as a matter of

Austin recruiting the best production man in the business, another dimension is provided by Lord Swinton, then Secretary of State for Air. In his memories he writes that: 'I very much wanted Lord in the aircraft picture, but we came to the conclusion that if he were agreeable we could use him better elsewhere, and *we arranged he should join Austins* [author's italics] to take charge both of airframe production and of engine and assembly work which that firm was to undertake.'[17] While this statement should not be taken too literally, it does, nevertheless, suggest a degree of governmental pressure on Austin to take on Lord as a supporter of its shadow factory scheme. Once ensconced, the new works director set about revitalising a sound but static business. By 1949 it had, in productive terms, overhauled Morris, a company that Leonard Lord now held firmly in his sights.

Lord's replacement at Morris Motors was Wolseley's pipe-smoking managing director, Oliver Boden, who didn't want the job. 'There's going to be a lot of heads rolling soon over some botch-ups, car engines in commercial vehicles and that sort of thing'[18] he told his friend John Howlett, founder of Wellworthy Piston Rings, who, like Issigonis, had learnt his engineering at Battersea Polytechnic. Boden knew that Lord 'had cut a few corners and then, when the birds come home to roost, he blames the people who let him do it.' But 'you don't refuse Morris, not when he's made up his mind.'

Robert Boyle, who, it will be recalled, was a Lord appointee, was an early casualty of the new regime and he left Cowley to return to Engines Branch. By World War Two Boyle was back at Rover and he was to be a key player in the design of the acclaimed 2000 model of 1963. Tom Brown also departed for Engines, where he became the Branch's assistant chief engineer. Cordey, after his spell on rear axles, may have been glad to find sanctuary at Wolseley. This left only Alec Issigonis as a member of Boyle's original team.

The move to Cowley had resulted in a temporary halt to the construction of the Lightweight Special because Alec and his mother had to move house and they found a new home in the village of Radley, near Abingdon, within easy driving of Morris Motors's works. It seems likely that, prior to their move, Issigonis disposed of his Austin Seven Ulster, although, as will emerge, he was to meet up with it again in wholly unexpected circumstances.

Issigonis and his mother once again followed the precedent they had established in Warwickshire of living in a semi-rural environment conveniently located a few miles away from Alec's place of work. Cowley is on the south-eastern side of Oxford and Radley some four and a half miles to the south of the city. It was just two and a half miles from the town of Abingdon, to where Morris's MG subsidiary had moved in 1929.

Radley at the time was a scattered community with a population of about

1,000 and, apart from agriculture, was dominated by Radley College public school, which had opened there in 1847. Mother and son were to rent a lodge, Oakdene, on the college estate and within the confines of Radley Park. However, the move necessitated Alec building a shed to house the Special and it lived outside until the work was completed. As will emerge, it was to inhabit one further location before its eventual completion.

Robert Boyle was replaced in 1936 by an individual whom managing director Oliver Boden had known well at Wolseley. Victor Oak, who was accorded the title of group chief engineer, was a capable and direct but pragmatic personality. During his final years as chief engineer at Ward End he had been responsible for the design of the Six saloon and Hornet sports car lines, and he had also worked well with Hubert Charles, MG's chief engineer, as Wolseley supplied Abingdon with its overhead camshaft engines.

To Vic Oak's eternal credit he recognised Issigonis's worth, or to quote a contemporary, he soon identified his 'creative potential.'[19] The author of these words is Jack Daniels, a 25-year-old draughtsman Oak assigned to Issigonis, who would transform his freehand sketches into engineering drawings. Often these would resemble parts of an automotive three-dimensional jigsaw, and they were becoming an increasingly important part of Issigonis's creative process. For Daniels this marked an association with 'Issy,' as he always described him, that was destined to endure for over 40 years. He recalls that the 'little sketches were quite accurate, you'd see a clear outline of what he wanted, the detail you had to sort out yourself afterwards.'[20]

Charles Griffin, Issigonis's right hand in the 1960s, says that he had 'a great reverence for his technique. He was a great sketcher, he didn't do any calculations, it was all in his eye, but if you went through something, stress-wise, you'd find it was a beautifully balanced piece of engineering.'[21] Alex Moulton put this intuitive gift down to his friend's Greek blood.[22]

As far as Issigonis was concerned, he said: 'I was not taught to do formal drawings – I devised my own technique. It was not so much to communicate with other people but to communicate with myself. The first sketch can be very, very informal – it's only for myself. But when it comes to doing a sketch for somebody who has to interpret my ideas, then I do formal sketches.'[23]

Jack Daniels's brief, he recalled, was to keep the mercurial Alec 'on the rails'[24] and he later reflected that 'most people found Issy hard to get on with but he and I just gelled!'[25] And as far as Issigonis was concerned, he had been assigned 'the best draughtsman in the country who was also an excellent mathematician!'[26]

William John 'Jack' Daniels, (1912–2004), born on 8 February 1912, left the Oxford Central School, where he shone at woodworking and engineering drawing and, at the age of 15 and a half in 1927, joined MG at its new factory at Edmund Road, Oxford, as its first unindentured apprentice. When MG moved to Abingdon in the autumn of 1929 Daniels was one of the first to arrive there and he joined the drawing office. His immediate superior was Keith Smith, but, following a contretemps with the management, he departed to be replaced as chief designer by George Gibson, who had previously been employed on the design of the R100 airship.

Daniels's worth soon came to the attention of Hubert Noel Charles, MG's talented chief engineer. Jack could not have had a better mentor. He also knew Vic Oak through MG's associations with Wolseley. But in the summer of 1935 Leonard Lord ordered that the Abingdon design office be closed. He disliked MG's creator, Cecil Kimber, but he also had a point because the business had returned a profit of a mere £419 in the five years of trading between 1930 and 1934 and recorded its biggest ever loss, of £28,156, during the first eight months of 1935.[27] MG, hitherto personally owned by Lord Nuffield, was now acquired by Morris Motors and thereafter design responsibility would be vested in its Cowley drawing office. All the technical staff were sacked, with the exception of Charles, Daniels and body engineer George Cooper, who were transferred to Cowley in mid-1935. Even Hubert Charles was distanced from the immediate design of MG cars, although he was retained in a consultative role. He did, however, move into the mainstream of Morris car design.

Jack Daniels then witnessed the various upheavals in that organisation and, although he was to strike up a good rapport with Issigonis, the latter did not get on with Hubert Charles, who had graduated with a BSc degree in engineering from London University, the very establishment that had failed to recognise Issigonis's worth in his youth. Perhaps when Alec learnt that Charles listed 'mathematics' as one of his hobbies, a subject that he loathed, that was the last straw!

His working association with Jack Daniels dates from 1937, when Vic Oak brought them together for what the latter described as 'the nucleus of a Design and Development team.'[28] However, Jack remained in the main drawing office, but was given a large full-scale drawing board to augment his existing flat equipment. For his part Issigonis took over an office in an adjacent area, to which workshop personnel were recruited.

As such they were to work on the development of the unitary body for the new Series M 10hp saloon, destined for the 1939 model year, which was Cowley's first monocoque. Built up from a total of 69 pressings, it was welded and fused together by Pressed Steel just across the road from the Morris works. It was not Britain's first unitary car, however. That accolade belonged to Vauxhall, General Motors's British satellite, which had, in October 1937, launched its revolutionary 10hp model, complete with Olley-designed ifs.

Issigonis, as Morris Motors's resident suspension expert, was also commissioned to design the company's first ifs system for the Series M that was announced in August 1938. This was to be allied with a rack and pinion steering gear that gained popularity in Germany following its appearance in 1932 on the front-wheel drive Adler Trumpf. Issigonis, thanks to John Morris's influence, would have been all too aware of its arrival on the Traction Avant Citroën and Morris's new 10 would have been the first British car to be so enhanced.

Alec was soon at work designing a coil and unequal wishbone unit in the Olley idiom, although the new car was not destined to be so equipped. It was not until 1958 that H.N. Charles revealed[29] that the design had proved to be unsatisfactory, or, as he tactfully put it, Issigonis's 'first attempts with coil springs were not up to our hopes… and I was forced, at a moment's notice, to perform the almost impossible feat of designing a softly sprung small car suspension using an ordinary front axle and radius rods to meet the emergency.'

Perhaps, characteristically, Issigonis had a different version of events, involving the presence at Cowley of a Chrysler with 'a very conventional beam axle… that rode almost as well as those with ifs… and the management said, understandably, that if American cars could manage so well with beam axles, then Morris engineers must follow suit.'[30]

H.N. Charles devised a conventional beam axle for the Series M which radically differed from its contemporaries by incorporating a transverse torsion bar cranked at either end and attached to the front axle by brackets. This prevented the axle from twisting under braking and has been a familiar feature of many British cars ever since. In addition to this feature, significantly Charles specified that the front springs be far softer than the rear ones and here Olley's influence is immediately apparent. He was flying in the face of orthodoxy but clearly Charles and Issigonis were thinking along similar lines.

As it happened Alec and Jack Daniels's efforts were not wasted because they continued their work and the ifs system would have featured on the Series III Morris 12 destined for the 1939 Motor Show that was cancelled because of the outbreak of World War Two. The new suspension/steering combination was also intended for a related MG-chassised version of the Series M, which was due to appear at the same event, but what was then designated the MG Ten saloon would not break cover until 1947 when it appeared as the Y-type. Issigonis's front suspension was also extended to MG's TD Midget sports car, was perpetuated on the MGA and survived, in essence, on the MGB, which endured until 1980.

Despite a busy work schedule Alec Issigonis had been able to take some time off during 1937 to attend the Monaco Grand Prix, held on 8 August. He was accompanied by George Dowson, who, it will be recalled, had been his companion at the German event two years before. After the war they drove to the event, non-stop from Calais, in a pedestrian side-valve Morris Minor. Dowson later recalled the run as being 'the longest journey of my life!'[31]

The 750 kilogram formula was intended to end in 1936 but it was extended for a further year. Mercedes-Benz's Max Wagner, assisted by a young Rudolph Uhlenhaut, had designed an entirely new car for the new formula. Its tubular chassis now featured ifs with softer coil springs than its predecessor, with unequal wishbones used in conjunction with a De Dion rear axle. Rather than being fitted with an intended V12 unit, instead a 5.6-litre twin overhead cam straight-eight unit was installed. With a theoretical output of 646bhp at 5,800rpm, it was the most powerful racing car the world had ever seen.

Mercedes-Benz ran a quartet of these cars at Monaco while rival Auto Union fielded a trio of 6-litre C-type mid-V16-engined racers. The latter had triumphed in three races during the season to the Mercedes-Benz's one. The German cars dominated the first three rows of the grid with the remaining three lines occupied by slower Alfa Romeos and Maseratis.

The celebrated street circuit, a 'race of 1,000 corners,' would present a fascinating spectacle. Once again Alec and Dowson arrived in time for practice and Issigonis recalled that 'even on the comparatively smooth streets of the town, and bearing in mind that speeds are low on this circuit, it was apparent that a substantial improvement in road holding [on the Mercedes-Benz] had been attained. Gone was the high-pitch frequency of the sprung mass, and the front wheels were tracking correctly.'[32] He no doubt approved of the fact that W.125s dominated the race, taking the first three places, with an Auto Union fourth and another W.125 fifth.

His impressions of the improvements apparent on the W.125 were confirmed at the Donington Grand Prix, held some two months later on 2 October. Thanks to the combined efforts of the RAC, J.F. Shields, the circuit's owner, Fred Craner of the Derby and District Motor Club and Richard Seaman, the English racing driver who in 1937 had joined Mercedes-Benz, the Germans were persuaded to send their two teams to Britain for the first time and spectators flocked to the Derbyshire circuit to see the Silver Arrows in action. Once again four W.125s and three Auto Unions ran and Alec positioned himself at the Melbourne hairpin to see how the cars behaved when their suspension was fully extended.

'The merits of well-appointed soft suspension were at last demonstrated to the racing world at large. The road-holding performance [of the Mercedes-Benz] was outstanding at the hump on the straight where it dips down to Melbourne Corner,' he enthused and contrasted this with the behaviour of the Auto Unions at the same place. 'They pitched so badly coming out of the bump that the rear wheels went clean off the road. Other cars running in this race were too slow at this point to show up suspension defects.'[33] Despite these limitations, Auto Union's star, Bernd Rosemeyer in a C-type, took the chequered flag, von Brauschitsch in the leading W.125 having burst a tyre, although Mercedes-Benzes were in second and third places.

In 1938 a 3-litre racing formula was introduced and Mercedes-Benz replaced its fabled W.125 with the equally successul W.163. After the war, in 1947, Issigonis had the opportunity to examine an example while it was en route to America. To him the well-honed aphorism of 'racing improves the breed' was 'so much nonsense. A quick glance around this 1939 Grand Prix car shows the student of design that the machine bristles with chassis and suspension details that were commonplace on the better types of transatlantic car in the mid-thirties.'[34] He cited the gas welding of the chassis and noted that the wishbone independent front suspension 'followed closely the layout employed by General Motors.' He was clearly unaware that Mercedes-Benz's work preceeded GM's, but his point was, nevertheless, still valid.

Issigonis never lost his love of these pre-war Grand Prix events. In addition to his regard for Rudolph Uhlenhaut and Ferdinand Porsche, the Beetle excepted, Christopher Dowson recalls: 'Alec's heroes included the drivers too, Bernd Rosemeyer, Rudolph Caracciola, Dick Seaman and Herman Lang.' After the war 'he also worshipped Fangio and Ascari too and, of course, Nuvolari.'[35] But Issigonis's interest in motor racing, although still apparent in the 1950s, waned in the following decade.

Alec was soon supporting a very different type of motor racing and followed John Morris's purchase from C.D. Wallbank in about 1937 of an Edwardian giant of a car. It was one of only six examples of the famous 'Blitzen Benz,' a 21.5-litre chain-driven monster, although this single long chassis 1912 car was bodied in Paris as a four-seater tourer and brought to England where it was raced at Brooklands by Captain Alistair Miller. It had covered its fastest-ever lap at the track in 1930 with a speed of 115.55mph, an impressive performance for a 18-year-old vehicle.

Morris then proceeded to make it race-worthy. The gearbox is the weak point on these monsters and, to the dismay of William Boddy, then editor of *Brooklands – Track and Air*, he discovered the ex-Count Zborowski Maybach-engined Chitty-Bang-Bang 1, which had been relegated to the sheds at the Surrey circuit used by shock absorber manufacturer/racing driver T.B. André. André was possibly related to Morris on his mother's side, and Morris acquired Chitty for spares and broke it up for its Mercedes gearbox, which, not surprisingly, then proved to be unsuitable.

In 1939 John Morris entered the Benz, sporting a massive pair of SU carburettors projecting from its bonnet, in the inter-club Stanley Cup meeting at Crystal Palace on Saturday 15 April. In the second VSCC handicap event at Stadium Dip the car's throttle stuck and Peter Hull, club secretary from 1971 until 1986, who witnessed the event, later wrote that 'the sight and sound of the vast Benz hitting the bank and rolling over on its side was most alarming.'[36] Fortunately neither the driver nor the car were seriously injured or damaged, but both featured in a photograph published in the *Sunday Pictorial* on the following day captioned 'A 'Smash' Finish!'

Morris and the Benz were sufficiently recovered to participate at the Midland Automobile Club's meeting at Shelsley Walsh on 3 June, the last gathering to be held there before the outbreak of war. The proceedings were opened by pre-1914 cars with Anthony Heal's 1910 10-litre Fiat fastest at 49 seconds, followed by John Morris who achieved 50.77.

During these years the demands on Alec Issigonis at Morris Motors were considerable and, inevitably, the completion of the Lightweight Special suffered. As a result, some time after his moving to Cowley, the car was transferred from Radley to a barn at George Dowson's Worcestershire farm where the work was finally completed.

The public had already been given its first sight of the car, although it was not yet named the Lightweight Special, as it was the subject of a two-page article in *The Autocar* of 4 June 1937, written and illustrated by technical artist John Ferguson. Although there were no photographs, Ferguson contributed an excellent cutaway drawing of the completed single-seater, describing it as a 'Featherweight Flyer for Sprint Events.' He credited Issigonis as its 'designer and constructor' – George Dowson was not mentioned – who had 'a fixed intention to cut down weight to the absolute minimum.' There is a suggestion of modifications being made to the front suspension, Ferguson hinting at 'certain problems' that 'were not fully understood' when it was originally laid out. However, 'in the light of recent progress some modifications will be carried out... in order to achieve better results.'

The engine had yet to run, although the car was clearly nearing completion as Ferguson reported that cloth, in the Mercedes-Benz manner, rather than leather, had been adopted for the seat as a weight-saving measure. (With use it was found that the cloth soon wore out and it was replaced by leather.) The aluminium body was similarly bereft of paint for the same reasons. Ferguson gave the single-seater's weight as 587lb, of which the engine, gearbox and blower accounted for 252lb, which compared with about 672lb for its Seven-based rivals. And the Lightweight turned the scales at approximately half that of Murray Jamieson's factory twin-cams, which weighed in at 1,092lb apiece. Austin tradition demanded chassis side members of 8swg steel with steel tubular cross members

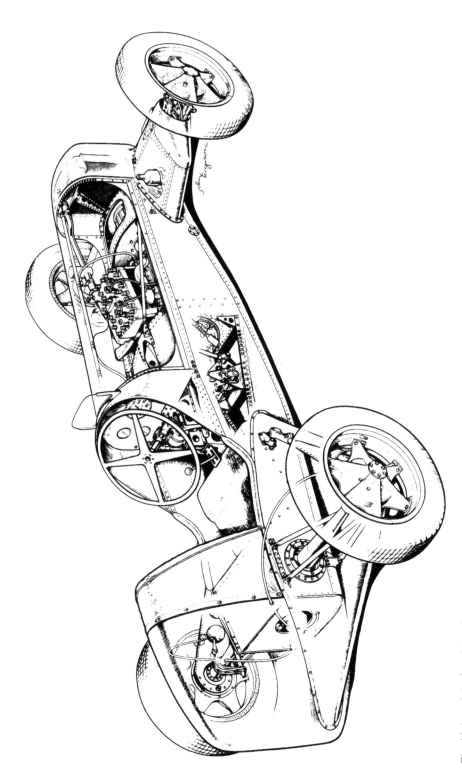

The Lightweight Special. A fine cutaway drawing by John Ferguson used to illustrate his article on the car in 1937. (*Autocar*)

hogged out of the solid and bolted up with 2BA pins, nuts and cotters. It would be another 16 months after the *Autocar* article before Issigonis and Dowson's efforts were seen in public for the first time. And on totting up what they'd spent on the car, Alec and George estimated a figure of some £300, about £8,800 at today's prices.

The venue for the Lightweight's competitive baptism was the Bugatti Owners' Club's new Prescott hillclimb in Gloucestershire, held on 25 September, that had only opened six months before. It was entered in the class for 750cc racing cars as an Austin Special but, alas, Dowson had the misfortune to crash during his first run. As *The Light Car* put it: 'everyone was anxious to see how J.M.P. Dowson's beautiful and exquisitely finished Austin Special would fare. Poor Dowson was fated to get no further than Orchard Corner where he demolished the barricade good and proper.'[37] It seems likely that the car's uncertain brakes were the culprit and after the war they were changed to twin leading shoe Lockheed hydraulics. 'Those didn't work either,' remembers Christopher Dowson, who drove the car in the 1970s. 'You only had to press the pedal twice and the drums expanded from the heat.'[38]

The Prescott incident was illustrated in the BOC's magazine *Bugantics*, which commented that '...it might have done well if it had not taken umbrage at our Maginot Line [a reference to the miles of underground concrete fortifications that then separated France from Germany] at Orchard Corner which put up a sturdy resistance to attack.'[39]

Did Issigonis and Dowson delight in the garden party atmosphere so prevalent at Prescott? Seemingly not. Many years later Issigonis disarmingly described his dedication to the Lightweight as 'pompous.' He and Dowson were agonising about the car's sensitivity to humidity and temperature and were 'busy as beavers with notebooks and pencils logging every detail.'[40]

Back the car went to the Dowson farm, where it was repaired, and the duo returned to Prescott in 1939 for the BOC's Open meeting held on 14 May, but George made, said *Motor Sport,* an 'indifferent' ascent. Next came International Day on 30 July, the event being marked by the appearance for the first time of two works twin-cam Austins. Bert Hadley in one of them won the 750cc class for racing cars with a climb of 47.76 seconds, which was a new record. C.D. Buckley in the other Austin was second, having recorded 49.36 and Dowson was third with 50.64. On this occasion the same magazine's correspondent was much impressed with his performance. 'The noise was immense and Dowson leaned out with his car on the corners... making artistry of his gear changes despite the between-the-legs location of the gear lever.'[41]

There was also a distraction for Alec Issigonis when he met up with an old friend.[42] An attractive young lady named Monica Strain was a club paddock marshal and *Bugantics* correspondent J.D. Aylward, who was classically inclined, was so enamoured by her appearance that he had on one occasion likened her to Venus. She had driven to the venue in her modified Ulster Austin which Alec immediately recognised as his old car.

It will be recalled that he had disposed of the Seven, probably in 1936, when he moved to Morris Motors. Soon afterwards it had been discovered in a West Midlands breaker's yard, either at Kidderminster or Stourbridge, by Barry Woodhead, who was running a Morgan trike-based sprint special named Chatterbox. Delighted to see that the Seven special was still fitted with its supercharged Ulster engine, he removed it, together with the gearbox, and duly installed the unit in his own car. He mentioned his find to Monica, who had a part-share in Chatterbox and lived in Seaford, Sussex. She had a penchant for Austin Sevens and her inventor father had bought her a tatty 1924 Chummy.

As it happened she possessed a spare 1931 engine and gearbox and decided – Monica was that kind of girl – to put castors on this thankfully compact unit, get on a train to the bemusement of the station staff, and there seek out the Midlands-domiciled engineless Seven. On arrival she found the scrap yard, single-handedly installed the engine and drove the Austin back to Sussex, knowing nothing of the car's history and its original owner. There was, apparently, no log book.

It was only when she attended the Prescott meeting that Issigonis saw the much-modified Ulster and identified it as his. The presence of the broomstick radius rods, which the car, to his horror, still retained, apparently clinched the matter! Monica had found the suspension modifications were only partially completed. In recent years Ulster historian Chris Gould has endeavoured to trace this car and managed to follow it as far as Charlwood in Sussex in the 1950s before the trail went cold.

Just five weeks after the Prescott event World War Two broke out and the Lightweight was retired to the Dowson farm for the remainder of hostilities. For his part Alec Issigonis had begun work on an all-new project at Cowley, which represented the starting point of his first production car. The Morris Minor was on its way.

Notes

1. Pomeroy, *op cit.*

2. Sir Miles Thomas, *Out on a Wing*, 1964.

3. I am indebted to Peter Seymour for this information which has been provided by John Lawrence, the archivist of Bablake School, and Leonard Lord's application, in his own hand, to join the Institution of Mechanical Engineers in 1919. He became a Graduate member in 1919 and a Full one in 1927.

4. Robert Jackson, *The Nuffield Story*, 1964.

5. Frank Woollard recalled in *Principles of Mass and Flow Production* (1954) that 'It would appear that these were the first automatic transfer machines antedating those recently made in America and this country by some 20 years. Unfortunately, in the state of the art at the time, they proved in practice to be over complicated. They were, therefore, divided into individual machine units and the automatic system was abandoned, to be revived 20 years later [at Austin's CAB facility].'

6. Thomas, *op cit.*

7. Spen King, who was told the story by Robert Boyle, *op cit.*

8. Maurice Olley, National Influence on American Passenger Car Design, *Proceedings, Institution of Automobile Engineers*, Volume 34, 1939–1940.

9. Turner, *op cit.*

10. Spen King, per Boyle, *op cit.*

11. *The Motor*, 1 September 1936.

12. I am indebted to Peter Seymour for this information.

13. Thomas, *op cit.*

14. Quoted in James Leasor, *Wheels to Fortune*, 1954.

15. Thomas, *op cit.*

16. Ibid.

17. Viscount Swinton, *I Remember*, 1946.

18. John Howlett, *The Guv'nor*, 1973.

19. Jonathan Wood, From MG to Minor, *Thoroughbred and Classic Cars*, April 1981.

20. Jack Daniels, *The Development of the Mini*, 1997.

21. Graham Robson, *The Anchorman*, Mini Magazine, October 1997.

22. Alex Moulton, *op cit.*

23. Jackson, *op cit.*

24. Wood, *op cit.*

25. Dave Daniels, *William John (aka 'Jack') Daniels*, 2004.

26. Turner and Curtis, *op cit.*

27. Jack Daniels, *Jack Daniels*, handwritten biographical account of his career at Morris Motors, no date.

28. Peter J. Seymour, article, *The End of Racing, Why was the MG Car Company Ltd sold to Morris Motors Ltd in 1935?*

29. H.N. Charles, letter, *The Motor*, 3 December 1958.

30. Barker, *op cit.*

31. Dowson, *op cit.*

32. Issigonis, A Revolutionary, *op cit.*

33. Ibid.

34. Ibid.

35. Christopher Dowson, *op cit.*

36. Peter Hull, *The History of the Vintage Sports-Car Club*, 1964.

37. *The Light Car*, 30 September 1938.

38. Christopher Dowson, *op cit.*

39. *Bugantics*, 1939.

40. May, *op cit.*

41. *Motor Sport*, September 1939.

42. I am grateful to Christopher Gould for this story which is based on his conversation with the late Monica Whincop, née Strain.

Chapter Four

THE WORLD CAR
FROM COWLEY

'We used to say at Morris that you would not be a successful car designer unless your model could be put together by a Bournemouth waiter.'[1]

Alec Issigonis

BECAUSE of the intervention of World War Two the Morris Minor had a protracted gestation. Indeed Alec Issigonis had begun work on what was to be coded the Mosquito prior to the outbreak of hostilities. It was the first production car for which he was wholly responsible and it looked as at home on a village green as it did in a busy suburban street. As such it was to become as identifiably British as the union flag or Giles Gilbert Scott's red telephone box.

Yet the Minor was conceived by an engineer of Greek and Bavarian parentage who had drawn his design influences from America, Central Europe and France. These had been brought together to create a skilfully packaged, integrated design that possessed individuality and, above all, charm – an elusive quality in any motor car – in abundance. In consequence it looked and, it should be said, handled like no other. Above all, it was to make money for Morris Motors and, arguably, represents Alec Issigonis's greatest achievement.

In his latter years the Minor's creator credited the sense of proportion expressed in his styling to his 'early exposure to the architectural treasures' of Smyrna.[2] 'I know nothing about architecture'[3] was one of his few recorded comments on the subject. But he was, of course, an architect in the automotive sense, in that he could could visualise a small car in its entirety and so arrange the 'furniture' to provide the maximum amount of interior space for its occupants.

It might be imagined that Issigonis, with his extraordinary creative powers, his grasp of perspective, his responses to visual aesthetics and, above all, his Greek blood, might relate to Georgian architecture, which relies for its visual impact on rules of proportion laid down by the Greeks and Romans of classical antiquity. Yet on the occasions that he visited MG's factory in Marcham Road, Abingdon, he would have had to drive past the town's magnificent 18th-century town hall, the work of Christopher Kempster, a pupil of the great Christopher Wren. It is unlikely that he gave it a second glance.

But Alec enjoyed relaxing in the *Belle Epoque* opulence of Monte Carlo and in the 1960s he spoke of his 'dislike for modern buildings.'[4] And if the houses he lived in are any guide, he clearly responded, consciously or otherwise, to the Modern Movement, given form by the products of the German Bauhaus school, which displayed a reaction to the decorative excesses of the 19th century by expunging all such features from its architecture. The result was a style wholly 20th century in concept, which was noticeable for the absence of external embellishments. It chimed with Issigonis's functionalism, which was later to be expressed in the Mini, both outside and in.

When Alec and his mother came to move from Radley to Oxford in 1938, they chose to rent a small apartment on the top floor in the newly completed three-storey Sollershott flats in the tree-lined Linkside Avenue, just off the Woodstock Road in the north of Oxford. Even today they sit a little uncomfortably among the gables, tiled roofs and bow windows of the neighbouring properties, thanks to their white brick construction, angularity, lack of external decoration and a starkness in accord with the European style of the day. With the exception of a slate roof – a flat one would have been more appropriate – they could have easily been transplanted from the suburbs of any European city.

Opposite the apartment was Linkside Lake, which had until the early 1900s been a clay pit from which Oxford facing bricks, yellow, like London stock, were made. The Victorian Gothic Randolph Hotel, which the Issigonises frequented over a period of a year, was built of them. The pit had filled with crystal clear water and, although some 50 feet deep, was a popular play place for many of the children growing up in the area. There they could swim, sail on rafts on sunny days and skate in the winter. Indeed, on a summer's evening, Alec and his mother would often sit on their third-floor balcony overlooking the lake watching the youngsters at play.

Number six Sollershott was destined to remain the home of mother and son for some 25 years and Jennifer Gilman, whose parents were family friends of

Alec's, retains clear memories of the flat, which she first visited in the late 1940s. 'It was very small and very spartan. When you entered, Mrs Issy's bedroom was to the right of the front door and Alec's on the left overlooking the front.'[5] The sitting room adjoined it and from there a glazed door opened on to the balcony. But when in the post-war years Jennifer's parents went on a visit to Paris, they sought out some of the restaurants recommended to them by Issigonis and were surprised to find that they were 'very expensive'. Morris Motors had probably footed the bill during its chief engineer's attendances at the capital's motor show, but such exclusive establishments made a dramatic contrast to the frugality of Alec's Oxford lifestyle.

Jennifer Gilman's recollections of the Linkside Avenue flat are shared by Malcolm Axtell, whose parents were neighbours of the Issigonises. He said of a visit in the 1950s: 'I remember it as pretty sparse with no real finesse to it. It's as though they'd collected furniture on the cheap. I don't think there was any interest in making it attractive or comfortable. It was dull with heavy stained doors, rather oppressive and with no light. The atmosphere was far from welcoming, certainly as far as the decor was concerned.'[6] Doreen Schreier was Morris's first engineering apprentice and would, in her later years, work unofficially for Issigonis. She was another visitor and remembers that Alec's 'mother "controlled everything". They lived very frugally. I think it was because they had once lost everything and possessions did not mean a thing. I remember that they had a little fridge there and it moved with them when they went to Edgbaston.'[7]

In a sign of the times, each Sollershott flat came with its own flat-roofed garage in matching white brick. At about the time of the move Issigonis was beginning work on the design of what was to emerge some 10 years later as the Morris Minor. In order to see why this vehicle was such a radical departure from previous small British cars, it is necessary for us to chart some of the design developments that were being undertaken by the motor manufacturers of continental Europe. For Alec Issigonis was to respond to them in a way which differed from many of his British contemporaries who invariably sheltered in the safety of existing themes.

Thanks to the advocacy of John Morris, the influence of Citroën's Traction Avant of 1934 on the Morris Minor can be taken as read, certainly as far as its rack and pinion steering was concerned. But as will emerge, Issigonis's conversion to its torsion bar suspension, which was such a significant feature of the Citroën's specification, proved to be more protracted.

As will have been apparent in the previous chapter, while Britain's car makers tended to remain faithful to the front-engine rear-drive concept, espoused so successfully by the immensely influential Model T Ford of 1908, across the

English Channel this orthodoxy was being challenged in many quarters. One of the most persistent champions for change was Joseph Ganz, editor of the German motoring magazine *Motor-Kritik,* who, by the early 1930s, was advocating 'inexpensive light cars with tubular backbone frames, air cooling, rear engines, and all independent suspension.'[8]

It was a creed that found an appreciative ear with the German-domiciled Austrian engineer Ferdinand Porsche, who in 1930 had set up a design bureau in Stuttgart. In 1934 what was designated Type 60 in his register eventually emerged as the state-sponsored Volkswagen, intended to sell for RM1000 (£83). Initiated by Hitler on his appointment as German chancellor in 1933, the concept took no less than four years to evolve, mainly because of delays in finding a suitably cheap engine. Franz Zaver Reimspiess's E-motor, adopted in 1936, was what the Continentals described as a boxer motor, a horizontally opposed four-cylinder unit which, for cost considerations in the VW, was air cooled and rear mounted.

What the British also called a 'flat' engine was not new. It had the virtue of being more compact than the usual inline engine, although this made it less accessible to the vehicle's owner and, the Volkswagen excepted, it tended to be more expensive to manufacture. Benz had featured such a twin in 1897, while in Britain first the exclusive Lanchester and later the utilitarian Jowett were the best-known exponents of the concept. It enjoyed greater popularity in Europe and, in Czechoslovakia, Hans Ledwinka's ingenious Tatra Type II of 1924 was a small car powered by a front-mounted, air-cooled 'flat twin' engine. It also featured a backbone chassis, to be so favoured by Joseph Ganz, and all independent suspension.

In Austria, in 1936, Steyr, an armaments manufacturer which began building cars in 1920, introduced its Kleinwagen, a small family car which was to have a profound influence on Alec Issigonis, although he would never admit as much. The fact that its designer had adopted a unitary construction body three years before Morris would have attracted his attention, as would the albeit crude all independent transverse leaf suspension.

But it was the car's low-mounted 'flat' four-cylinder engine, located well ahead of the theoretical front axle line, that would have particularly interested him although, as will emerge, chance had played a role in the choice of power unit. The designer, Karl Jenscke, a pupil of Ledwinka, had worked for Steyr in 1916–21, and was 'an enthusiastic glider pilot and at some time in 1935 he decided to motorise his glider.'[9] Assisted by his engine designer Karl Wagner, he recalled that they had 'developed a horizontally opposed two-cylinder engine for the job. Suddenly we had an idea. This would be an ideal power source for a small car.'

This was the Type 50 two-door saloon and its engine was a 984cc side valve flat four. Ingeniously, the radiator was mounted behind, rather than in front of, the engine thus making a compact unit. Endowing the car with a low centre of gravity, significantly it was mounted well to the fore so making a positive contribution to the Steyr's road holding.

Morris Motors purchased one, which was road tested, stripped down and a report prepared. Eric Moore, who had joined its experimental department in 1936, 'always had the impression that Alec Issigonis was responsible for bringing it in.'[10] It will come as no surprise to find that a Traction Avant Citroën was similarly appraised and an SS100 sports car was likewise evaluated. Such evaluations are commonplace today but the presence of these cars at Cowley indicates an element of pragmatism in Alec Issigonis's thinking that was noticeably absent from his later years.

In all some 13,000 examples of the Type 50 and its 55 derivative were produced by the time that production ceased in 1940 but another Continental small car, produced across the Alps in Turin, was destined to be more enduring. Alec Issigonis, with his preoccupation for small car design, would have studied Fiat's new 500, then the smallest production four-cylinder car in the world, and the most significant since the Austin Seven, with the keenest interest. Immediately branded by the public *Il Topolino* or 'Mickey Mouse,' it was the brainchild of Dante Giacosa, who, perversely, had previously been concerned with Fiat's aero engine design.

Although he contemplated using a flat four like the Steyr's, Giacosa discounted it on the grounds of cost. Instead he used a conventional side valve four-cylinder engine of a mere 569cc but, like the Austrian car, the power unit was mounted well forward, ahead of the transverse leaf ifs. The radiator was similarly mounted behind the power unit to allow for an aerodynamically refined cowl.

It was for packaging rather than handling reasons that the engine was so located and the 500 could be pushed to 55mph, although performance fell off somewhat with a full complement of two adults and two children in the back. The saloon body accordingly had only two doors and, as a concession to the Italian climate, there was an all important rollback sunroof. The overall length was just 10ft 6.5in. To keep the wheels in proportion, Giacosa also decided to use smaller rims than the norm and commissioned Pirelli to produce, for the first time, 15in tyres. A landmark in small design, it was, above all, cheap to run and operate.

Il Topolino was Fiat's first small car and it proved to be an outstanding success. Some 122,000 had been completed by the time production ceased in 1948. Giacosa would become Fiat's engineering supremo and, although he never possessed the same corporate power as Alec Issigonis was destined to exercise, the latter regarded him as his greatest rival.

In the meantime, in 1938 Ferdinand Porsche's engineers had completed the design of the Volkswagen, although then named the KdF-Wagen (The Strength-Through-Joy car) by the Nazis, unveiled at the 1939 Berlin motor show, held in February and March of that year. One of the many visitors who attended was Alec Issigonis and, recalling the occasion and the car's subsequent history, he reflected that it was 'successful because it looks so unusual even though the engineering is so terrible. Not that it was badly built but the rear engine and air cooling is so bad. Porsche was not an engineer, he made his team do the designing. He got Hitler's eye and suggested a people's car [in fact the reverse of the truth] and that was it. I saw it at the Berlin motor show... it was really terrible.'[11] Despite his disdain for the Volkswagen and its creator, the Beetle does share one common feature with the Morris Minor, its torsion bar suspension. Porsche, the patent holder, prudently incorporated it in the design. It did, however, take Issigonis some time to be convinced of the worth of his invention.

He was no doubt delighted to find that his suspension and handling guru, Maurice Olley, had returned to Britain from America in 1936 to join Vauxhall. This did not prevent Rolls-Royce's works director Ernest Hives fruitlessly attempting to lure him back to Derby as chief engineer of the newly formed chassis division. In February 1938 Olley addressed the Institution of Automobile Engineers on the *National Influences on American Car Design* and only an extraordinary reason would have prevented Issigonis from being present at the IAE's headquarters in London's Hobart Place to hear his hero present the paper in his customary entertaining yet incisive manner. Above all, Olley's presence in Britain provided Morris's resident suspension expert with the opportunity to establish direct contact with him.

As mentioned in the previous chapter, Olley's influence was to be found in Hubert Charles' front suspension of the Series M Morris Ten announced in August 1938, but it did not extend to the Series E Eight, launched at that year's Motor Show. The latest model in Cowley's best-selling line, it was a wholly conventional design which still retained the familiar mechanical layout of chassis frame, all round half elliptic springs and 918cc side valve four-cylinder engine, the latter tucked away beneath a new alligator bonnet. However, its styling by Morris's chief body engineer, Leslie Hall, did offer a concession to modern trends. There were no running boards and the hitherto free-standing headlamps were, for aerodynamic considerations, now faired into the front wings. With close on 55,000 examples completed by 1939, it was to maintain Morris's position as Britain's premier motor manufacturer.

The Eight was the smallest capacity car in the range. In the meantime Issigonis had been preoccupied with a project close to his heart, having in 1938 been promoted to the post of project engineer in the experimental department. There he designed a baby car with, remembered Jack Daniels, 'accommodation for two adults and two children, rather like the original Austin Seven seating specification.'[12] This would have been powered by a 600cc two-stroke engine, probably inspired by the popularity in Germany of DKW's front-wheel drive F1.

Issigonis was not responsible for the design of this Cowley-built two stroke, it having sprung from the creative brain of his friend John Morris. As SU was owned by Morris he was therefore privy to the secrets of the design and development department of Morris Motors. The unit developed about 16hp and was 'an opposed piston, two stroke engine with a Scotch crank, an alternative way of converting reciprocating motion to rotary motion using two crankshafts and sliding blocks, instead of one orthodox crankshaft.'[13]

Gerald Palmer, the author of these words, worked on this engine and was recruited to Morris Motors by Vic Oak in 1938, a further endorsement of his appreciation of engineering talent. Coincidentally, Palmer had been recommended to Morris, via MG, by the very same Brian Robbins who as secretary of the Institution of Automobile Engineers had in 1928 been instrumental in starting Alec Issigonis on his motor industry path.

John Morris's engine was tested in a Series E saloon but, Daniels remembers: 'despite our efforts we could not overcome the age old deficiencies of a two stroke, such as four stroking and excessive fuel consumption.'[14] Morris Motors's vice chairman, Miles Thomas, of whom more anon, recalled that 'anything over 2,500rpm it ran like a dream, very smoothly with plenty of torque. Below 1,000rpm it stuttered badly and was far too rough for commercial acceptance.'[15]

When all these factors were taken into consideration it was decided to abandon the project although, historically, it marks the starting point of the Mini project. Gerald Palmer remembered that Alec Issigonis was at the time 'obsessed with the concept of a very small car, which he called his "charwoman's car" and often talked to me about it.'[16] Its day was yet to come.

It says much for Vic Oak's magnanimity that Issigonis was able to begin work on what would be a successor to the Series E Eight. He therefore turned to a design that, in any event, had been gestating alongside the baby car. Unlike its predecessor, on which he collaborated with John Morris, this would be wholly his work and, just as he had done with the Lightweight Special, he had responsibility for both the car's styling and mechanicals. Such commissions had hitherto been the respective domains of Leslie Hall and Stan Westby.

In his later years Issigonis recalled 'that there was no day'[17] he could pin down as the conception date of the Minor. He said 'the idea was there before the war' and the car was forming itself on his sketch pad all the time. This is confirmed by a series of drawings on which he set down the design of the Steyr-inspired flat flour engine intended for the model. On one of these, today in the ownership of the author, Issigonis, in his own hand, has added the date of 1939. This infers the overall design of the engine was in being before the war and the existence of other sketches in the series suggests that there was much more besides.

Had the Minor been so powered, it would have been the most mechanically unorthodox car ever to have then been offered for sale by a mainstream British car manufacturer. There were existing engines available of course; the 918cc Eight was being made in side and overhead valve forms, the latter for the Wolseley Eight. But Issigonis was intent on reaping the full benefits of the flat four's low centre of gravity and its compactness, which would have benefited the car's handling and internal accommodation. Although such work was, ostensibly, the responsibility of Morris's Coventry-based Engines Branch, he undertook the design of the power unit himself.

The combined crankcase and block was of cast iron and the cylinder heads were made of the same material with the sparking plugs positioned near to their upper faces and inclined for accessibility. Issigonis was no doubt intent on keeping the unit as short as possible and only specified a two-bearing crankshaft, which proved to be the unit's limiting factor. Peter Tothill, who joined Morris's experimental department in 1950, had heard that the flat four's 'crank worked like a skipping rope and loosened the flywheel.'[18] However, the first one was not built until 1945, experimental cars being powered by Morris Eight engines.

It was not just the power unit but its location which challenged British orthodoxy. As Issigonis would later recall: 'In my suspension work, I found by experiment [on the Series M] that cars always ran much straighter and were more directionally stable if I put a couple of sand bags on the front bumper. I kept this very much in mind when I started the design of the Morris Minor in which the engine was outrageously far forward, in front of the front wheels.'[19] A logical development of this location would have been front-wheel drive but, as Issigonis later conceded, 'I did not know how to do it at the time.'[20]

Alas, this work was halted by the outbreak, in September 1939, of World War Two and, as will emerge, although Issigonis would become side-tracked, the car project received a fillip by the unexpected death, on 6 March 1940, of Oliver Boden. It will be recalled that he had replaced Leonard Lord as managing director of Morris Motors in 1936 and had subsequently been appointed Lord Nuffield's deputy. Only in his 54th year, he died suddenly in his car on his way to a Birmingham railway station to attend a London conference. Miles Thomas, his replacement, was in May to rename the businesses the Nuffield Organisation. Not only did he become deputy chairman, but he also soon recognised the abilities of 'a shy reserved young man named Alec Issigonis.'[21]

The picture that Thomas paints of the engineer does not chime with the one that those who knew him in his later years would recognise. 'Alec always used to put his suggestions forward in a most tentative way,' Thomas remembered, 'he

1) 1st British car
to exceed over 1 million
car of the same series.

2). 1st car to use 14" wheels
all cars up to that type
used 16" wheels.
— This created quite a
stir at the time amongst the pundits!
The reason for this was both technical &
aesthetic. — Increased room within
the car, and gave external appearance of
greater length.

3) 1st car to have head lamps built
into front grill. — This had to be
changed later for legislation reasons
quite unnecessarily.

4) 1st car in Britain to use torsion bar
independent front suspension.

5). 1st car in Britain to use rack &
pinion steering.

⑥ First car in England to
have more heavy weight
distribution. — Giving good
directional stability in strong winds
— Basic understeer. — Opposite to Beetle Philosophy

A description by Alec Issigonis in his usual blue Pentel in which he extols the salient points
of the Morris Minor. (*Author's Collection*)

had some very fundamental new ideas about motor car construction…'[22] Once again fate had played a role in Issigonis's life because Thomas was in a position to turn his dream into reality.

William Miles Webster Thomas (1897–1980) had worked for Morris since 1924. Unusually for a Morris Motors executive he was the product of a public school education at a time when most of its managers had, like its chairman, been schooled locally, followed by practical experience on the shop floor. Thomas had attended Bromsgrove School, founded in 1553, but he had no doubt redeemed himself in William Morris's eyes by serving a five-year apprenticeship with the Birmingham engineering company of Bellis and Morcam, which made pumps.

During World War One Miles Thomas had served in German West Africa; in Egypt he had been commissioned in the Royal Flying Corps and he had flown aircraft in Mesopotamia, Persia and Southern Russia. In 1918 he was awarded the Distinguished Flying Cross.

Thomas, fascinated by motor cars, became a motoring journalist, joining *The Motor*, published by the Temple Press, in 1919, and was subsequently promoted to the editorship of *The Light Car*. In that capacity he met William Morris, who offered him a job at Cowley as a publicity adviser. Thomas joined the business late in 1923 and started *The Morris Owner* magazine. In 1927 he was appointed a director and sales manager of Morris Motors. However, he left Cowley in 1933, following Len Lord's arrival, recognising that 'big as it was, Cowley was not big enough for both of us'[23] and, at Oliver Boden's suggestion, Thomas went to Morris Commercial before transferring to Wolseley. When in 1936 Boden left for Cowley to take Len Lord's place as managing director, Thomas replaced him at Ward End.

Aged 43 at the time of his appointment in 1940, Miles Thomas's promotion made him Lord Nuffield's heir apparent. The company's most able executive, he was dynamic, an excellent communicator, worldly and pragmatic and in 1943 would be knighted for his services to the war effort. Geoffrey Rose, who had joined Wolseley as an engineering apprentice in 1934, remembers Miles Thomas as 'a good manager of people. He also generated a team spirit in a way that others didn't. When in 1939 I joined the Territorial Army, every six months or so those of us in the services had a note from him asking "how are you doing? What is happening?" He'd got that touch and inculcated a sense of loyalty which had great impact on us younger people. He had a flair for publicity, was a bit of showman and ran a beautiful red Wolseley Super Six.'[24]

Alec Issigonis could not have had a better champion and Thomas, once ensconced at Cowley, recognised that, despite the ongoing war, 'I was particularly concerned to get a low priced four-seater saloon developed.'[25] Also, significantly, he was looking to develop an export potential for the car, reflecting in his memoirs 'we also decided that we must have an engine that attracted low rates of taxation under the RAC horsepower and yet would give bonus power for overseas use.'

This provision was in itself exceptional. Before the war the British motor industry had a decidedly lukewarm attitude to exports. Dudley Noble, who worked for both Rover and Rootes, probably spoke for most of his colleagues when he revealed that 'sales abroad were looked upon as a damned nuisance.'[26]

Miles Thomas was the first to recognise that the car Alec Issigonis was proposing would 'clearly have to be unconventional'[27] but backed the design to the hilt. The vice chairman's endorsement gave the project a corporate status it had not previously enjoyed and it was accorded an official start date of 1941. It was probably at Thomas's suggestion that it was accorded the code name of Mosquito, de Havilland's famous wooden framed fighter-bomber having made its appearance that year.

In his later life Issigonis was wont to paint the picture that he alone had been wholly responsible for the Minor's design and, indeed, he was. Having said that he was always reluctant to acknowledge a debt to any other individual and he was fortunate to have the continued support of his immediate superior, Vic Oak. He had, as Gerald Palmer wrote in 1958, played 'a not inconsiderable part in guiding the design of the Minor along *sound and practical lines* [author's italics] and laying the foundations for the astonishing commercial success that this car has enjoyed.'[28] Above all Oak was able to control Issigonis. Peter Tothill recalls that 'he was very much John Blunt, and I had it on good authority that, when they were discussing some new model, he lost patience with him and said "stop f***ing about Issy, I want this in production on Monday."'[29]

Nonetheless, work proceeded on the Mosquito project. The styling was finalised by 1942 when a model was made of the design that bears, with some exceptions, a remarkable similarity to the finished product. In his later years Issigonis would not consider himself a 'stylist,' declaring 'I am an engineer,'[30] but the Minor was undoubtedly styled and he was the individual responsible!

What were his influences? He was characteristically coy about revealing them but did go as far as conceding that the Minor was 'American influenced by the Cord to some extent.'[31] This would have been Gordon Buehrig's coffin-nosed Cord 810 of 1935, which would have a profound impact on US styling thereafter.

Issigonis was not alone in casting his eyes across the Atlantic. Stylists of family cars throughout the British motor industry were looking to Detroit for their visual inspiration, and many vehicles made their debut at the same 1948 Motor Show where the Minor was unveiled.

For his part Issigonis had clearly been looking at such cars produced during 1941 and just one was the Packard Clipper, which was unveiled in April of that year.[32] Ironically Dutch Darrin, who is credited with having made a major contribution to its lines, had only recently returned to America from Paris and the Clipper contains its fair share of European influences. Its contribution to the Minor is mainly to be found below the waistline, namely in the subtle way in which the bottoms of the doors are flared outwards to conceal vestigial sills.

There are more direct European styling cues apparent. Issigonis was to claim, correctly, that the Minor was 'the first car in England to have front wings as part of the front doors'[33] although Gerald Palmer's Jowett Javelin, probably inspired by the as yet unseen Minor, also featured them and reached the public first. For his part Issigonis cited an unnamed American source for the feature but he could also have been inspired by Hans Ledwinka's Type 87 Tatra of 1936, a rear-engined, backbone-chassised, be-finned aerodynamic saloon that looked more aeroplane than car. Its front wing pods were extended into the adjoining doors, which also contained recessed handle apertures, just like the Minor's.

Like Dante Giacosa's experience with the 500, the Minor's creator also found that the existing wheels were unsuitable for his purposes. The Morris, recalled Issigonis, 'was the first to use 14in wheels when all other [British] cars of that type were using 16in wheels. This caused quite a stir at the time amongst pundits! The reason for this was both technical and aesthetic. It gave increased room within the car and gave the external appearance of greater length. This was terribly important. It meant that from any distance the car was in proportion. Of course at the time there were no such wheels and no such tyres but Dunlop immediately co-operated.'[34] He placed these wheels 'near the outside edges of the body, 1⅛in from the edge of the tyre to the bodywork. I kept the bottom edges of the body straight and parallel to the ground like running boards.'[35]

Those 14in wheels were located, as far as practicable, at each corner of the Mosquito, a position that was to feature on every subsequent model with which Alec Issigonis would be directly involved. To him a car was 'a dynamic device,' and such a feature represented 'the essence of elegance. A lot of overhang front and rear is technically unsound.'[36] So his cars were from the outset imbued with an inherent stability which, he recalled, 'is so typical of cars [built] in the 1920s.'[37] It had then been much easier to express because the boot was yet to become fashionable. Although destined to be eroded in the 1930s, the wheel-at-each-corner approach was vigorously displayed on the Traction Avant Citroën, a car which Alec Issigonis had driven and much admired.

In January 1942 his colleague Gerald Palmer left Cowley to join the small Jowett company based at Idle on the outskirts of Bradford, Yorkshire. Like Issigonis, he was able to visualise a complete car, was no mean stylist and in 1950 had even designed his own home, Orchard House, at Iffley. Not surprisingly he titled his autobiography *Auto-Architect*.

Once ensconced in Jowett's factory, Palmer designed the Javelin saloon, much praised for its performance and handling, which reached the public early in 1948, some 10 months ahead of the Minor. Like Issigonis, Gerald Palmer was also inspired by the Type 50 Steyr, the only significant difference being that, unlike the car from Cowley, its forward-mounted horizontally opposed engine reached production, as did the rear-mounted radiator. However, it did suffer from mechanical shortcomings and highlighted Palmer's limitations, like Issigonis's, in the field of engine design. It similarly shared torsion bar suspension with the Minor, although Palmer was also able to retain transverse bars at the rear.

A pre-production Minor, a shiny black two-door saloon, coded EX/SX/86, was completed during 1943. Although there were many detail differences between it and the production model, the principal one was that it was a significantly smaller car than the production version, having a width of 4ft 9in, which was the same as the Series E Eight. The headlamps were concealed in the manner of the pre-war Peugeot 402, behind the front oval grille, and its vertical slats tended to underline its narrowness, the nose coming to a pronounced point. The top of the bonnet was heavily louvered because the radiator, à la Steyr, was located behind the engine rather than in front of it.

If the body reflected American influences, they were also to be found inside the Mosquito, with the presence of a steering column gear change. A three speed box was fitted, and, accordingly, a bench-type front seat featured. The vertical radiator slats were echoed by similar moulding in the middle of the fascia. Also, significantly, the instrumentation was designed so that the car could be produced in left-hand drive form from the very outset, the hooded speedometer being balanced by a similarly sized clock on the passenger side.

And then there was the all important matter of suspension. As will have been apparent in the previous chapter, Issigonis, with John Morris's prompting, required little encouragement to recognise the worth of the torsion bars used in the Traction Avant Citroën. But as a dedicated disciple of Maurice Olley, as his work on the aborted Morris Ten system in 1938 revealed, he was still a trenchant advocate of the coil and wishbone system. Why then was the Minor not so equipped and, instead, ended up with torsion bars? Who could have changed the mind of this most dogmatic of automobile engineers?

To answer this question we must briefly retrace our steps to 1935 when, at the MG factory at Abingdon, chief engineer Hubert Charles created the ingenious R-type 750cc single-seater racer. Introduced in April of that year, what had been designated EX 147 featured a backbone chassis and all round independent suspension with equal length wishbones front and rear respectively serviced by longitudinal torsion bars. The system did have teething troubles: the car rolled excessively on corners, on account of its equal, rather than unequal, wishbones, and the frequency of the rear bars was greater than those at the front. These were no doubt the reasons why Issigonis was not impressed by the R-type! The shortcomings could have been quickly corrected, but the concept was not fully developed because, on 1 July 1935, Leonard Lord, as managing director of Morris Motors, put an end to MG's racing activities. 'That bloody lot can go for a start'[38] was his characteristically robust response when he viewed the newly-minted R-types in the Abingdon racing shop.

The MG had not escaped the attention of Ferdinand Porsche, inventor of the torsion bar, and although Charles had patented his design, some of its features were opposed by the Austrian engineer. As Charles later put it, 'time was needed to decide the issue between his work and mine.'[39] The system was to have been extended to a 3.5-litre MG saloon designated EX 150, but this remained a paper project. In any event no production Morris or MG was fitted with ifs before the war, but this did not prevent H.N. Charles from undertaking experiments following his move to Cowley in the summer of 1935.

Issigonis was to correctly claim that 'the Minor was the first car in England to have nose heavy weight distribution giving good directional stability in strong winds.'[40] True, but once again Palmer's Javelin reached the public first. 'It also had basic understeer and this is exactly opposite the Beetle philosophy. You know, fundamental understeer is much safer than oversteer. I tried a two-seater BMW before the war with pronounced oversteer and I found it almost impossible to drive.'[41]

This statement took no account of experiments that were undertaken at Cowley prior to Issigonis's arrival at the end of 1936. H.N. Charles recalled that, following his transfer there, he undertook 'most careful basic investigations of car stiffness, and the meaning of weight distribution, including the swinging of entire cars on giant coil springs.'[42] (This may well have been initiated by Robert Boyle, as similar experiments were also being undertaken by General Motors in America).

Charles continued: 'From all this data we commenced to have a picture of how to design a small car which could have nice road manners, which was in any event the object of the exercise. *It was at that point Alec Issigonis joined our team*' (author's italics) and he was '…intensely keen on independent front suspension with coil springs… Like most creative workers he was very receptive, and eventually fell for my own great interest in torsion bars and their associated general effects.' For his part, Charles acknowledged that, conversely, he 'fell for [Issigonis's] studies of coil springs…'[43]

As far as the evolution of the Minor was concerned, Charles could, with justification, claim that 'Alec Issigonis and I are entitled to the satisfaction of having given such 'manners' to several British small cars as to make them a world-beating success.'[44]

In the immediate pre-war days, as *Motor's* Philip Turner has pointed out, 'the road holding and handling of most family saloons could only be described by that hideous word "acceptable". It was a widely held view in the British motor industry that customers for their small saloons did not "want" good handling and would not appreciate it if it was provided.'[45]

As originally conceived the Minor, like the R-type, was intended to possess all round torsion bars, although the rear system, which featured a live axle, radius arms and 'bent' bars, was eventually deleted on cost grounds. (A 'bent' system, although for an ifs design, was patented by Issigonis and Morris Motors in 1945). Their place was taken by conventional half elliptic springs.

The front system entered production very much as Issigonis had designed it. Its most distinctive feature is a long swivel pin which Jack Daniels says was adopted for two very sound reasons. First, it was to keep the cornering loads of the upper wishbone to permit the use of a single arm and *minimise manufacturing costs* (author's italics) and second to reduce the significance of mounting tolerances to a point where separate adjustments for caster and camber would not be required. Rack and pinion steering in the Citroën manner was adopted.

Meanwhile there was a war to be won. Both Issigonis and Daniels were in a reserved occupation. But because Cowley was an assembly rather than manufacturing plant it did not initially have the facilities to take on military contracts.[46] In an attempt to interest the army, they designed and built a small armoured car for one man using the unitary con-struction methods pioneered in the Series M. Power was provided by

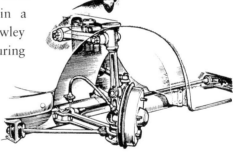

The Morris Minor's distinctive independent torsion bar front suspension. (*Autocar*)

its engine, which drove all four wheels, and the suspension was all independent. At the front the medium was bent torsion bars and this is significant for being the first occasion that Issigonis applied them to a completed vehicle. Coil springs featured at the rear. Steering was by rack and pinion. The driver operated an aircraft-style joystick – here Issigonis's interest in aviation is immediately apparent – to fire the two machine guns.

Daniels recalls[47] that the military then required that a turret be added for a second occupant, the vehicle being christened Salamander, and then came a further request for accommodation for a third person, at which point the project was passed on to the main drawing office, although it never entered production. But in 1941 Daniels and Issigonis went their separate ways. Jack moved elsewhere in Cowley and would only occasionally 'see Issy except for a couple of relatively minor jobs.'[48]

For his part Alec was responsible for the design of what can be seen as a derivative of the armoured car in the shape of the Morris Light Reconnaissance Car of 1941, with a unitary hull and powered by a rear mounted 3.5-litre Morris Commercial four-cylinder engine. In its original Mark I form only the rear wheels were driven, but suspension was independent at the front. For this Issigonis retained coil springs, although they were augmented by an anti-roll bar in the manner of Charles's Series M. More significantly the kingpin and upper and lower links bear a remarkable resemblance to those used on the Morris Minor. However, a Mark II version was a four-wheel drive vehicle and had a cart sprung front axle.

In all 2,200 examples of both versions of the reconnaissance vehicle were built at Cowley, although other projects that occupied much of Issigonis's time towards the end of the war never attained production. One was an amphibious version of Landcart, a miniature Jeep, intended for use in the jungles of the Far East. The component parts were to be contained within a cylinder and then dropped from an aircraft, to be reassembled on the ground. Issigonis designed the Gosling, powered by a single-cylinder two-stroke 500cc Villiers engine. Eight inch diameter wheels were specified by the engineer, who would later pioneer 10in ones on the Mini.

Another productive dead-end with which Issigonis was involved was Nuffield Mechanizations's four-wheel drive Gutty, an experimental British version of the Jeep of which three examples were completed in 1946/47. Of stressed skin unitary construction, power was provided by a dry sump 1.8-litre version of the flat four unit intended for the Mosquito, while the all independent suspension used longitudinal torsion bars with the same associations. But the engine continually overheated and the bars detached themselves from their mountings. The War Office was unimpressed, declaring that the Gutty exhibited 'serious defects,'[49] although the concept was revised with a conventional chassis as the Rolls-Royce-engined Wolseley Mudlark of 1949, which was the precursor, following the creation of BMC, of the 1952 Austin Champ.

The war had, of course, put paid to Issigonis's hillclimbing activities. These had been held at weekends and prior to that practically all of his spare time was spent working on the Lightweight Special. But with the coming of hostilities, he was ready to leave the confines of the Sollershott flat and have a lunchtime drink on a Saturday with Maurice Connelly, who was the patent agent at Pressed Steel, which had its factory close by Morris Motors's Cowley Works.

Maurice, his wife Dorothy and their young daughter Jennifer lived in Banbury Road, Oxford, within walking distance of Linkside Avenue. Today, as Jennifer Gilman, she remembers, 'he always drove, never walked. He and my father used to go for a drink at the Friar Bacon, a pub nearby at Cutteslowe. They were good friends and would usually enjoy their beer although on high days and holidays Alec would persuade my father to have a gin and French after their beer. His would be on the strong side!'[50]

Issigonis clearly enjoyed Maurice Connelly's company and it was reciprocated. 'He was part of the family,' recalls his daughter. 'Alec, it was never a case of Uncle Alec, was wonderful with the young even though I was a girl and didn't know about engines.' As will become apparent, Alec Issigonis was able to establish a special rapport with young people and his god-daughter, Penny Plath, née Dowson, believes: 'it would have been wonderful if he had had children.'[51] Alex Moulton says that Issigonis enjoyed being with children because his own childhood had been such a solitary one.[52]

Jennifer Gilman has happy memories of the designer of the Morris Minor 'sitting on our step drawing me Spitfires. This would have been in 1943 when I was five. During the war Pressed Steel made parts for Spitfires and I can still remember that it had a special curved wing. Sometimes he would draw motor cars. I used to have wodges of them.'[53]

Later, in 1948, when she visited the Issigonises at their Sollershott flat, she met Alec's mother, who was then 52 years old. 'When you're 10 she seemed so ancient but she was a very bright, intelligent lady.'[54] However, young Jennifer was rather taken aback by her habit of 'suddenly flinging herself down on the floor. She always used to sit on the floor by the fireplace and she would knead her hands – they were large, just like Alec's – which she said would prevent her from getting arthritis. There was a rug by the fire and she used to sit on the side of it. I never saw her sit on a chair. She used to smoke an awful lot.'

When Alec Issigonis went for his Saturday lunchtime drink with Maurice Connelly he sometimes arrived in an experimental Morris Minor and it was probably EX/SX/86, which he was running throughout the war. By 1944 it had been resprayed a more anonymous grey, so it could have been easily dismissed as having a military application for road testing, and the brightwork similarly disguised. Issigonis was clearly still unhappy with the grille, which was reworked in a rectangular shape with horizontal slats. The bonnet was now revised; the louvres were deleted, which reflected the fact that the radiator itself had been repositioned in a conventional position because of persistent overheating.

In 1944 a new player joined the small Mosquito team. Reg Job was the son of a wheelwright in the village of Claverton, near Warwick. After serving an apprenticeship with a local coachbuilder he went to Armstrong Siddeley in nearby Coventry and joined Pressed Steel in 1934 at the behest of its manager, W.C. Marton, who had also worked for that Coventry company. In 1939 he crossed the Oxford bypass and joined nearby Morris Motors. He was seconded to the Mosquito project because of his familiarity with designing complete body shells.

He later recalled that he had 'been given a one-twelfth scale model. And that was what I started with. And so I blew that up to full size... on linen backed cartridge paper... the Minor is such a beautiful shape... We tried to alter it once or twice but it's impossible to alter it because if you do anything to it you spoil it completely. That's because one part bears a resemblance to the rest of it.'[55] It was a view endorsed by the Midlands-based director of the Morris Bodies' pattern shop, who told Job: '... you needn't have bothered to come, it's absolutely perfect – I've never known a body model to be without some alteration...'[56]

Just prior to the end of the war in 1945, Jack Daniels was able to rejoin Alec Issigonis. He was pleased to find that, in the interim, the development shop facilities had been much improved by the installation of such equipment as 'a dynamometer, bump rigs, shock absorber testers, together with the staff to use them.' This consisted of C. Hosking (rigs), T. Dixon (dampers) and L. Wright (testing). Issigonis had, in the meantime, taken R. Parker, 'a young newcomer,' formerly an office boy, under his wing to school him in the disciplines of draughtsmanship.[57]

In retrospect Jack Daniels, who had been concerned with such heavyweight projects as the stillborn Argosy amphibian and the 85-ton Tortoise tank, of which 25 were completed, thinks that he 'may, just possibly, have introduced a modicum of over-engineering'[58] into the Minor's unitary body, the complete car turning the scales at a little over 15cwt. This does go some way to explaining why so many examples are still on the road! He also recalls 'lengthy discussions with A.V. Oak' who in 1943 had been promoted to the post of technical director of Morris Motors. With the war coming to an end in 1945 the prospects for the Morris Mosquito looked good. A worldwide pent-up demand for motor cars was in the offing and Cowley was well placed to satisfy this need with Issigonis's new model.

Prior to the outbreak of war in 1939 Morris had offered a five-car range. When it resumed production in the autumn of 1945 this was reduced to just two, the Series M Ten and the Series E Eight, the latter having outsold the larger model at the rate of about two to one. Both, however, were to sell strongly in about equal volumes after the war, on account of a world shortage of cars following the decimation caused by six years of conflict.

In 1946 a further two Mosquito prototypes, EX/SX/130, significantly a left-hand drive car, and 131, a conventional one, were completed. By this time a grille with vertical slats had been reintroduced, although the headlamps were now contained within the extremities of the grille surround and were no longer obscured by it. The lamp units themselves had a section removed at their rear and Issigonis was particularly proud of the fact[59] that at night they illuminated the engine compartment.

Returning to the Cowley experimental department after war service, Eric Moore had his first encounter with Alec Issigonis. 'I found him very quiet and very polite, I liked him and he was easy to talk to. He was obviously a clever man although some people thought he was a bit odd. He was always sketching! I'd say he was a good communicator on a one-to-one level but not a leader. He was too reserved, a very private person.'[60]

Another visitor that Moore regularly encountered in the experimental department, usually in the engine test shop, was Alec Issigonis's friend, John Morris. During the war he had played a key role in improvements to the power unit of another Mosquito, de Havilland's aircraft no less, that was the first recipient, in 1944, of SU's direct fuel injection system for its Rolls-Royce Merlin engines.

Eric remembers that Morris invariably arrived in a Traction Avant Citroën. 'I was surprised in a way they were friends, he seemed far too outgoing for Alec. John Morris used to have a stock phrase when he was adjusting the needle of an SU carburettor, "just half a thou" was the clearance invariably required!'

Doreen Schreier, who went to Cowley in 1942, recalls that 'John Morris was often there. He and Issy were like a comedy act. I can remember Clive Morris, who was in charge of test shop, one day found a 10 shilling note on the ground. On the next occasion Clive saw him he asked whether it was his. "I'm always losing those" Morris said and pocketed it.'[61]

As far as the experimental department was concerned, says Moore, they thought the Mosquito 'the cat's whiskers.' It will have been apparent from the car's evolution, that the Mosquito project was driven by Sir Miles Thomas, vice chairman of the Nuffield Organisation. But what of the chairman, Lord Nuffield? In the victory year of 1945, Britain's leading motor manufacturer would celebrate his 68th birthday and, while he told his deputy that he would leave the running of the business to him, he invariably countermanded or contradicted Thomas's orders, often from a distance. Since the late 1920s he had delighted in taking long annual sea cruises to Australia and he was absent from Cowley throughout many of the crucial months of 1947.

Lord Nuffield had no contact with Alec Issigonis until long after the Minor had entered production and positively disliked the model and its appearance. His oft-quoted remark, 'it looks like a poached egg'[62] filtered through to its creator and was prompted by the fact that the car lacked a traditional radiator. Morris's interest in radiator design had been expressed from his first days as a car maker when in 1912 he had launched the 'Bullnose' Oxford, its distinctive radiator being such a memorable feature of the model. Peter Tothill confirms the chairman's attitude to the Minor. 'He hated the Minor to such an extent that he wouldn't have one and would drive his Wolseley Eight into the factory every day. Then he got another one built from spare parts. He wanted a small car but didn't want the Minor.'[63]

There can be little doubt that the ingenuity and innovation that Issigonis had lavished on the design completely bypassed his chairman. Even worse, Lord Nuffield set out to destroy the project, a vendetta which very nearly succeeded. He seemed content to rely on the commercial success of the wholly conventional Series E Eight that was selling strongly, along with practically every British car, in those car-hungry early post-war years. He took no account of the growing strength of the rival Austin company that was being revitalised by an aggrieved Leonard Lord, who was determined that the pole position Morris had enjoyed within the British motor industry since 1935 would soon be overhauled. Nuffield, however, was not alone in his dislike of the Minor. 'None of the directors were very keen, from Donald Harrison, (the sales director) downwards,' recalled Issigonis.[64]

On a broader front, the newly elected Labour Government was becoming more closely involved with the affairs of the motor industry as it was recognised that export potential could generate, in particular, much-needed dollars for an Exchequer effectively bankrupted by war. The car makers were therefore allocated supplies of steel on the basis of their sales overseas. It was also for this reason that the horsepower tax, which unduly penalised larger capacity engines more favoured in overseas countries, was abolished to be replaced from 1948 by a flat rate system. Sir Miles Thomas was in the vanguard of representations to Chancellor of the Exchequer Hugh Dalton to these ends.

There was more. A policy was spelt out by the president of the Board of Trade, Sir Stafford Cripps, who, in November 1945, told a Society of Motor Manufacturers and Traders (SMMT) dinner: 'We must provide a cheap, tough good-looking car of decent size – not the sort of car we have hitherto produced for smooth roads and short journeys in this country – and we must produce them in suitable qualities to get the benefits of mass production.'[65] He might have been describing the as yet unnamed Morris Minor, although his words fell on deaf ears as far as Lord Nuffield, who was always suspicious of any governmental intervention, particularly if it was a Labour one, was concerned.

Cripps went on: 'We cannot succeed in getting the volume of exports we must have if we disperse our efforts over numberless types and makes.' This was a reference to the fact that in pre-war days the British-owned sector of the industry had produced a multifarious range of models. In 1934, for instance, Austin offered no fewer than 50 different lines and Morris even more. Although some much-needed culling subsequently took place, this contrasted with the more financially-aware Ford and Vauxhall makes in the American-owned sector, which in 1939 only offered variations on two rationalised models apiece.

Sir Stafford also spoke of export quotas and revealed that the lowest possible figure then being contemplated by the government was 50 percent. This produced a response of 'No' and 'Tripe' from the audience, to which Sir Stafford bit back: 'I have often wondered whether you thought that Great Britain was here to support the motor industry, or the industry was here to support Great Britain. I gather from your cries you think it was the former.'[66]

In August 1945 a launch date of January 1947 had been scheduled for the Mosquito and in February 1946 a target of 250,000 over the following three years was projected. The next month Sir Miles spoke to his co-directors of the car representing a 'new era for the Nuffield Organisation'[67] but in June 1946 the hand of the chairman was apparent: because of healthy sales of the Series E, the date was put back to July 1947. The same month Victor Riley proposed, as a sop to the chairman, a Wolseley version, complete with traditional radiator. Fortunately the Minor was back in front in September but the launch date had slipped to January 1948.

Miles Thomas was in America in the autumn of 1946 but, on his return on the *Queen Elizabeth* in November, *The Autocar* reported that 'optimism was the keynote'[68] of his address to the press when he spoke of a Nuffield 'People's Car,' which we now know to have been the Morris Minor, that was then undergoing 'exhaustive tests.' The name was inspired by the Volkswagen and in 1945 Dennis Kendall, the MP for Grantham, had launched what was heralded as a British 'People's Car' that never reached production. But the phrase caught the public imagination and the magazine reported that it was 'known in Coventry [sic] that for some time experiments have been made by Morris engineers with a 'flat four' or horizontally opposed, water cooled side valve engine.' It recognised that the production date of the new Morris was 'dependent on several factors,' but it 'was unlikely to be in the public's hands before 1948.'[69]

By the summer of 1947 a pre-production Mosquito successfully completed a 10,000-mile 10-day test, much of this being undertaken by Issigonis himself. This was despite the fact that in June Lord Nuffield was fighting a rearguard action for the Series E, which he proposed be fitted with the Minor's ifs and a revised radiator. An experimental car was duly built but Vic Oak protested that the resulting model would have been prohibitively expensive.

At the same time it was decided to scrap the flat four engine programme and, instead, the Mosquito was to be fitted with the Series E unit and its four-speed gearbox. In retrospect this was, by default, a wise decision, because the original unit had revealed the limitations of Issigonis's expertise in engine design. The reasons, according to its instigator, were 'on the grounds of the cost of tooling and the development of the two bearing crank.'[70] For 'development' read 'limitation'.

The 918cc side valve Eight unit, which dated back to 1935, was, by contrast, wholly conventional, but above all it was a proven unit that imbued the Minor with an element of reliability it would probably not have enjoyed had the flat four been retained. For his part Issigonis dismissed it as '... a terrible old thing. But, well, we had no option.'[71]

As it happened the switch of engine gave him the opportunity to widen the Minor's body at this late stage, as he believed the original was too narrow. The episode has now entered Morris Minor lore and I can do no better than cite the reasons for his decision by quoting his own words. 'Proportions are everything. When I study a car to assess its looks I don't say: "It's pretty" or "It's well styled"; I say "Does it look elegant?" In other words, are the proportions right? The Ancient Greeks knew all about this – the columns in their ancient temples have perfection of proportion. Being Modern and only half Greek, I have inherited no more than an average instinct or flair for aesthetics.'[72]

One of the Mosquito prototypes was therefore cut in half and the two sections mounted on trolleys that were moved backwards and forwards by mechanics. Relying on his eye, Issigonis experimented until the proportions were to his satisfaction, whereupon the halves were welded in place and secured by steel plate. The revised body was four inches wider that the original, what Issigonis later described as 'a hand's width' to Christopher Dowson.[73] Although the tooling had already been completed, the extra spacing only showed on the bonnet but did not detract from its appearance. However, the bumpers required a spacer to accommodate the car's increased width.

The steering rack for the Minor was to be made by Wolseley and Geoffrey Rose, who had returned to Adderley Park in 1946 a demobbed Lieutenant Colonel after war service in France and Germany, became personal assistant to production manager Bill Hartley. 'One day, probably late 1947, he said to me "be available this afternoon. Alec Issigonis is coming up to talk about the rack and pinion steering unit for the Morris Minor." We sat in Bill's office and Alec produced a prototype rack. It was to be the first one we'd ever made. To us he was an up-and-coming chap and much admired. He had a very retiring sort of attitude when he was talking but there was steel behind his words. He very quickly realised that we knew what he was talking about and he was determined to have what he wanted.[74] This was pretty unusual. The normal attitude was "these people are supposed to be the experts. Let them get on with it." Alec wanted to know exactly how it was going to be done. It was typical of his general approach.'

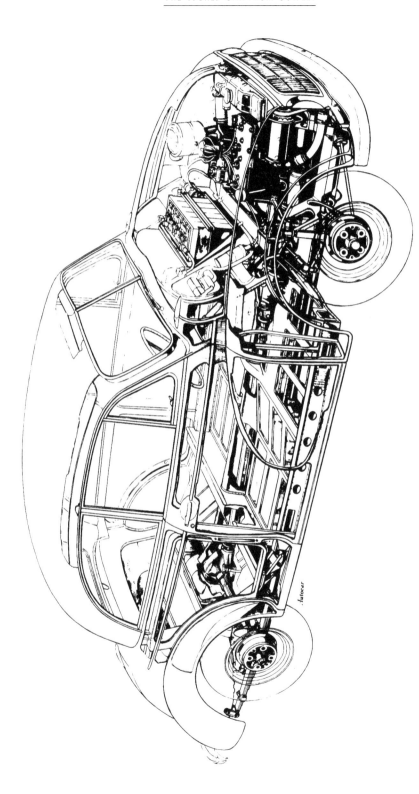

The Morris Minor of 1948, the work of *The Autocar's* incomparable technical illustrator Max Millar, which reveals the forward mounting of its engine and the torsion bar of the independent front suspension, which was attached to the body sub structure just below the driver's seat. (*Autocar*)

While Issigonis was busy putting the finishing touches to the Mosquito, over at the Austin factory at Longbridge work was nearing completion on the first wholly new Austin of the post-war years. Launched in September 1947, the A40 saloon was produced in four-door Devon and two-door Dorset guises. But beneath corporate stylist Dick Burzi's fashionably transatlantic lines, which owed much to Chevrolet's 1940 styling, was a traditional chassis frame and power was provided by a new 1.2-litre engine, Austin's first overhead valve car unit. Independent front suspension was, thanks indirectly to Issigonis, a wishbone and coil spring system, because it was the work of his former colleague Hubert Charles, who also had a hand in the new power unit. He had left Cowley in 1938 to become chief engineer of Rotal Airscrews and in 1941 had arrived at Longbridge to introduce some science into Austin engineering and set up its first development department.

Destined to be the fastest selling Austin of its day, thanks to a strong export performance, no fewer than 270,000 units had been completed by the time production ceased in 1952. Having said that, the A40 was a traditional, dependable model in the best traditions of the marque, but it was heavy at close on a ton, and although not directly competing with the Minor, it conspicuously lacked its flair and ingenuity.

Leonard Lord had also consolidated his hold on Longbridge. Lord Austin had died in 1941 and his place as chairman was taken by Ernest Payton, who shared the managing directorship with a newly promoted Lord. Payton had joined the board in the dark days of 1921 when the business was briefly in receivership. A financier and property developer, he had brought a much-needed fiscal element to balance Sir Herbert Austin's engineering instincts, although it was not long before he clashed with the abrasive Lord.

In 1945 Payton had tried to woo Sir Miles Thomas, whom he regarded as 'the best commercial man in the business',[75] to Longbridge to work in tandem with his old adversary. But Sir Miles declined, revealing in his memoirs that he 'could not let W.R. [Morris] down' although he also clearly had apprehensions about sharing a bicycle made for two with Leonard Lord.

Payton himself retired as chairman in November 1945 and died early in the following year. His place had been taken by Lord, then aged 49, who also continued in the post of managing director, and he dominated a board that consisted of just four directors. In 1949 his colleagues granted him the equivalent of £100,000 (over £2 million by today's values) binding him to the job, it being conditional on him not taking up a motor industry post anywhere in the world. He had reached the pinnacle of power at Longbridge and now looked to Morris – 'those buggers in the country' – as he dismissed them, to ultimately give him control of Britain's two largest indigenous car companies.

At Cowley Sir Miles Thomas was becoming increasing frustrated by Lord Nuffield's hostility to the Mosquito and, on 14 October 1947, three days after his chairman's 70th birthday, he penned a memorandum to him specifically relating to the model. The hostile climate surrounding the car is encapsulated in its second paragraph: 'At Nuffield Metal Products I was perturbed to see what Mr Tolley graphically called "the graveyard of the Mosquito" – a pile of tools that had never been used and clearly represents much locked-up capital.'[76]

Thomas recalled that 'I should have been by now deaf as well as blind if I could not have seen that all was not well between the chairman and myself.'[77] For his part Nuffield, 'whilst he could stomach his executives making mistakes, did not like being challenged.'[78] Deeply distrustful of politicians, particularly Socialist ones, he was also riled by his deputy's friendship with Ernest Bevin, secretary of the Transport and General Workers Union and Minister for Labour in Churchill's wartime coalition, who was by then showing his mettle as an outstanding Foreign Secretary in Attlee's post-war administration.

It was against this background that, on 17 November 1947, Sir Miles Thomas resigned as vice chairman of the Nuffield Organisation after 24 years in the British motor industry, never to return. Although Peter Tothill did not join Morris until over two years later 'it was still spoken about when I arrived. This was because, within half an hour of his departure, Lord Nuffield got someone from the maintenance department to take Sir Miles's name off the door of his office.'[79]

Nuffield's worst fears were confirmed when in 1948 Thomas was appointed vice chairman – he soon took the chair – of the nationalised British Overseas Aircraft Corporation (BOAC), where his global perspective could be played out. Subsequently Sir Miles became chairman of the British arm of the American Monsanto Chemicals. He was made a life peer in 1971, becoming Lord Thomas of Remenham. He died at the age of 82 in 1980, the best leader the British motor industry never had.

A revitalised Morris Motors, headed by Sir Miles Thomas and concentrating its efforts on the Minor with its enormous export potential, would have underpinned Morris Motors's position as Britain's principal car maker. And what was to prove a calamitous takeover by Austin in 1952 to form the British Motor Corporation might have been averted.

Sir Miles's replacement as Morris's vice chairman was the bespectacled, diminutive figure of 51-year-old Reginald Hanks, whose appearance, that of a local bank manager, belied his resolve. Locally educated at New College School in Oxford, he had served an apprenticeship with the Great Western Railway at its Swindon works. Joining Morris in 1922 in the technical services department, he had been general manager of Nuffield Metal Products between 1941 and 1945 and that year became general manager of Nuffield Exports. He had been made a

Morris director in August 1947. For his part Alec Issigonis was delighted at the appointment. 'He hadn't the vitality of Miles, you know, he was very steady going. But I knew Reggie Hanks both socially and professionally much better than I did Miles Thomas.'[80]

They shared a passion for steam engines, both model and full-size, and Issigonis was to spend some of his evenings pursuing his hobby of building miniature steam engines, even though a third-floor flat precluded him from using them. 'I build steam locomotives, I have built a great deal of track, but I have not laid it down yet, as I have no special place for it.' he lamented. 'I do my model work on the dining-room table, and the soldering on the gas stove! I buy certain parts from a man in Oxford, but I do all the sheet metal work myself.'[81]

Hanks lived nearby in Lonsdale Road and Christopher Dowson can recall, as a child, riding on his train: 'the track was on triangulated uprights that went all around his garden.'[82] The vice chairman's enthusiasm for steam even extended to his company car, a commodious Morris 14, which was modified to echo his first love. Eric Moore remembers that he 'had a small handle added to the steering wheel, just like that on a steam traction engine. And the horn was operated by a little chain, rather than the usual button.'[83] This minor eccentricity apart, although 'Hanks was short in stature, he had a presence,' recalls Peter Tothill.[84]

Sir Miles Thomas's resignation was to have repercussions for Morris Motors because a few weeks later, in December 1947, a swathe of ageing directors resigned. Hans Landstad, Victor Riley, Harold Ryder and Carl Skinner all departed, leaving only Vic Oak and the newly appointed Sydney V. Smith, who became director of assembly facilities, as survivors. On 19 December 1947 the old board gathered for the last time and, following Thomas's departure, the Mosquito name was finally laid to rest. Issigonis's car then officially became 'the Morris Minor', which revived the name of the model built at Cowley in the 1928–34 era. Up until this point there were thoughts of elevating its factory coding to a model name, although calling a car destined for export markets after an insect that carried malaria was hardly diplomatic!

If Lord Nuffield had thought that Sir Miles's departure had spelt the end of the Minor, he was mistaken. Hanks, although a less charismatic figure than his predecessor, was a steadying influence on the business at a crucial time, recognised Issigonis's worth and pressed ahead with the project. Less desirably, his was a more parochial outlook than his predecessor's and, in consequence, lacked Thomas's global aspirations. Nevertheless, after a protracted gestation, the public got its first official glimpse of Cowley's new Minor, allocated the Series MM designation, in two-door saloon and touring forms, when it dominated Morris's stand at the 1948 Motor Show.

Notes

1. Graham Turner, *The Car Makers*, 1963.
2. Rob Golding, *Mini*, 1979.
3. Jackson, *op cit.*
4. *The Mini Man*, Channel 4, 1998.
5. Jennifer Gilman, interview with author, 2004.
6. Malcolm Axtell, interview with author, 2004.
7. Doreen Schreier, interview with author, 2004.
8. Michael Sedgwick, *Cars of the 1930s*, 1970.
9. Ralf J.F. Kieselbach, *Stromlinenautos in Europa and USA*, 1982.
10. Eric Moore, interview with author, 2002.
11. Christy Campbell, The Making of the Mini, *Thoroughbred and Classic Cars*, September, 1979.
12. Wood, *MG to Minor*, *op cit.*
13. Gerald Palmer, *Auto-Architect*, 1997.
14. Wood, *op cit.*
15. Thomas, *op cit.*
16. Palmer, *op cit.*
17. Christy Campbell, The Birth of the Morris Minor, *Thoroughbred and Classic Cars*, July 1978.
18. Peter Tothill, interview with author, 2004.
19. Turner and Curtis, *op cit.*
20. Pomeroy, *op cit.*
21. Thomas, *op cit.*
22. Ibid
23. Ibid.
24. Geoffrey Rose, interview with author, 2002.
25. Thomas, *op cit.*
26. Noble, *op cit.*
27. Thomas, *op cit.*
28. Gerald Palmer, letter to *The Motor*, 3 December 1958.
29. Peter Tothill *op cit.*
30. Paul Skilleter, *Morris Minor*, (third edition), 1989.
31. Campbell, *op cit.*
32. For an account of the other stylists involved in the design of the Clipper, see *Packard, A History of the Motor Car and Company*, 1978.
33. Campbell, *op cit.*
34. Ibid.
35. Turner and Curtis, *op cit.*
36. Sir Alec Issigonis, Elegance of the Twenties, *Autocar*, 12 November 1977.
37. Ibid.
38. Quoted in Wood, *MG from A to Z*, *op cit.*
39. H.N. Charles, letter, *The Motor*, 3 December 1958.
40. Campbell, *op cit.*
41. Ibid.
42. Charles, *op cit.*
43. Ibid.
44. Ibid.
45. Philip Turner, The Man Who Made Motoring Fun Again, *Motor*, 8 January 1972.

46. Daniels, *op cit.*
47. Ibid.
48. Ibid.
49. Quoted in Gutty, *Classic Military Vehicles*, November, 2003.
50. Jennifer Gilman, *op cit.*
51. The Mini Man, *op cit.*
52. Alex Moulton, *op cit.*
53. Jennifer Gilman, *op cit.*
54. Ibid.
55. Quoted in *Making Cars*, Television History Workshop, 1985.
56. Skilleter, *op cit.*
57. Jack Daniels, *op cit.*
58. Ibid.
59. Campbell, *op cit.*
60. Eric Moore, *op cit.*
61. Doreen Schreier, *op cit.*
62. Turner and Curtis, *op cit.*
63. Peter Tothill, *op cit.*
64. Skilleter, *op cit.*
65. Quoted in Wood, *Wheels of Misfortune*, 1988.
66. Ibid.
67. Skilleter, *op cit.*
68. *The Autocar*, 29 November 1946.
69. Ibid.
70. Skilleter, *op cit.*
71. Ibid.
72. Barker, Alec Issigonis, *op cit.*
73. Christopher Dowson, *op cit.*
74. Geoffrey Rose, *op cit.*
75. Thomas, *op cit.*
76. Skilleter, *op cit.*
77. Thomas, *op cit.*
78. Leasor, *op cit.*
79. Peter Tothill, *op cit.*
80. Skilleter, *op cit.*
81. Ullyett, *op cit.*
82. Christopher Dowson, *op cit.*
83. Eric Moore, *op cit.*
84. Peter Tothill, *op cit.*

The Sollershott flats in Linkside Avenue, Oxford, where Alec Issigonis and his mother lived from 1938 until 1963. Number six is on the top floor on the left-hand side. Mother and son often used to sit on the balcony doing their crosswords. (*Author*)

The unitary construction Type 50 Steyr of 1936, a two-door four-seater saloon which provided the mechanical inspiration for the Morris Mosquito, later the Minor, on account of its "flat" four-cylinder engine that is mounted ahead of the front axle line. Steering was by rack and pinion. This car similarly influenced Gerald Palmer in his design for the Jowett Javelin. (*Author's Collection*)

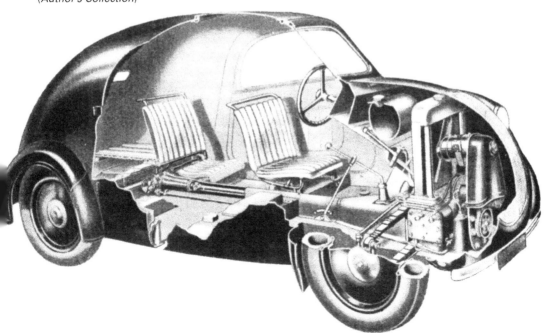

The Salamander, which started life as a speculative armoured car project by Alec Issigonis and Jack Daniels in 1940. This is the first occasion that Issigonis applied torsion bar independent front suspension to a completed vehicle although the project never attained production status. (*Peter Seymour*)

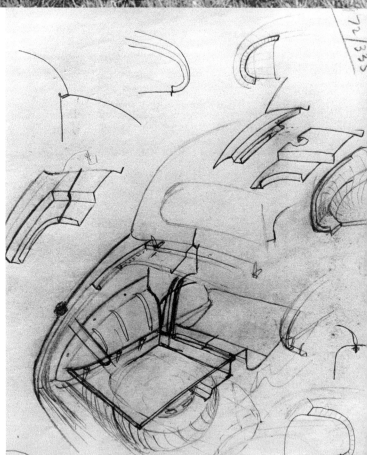

72/335

A drawing by Alec Issigonis showing the rear construction of the Morris Minor. (*Author's Collection*)

A model owned by Jack Daniels of the Morris Mosquito, circa 1941. Note the louvres on the top of the bonnet which indicated that the radiator was mounted Steyr-like behind the flat four engine. (*Author's Collection*)

The Mosquito in its original form, prior to Issigonis adding an extra four inches to the width, and the rear bumper accordingly lacks a spacer. This is probably the second experimental car built, EX/130, a left-hand drive example completed in 1946. Note the single rear light which never reached production. (*Barry Blight*)

What may be the first experimental 'wide' Mosquito of 1948. Note the apparent absence of a spacer between the two halves of the bumper. The bonnet hump also appears to be slightly higher than that of the production Minor and the contours of the front wings also differ. (*Barry Blight*)

Issigonis's masterpiece, the Morris Minor, was Britain's most popular car of the 1950s. Created for world markets, its full potential was never fully exploited by its manufacturer. (*Barry Blight*)

George Dowson photographed by Murray Hardy in the Lightweight Special at Prescott on 23 June 1946. This was the occasion when strands of rubber were removed from the rear suspension to create negative camber. The blanked-off carburettor intake on the offside suspension binnacle indicates the presence of the Wolseley ohc engine. (*Bugatti Owners' Club*)

Alec Issigonis (centre) and George Dowson (left) loading the Lightweight Special on to its trailer at the Vintage Sports-Car Club's Elstree Speed Trials held on Easter Monday 1946. The marshall on the right was one of a number supplied by the North London Enthusiasts' Club. (*Bugatti Owners' Club*)

A mini car before the Mini. Ian Duncan with the Duncan Dragonfly in the summer of 1948, which in some respects anticipated the Issigonis baby, on account of its front-wheel drive, transverse two-cylinder engine, small 12in wheels and Moulton rubber suspension. The location is Swannington airfield in Norfolk, where Duncan bodied Healey 100 chassis, an example of which is in the background. The Dragonfly was seen by Leonard Lord and bought by Austin later in that year for £10,000. (*Author's Collection*)

Inspiration for the Mini name and the car? Laurence Pomeroy's imaginary front-wheel drive transverse engined Mini-Motor of 1939, with its original caption, which appeared in the 7 February issue of *The Motor*. (*Autocar*)

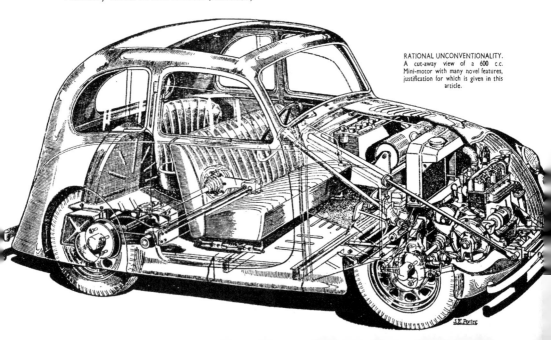

RATIONAL UNCONVENTIONALITY. A cut-away view of a 600 c.c. Mini-motor with many novel features, justification for which is given in this article.

BMC's controversial chairman Leonard Lord (right) who impulsively commissioned the Mini from Alec Issigonis in 1957, so switching the corporate emphasis from rear to front-wheel drive. He is seen here in company with Harold Hastings (left), Midland Editor of *The Motor,* and its editor Christopher Jennings. (*National Motor Museum*).

George Harriman, when vice chairman of the British Motor Corporation in 1957. Promoted to chairman in 1961, he and Alec Issigonis were to run BMC for much of that decade.
(*Author's Collection*)

The Trout at Godstow, Oxford, the Thames-side pub where Alec Issigonis was a 'regular' from the 1950s until he left the area in 1963. (*Author*)

Issigonis relaxing with friends on the terrace of the Trout in the 1950s. (*Christopher Dowson*).

Chapter Five

THE GREEK GOD

*'None of the directors were very keen… "This thing"
that Issigonis is doing they would say. It was because
it didn't look like any other car.'*[1]

Alec Issigonis

T HE TITLE for this chapter is not a reflection of the author's penchant for alliteration. It is the name accorded to Alec Issigonis by his contemporaries at Cowley, following the success of his first car, the Morris Minor. Not only was it the most outstanding British family model to be exhibited at the 1948 London Motor Show, it was also the most technically advanced small car in the world.

As the quotation at the beginning of this chapter reveals, Morris Motors failed to recognise the Minor's true worth, an indifference which today can be identified as one of the many tragedies that has punctuated the British motor industry's turbulent history. This was despite the fact that the world was desperate for new cars and, with many European car factories decimated by war, the Minor's export potential was accordingly never fully exploited. Although this was a world resentful of Germany's all too recent military aggression, it was a gap ably filled by the Volkswagen Beetle.

Yet if Morris 'had concentrated on the Minor and developed it year on year as the Beetle has been developed,' as Philip Turner, a respected commentator on *Motor* magazine observed in 1972,[2] it could have become 'the British equivalent of Volkswagen, in which case British Leyland would be owned by Morris Motors and not vice versa.'

But in 1948, the year in which the Minor was launched, Volkswagen built just 19,244 cars. In the same period 68,772 Morrises left Cowley and Alec Issigonis was on the company's stand with Jack Daniels at that year's Motor Show when the chief engineer of General Motors was introduced to them. After examining the car, Daniels remembers, 'His words of praise for its superb packaging gave immense pleasure to Issigonis. I too felt a measure of pride.'[3] In celebration of the Minor's reception, Issigonis was awarded a £100 bonus which he spent on a pearl necklace for his mother, perhaps in recompense for the solitaire ring she had sold 18 years before so that he could buy his Austin Seven Ulster.

The Autocar was ecstatic and dedicated a leading article to the Minor, describing it as a 'masterpiece of car engineering.'[4] Its road test, published in the same issue, concluded, 'The new Minor can, without hesitation, be awarded full marks, especially for suspension, steering, stability and general road worthiness.' Its appearance was 'cherubic,' a description not usually allocated to a motor car. Top speed was 62mph.

The new model was also driven on its introduction by motoring journalist Philip Turner, a friend of Issigonis. 'I met him frequently at those early post-war sprint meetings which for a time were the only form of motoring sport in Britain... Mrs Kay Petre, ex-Austin works driver and *Daily Sketch* motoring correspondent, used to attend meetings amply supplied with picnic lunch and used to take pity on poor, starving bachelors such as Alec and me, so that many a meal we shared out in the open, thanks to her hospitality.'[5]

In 1948 Philip, following three years on *The Autocar,* had been appointed technical editor of *The Garage and Motor Agent* and it was in that capacity that he attended the first Motor Show press day, held in the autumn of 1948 at the newly opened Goodwood circuit. Turner later recalled his first impressions of the Minor.

The demonstration car had been late in arriving and 'Issigonis drove the Minor into the Paddock... therefore I knew him well enough to snatch the car almost before he was out of the driving seat. To this day [1972] I can remember most vividly the absolute revelation of those first few laps... for here was a car head and shoulders above all its rivals. Only the knowledge of so many impatient fellow scribes awaiting their turns dissuaded me from exceeding my quota of laps.' Such was the impact the Minor had on motoring correspondents. Indeed Harry Barber, managing director of Pressed Steel, who had worked closely with Issigonis when the latter had moved to Alvis, once told Turner that he was sure that it was 'the tremendous enthusiasm of the motoring press for the Minor that made it such a success.'[6]

Peter Tothill arrived at Cowley in 1950 when Issigonis's star was in the ascendancy. 'He had a nickname, he was known as the Greek God. But it was difficult to get near the guy, he was regarded as a bit of a boffin who didn't have his feet on the ground although he was a brilliant innovator and lateral thinker. He would never have fitted in at either Ford or Vauxhall.'[7]

The Morris Minor saloon was priced at £358 and Gerald Palmer, later to become a Cowley-based BMC executive, knew that in the 1950s Morris was making a respectable profit of about £40 on each one it built.[8] As will emerge, the Mini, born of an Austin-dominated corporation, was flawed in that regard because it was over-engineered and seriously under-priced. Why therefore did these shortcomings not affect the Minor?

There were two principal reasons. Firstly, Issigonis's talents were held in check by Vic Oak, his technical director, who was able to channel his subordinate's extraordinary talents along commercial lines. The deletion of his wholly new flat four engine not only imbued the Minor with reliability, but its replacement by the existing Morris Eight unit was also to the benefit of the model's profitability. Similarly the fitment of cheap, conventional rear leaf springs, in place of Issigonis's preferred torsion bars, was financially beneficial. Even if the last-minute body widening added modest extra cost, the Minor undoubtedly benefited as a result.

Secondly, William Morris, who had founded the business in 1912, while having a natural instinct for a car's mechanicals, also, crucially, possessed a formidable grasp of finance. Unlike practically all of its contemporaries, the original 'Bullnose' Oxford of 1912 was assembled from bespoke parts supplied by outside contractors at a time when the overwhelming majority of the constituents in the British motor industry misguidedly believed that as much of a car as possible should be made on the premises.

By the 1920s Morris had some 200 suppliers and obtained 60 days credit from them and was able to build a Bullnose in just six. It was a formula that produced a business built on the solid foundations of mechanical and financial engineering and by 1923, with pre-tax profits of £927,000, Morris was running the most profitable car company in the country. His fiscal control was absolute and each division of his empire was required to produce detailed quarterly trading statements so the chairman could see instantly how it was faring. Less desirably, Morris had had to buy his principal suppliers when they could not keep up with demand for the Bullnose and by the early post-war years he owned no fewer than 16 factories scattered across Oxford and the industrial Midlands.

Such tight monitoring, employed in tandem with a dominant position in the British car market between the wars, was to bring Morris's founder great personal wealth, particularly after the business went public in 1926. Lord

Nuffield, as he became, was Britain's best-known benefactor, giving away a total of £30 million in his lifetime. By contrast, Austin, established by that champion of engineering orthodoxy, Herbert Austin, was less profitable and accordingly produced as much of the car as possible at Longbridge, his only factory. When Leonard Lord took over the helm at Austin, his pricing policy went along the lines of 'What's Morris's bloody figure? Right, make ours £5 less.'[9] Apparently imprecise, it was no doubt based on his knowledge of Nuffield's more perceptive costing methods.

Issigonis had also scaled up the Minor design to create the Series MO Oxford, although it has to be said that the lines did not enlarge particularly well, which underlined the fact that his remarkable gifts could only express themselves in the creation of small cars. Interestingly, at the time Philip Turner remembered that it was believed 'the Oxford would far outsell the Minor... when the general opinion was that the medium sized family saloons would be the big sellers, both in home and export markets.'[10]

The Oxford, with its American-inspired steering column gearbox, was a roomy six-seater intended for export. It only survived until 1956 and the 160,000 sold was a reflection of a seller's market. It was, in truth, a rather gutless performer, a consequence of it weighing close on a ton and being powered by a 1.5-litre side valve engine. Mention should also be made of the Wolseley MS version of the Oxford, for which, as a concession to Lord Nuffield, a traditional radiator shell was incongruously grafted on to the Issigonis-executed lines. Just 12,400 were built in five years.

The Minor, however, was an instant hit, although production did not begin to build up until 1950 when some 48,000 were built. Both saloon and tourer were displayed in left-hand drive forms and the Nuffield Organisation's advertisement in the 1948 Motor Show catalogue echoed the export-conscious mood of the time when it proclaimed: 'The New Morris Cars answer demands of world motorists.'

While the words were brave, in reality the full export potential of the Minor as a global car was never exploited and the opportunity would be seized by the German Volkswagen company. Based in a bomb-damaged plant completed as recently as 1940, the VW factory was located at Wolfsburg, a town so named by the British as Lower Saxony fell within its Military Zone. It is for this reason that, in a supreme twist of irony, Morris Motors had been offered the Volkswagen as part of the spoils of victory. The car, with its noisy, air-cooled, rear-mounted engine and, to British although not Continental eyes, unconventional appearance, would have come complete with the services of its designer, Ferdinand Porsche. In any event Cowley already had its own 'People's Car' and the offer was refused, although a Volkswagen was dismantled and inspected within the confines of Morris's experimental department.

In January 1948 Volkswagen acquired a new general manager in the shape of 47-year-old Heinz Nordhoff, who had learnt his automobile engineering in the cost-conscious environment of General Motors's Opel subsidiary, where rationalisation was the order of the day. Global in his view, fluent in English and with a passion for Impressionist art, he was the quintessential product of Germany's formidable system of technical education.

Nordhoff was to take two inspired decisions that were destined to ensure that the Volkswagen Beetle would become the most popular car in the history of the automobile. Crucially he opted to produce, just as Henry Ford had done with the Model T, one model, although there would be a better equipped export version. He also decided not to change the VW's appearance. Although Nordhoff recognised that the car then 'had more faults than a dog has fleas... Professor Porsche had worked something into it which made this diamond very much worth our while polishing.'[11] He therefore decided to refine it organically, from the inside outwards, and by 1981 it was calculated that only one of the Beetle's 5,115 parts was common with its 1945 forebear, namely the rubber bonnet seal.

Just as Ford had done, Nordhoff recognised that manufacturing economies could be reaped from volume production and this meant a strong overseas market. The first Volkswagens to be exported went to Holland and on 1 January 1949 America received its first official export. Such would be its penetration of the US market that, thanks mostly to the vehicle's phenomenal reliability, impressive sales and service support, demand would not peak there until 19 years later when in 1968 a total of 423,008 Beetles found buyers. Morris's best year for transatlantic sales had come nine years before in 1959 when a mere 14,991 cars were sold, the overwhelming number of these being Minors.

In a European context in 1957 Volkswagen had, thanks to the success of the Beetle, overtaken the British Motor Corporation, of which Morris was an integral part, to emerge as the Continent's largest car maker. As such it symbolised what Germany called the *Wirtschaftswunder* and the English-speaking world spoke of as the Economic Miracle. In 1973 the Beetle overtook the Model T Ford as the most popular car in the history of the automobile. The 20 millionth example was completed in Mexico in 1981 and the car finally ceased production in 2003, some 65 years after it had first made its public debut. Such production levels meant that between 1965 and 1968 and in 1971, over a million Beetles were produced each year. By contrast, it took Morris 12 years to manufacture a million Minors, the first British car to attain this figure. It was only then that 83-year-old Lord Nuffield spoke to Alec Issigonis and, as Alec recalled 'he had the grace to thank me.'[12]

Although the development of the Volkswagen was a copybook exercise in vehicle refinement, the Morris Minor did itself evolve. Indeed American export sales were to have an impact on the car's appearance because one of the requirements of the Californian market was that the headlamps had to be raised. Much to his sorrow Issigonis had to transfer them from the radiator grille to the wings, which coincided with the arrival of a four-door version of the car. 'I regret it very deeply… it was all due to some completely nebulous American regulations and it was completely unnecessary. And do you know it knocked 1.5mph off the top speed?'[13] The new headlamps appeared in the four-door Minor at the 1950 London Motor Show. This also flew in the face of its creator's wishes because 'Issigonis believes that, for a small car, two wide doors giving easy access to the most-used front seats are preferable to four rather restricted openings.'[14]

Further concessions to the export market took longer to evolve and the Minor did not receive a left-hand door lock to match its left-hand drive until late into its export life. Previously the driver was required to open the passenger door and then unlock the opposing one from the inside, before walking around to get into the car.

The Minor was sold in outlets other than America, being produced in CKD (Completely Knocked Down) form in the traditional Empire markets, namely Australia, New Zealand, South Africa and India. Closer to home it was also assembled in Holland and the Republic of Ireland.

One country where for a time during the 1950s the Minor successfully challenged the Volkswagen was Denmark, a member of EFTA, the European Free Trade Area, set up by Britain in 1957 to challenge the European Economic Community. Rogers Sogaard, formerly technical editor of the Danish motoring magazine *BILEN*, recalls[15] that during that decade 'every third car selling in Denmark coming from Britain was mainly a BMC product and the Morris Minor was the most popular model. It was seen as the English Beetle and in the 1950s fought the Volkswagen with some success. The Minor was recognised as a roadworthy car, price worthy and relatively simple to maintain. Although its reliability did not compare with that of the Beetle, many buyers preferred it because it was English, not German. Five years of wartime occupation were still in the minds of many Danes.'

Over the years a few minor problems have emerged. An MM driver will tell you that it is not possible to steer with the driver's quarter light open. 'One of my mistakes I'm afraid,' Issigonis later conceded. Another was the 'threaded king pins – they only go wrong because people don't look after them properly.'[16]

The most significant change to the Minor mechanicals had occurred in July 1952 when, following the creation of the BMC earlier in the year, its side valve Morris engine was replaced by the then rather indifferent 803cc overhead valve Austin unit powering the A30, Longbridge's rival to the Minor, which survived until 1959. The intended Nuffield replacement, the ohv Wolseley Eight engine, was therefore sidelined.

The Austin unit came complete with the attendant gearbox and rear axle and Peter Tothill remembers that 'the first day we ran the Minor with these units, it broke a gearbox and by the end of the week three had gone. We were so concerned that we had a special bell housing cast to attach the Morris gearbox to the Austin engine. It never happened and the problems were resolved but the original A Series engine was a very fragile thing.'[17]

A van version of the Minor also arrived in 1952 and a Traveller estate car with a composite wood and metal body followed for the 1954 season. The 1957 Minors were known as the Morris 1000, on account of the bigger bored and much improved 948cc engine, and it was enlarged to 1098cc for 1963. That was to be the last significant mechanical change made to the model, which survived until 1971. Even then much of the Minor's 1948 specification, including the provision of a starting handle, long after one had ceased to be offered by its competitors, was still part of the specification.

Such developments, or the lack of them, were for the future. In December 1948, soon after the Minor's triumphal launch, Alec Issigonis was promoted to the position of chief engineer of Morris Motors, just a month after he had celebrated his 42nd birthday. Although Cowley's total output of cars produced during the year would in 1949 be overhauled by Austin, in 1948 Morris was not only Britain's, but also Europe's most productive car maker. It was an extraordinary achievement for Issigonis, a man with a notable lack of academic and technical education in the conventional sense, who 26 years before had arrived in Britain as a near-penniless refugee.

In announcing the news, Morris made clear that Issigonis's motorsport activities were now at an end 'owing to increased duties laid upon him by his new appointment, he will no longer be able to devote any time to racing.'[18] These had restarted in 1945 when the Lightweight Special, which had spent the war years in the safety of George Dowson's Pershore farm, was dusted off and readied for action. Serving in the RAF during the war, Dowson had married Ida, universally known as Max, and they were to have two children, Penelope and Christopher, who were destined to became part of Alec Issigonis's extended family.

Dowson had driven the Lightweight pre-war but it was now Issigonis's turn to take the wheel and he was soon to prove his abilities as a racing driver. He drove the Special in the first English sprint meeting to be held after the war, on 28 October 1945, at Filton Airfield, staged by the go-ahead Bristol Aeroplane Company Motor Sports Club, of which more anon. 'The independent suspension for all its four wheels proved a boom and a blessing to the "Lightweight Special" over the bumps,' reported *The Autocar* and 'its Austin engine had a healthy snarl as A. Issigonis won the 1100cc racing class with it.'[19]

The magazine was not to know it but by this time the Special had a new engine, the diminutive Longbridge side valver having been replaced by another 748cc unit, this time courtesy of the Nuffield Organisation. Then still on the secret list, there were, according to Issigonis, 'six engines built. Wolseley kept three for test bed work and three were sent to Cowley which the Morris management gave me.'[20] It was a prototype overhead camshaft Wolseley four-cylinder engine, courtesy of the corporate Engines Branch, but not proceeded with and it drove, by chain, the Zoller supercharger, which blew at 24psi. The SU carburettor was now directly attached to the blower, so negating the unit's earlier location in the offside suspension binnacle, the original intake then being blanked off. A further modification was that the gear lever now resided externally on the offside of the cockpit. The aforementioned modifications to the brakes were effected at the same time. As a consequence of these changes the car became less of a Lightweight, the cast iron engine contributing to it now turning the scales at some 750lb.

A pent-up enthusiasm for motorsport following the war years was reflected by the large crowd of spectators, estimated at 10,000–15,000, who attended the VSCC's Elstree Speed Trials, held on a slightly uphill aerodrome runway on Easter Monday 1946. The Lightweight was entered and on this occasion Dowson, 'remarkably fast and steady,' won its class at 16.4 seconds which was deemed 'quick for a 750cc car'.[21]

Although designed for sprints and hill climbs, the car was entered for Britain's first post-war race meeting organised by the Cambridge University Automobile Club and held at Gransden Lodge airfield on 15 June 1946. This time Alec took the wheel and the event for 750cc racing cars was, by all accounts, 'a gift for the Lightweight Special driven by its designer Issigonis.'[22]

At a Bugatti Owners' Club meeting at Prescott on 23 June 1946, Alec made a remarkable, if accidental discovery. 'In the course of a very muddled day during practice at Prescott we found the car almost uncontrollable,' he related.[23] 'When one is such a state of confusion one tends to do the most unexpected things, in the course of which we accidentally lowered the back of the car very considerably.' This was achieved by the simple expedient of removing a strand or two of rubber, *Motor Sport* commenting that Dowson then stowed the discarded material in his pocket![24] Issigonis continued: 'practice time was running out and it was, therefore, essential to do a few runs with the car looking ridiculously knock-kneed. The benefit of the highly negative camber rear wheels was astonishing,' Dowson had the Specials class to himself and made an excellent time of 50.05 seconds. 'This accidental discovery... taught me a fundamental lesson long before the practice became commonplace in racing car design.'[25]

Later in 1948, while Dowson had to concentrate on the family farm and Issigonis was fully occupied seeing the Morris Minor into production, the car ran in only one trials meeting, the last of the year held on 9 October at Weston-super-Mare. There,

John Bolster reported with delight, 'it managed to beat my unsupercharged 2-litre special.'[26] Thereafter the Lightweight went into retirement. The reason, according to George Dowson's son Christopher, was that it was being 'regularly beaten by John Cooper's 500s and a certain Stirling Moss! Alec used to call him "The Boy" and the cars "Bloopars".'[27] In 1950 *The Autocar's* John Cooper reported the news, lamenting 'there seems no hope that it will appear much… in the future.'[28]

Relegated to The Poplars farm, the vehicle remained incarcerated until 1959 when, encouraged by Christopher, George entered it for a meeting at Shelsley Walsh and his son, who was to emerge as no mean hillclimber in his own right, invariably took the wheel from the late 1960s until 1976. 'Alec took a real interest in the car when I was driving it and even worked out a different hysteresis for the rubber suspension in a bid to improve the handling. Not that it did! The only thing that made it handle at all was the strength of the bonnet straps.[29] Mechanically the weakest point on the Lightweight was the differential which, being Austin Seven-based, was forever breaking. It was a nightmare to work on because everything had a dual purpose, being stressed. It took a week of work to take it apart, there seemed to be thousands of 2BA bolts to undo. And it took another two weeks to put back together again.'

In 1961 Alec Issigonis, then basking in post-Mini euphoria, together with 15 other pre-war drivers and their cars, was reunited with the Lightweight at the VSCC's Oulton Park race meeting. Subsequently, in 1976, at his request, it went on display at the Stratford Motor Museum. However, after George Dowson's death in 1979 Christopher became the owner. 'Alec formally gave me the Lightweight… sadly, I had to sell it in 1997 to Iain Cheyne to pay school fees. It is in very good hands.'[30] Happily, the new owner continues to campaign the car at VSCC events. In later years Issigonis was publicly dismissive of the Lightweight as 'a frivolity of my life. It was not so much a design exercise as a means of teaching me to use my hands. George and I learnt the hard way how to build something for ourselves from scratch.'[31]

However, Issigonis's sprint and hillclimbing activities were to be indirectly responsible for him meeting, in 1949, Alex Moulton, who was to become a close friend and engineering colleague in an association that was destined to last for some 15 years. Alec Issigonis had got to know Joseph (Joe) Fry and enjoyed the company of his cousin David and the latter's wife Joy. The enterprising Frys had created a fearsome hillclimb car named the Freikaiserwagen, on account of the mid location of its engine in the manner of the Grand Prix P-Wagen Auto Union.

Dating from 1936, in its original form it was the work of its owner David Fry, the 18-year-old son of Cecil, chairman of J.S. Fry Ltd, famed Bristol-based chocolate manufacturers, and seasoned special builder Dick Caesar. Based on a chain-driven GN chassis, to which Morgan independent front suspension was grafted, power came from a V-twin water-cooled Anzani engine.

A chance meeting of the cousins at that year's Backwell hillclimb resulted in Joe, educated at Uppingham and Cambridge and rarely seen without a cigarette in his mouth, taking a £100 share in the car which, by reason of its antecedence, was informally named Porsche. Both were excellent drivers but David weighed some 16 stone and Joe was nearly half his weight (9 stone) and he invariably drove the car, which he progressively improved and refined. A major reworking in 1937 saw the replacement of the original engine with a 1100cc Blackburne unit. John Bolster considered it to be 'the most successful of all sprint specials.'[32]

In a broader context the Friekaiserwagen can be seen as the precursor of the 500cc racer, a movement which began in the West Country. The formation of the 500 Club in December 1945 by the Bristol Aeroplane Company Motor Sports Club marks a tangible starting point and 'the Bristol boys' were to bring participation in motorsport to the masses. The principal rule – in truth there were very few rules – was that the single-seaters would be powered by an unsupercharged engine limited to 500cc. As there were no car units of that capacity available, this meant a motorcycle engine and most constructors turned to the ubiquitous JAP, the variant created for speedway racing proving to be the most suitable power source.

Invariably located behind the driver in the manner adopted in 1946 by Harrow motor engineer Colin Strang, these light single-seaters enjoyed great popularity in the early post-war years. Indeed Gregor Grant, in recording the formative years of what was to emerge in 1950 as Formula 3, lamented Issigonis's absence, from an engineering standpoint, from the 500cc scene. 'What a wonderful "500" would result if Alec Issigonis took a hand! In fact, I shouldn't be in the least bit surprised to hear that Issigonis had actually designed a half litre machine.'[33]

The 500s were invariably one-offs but from 1946 Charles Cooper of Surbiton, Surrey, began to produce, for his son John, JAP-powered cars based on two Fiat 500 chassis mounted back to back to reap the advantages of its ifs. Another car followed for John's friend Eric Brandon and in time Cooper was dominating the field, to the eventual total of some 360 cars completed. Later to graduate to For-mula 1 cars, which perpetuated the 500's mid location, John Cooper's association with Alec Issigonis dates from these years. Their paths were destined to cross again in the early 1960s, in an alliance that was to give birth to the Mini-Cooper.

The Freikaiserwagen was rebuilt on three occasions in the post-war years, in the winter of 1947, the spring of 1948 and the winter of 1948/49. During this last reconstruction its Blackburne engine was enlarged to 1250cc, two-stage supercharging was adopted and the cockpit was moved further forward. It was then that Joe accorded responsibility for the car's development to four individuals. They were, in his own words, David Fry, Dick Caesar, the well known tuner Robin Jackson and Alec Issigonis. 'They have the brains: I pick them.'[34]

Issigonis's principal contribution was to the rear suspension which, like the Lightweight, was rubber strands in tension that replaced the original quarter elliptics in 1947 when a new tubular chassis was created. This was refined at the end of that year so that they 'only support the car but do not resist it tipping to either side, the front wheels performing the whole of that duty.'[35] It turned the scales at just 570lb.

Joe Fry had been the fastest special at Shelsley Walsh in 1947 (40.61 seconds) and the revised car appeared at the same venue in June 1949 where he beat Raymond Mays's record. Simultaneously yet another member of the Fry family put in an appearance, in the shape of David's younger brother, 24-year-old Jeremy, who had already been roped in to assist with the preparation of the Freikaiserwagen but was driving his own impressively prepared cream-coloured 500cc racer, designed and built for him by Keith Steadman. Like his cousin's car, it was powered by a Jackson-prepared Blackburne unit. Probably the only 500 racer of its day to feature separate chassis for engine and transmission, it was also the lightest, weighing only 470lb.

The car bore the unusual moniker of Parsenn, which was adopted because the Fry family enjoyed skiing as a pastime in the Swiss province of that name. Jeremy held the class record at Bouley Bay and put up a good showing at Shelsley Walsh. Gregor Grant wrote at the time that 'young Fry has shown great skill in handling the car and is one of our most promising hill-climb drivers. Parsenn is undoubtedly one of the fastest non professionally built "500s".'[36] For his part Jeremy Fry continued to run Parsenn for the remainder of the season but thereafter concentrated his energies on a Bristol-based engineering business which specialised in the manufacture of valve guides. In 1959 it moved to Bath and today Rotork Actuation is a leading supplier of pipeline components to the global gas and oil industries.

The Fry family thus had a great impact on motorsport in the early post-war years, and on Alec Issigonis. However, he was not the only enthusiast to be expounding the virtues of rubber suspension as it had featured on the the Fry-sponsored Parsenn and here the influence of Alex Moulton, of Spencer Moulton, becomes apparent. Its independently sprung front wheel used rubber in torsion while the swing axle rear employed rubber in compression.

It was therefore inevitable that Moulton and Issigonis would encounter each other at some point, and they did so in 1949. 'I said to David Fry. 'I would like to meet this Alec Issigonis I've heard all about. He sounds an interesting man,' Moulton recalls.[37] 'So we drove over to Cowley to meet him and, although I was some 14 years younger, he recognised in me and me in him a fellow spirit. We sparked off each other. We had lunch in the senior managers dining room, a nice oak panelled room and had a lot of gin and tonic, I was really quite away by the end. These were the days of serious lunches. That was the start of it and I used to go back to his mother's flat in Oxford.'

Moulton was at the time 29 years old and Issigonis 43, but not only were they both named Alexander, although one was Alec and the other Alex, they also shared a superficial resemblance. Coincidentally, this was not the first connection between the Issigonis family and Moulton's family business. Fifty-three years before, in 1896, Alexander and Alfred Spencer, of Spencer Moulton, had been two of five seconders[38] to have backed Alec's uncle George Issigonis's successful application for associate membership of the Institution of Mechnical Engineers.

Both were engineers and suspension specialists, although Moulton's qualifications were the greater, and both had complemented theory with practical experience. Alec and Alex shared a similar regard for Maurice Olley and both, at varying stages in their respective careers, had recognised the potential of rubber suspension. If Issigonis lived in a small two-bedroom flat and Moulton occupied a fine Renaissance house, no matter. There was so much to discuss!

'I was very much his disciple, I learnt so much from him and I was able to give him things that were outside his particular knowledge. I've had two engineering gurus in my life, number one was Sir Roy Fedden, chief engineer of Bristol Aeroplane Company, I was his PA during the war, and number two really was Issigonis. He had a very good mind, although he was only modestly educated at Battersea on rudiments. He read and read, he idolised the works of Olley, and was very knowledgeable on cars.'[39]

There were downsides. 'He was very opinionated and he wouldn't give credit to anyone else who was working with him, unless they were of a manifestly lower status. He wouldn't even allow the name of Fiat's Dante Giacosa, who was a very great man, to be mentioned as another car designer.'

Alexander (Alex) Eric Moulton was born on 9 April 1920. His father, John Coney Moulton, DSc, a distinguished scientist and entomologist, died young and Alex was brought up in the Victorian atmosphere of his grandfather's house. This was The Hall at Bradford-on-Avon, built in 1598–1601 by the Smythson brothers for John Hall, a wealthy local clothier. Alex's great-grandfather, Stephen Moulton, had in 1848 established a factory for the production of rubber in the town. This followed the decline of the local woollen industry and in 1846 he bought the Kingston Mill for this purpose. The railway boom of the time saw the company start producing rubber goods for railway rolling stock, especially buffer springs. Moulton also bought what today is known as The Hall, where Alex Moulton has lived throughout much of his life. Alex looks back on a 'supremely happy' childhood there.[40]

However, the buoyancy of the Victorian years gave way to the relatively less prosperous times of the interwar years. Instead of following his father to Eton, Alex was sent to Marlborough, which he much enjoyed. By this time he had decided on his career as a design engineer. He was soon devouring books and magazines on engineering. 'Those wonderful cutaway drawings in *The Autocar* for instance...' and he began to hero-worship giants of the engineering world. He particularly admired the commanding figure of Roy Fedden, chief engineer of the nearby Bristol Aeroplane Company, begetter of the mighty Pegasus and Mercury sleeve valve radial engines, and Nigel Gresley, his opposite number at the London North Eastern Railway.[41]

At school Alex Moulton had enjoyed some distinction for being the only pupil to return each term with a lathe, a pre-1914 3.5in Drummond, which was set up in the woodworking shop and produced the parts for a steam car which he built at the age of 14, keeping *Steam Car Developments* magazine informed of his progress. He actively continued with these experiments until 1951.

Between finishing at school and going up to King's College, Cambridge, where he was to read engineering, the young Moulton's practical skills were honed during a premium apprenticeship at the Sentinel Works in Shrewsbury which made steam wagons. He began his studies at Cambridge but then the war, and fate, intervened, because Moulton had the opportunity of working for his childhood hero, Roy Fedden, as his personal assistant. His predecessor, the talented Adrian Squire, who is best remembered for producing the rare, costly but visually stunning Squire sports cars in 1934–36, had been sadly killed in a daytime raid on Filton in September 1940 and Alex Moulton, aged only 20, took his place. It was a rare opportunity for an ambitious young man with an enquiring mind who was intent on becoming an engineer.

 Subsequently, in 1942, Fedden, who was knighted in that year's New Year Honours List, had a major falling-out with his employers and departed in October to become special technical adviser to Sir Stafford Cripps, Minister of Aircraft Production, and Moulton also left. In 1943 Roy Fedden Ltd was established and produced what its founder deemed to be a British 'People's Car' in the spirit of the Volkswagen. The initial work was undertaken at the Bristol flat that Moulton shared with Ian Duncan, who had joined the Aeroplane Company just prior to the outbreak of war and became the project's chief engineer.

Unfortunately the Fedden proved to be a flawed design. A four-door saloon, it was influenced by the Volkswagen in having a rear-mounted power unit. But this was Fedden's beloved sleeve valve radial, a 1.6-litre three-cylinder unit, with drive being transferred to the rear wheels via a torque converter. Suspension was by unequal wishbones at the front and a swing axle and trailing arms at the rear. The medium was aircraft-related in that it was Lockheed oleo-pneumatic struts, which had been used for undercarriages, although they began to leak when applied to a car. They were replaced, significantly in the light of future events, with rubber suspension for which Alex Moulton was responsible. The material being used in compression, it took the form of a pile of rubber pastels slotted onto a central tube.

A single Fedden, 1Ex, was built and extensively road tested by Ian Duncan early in 1946. He recalled a memorable encounter on a lonely Cotswold road when he noticed another strange vehicle approaching. Both drivers stopped, got out of their respective saloons and, almost without a word, carefully scrutinised the other's vehicle. The 'other' car on this occasion proved to be an experimental Morris Minor being put through its paces by Alec Issigonis.[42] He remembered this encounter and later told Moulton that 'he knew at once the Fedden would be an enormous disaster.'[43]

Indeed, it soon became apparent that something wasn't 'quite right' about the Fedden's handling, the combination of the high-mounted radial and swing axle. The project came to an abrupt halt in mid-1946 when the prototype crashed at Stoke Orchard aerodrome where it was undergoing tests. Duncan had a row with Fedden, left and, gathering some members of the design team, took himself off to the small town of North Walsham in Norfolk. There they began work on an advanced small front-wheel drive unitary construction car which was named the Duncan Dragonfly.

Alex Moulton had, in the meantime, returned to Cambridge in 1944 to successfully complete his studies there, gaining an MA in 1949. Although he was tempted by the dawning of the jet age at Bristol, 'the call of the house at Bradford proved too strong; it was empty then and very run down. I felt that I might in some way combine its support with entering the firm founded by my great-grandfather which had its works adjacent.'[44]

This he did, becoming the business's technical director, having initiated the building of a research laboratory there. He steeped himself in rubber technology because he had decided to devote himself to developing a rubber spring for use in motor cars.

Moulton's research was concentrated on methods of bonding or chemically attaching rubber to metal, a process not widely used at the time. 'This enables rubber to be strained in shear as well as compression as hitherto.' From this research sprang a family of rubber springs of which the best known was Flexitor, in which a sleeve of rubber is twisted in torsion. It was to find application on trailers and caravans, but Alex Moulton's ambition at the time was 'to get it adopted for motor car suspensions.'[45]

In 1948, although only used in compression, rubber was used on Ian Duncan's Dragonfly, which was completed in that year. The car's key features, namely its diminutive 12in wheels, rubber suspension, front-wheel drive, transversely located engine and doors, which contained sliding windows with pockets below, can, in some respects, be seen as anticipating the Mini. It was a car of which Alec Issigonis was, characteristically, dismissive.

The comparison between the two is attractive but the significant difference was that the Dragonfly accommodated three people on its single seat. With an overall length of 10ft 9.5in, it was 9.5in longer than Issigonis's baby four-seater of 11 years later. Stylist Frank Hamblin's visual inspiration had been the dodgem cars seen at a local fairground. Mechanicals were the responsibility of Alan Lamburn and Moulton contributed the suspension medium, which, like the Fedden, used rubber pastels front and rear although it respectively featured wishbones and a dead rear axle located by Panhard rod. Power was provided by a 500cc two-cylinder BSA motorcycle engine, which progressively Lamburn mounted well to the fore, making the Dragonfly nose heavy to reap the tractive advantages of front-wheel drive.

Unfortunately Ian Duncan had diversified into the construction of car bodies, fell foul of the Inland Revenue and was forced to sell the Dragonfly. He took it to Austin and chairman Leonard Lord was impressed when, recalled Duncan, 'it went up Lickey Hill outside the factory quicker than an A40.'[46] Austin paid £10,000, over £200,000 by today's values, for this prototype and Ian Duncan's services. However, the model that finally emerged from the Dragonfly was the wholly conventional Austin A30 of 1952. The baby car was relegated to one of the many wartime air-raid tunnels on the site and it was subsequently destroyed. Virtually nothing now remains of this pioneering front-wheel drive prototype, although the author has two of its Moulton rubber suspension rings given to him by Alan Lamburn.

Alex Moulton's 1949 meeting with Alec Issigonis was also to take forward his work on rubber suspension even though he recalls that Morris's chief engineer was initially sceptical of its virtues, despite having used it on the Lightweight Special. 'He said he didn't like rubber, it was "not a serious material",'[47] although he was probably responsible for sanctioning a research programme using rubber springs which was undertaken by Jack Daniels after Issigonis had left Cowley in 1952. A Minor was duly modified with Flexitor units at the front while a new type of rubber spring, that of Rotashear, featured at the rear. In retrospect these experiments mark the starting point of what was to emerge in 1959 as the Mini's rubber suspension. 'We ran a proper test at MIRA on the pave, it did 1,000 miles without any trouble at all, 500 miles was the norm, which was a total vindication that, if you do it properly, rubber is a very serious suspension material.'[48]

To Moulton this represented 'the key experiment on rubber suspension. I believe that in every innovation there *should* be a key test, experiment or observation from which the innovator can know whether success or failure is likely. I am speaking in the technical sense: a commercial success may be another matter.'[49]

In the meantime, in 1951, Alec Issigonis had begun work on an experimental front-wheel drive version of the Morris Minor, a vehicle which, in retrospect, represents a stepping stone between that car and the Mini. Unlike the Traction Avant Citroën, which was powered by an in-line engine, this was mounted transversely across the engine compartment in the manner of his later BMC baby. Peter Tothill remembers the car well. 'It was a two door black saloon built in the development section of which Jack Daniels was in charge. Prototypes were made there. This was separate from experimental which tended to deal with pre-production and production cars.[50]

'This Minor had a transverse side valve engine and end-gearbox with a final drive off the gearbox.' The joints at the hubs were a combination of Hardy Spicer and a special sliding Cardan one. 'But because there were no constant velocity joints on full lock it kicked on corners. There was just a tube in place of the original rear axle. I have to say that the car wasn't taken particularly seriously at the time.'

So where did the inspiration for such a development come from? In truth cars fitted with transverse, as opposed to 'north/south' engines, are almost as old as the automobile. The American J. Walter Christie's monstrous front-wheel drive racer of 1904 is the most celebrated example and, interestingly, its creator was at Cowley early in 1937 to discuss tank design with Morris Motors. Did he, the pioneer of transverse-engined front-wheel drive, and Issigonis, who took the concept to the wider world, ever meet?

What is more likely is that Morris's chief engineer had been influenced by his friend Laurence Pomeroy. Following his production of the Zoller supercharger in Britain, in 1936 Pomeroy had travelled to Germany to consult with Faudi Feinbau in Frankfurt, who held the Zoller patents. He did not return to Britain until 1937 when he joined the staff of *The Motor* as its technical editor. Thereafter he contributed articles in which technicalities were presented in a straightforward and readable manner on a wide range of subjects which invariably contained a strong European perspective.

Writing in *The Motor* of 7 February 1939, he headed the second instalment of a two-part article *Is The Unconventional Car Justified?* His imaginary saloon was a front-wheel drive vehicle, illustrated by a cutaway drawing, and bristling with Continental influences. Its two-door body was clearly Fiat 500-inspired, while the torsion bar suspension and rack and pinion steering were in the Citroën Traction Avant idiom.

Above all, Pomeroy wrote that, having opted for front-wheel drive, 'it seems to me that one might well take advantage of having a small engine *by placing it athwart the frame instead of in line with it as normal.*' (Author's italics.) This location was not driven by a desire 'to save space' but to improve weight distribution, so reaping the benefits of front-wheel drive and reducing noise levels. Knowing Issigonis's preoccupation with small car design and as a friend of Pomeroy, it is impossible for him to have been unaware of this automotive castle-in-the-air which its creator christened a Mini-motor…

A further influence may have been provided by the front-wheel drive Dechaux prototype chassis exhibited at the 1947 Paris motor show, which used a transversely located air-cooled engine. Its automatic gearbox may have been located in the sump, thereby anticipating the Mini. It never attained production and Charles Dechaux later turned his talents to helicopter design.

Issigonis was probably unaware of the fact that his great rival, Dante Giacosa at Fiat, had in 1947 produced a prototype of a transverse-engined front-wheel drive car with the diminutive 600cc four-cylinder engine located horizontally ahead of the front axle line. What was designated the '100 E1' remained stillborn but in 1948 Citroën had followed its Traction Avant with the 2CV, a small front-wheel drive car to which Alec Issigonis, John Morris and Alex Moulton could positively respond, although their enthusiasm was not widely shared by their British contemporaries. Maurice Platt, soon to be appointed Vauxhall's chief engineer, recalled that the 'freakish' Citroën 'was viewed derisively by engineers and journalists alike because of a skimped specification and bizarre appearance.'[51]

Chunky, spartan and with mechanically interconnected all independent suspension, in his later years Issigonis would recognise its 'tremendous character, having been designed for a purpose it fulfils admirably.'[52] But unlike the Traction Avant engine, the 2CV's power unit was located, to the benefit of its road holding, ahead of the front-wheel line, making it the first significant production car to do so.

Yet for all its individuality, the Citroën did not begin to take account of the space-saving advantage reaped by the use of a compact 375cc water-cooled horizontally opposed two-cylinder engine. Then in 1950 such a vehicle did appear from an unexpected quarter. The Swedish Saab company joined the ranks of the world's motor manufacturers and introduced a car that did precisely that.

A new recruit to the ranks of the motor industry, this was a business that in 1914 had begun to manufacture aircraft and after World War Two had decided to diversify into car manufacture. The prototype 92 model was completed in 1946 although series production did not begin until 1950 and its specification shared some similarities with the Minor's gestation. The front-wheel drive Saab drew on the pre-war German DKW technology and was therefore powered by a transversely mounted two-cylinder two-stroke engine, although of 764cc, with its gearbox attached to the end of the unit. On the DKW little attempt had been made to capitalise on the space-saving attributes of the layout but the Saab 92 did, its aerodynamically refined unitary construction two-door saloon body reflecting Saab's aviation parentage. All independent suspension was by transverse torsion bars.

However, Issigonis was unable to oversee the completion of the front-wheel drive Minor before fate intervened. Leonard Lord was endeavouring to effect a 'merger' between Britain's two largest car makers and this finally came to fruition in February 1952 when the British Motor Corporation was formed, becoming Britain's, and indeed Europe's, largest car company in productive terms. Seventy-four year old Lord Nuffield was ostensibly chairman but he stepped down in December of that year to become BMC's president. Thereafter he played no part in corporate affairs as Austin effectively took over Morris with Leonard Lord as chairman and George Harriman, his protégé, as deputy.

By this time Alec Issigonis had left Cowley. No doubt apprehensive about Lord's arrival, he had been urged to do so by Reginald Hanks. As it happened Issigonis had already heard from Donald Healey that Alvis in Coventry was thinking of producing a V8-engined car. His contact with Healey sprang from their discussions for creating a 'super sports' Morris Minor. In the meantime Healey had established a dialogue with Alvis regarding the use of its power unit in one of his models.

Soon after BMC's creation, in the spring of 1952, Alec Issigonis had asked Gerald Palmer, who in July 1949 had returned to Cowley after seven and a half years years with the modest Jowett concern, 'what it was like to work for a small company?'[53] Palmer was somewhat surprised by this question because 'small cars, which were his speciality, needed to be produced in large quantities which were beyond the resources of a small firm. I told him what it was like as best I could, stressing that you were your own boss!'

In fact Issigonis had wasted little time in approaching Alvis and was offered the job. To Gerald Palmer's and 'I believe everyone else's astonishment, a few days later he resigned from Morris Motors.'[54] In any event rumours to that effect had been circulating at the Geneva Motor Show which had opened on 28 March.

Issigonis's appointment was announced by Alvis to the motoring press in the second week of April and his contract took effect from 5 June. Morris had lost its greatest asset, for its chief engineer was to join the respected Alvis company in Coventry which, as Palmer had predicted, had never built a small car and was then producing a traditional, well appointed, 3-litre saloon.

So Alec Issigonis departed after over 15 years at Cowley. He had joined as a design draughtsman and left as its chief engineer, leaving behind the Morris

Minor, which was destined to enjoy something of a Cinderella existence for the remainder of its production life. Sadly it was a victim of personalities who played out a scenario of indifference, the British motor industry's innate parochialism, arrogance and downright hostility.

Miles Thomas, who had been in a position to develop the car and enhance its global status, had also departed and Geoffrey Rose recalls that, once a project had been completed, Alec Issigonis himself tended to lose interest in it and move on to the next assignment. The Minor had been opposed by Lord Nuffield and BMC's Leonard Lord, although he recognised that it was Morris's best-selling model, at best looked upon it with suspicion and was to try, fruitlessly as it transpired, to replace it. Little wonder, with such a troubled conception and formative years, that the car was destined for such an unfulfilled history.

Despite being so disadvantaged, Minor production peaked in 1958 when some 113,000 examples were built. That year Philip Turner conducted a detailed interview with Alec Issigonis, who had by then returned to the BMC fold, which was published in *The Motor* of 12 November 1958. *A Minor Miracle* chronicled the model's birth and evolution, and it contained, characteristically, what might charitably be described as an excess of 'Vitamin I'. This prompted letters from Hubert Charles and Gerald Palmer; the latter, in particular, believed that Vic Oak's role had been excluded from the story and he duly redressed the balance on his friend's behalf.

Palmer subsequently stated that he had 'got on well with Issigonis – we shared an arrogance common to designers, he possessing it more deservingly and openly than me, and it increased with his success.' But the Issigonis-infused article on the Morris Minor 'reminded me of a Coward play; written by Noel, acted by Noel, directed by Noel...'[55]

Notes

1. Skilleter, *op cit.*
2. Turner, *op cit.*
3. Daniels, *op cit.*
4. *The Autocar*, 26 November 1948.
5. Turner, *op cit.*
6. Ibid.
7. Peter Tothill, *op cit.*
8. Palmer, *op cit.*
9. Graham Turner, *The Leyland Papers*, 1971.
10. Turner, *op cit.*

11. Quoted in Jonathan Wood, *The Volkswagen Beetle*, 1983.
12. Campbell, *op cit.*
13. Ibid.
14. Philip Turner, A Minor Miracle, *The Motor,* 12 November 1958.
15. Rogers Sogaard, communication with author, 2004.
16. Campbell, *op cit.*
17. Peter Tothill, *op cit.*
18. *The Autocar*, 19 December 1948.
19. *The Autocar*, 2 November 1945.
20. Alec Issigonis, note to Christopher Dowson. The Austin Seven engine parts went to 'the ex-Brettel car,' see Moores, op cit.
21. *The Autocar*, 26 April 1946.
22. *The Autocar*, 24 June 1946.
23. Pomeroy, op cit.
24. *Motor Sport*, July 1946.
25. Pomeroy, Ibid.26. Bolster, *op cit.*
27. Christopher Dowson, *op cit.*
28. Cooper, *op cit.*
29. Christopher Dowson, *op cit.*
30. Ibid.
31. Barker, *Alec Issigonis, op cit.*
32. Bolster, *op cit.*
33. Gregor Grant, *500cc Racing*, 1950.
34. Dennis May, Sportrait, Joe Fry, *The Autocar,* 28 January 1949.
35. Bolster, *op cit.*
36. Grant, *op cit.*
37. Alex Moulton, *op cit.*
38. His three other seconders were Egypt-based James and Francis Peacock of the Egyptian Light Railway and James Gresham of the Craven Iron Works, Salford, Manchester.
39. Moulton, *op cit.*
40. Dr Alex Moulton, Innovation, *Journal of the Royal Society of Arts*, Volume 128 (1979–1980).
41. Ibid.
42. Jonathan Wood, Pursuit of a Dragonfly, *Thoroughbred and Classic Cars*, June 1976.
43. Alex Moulton, interview, *op cit.*
44. Moulton, Innovation, *op cit.*
45. Ibid.
46. Jonathan Wood, Pursuit of a Dragonfly, *T and CC*, July 1976.
47. Alex Moulton, interview, *op cit.*
48. Ibid.
49. Moulton, Innovation, *op cit.*
50. Peter Tothill, *op cit.*
51. Platt, *op cit.*
52. Issigonis, Elegance... *op cit.*
53. Palmer, *op cit.*
54. Palmer, *op cit.*
55. Ibid.

Chapter Six

ALVIS INTERLUDE

'I was never happy with that car.'[1]
Alec Issigonis

I T WAS a bold idea by Alvis's chairman, John Parkes. The car that Alec Issigonis was commissioned to design, a V8-engined sports saloon, would have used a Pressed Steel unitary construction body and initially a projected 5,000 would have been built every year. This was a hitherto unprecedented rate for the Coventry company and, had it been successful, could have secured the future of the Alvis car.

But what was designated the TA350, of which at least one example was completed, highlighted not only Issigonis's considerable strengths but also his weaknesses. Stylistically the saloon lacked the flair and the originality that had been so apparent in the Morris Minor. Neither did its appearance chime with Alvis's reputation as a manufacturer of fast, stylish cars for a discriminating clientele. More positively this commodious car underlined its creator's outstanding abilities as a packager (he hated the word, preferring designer) but, less happily, its V8 engine underwent an unnecessarily protracted gestation. Of far greater significance was its innovative, interconnected, all independent suspension, the work of Issigonis's friend, Alex Moulton.

Alvis had an impressive pedigree. It had begun to build cars in 1920 but, like so many specialist manufacturers, had never possessed a bodyshop. This did not present a problem between the wars when the motor industry was served by coachbuilders aplenty, but their numbers were drastically reduced in the post-1945 world. Alvis's four-cylinder overhead valve 12/50 model of 1923, the work of chief engineer George Smith-Clarke and his chief draughtsman William Dunn, with its delightful polished aluminium 'duck's back' body by Cross and Ellis, was one of the most memorable and best British sports cars of the 1920s. It was not cheap. The 12/50 sold for £550 at a time when Britain's most popular car, Morris's 'Bullnose' Cowley, cost just £299.

A six-cylinder Alvis, the Silver Eagle of 1929, paved the way for a succession of high-speed tourers of the 1930s and the Speed 20 and 25, Crested Eagle and 4.3-litre underpinned Alvis's reputation for producing soundly engineered performance models. Always in the forefront of technical innovation, in 1933 Alvis offered Britain's first all-synchromesh gearbox and the unit had a list price of £80 at a time when the cheapest Austin Seven could be bought new for £100!

The Alvis factory faced the Holyhead Road and was located alongside the railway line, which ran from Coventry to Nuneaton. Indeed, the bridge that carried the track bore for many years an Alvis advertisement featuring its famous red triangular badge, a display which, for a generation of motorists, underlined Coventry's undisputed position as Britain's motor city of the interwar years. But like so many of its contemporaries, the manufacturer of 'The Car for the Connoisseur' had experienced switchback fortunes. In 1924 a receiver was appointed on account of debts of £219,000, although the business was reconstructed.

Yet Alvis's founder, T.G. John, was nothing if not pragmatic, and in 1935 and with war clouds gathering on the horizon, he decided to diversify into aero engine and armoured car production. In 1936 the firm's name was accordingly changed from the Alvis Car and Engineering Company to a less automotively committed Alvis Ltd. Although these developments took the business deeply into the red, it returned to profitability in 1939.

In adopting aero engines, John was moving into familiar territory because during World War One he had been chief engineer of Siddeley-Deasy, which built the Siddeley Puma radials. In August 1935 Alvis took a licence on a number of Gnome-Rhone (G-R) engines and a new factory was built to the west of the old for their manufacture. In addition sub-contract work was secured from Rolls-Royce and de Havilland, the latter order being placed by its general manger, one John Parkes.

Despite Alvis endowing its aero engines with the classically-inspired Greek names of Pelides, Pelides Major, Alcides and Maeonides, the expanding Royal Air Force did not respond to these French-designed Alvis-built radials, reputedly because G-R had fobbed Alvis off with their most antiquated designs. Far more promising was the Leonides, the work of Alvis's own George Smith-Clarke, a conventional nine-cylinder radial which ran for the first time in 1936. Development continued throughout the war although production would not begin until 1947.

It was much the same story with Alvis's diversification into armoured vehicle production. Beginning in 1936, the Alvis-Straussler car proved to be a stillborn project and the company would not begin to reap the rewards of John's initiative until after World War Two. John Parkes, who was then running the company and, no doubt with both projects in mind, was wont to quip that Alvis had immense experience of knowing what *not* to make.

In the 1930s the mainstay of the company's business was still the production of its well engineered, sporting cars. Nevertheless, T.G. John was all too aware of its lack of bodyshop, and just before the outbreak of war in 1939 he laid out his strategy for the following decade. This envisaged producing a more rationalised range of cars using a single chassis with a choice of 14 and 20hp engines. The firm had, on average, produced about 600 chassis per annum and had only breached the 1,000 barrier in 1927 and 1934. John's aim was to increase output to 3,000 cars per annum and the company would build its own bodies using bought-in pressed steel panels.

This plan was set aside by the outbreak of war. The car factory was destroyed by enemy bombing in November 1940 and although the nearby aircraft facility was damaged it was soon back in production. Its work principally consisted of manufacturing parts for Rolls-Royce's Kestrel, Merlin and Griffon aero engines. In total Alvis was responsible for the running of 21 factories during hostilities, which mostly produced aero-related products and employed some 3,000 people.

T.G. John died at the age of 65 in 1946 at his home, Rouncil Towers, in Kenilworth. He had in any event retired in 1944, and in 1946 John Joseph Parkes took over as Alvis's chairman and managing director. He joined the company from Airwork, where he was technical manager and test pilot, and prior to that, as has already been noted, de Havilland. However, he had begun his career in the Coventry motor industry, having served an apprenticeship with Swift and worked for Rootes in 1927/28, prior to switching to aircraft. Like so many of his contemporaries, Parkes's management style was autocratic, but his experience of both the automotive and aviation sectors made him well qualified to take over the running of Alvis.

Car production restarted in 1946 with the appearance of the 1.9-litre four-cylinder Fourteen, known internally as the TA14, which was based on the 12/70 model of 1938. The overwhelming majority were fitted with a four-door traditionally styled saloon body by Mulliners of Birmingham. Thanks to the acute shortage of cars that characterised the early post-war years, it proved to be the most popular Alvis to date, despite its dated mechanicals, which uncharacteristically retained all round cart suspension. Nonetheless, by the time production ceased in 1949 a total of 3,227 examples had been completed.

In 1950 the Fourteen was replaced by the outwardly similar 3-litre, or TA21, mechanically an all-new model and the work of William Dunn, who in 1950 had taken over from Smith-Clarke as Alvis's chief engineer. Still retaining a separate chassis, although now enhanced with independent front suspension, its six-cylinder overhead valve engine was designed by Chris Kingham, who had joined the company in 1946.

The problem, as ever, centred on bodywork. Alvis had approached Briggs Motor Bodies, the Dagenham-based mass producer, and although it quoted a price of £65 per unit, it would have meant the company taking 10,000 over a three-year period.[2] In 1947 the firm again requested a quotation from Briggs to manufacture the body for the new car but the rate of 100 shells a week and tooling costs of £150,000, with each completed body costing £200, was quite beyond Alvis's resources. In 1947 it had returned a net profit of just £19,000. It therefore had little choice, and with some misgivings reverted to Mulliners, its supplier since 1937 and with whom relations had at times been strained. However, Alvis cars were soon playing second fiddle to the company's aero engine and armoured vehicle manufacture, which built on the foundations laid so assiduously by T.G. John before the war.

In 1947 Alvis began to market the Series 500 Leonides for aeroplanes and the Series 520 for use in helicopters and their first respective applications were in the Percival Prince and Westland Siksorksy WS-51. The Leonides proved to be an outstanding unit and it was destined to be Britain's last high-powered piston aero engine. Production continued until 1966.

It was in the same year of 1947 that Alvis was awarded a contract by the War Office to design, develop and produce a range of military vehicles. The Saladin armoured car of 1950 was the result, from which sprang the Saracen armoured troop carrier, the Salamander fast cross-country fire tender and the Stalwart load carrier. All were powered by straight eight Rolls-Royce engines.

With aero engines and armoured cars beginning to move centre stage, Alvis cars, until then the mainstay of the business, were downgraded in importance and 1948 was the last year that the division contributed any profits, having during that year produced a record 1,143 chassis. Indeed, the directors began to question the worth of continuing but John Parkes believed it should be maintained for two reasons. Firstly, they absorbed overheads from other departments, and thus gave the company a negotiating edge when bidding for contracts. Secondly, the cars, the quality of reputation of which was not in doubt, maintained 'prestige and goodwill' for Alvis, particularly in its aviation work.[3] There are parallels here with Rolls-Royce, which at this time continued to manufacture 'The Best Car in the World' at a loss, alongside its mainstream and profitable aero engine business.

Alvis's profits were creeping up, particularly from 1950 when the company had a full order book for both its aero engines and armoured vehicles, which were produced in the same factory. That year the net surplus stood at £26,000. It increased to £48,000 in 1951 and virtually trebled in 1952 to a figure of £142,232.

It was against this background of rapidly improving finances that Parkes appears to have changed his mind as far as Alvis's newly formed Vehicle Division was concerned. The 3-litre was a traditional car which retained the separate chassis that had been an Alvis feature since the marque's inception. But the mechanically unrelated, economical V8-powered sports saloon, capable of over 100mph, that he envisaged would be based on a unitary construction body. This would allow Alvis to 'enter the passenger vehicle industry on a much larger scale than hitherto.'[4]

Interestingly, the initial projected production figure of 5,000 per annum over a five-year period, which represented 100 cars a week, was precisely the quantity Briggs had specified when it was approached for a quotation for the 3-litre's body. But Lt-Col John Chaytor, who was an Alvis director and since 1929 had been chief constable of the North Riding, believed that the intended output figure should be doubled to 10,000 units per annum.

Although from an engineering standpoint a V8 engine has the advantage of being compact and mechanically well balanced, it was still relatively rare in Britain. Although Ford-England had offered a variety of parentally-designed side valve V8s from 1932 until 1950, demand had always been modest on account of the combined disincentives, in British eyes, of excessive fuel consumption and a high horsepower tax rating. However, the latter constraint was eliminated by introduction of the flat rate of 1948.

Across the Atlantic the V8 was to effectively replace the straight six among the ranks of America's Big Three motor manufacturers during the 1950s. In 1949 Cadillac, a side valve V8 exponent since 1914, had introduced a new high compression, overhead valve design and it was soon to be followed by Chrysler. Despite these US initiatives, it seems more likely that Parkes sought inspiration for his V8 closer to home. In 1951 Rolls-Royce, a company with which Alvis had the closest of ties, had begun work on the design of an alloy wet liner overhead valve V8, eventually to be of 6.2-litre capacity, although it would not replace its straight six engine until 1959.

When Alec Issigonis, then basking in the glory of the Morris Minor's success, applied for the post of what was grandly described as 'Engineer in Charge of Passenger Car Design', John Parkes was no doubt delighted to offer him the job in the knowledge that he had secured the services of one of the world's leading car designers at a salary of £2,500 a year,[5] some £40,000 by today's values. Issigonis's five-year contract, the norm at Alvis, ran from 5 June 1952. But Parkes was probably unaware of his new recruit's emotional commitment to small cars and the limitations of his abilities as an engine designer, to which the Morris's stillborn flat four bore testament.

For Alec the assignment represented a welcome and timely refuge from Cowley, then falling under Leonard Lord's Longbridge-based regime, and any automobile engineer relishes the opportunity of being offered a clean drawing board on which to begin work. The project was, nevertheless, about as far removed from the 'charwoman's car,' of which he had talked so enthusiastically with Gerald Palmer, as could be imagined.

Issigonis's intention would be to repeat the formula of creating a small, closely-knit team of the type that had so successfully seen the Morris Minor into production. And, similarly, he would bear responsibility for the entire project, with one notable exception. For while he would be undertaking the design of the mechanicals, engine, interior and styling, he would be working closely with Alex Moulton on the car's all independent suspension.

So in June 1952, some 14 years after leaving Coventry, Issigonis returned to the city which had marked the true start of his career in the British motor industry. However, he and his mother continued to rent their Oxford flat. During the week he lived locally in a motel on the outskirts of Coventry and returned to Linkside Avenue on Fridays to spend his weekends there.

On arrival at Holyhead Road, Issigonis was assigned a first-floor facility at the front of the building near to the corporate drawing office that faced the Carbodies coachbuilding works on the other side of the road. Daily contact with Alvis's newest recruit had been delegated to Arthur Varney, who, along with Smith-Clarke and Dunn, had joined the company in 1922 and was responsible for the design of Alvis's celebrated all-synchromesh gearbox. In 1950 Varney became chief engineer of the company's Aero Engine Division and, in his recollection, Issigonis 'for a while worked by himself drawing... on pieces of paper stuck on the corner of his desk.'[6] In due course he revealed something of his life to Varney: 'he told me that he and his mother came as penniless refugees to England' and that 'his mother was a chain smoker of black cigarettes and always sat on the floor'.

Another employee who was to enjoy similar conversations was chief aero engine development engineer George Clarke, who was Smith-Clarke's nephew and had joined the company in 1940. He remembered that 'when asked where he came from, [Issigonis] replied on most occasions it was Asia Minor. He really appeared to be quite an introvert but, nevertheless, he became very interesting to talk to when he settled in at Alvis.[7] Alec was a very shy person but when he developed friendships, he enjoyed talking, especially at lunchtime in the dining room. We all had to help him finish his [Daily Telegraph] crossword before we could have lunch'. Issigonis always did the smaller of the two puzzles. During his working hours Clarke recalled that Issigonis 'kept a leather-bound diary in which he recorded notes and sketches of the design features that he worked on each day.'

The nucleus of Issigonis's small team was assembling in a separate office nearby. Fred Boobyer, whose speciality was bodywork, came to Alvis from Austin. Body engineer John Sheppard had joined as a draughtsman in 1946 from A.P. Metalcraft, a business which produced coachwork for Lea-Francis in Coventry. For his part Sheppard was to work for Issigonis for most of his career in the motor industry. He recalls that he awaited his new boss's arrival with 'deep trepidation. He'd just done the Morris Minor and was like a God. In fact I found him very pleasant, even if he got me smoking. He used to say "I can't think without a cigarette".'[8]

Soon afterwards this duo, plus their secretary, moved to another, more secluded location at the back of the building on the ground floor under the assembly shop, where Saracen armoured cars were under construction. 'It was very noisy,' remembers Sheppard. 'Issigonis was in with us and there was a workshop next door to do any work we needed.' The group's seclusion from the rest of the car workforce resulted in them being known as 'the cell'. Issigonis would adopt this name and take it with him when he moved to BMC.

They were soon joined by Alvis's engine designer, an engineer of considerable experience in his chosen field. Christopher Dixon Kingham, like Sheppard, would work for Issigonis for the next 20 or so years. He had joined the company from the Smethwick-based Midland Motor Cylinder Company, which made engine blocks, where he gained practical experience in the pattern shop and die design office, a hands-on qualification that would have impressed Issigonis. Hampshire-born Kingham had learnt his engineering as a pupil with John Thornycroft, the Basingstoke-based commercial vehicle manufacturer. His father, Robert, a barrister, had been knighted in 1945 for his years as secretary of the National Savings Committee.

Then there was Alvis's chief body engineer, Harry Barber, appointed in 1945, formerly of Austin, a firm he had joined in 1932, and no mean stylist in his own right. Bill Cassells was a transmissions specialist while Harry Harris's responsibility was suspension and steering.

Discussions were soon underway amid a haze of cigarette smoke. 'Chris Kingham smoked, in fact he got Issigonis to switch from Gold Flake to Senior Service,' recalls John Sheppard. 'He would get us together and say "let's have a think tank." He was brilliant at sketching, sometimes in pencil or he used a pen that produced what looked like a charcoal finish.'[9]

Initially accorded the designation of TA 175/350, the Alvis project was so identified because the original intention was for the car to be produced in two versions, with a choice of engines: a 1750cc four-cylinder unit, which was to have been one bank of the V8, in addition to the mainstream 3.5-litre one. Although it was still being so described in 1954, the smaller engine was never built and the TA350 designation thereafter sufficed.

Despite being of a larger capacity than the 3-litre, the TA350 was a shorter car, having a projected overall length of 14ft 6in, some eight inches less, but it was considerably wider at 6ft 4in, which compared with the six's 5ft 6in. The front and rear tracks of 4ft 7in were about the same.

As Issigonis remembered the Alvis, it was a four-door five-seater saloon, 'very small and compact, like a Lancia Aurelia in appearance but very, very spacious inside with hardly any propeller shaft tunnel.'[10] The projected weight of 21cwt was a reflection of its unitary construction. The 3-litre, by contrast, turned the scales at 28.5cwt. Alvis's intention was to launch its new car at the 1956 London motor show.

The use of a V8 had, of course, been a prerequisite of the specification and Issigonis decided, adventurously, to use as he later described it, 'a barrel crankcase for the engine, like the Miller racing engines, but it was a ghastly mistake, for we could never keep the engine quiet.'[11] Chris Kingham, who had the unenviable task of attempting to make the 90 degree alloy unit work, remembered having 'monumental problems,' the basic flaw of the design being 'an inherent lack of rigidity.'[12] Arthur Varney cast an informed eye over the engine and recalls that 'the crankshaft main bearings were housed in circular cast iron discs so that the shaft and its bearings could be passed into the crankcase from one end and into matching circular holes at each bearing station. The cast iron discs were pegged into the casing.'[13]

The pistons ran in wet cylinder liners and at the top end of the engine was a single overhead camshaft per cylinder bank, which reflected the car's sporting requirements. At this time chain-driven camshafts were the norm but Issigonis was insistent that more efficient gears be used, even though they added to cost, complication and noise levels. Skew gears of the Wolseley type were therefore adopted. Each camshaft initially ran in its own closed tunnel but this meant that there was no way of adjusting the tappets. This was subsequently dispensed with and a conventional bucket system of tappet adjustment introduced.

The aim was for a respectable fuel consumption of 27mpg, so the valves were on the small side and for the same reason initially only a single 2in SU carburettor was adopted. Here John Morris reappears on the scene. (Alvis was an established customer for its carburettors and fitted SU fuel injection to its Leonides helicopter engine.) Fed through an eight-branch manifold it was, inevitably, named Octopus. Unfortunately the engine only developed 100bhp in this form and the single SU was replaced by a twin carburettor layout which pushed the figure up to a more respectable 124bhp.

The TA350's transmission was similarly adventurous, although precise details of its design still remain unclear. There was a Smiths Selectadrive centrifugal clutch at the engine end which drove 'a high speed propeller shaft connected to the gearbox/rear axle differential unit,' remembered Clarke,[14] which suggests Lancia Aurelia influence, and was adopted for the twin reasons of space saving and weight distribution. This gearbox was an Alvis-made two-speed unit, but there were four speeds because of the presence of a Laycock overdrive system under the front seats. The rear wheels were driven by universally jointed drive shafts. Front-wheel stations also broke new ground. Clarke recalled that they were 'experimental one piece bearing assembly,' a design that in later years would become the norm. This was instead of the two bearings then current. Conventional steel wheels were used and the TA350 was shod with 6.40x15in tyres.[15]

But the Alvis's truly innovative feature was to be its interconnected all independent suspension. On this Alex Moulton worked with Issigonis, and Chris Kingham recalls that 'the two of them sparked genius off each other – I don't think either of them would have been so fruitful mentally without the other.'[16] The layout was conventional enough: upper and lower wishbones, plus an anti-roll bar at the front. Steering, following Morris Minor precedent, was by rack and pinion. Semi trailing arms were used at the rear.

The medium Moulton adopted was of the greatest significance and built on the work he had originally undertaken with the Flexitor system at Morris. In its original form the Alvis was fitted with conical rubber springs, similar to those later used on the Mini, although Issigonis remembered them as being 'too hard; we really wanted something more supple like torsion bars.'[17] He and John Morris had, it will be recalled, conceived a torsion bar-based interconnected design some 20 years before.

Moulton accorded his springs the name of Diablo because, when placed back to back, they resembled the old 'devil-of-two-sticks' game of a diablo top suspended on a string. But, recalled Moulton, 'it did not take us long to realise that, by inverting the rubber springs, the volume between would form a displacer for *fluid* interconnection of the suspension front to rear.'[18] The medium used was water and the experimental conduit was ⅝in bore copper tubing. The 7in diameter Diablo springs were 'fitted in tandem pairs on each wheel… mounted back to back and were, in effect, struts compressed by swinging arms in the suspension mechanism…'[19]

The limitation of a conventional suspension is that the front and rear springs have to differ in frequency to minimise pitching. In consequence a car's rear seat passengers suffer an inferior ride to the front ones. On an interconnected system, as Alex Moulton describes it, 'pitching is minimised and the motion is harmonic and jerk-free.'[20] On the debit side was cost and complication.

His inspiration, says Moulton, was the Citroën 2CV, which used an all independent, interconnected but basic mechanical system, and the ensuing dialogue included Issigonis and John Morris. 'I bought one, a little van, and took measurements of its mechanical interconnection. We said, us three, "it's a marvellous damn thing but a primitive way of doing it by rods and springs." I came up with the solution at Spencer Moulton.[21]

In the light of the Alvis suspension's antecedence it will come as no surprise to find George Clarke recalling a visit to the corporate experimental workshop where he encountered Moulton and Issigonis with 'a 2CV being stripped down,'[22] so that its suspension could be closely scrutinised. This was not the first occasion that Clarke had seen such a Citroën at Holyhead Road. 'John Morris used to run one which had a 16lb Calor Gas cylinder in the passenger seat feeding gas to a modified carburettor!'

Above all the work that Moulton undertook at Alvis marks the birth of what was to evolve into the Hydrolastic system introduced on the Morris 1100 in 1962, which was to develop into the Hydragas layout employed in the Austin Allegro and Metro. And the TA350, scheduled for introduction at the 1956 Motor Show, would have been the first British car to be so enhanced, just a year after Citroën's DS, the long-awaited successor to the Traction Avant, had made its sensational debut at the 1955 Paris Motor Show. And across the Atlantic in America earlier in the same year Packard had introduced an interconnected torsion bar system on which ride levels were compensated by an electric motor.

If the Alvis suspension broke new ground and the transmission was radical, the same could not be said for the TA350's appearance. The lines of the wheel-at-each-corner four-door saloon highlighted Issigonis's limitations as a stylist, particularly of larger cars, a shortcoming that would become all too apparent in his later years at BMC. Stressing the Alvis's visual resemblance to the Lancia Aurelia in the quotation cited earlier in this chapter amounted to little more than wishful thinking. Unfortunately no photographs of the car survive, but those who saw it recall that the car closely resembled one of Morris Motors's latest products. After the car's completion, Issigonis asked Gerald Palmer, his one-time colleague at Cowley, to view the TA350 and his recollection was of a saloon 'of not very striking appearance, rather like the Morris Oxford Series 11 [of May 1954] and not likely to appeal to traditional Alvis clients... but its outstanding feature was undoubtedly four-wheel independent suspension... at the time being developed by Alex Moulton and Issigonis...'[23]

Freddie Boobyer was responsible for producing the body drawings but 'the shape of everything was determined by Alec Issigonis,' recalled Harry Barber, 'You can honestly say that it was "his" car. But he wasn't really interested in styling as such. It was more a question of achieving the best utilisation of space.'[24]

To Alex Moulton, the Alvis 'looked unstyled, like an engineering drawing.'[25] Distinctive features were curved window glass and the wheel arches and sills were bolted in place to facilitate repair work in the event of a crash. These were features also inherited from the Morris.

Originally the front of the TA350 featured a curious combined grille and bumper which could be likened to a dog clutching a bone in its mouth. Again there are echoes of this treatment in the Series 11 Oxford, but while the Cowley design had achieved production status, the Alvis board was far from impressed. Chris Kingham remembered that sales director Stanley Horsfield, who had been in the job since 1933, 'went purple in the face and said it wasn't an Alvis at all.'[26] What was required was a proper radiator grille and this was duly introduced. It lifted in the Mercedes-Benz manner, with the bonnet, and was surmounted by Alvis's familiar triangular badge. This change was effected by John Sheppard, whose principal role was the body substructure. Its torsional stiffness, of 11,000lb/ft, was 'high by modern standards.'[27]

A V8 is, by nature of its configuration, a compact unit and with the gearbox tucked away at the rear of the car, both components made a positive contribution to the roomy interior. Able to accommodate five, it pre-dated to some extent the driving compartment of Issigonis's Austin 1800 for BMC, certainly as far as the space between the bench-type front seat and dashboard was concerned! The instrument panel was therefore sparsely furnished with two large dials in the centre. Although flanked by two glove compartments, they lacked covers, which provided the fascia with an unfinished appearance. Here again the Morris Oxford's dash provided a precedent. This contrasted with the handsome fascia of Alvis's 3-litre saloon, which was faced with wood, comprehensively instrumented with black-faced instruments and with a lockable glove compartment. The only hint of luxury in the TA350's interior was provided by the laminated wood-rimmed steering wheel.

The bench front seat also followed Cowley tradition, but while the Oxford used a steering column gear change, the Alvis's lever was to the right of the driver, a traditional placement for the control which harked back to the 1920s. For the record the handbrake was so positioned on the Morris. The Alvis, by contrast, had a Ford-style dashboard-mounted umbrella lever.

So much for the body structure. In the meantime three experimental V8 engines had been built and one of these ran for the first time in October 1953 when it was found that the valve gear was excessively noisy. This was modified and the changes incorporated in the second and third units. George Clarke also recalled that the 'sealing of the cylinders was defective'[28] and this shortcoming was, in due course, resolved. But it was not long before more serious problems began to be detected.

Teething troubles are inevitable in such a programme, this being the object of the exercise, but far as Arthur Varney was concerned, the V8 engine was a 'failure.'[29] This was on account of the fact that 'it could not be rid of vibration.' In the end 'Issigonis resorted to drilling holes in the flywheel at random in an effort to overcome the difficulty but he did not succeed.' In Varney's opinion 'the trouble was in the crankshaft mounting,' the result of a differential of expansion between the cast aluminium crankcase and the cast iron discs which 'became loose when the engine became hot. It was a difficulty that was never overcome and perhaps it was never realised as one, for aluminium discs were never tried.' Nonetheless, by November 1953, the engine had completed 300 hours of testing and, although the team persevered with the barrel crankcase, early in 1955 it was replaced by a conventional one designed by Chris Kingham, with the assistance of the Alvis foundry.

In 1954 the V8 engine was unexpectedly the subject of evaluation by a rival car company. During that year John Parkes began what proved to be a fruitless dialogue with David Brown, who owned Aston Martin, about a possible merger of the two businesses. Brown had known Issigonis for some years and was therefore greatly interested in the TA350 project. The W.O. Bentley-designed Lagonda twin overhead camshaft six-cylinder engine, then used in the Aston Martin DB2 line, was reaching the end of its development life and a new V8 with a sporting potential could have been used by both companies.

So, under cover of darkness, a lorry arrived at Holyhead Road and transported one of the precious engines to Aston Martin's factory at Feltham, Middlesex, where it was subjected to a testbed evaluation. But chief engineer Harold Beach was unimpressed and thought the engine poor. 'It had a dreadful crankshaft, like a piece of bent wire. We had no use for it and sent it back to Alvis.'[30]

Although Issigonis was wholly committed to the project, George Clarke believed that he still hankered after designing a small model, 'a car he thought was *really* required.'[31] This would have had 'a wheel-at-each-corner and a very large passenger compartment. Mr Varney told me that one day he was talking with Alec about an idea that he had worked on where the engine was mounted transversely.' This 1000cc front-wheel drive design had been executed before the war, and the drawings had been destroyed in the Coventry Blitz. 'Alec took due note and made a record in his book.' Any thoughts that this project had any bearing on the Mini can be discounted, because the design of the front-wheel drive Morris Minor had already been completed by the time Issigonis left for Alvis.

In July 1953 the company had recruited Bernard Miles, formerly chief engineer of the Birmingham branch of the American Cincinnati Milling Machines, as its chief production engineer, a new appointment which carried a salary of £2,000 a year. Prior to that he was chief planning engineer at de Havilland's propeller division and knew John Parkes there. His responsibility was for Alvis's Aero Engine and Vehicle Divisions, and thanks to his specialist knowledge of machine tools, he would become closely involved with planning for the V8 saloon.

After spending the working week in Coventry Alec Issigonis returned to his Linkside Avenue flat for the weekends. It will be recalled that, during the war, he had made friends with Maurice and Dorothy Connelly and their daughter Jennifer. As it happened they also had friends, the Axtells, who lived in Linkside Avenue, at number 36 on the same side as the Issigonises' flat, but who had a secondary garden on the other side of the road that ran down to Linkside Lake.

Graham Axtell was a director of the respected Oxford building business of Symm and Company. And to his sons, Malcolm and Peter, the lake represented a wonderful play area. They were often joined there by Jennifer Gilman, who remembers: 'You'd go by and see Alec and his mother sitting on their balcony doing their crosswords. They were great crossword people. We used to swim in the lake and Alec would appear. He used to wander down and see the children and he was always so interested in everything we'd done.'[32]

Malcolm Axtell recalls that Issigonis noticed 'my late brother and I making carts and carriages out of all sorts of things, anything we could find. Little did we know that Alec was observing us with his engineering interest. We made a sedan chair once which rather intrigued him.'[33] He became a frequent visitor to the Axtell household and, to the delight of the boys, took them to practice days at Silverstone. 'We went to the British Racing Drivers' Club enclosure where we were introduced to many grand prix drivers of the day. On one occasion we met Stirling Moss.'

At this time Issigonis's dress sense was what might be described as distinctive: semi-formal but essentially low-key. 'Alec used to wear rough wool greeny, browny rather murky colours, a tweed jacket, not very attractive in my eyes, and not always that well fitting. His ties were muted of woven wool with browns and khakis and greens and he wore darkish shirts. The effect was all rather relaxed and easy and finished off with brown shoes. He would not have won a prize for the best dressed man! I never saw him in a sweater, always a coat and tie. He was not a dresser-upper and very retiring and did not like the limelight.'[34] To Jennifer Gilman 'he was the first person I ever saw in a bow tie. He used to wear them quite a lot. His shirts were either Clydella or Vyella. He also had half glasses which would be perched on his nose.'[35]

With Alec away in Coventry during the week, Hulda Issigonis was befriended by Malcolm's mother. 'She was probably quite lonely but she got used to being lonely. There was a lot of mutual respect between mother and son. She was very proud of him and he was very appreciative of the sacrifices she had made. Later we used to see her sometimes midweek. I remember when I was learning to drive with my L plates on, my mother and I went all over the Cotswolds with Hulda in the back of the car.[36] Sometimes there would be visits to the Randolph Hotel, it was rather grand in those days. Hulda used to treat my mother to lunch there and she would recommend and always drank Beaujolais. "It's a wonderful wine," she would say. "You're always safe with Beaujolais".'

Jennifer Gilman 'was quite sacred of her. I must have been 17 and one evening I was swimming in the lake with Mark Ransome, who was a cousin and staying with them. We hadn't had any supper and Mark suggested that I went back to the flat with him for something to eat. We opened the door and Hulda said "I don't want you in here. I haven't got room for you." She was quite intimidating.'[37] Christopher Dowson agrees. 'I found her rather terrifying, although I always remember her liking for fresh green figs.'[38] Hulda's groceries came courtesy of the Co-Op at nearby Summertown. Her milkman, Ken Jones, recalls that she used to give him her order mid-morning and, once a week, he would deliver to the Sollershott flat.[39]

When Alec returned for his weekends in Oxford he invariably arrived in an Alvis and, in April 1954, some 18 months into the project, the company's directors commissioned a report on the car. Entitled *Scheme for the Production of Passenger Car TA350*, it was completed in April 1954 and there were clearly some apprehensions on the part of its author about the viability of Issigonis's power unit. He declared: 'it may in some quarters be felt that the high cost and relative immaturity of the V8 engine should guide us towards a conventional or less costly power unit.' But it was recognised that if this was adopted 'the entire design concept of the vehicle is materially modified, leading us to a type of vehicle which is universally manufactured at the present time.' The same applied to the Moulton suspension. Nonetheless it was recognised that, if the estimated selling price of £850 was to be maintained, 'material and manufacturing costs... have got to be reduced by approximately 8 percent.'

By this time the V8 had undergone 360 hours of bench testing. An output of 124bhp at 4,000rpm had been achieved and estimated road load economy of 29mpg at 50mph was recorded. The unit had a dry weight of 400lb. According to the report, the demands of fighting vehicles and Leonides aero engine production, then running at 25 units a month, and its 14-cylinder Major derivative at 12, would mean that 'there was very little in the way of plant and equipment available to transfer to the car project.' It would therefore have been necessary to acquire some 150,000sqft of factory space.

The projected costs made sobering reading. These were put at £2,243,037[40] in a year in which Alvis's net profits dropped to £102,000. The total was broken down to £751,147 for machine tools – here the hand of Bernard Miles is apparent

– with plant and equipment and jigs and fixtures totalling £263,150. Each car would have cost £698 to manufacture. Of this amount, the body unit would have accounted for £225, the raw materials for the engine and gearbox £55 and finished material £71. A further £31 was allocated to machining and £2 6s for assembly. The next most expensive item would have been the front and rear suspension units, which together cost £45.

Bearing in mind these figures, it is a moot point whether, had the car entered production, Alvis would have built the engine in-house. Its well-established sub-contract work for Rolls-Royce was lucrative and prestigious, and it was perhaps for this reason that there were thoughts of sub-contracting the V8 to Maudslay. The commercial vehicle manufacturer had been based in Coventry until 1953 but production had all but ceased and it was specialising in component production.

Above all, the report estimated that it would take two years to obtain the necessary plant and equipment and to complete work on the project. Otherwise, the writer cautioned, 'it would be necessary *to give instructions as early as possible this year* to meet August/September 1956' (author's italics). There is no indication that such instructions were ever issued, which suggests that although the project was officially halted in 1955, it had actually stalled in 1954, before the prototype saloon was even on the road.

Having said that, the intention in 1954 was to produce some 7,000 cars a year, an increase on the original of half as much again, so perhaps Col Chaytor's optimism had been shared by his colleagues. These would be produced at the rate of 75 cars a week for 20 weeks, and 188 for 29, the seasonal requirements of the market dictating the shift in manufacturing levels.

The all-important matter of the body would be allocated to Cowley-based Pressed Steel. This followed Briggs being acquired by Ford in 1953; BMC wasted little time in following suit by annexing Fisher and Ludlow, to the detriment of Standard Triumph. As will emerge, the latter acquisition was to have a direct impact on Alvis. Such rationalisation therefore left Pressed Steel as Britain's only significant independent provider of bodies to the motor industry. It quoted a figure of £350,000 to £375,000 for tooling the TA350's body, with £118 per body-in-white, although it had been responsible for the production and trim of the prototype shell which had been completed by the time of the April 1954 report.

It was proving to be a difficult year for Alvis's Vehicle Division. In October it was forced to discontinue production of the 3-litre, following Mulliners' agreement in June to allocate all of its body production to Standard Triumph as a direct result of it having lost the services of Fisher and Ludlow. Then, from January 1955 Tickford, which built the drophead version, was acquired by David Brown for Aston Martin, which closed that outlet.

Happily, this was not to be the end of the 3-litre, because the Swiss coachbuilder of Graber had since 1950 been offering an elegant two-door saloon on the TA21 chassis which was as stylistically modern as Mulliners' rendering had been antiquated. Here at last were lines in the best traditions of the marque and Alvis acquired Graber's manufacturing rights and tooling. Although Willowbrook of Loughborough, which built coach bodies, took over production of what was termed the TC/108G in 1956, it cost a pricey £3,500 and only 30 were made. Series manufacture did not get underway again until October 1958 when Park Ward, Rolls-Royce's north London-based subsidiary, took over the production of what was designated the TE21, costing £500 less than its predecessor.

This is to anticipate events, because in the summer of 1954 the Alvis board was still contemplating the future of the TA350 and Issigonis reported that the car was still experiencing a number of 'minor mechanical problems, but the only serious defect was the directional stability of the car.'[41] However, one car was on the road by the end of that year and was being subversively transported at night to the Motor Industry Research Association's circuit at Lindley, near Nuneaton. Although the intention was to cover 1,000 miles in a single night, the best the team achieved was 895.

To confuse the curious the Alvis was endowed with a cardboard octagonal shape at the point where the badge would have been to give the impression that it was an MG prototype. Issigonis was a member of the driving team and John Sheppard remembers being his passenger during high-speed testing. 'He asked me to light him a cigarette but then decided to do it himself which meant he took both hands off the wheel at 100mph while we were going round the top of the banking. Although I was apprehensive, he reassured me that 'centrifugal force' would take care of things.'[42] Other members of the driving team included Chris Kingham, Harry Barber and Mike Parkes, son of John Parkes, who would later become a Ferrari Formula 1 driver.

Kingham was later to recall that the TA350's 'road holding and the handling were absolutely marvellous and it was certainly exhilarating driving round MIRA flat-out which was 100mph.'[43] For his part, Alex Moulton's first experience of the car had proved to be 'an absolute revelation'. Its interconnected system endowed the Alvis with what he described as 'a big-car ride.'[44] Rowland Simmons of Alvis's service department also had an opportunity to take the wheel and remembered that 'it went round corners as if it were on rails.'[45]

Inevitably mechanical teething troubles emerged during this evaluation. Arthur Varney remembered that there were 'transmission problems… centred in the mounting of the drive pinion. It ran in bronze bushes and used a bronze thrust washer to take care of the driving pinion thrust. Mike Parkes could wear an assembly out in a [night's] test run. The solution to the problem, I believe, was to use a ZF gearbox mounted in the normal position and to build a new pinion assembly in the gearbox casing. This used the normal Timken tapered roller bearing to take care of the thrust and radial loads.'[46]

It was against such a background of exhaustive testing that a radical redesign of the car's mechanicals was completed by the end of the year, which not only applied to the engine but also addressed problems which had emerged with the transmission and, to a lesser extent, the suspension. Originally run on trade plates for circuit testing, the revised maroon saloon was registered PVC 835 on 12 February of that year, while the chassis and engine number were given on the registration documents as TA501. Under the cover of darkness, road evaluation began at the mysteriously named 'point X' near Cirencester.

By this time the Alvis board's cold feet were becoming even more apparent and members began to doubt whether they could sell even 2,000 cars a year. Then, crucially, in June 1955, Pressed Steel's tooling estimate rose from £350,000–375,000 to £620,000, and the price per body leapt to £233. This was dependent on production of less than 5,000 shells per annum. The only way to make the project viable was to build the car at the rate of 500 cars a year and double the selling price, which would have defeated the object of the entire exercise.

In a last ditch gesture, the ailing Singer company, which had always produced its own bodies from its plant in Canterbury Street, Coventry, was asked to quote for the job. It came up with a figure of £300,000 for the tooling, which was considerably less than Pressed Steel's. This was on the basis of a production rate of 40 bodies per week but it did not provide a price per body figure, only revealing that its SM1500/Hunter body cost £365.[47] In any event, in December of that year Singer succumbed to takeover by Rootes.

Pressed Steel's decision in June 1955 marked the end of the Issigonis Alvis and it also had the virtue of providing a face-saving excuse to the board. The decision was not made public until the company's annual meeting, held in November, when John Parkes declared: 'the equipment to make it has doubled in price since the original estimate was made.' Instead Alvis's 'motor engineers will concentrate on improving the design of its well proven 3-litre model.'[48] This decision was made against net profits for the 12 months to 31 July of £159,482. Alec Issigonis no doubt read with interest the comments of *The Daily Telegraph's* City Editor, who noted that Alvis's balance sheet 'showed up its bank limitations only too well. True, the net bank overdraft has been reduced but it still stands at £643,000, and capital commitments, even allowing for the dropping of the new model, total £96,000.' Its banker had already refused to allocate funds specifically for the project.

George Clarke remembered that 'Alec became quite disenchanted'[49] by the decision, although in later years Issigonis had no regrets. 'No, I'm glad it didn't happen,' he told Philip Turner. 'I was never happy with that car, you know.'[50]

In truth the decision marked the end of Alvis as a car maker. For although the 3-litre, then in abeyance, would be revived in 1956 and continue in production for a further 11 years, its design dated from 1950 and it became progressively outdated as the years passed. The last example of what had become the TF21 was completed in August 1967. After 47 years the Alvis car was no more. Aero engines had been discontinued in 1966 and although Alvis survives to this day as a producer of military vehicles, these are made at a different Coventry location. The company left its Holyhead Road home after 70 years occupancy in 1991 and the factories were demolished. Today the appropriately named Red Triangle shopping centre occupies the site.

Alvis estimated that it had spent £76,186,[51] the equivalent of £1.1 million by today's prices, on the project and the company then went to great lengths to ensure that any trace of the TA350 was expunged from the corporate record. Photographs and drawings of the car were destroyed although some items of paperwork of the type quoted in this chapter survive, but only because they were retained by their recipients. All that otherwise remains, with the exception of the few fragments mentioned later, are the notebooks and memories of those who were involved in the TA350's design.

In the absence of any official records some doubts have been raised in recent years about the precise number of TA350s built. Both Chris Kingham and John Sheppard state that there was just the one, with the latter recalling that there were suffcient parts for a second. Arthur Varney believed that there were more, and also recalled that 'when Alvis cleared out their parts stores to pass the contents to Red Triangle [formed in July 1968], the maintenance engineer, a man named Charlie Chere asked works director, H.J. 'Nick' Nixon,[52] what to do with the cars and he replied "burn them", which Charlie promptly did by soaking them with petrol and setting them alight. I didn't see this but it grieved me to know that nice cars, even if they didn't work very well, were so treated.'

However, Alvis apprentice Keith Moore only remembered seeing a single prototype stored in a hangar belonging to the company's Alvair subsidiary at Bagington airport on the outskirts of the city. 'As I recollect, it was a burgundy/maroon colour. Eventually it was taken to the Holyhead Road and the V8 engine removed. [This may have been for Mike Parkes's special, see below]. The rest of the car was cut up using a cutting torch and thrown on the scrap heap. I rescued the now bent badge that had been fixed to the front of the bonnet. The badge was much smaller than the standard one.'[53]

It seems therefore that Moore's memento is about the only surviving piece of the TA350, although Alex Moulton still retains some suspension parts. A spare engine survived for a time in a special built by Mike Parkes, co-designer of the Hillman Imp. Built in conjunction with Tim Fry, the other half of the Rootes small car team, it was a project of which Issigonis would have approved, being of plywood monocoque construction and accorded the name of Gaboon, which was the name of the material. But it was, in due course, scrapped and the engine went with it.

It was not long before news of the TA350's demise in the summer of 1955 reached the ears of Sir Leonard Lord, as he had become in 1954, chairman of the British Motor Corporation. As will emerge in the following chapter, by the autumn of 1955 he was beginning to reappraise his engineering strategy and, from a technological standpoint, bring BMC more into line with its counterparts in continental Europe.

Using John Morris, who was, in any event, a BMC employee, as an intermediary,[54] Issigonis was approached with a view to him rejoining the Corporation. But he was initially wary. After all, he had left Cowley because of Lord's anti-Morris stance and for his reputation for interfering in both the stylistic and engineering gestation of new models. If he did return to the BMC fold, Issigonis insisted that he be given a completely free hand, to undertake, without interference, the design of a new generation of cars. Although this flew in the face of all his interventionist instincts Lord agreed to the condition, but it was a decision that would have ramifications, not only for the British Motor Corporation, but for the entire indigenous automobile industry for many years to come.

On 17 November 1955, the day before his 49th birthday, Alec Issigonis was given a month's notice by Alvis. A brief statement, issued jointly with BMC, stated that 'Mr A.A. Issigonis will join the staff of BMC. He was formerly a member of the staff of Morris Motors Ltd.'[55] An addendum to his contract, dated 30 November 1955, released him from its provisions, other than him agreeing to keep Alvis's secrets and to hand over any inventions arising from the project,[56] although he arrived at Longbridge with sheaves of TA350 drawings.

So, after three and a half years in Coventry, Issigonis would be working for Leonard Lord at Longbridge. It will recalled that he had nearly done so in 1936, although he arrived at Morris Motors after Lord's departure. Now, 20 years on, he had been granted powers unrivalled by any of his European contemporaries, with the exception of André Lefebvre at Citroën. But the success of the Morris Minor and failure of the Alvis TA350 had starkly displayed the parameters of Alec Issigonis's extraordinary talents.

Notes

1. Turner and Curtis, *op cit.*
2. John Price Williams, *Alvis The Postwar Cars*, 1993.
3. Ibid.
4. Ibid.
5. Ibid.
6. Arthur Varney, letter to Kenneth Day, 1989.
7. George Clarke, unpublished memoirs.
8. John Sheppard, interview with author, 2005.
9. Ibid.
10. Turner and Curtis, *op cit.*
11. Ibid.
12. Jon Pressnell, Alvis V8: the true story, *Classic and Sportscar*, November 1992.
13. Varney, *op cit.*
14. Clarke, *op cit.*
15. The stillborn four would have used 5.90x15 covers.
16. Pressnell, *op cit.*
17. Turner and Curtis, *op cit.*
18. Alex Moulton, Innovation, *op cit.*
19. Moulton Rubber Springs, *Automobile Engineer*, January 1962.
20. Alex Moulton, *Automobile Engineer*, September 1962, *op cit.*
21. Alex Moulton, *op cit.*
22. Clarke, *op cit.*
23. Palmer, *op cit.*
24. Pressnell, *op cit.*
25. Quoted in Williams, *op cit.*
26. Pressnell, *op cit.*
27. *Scheme for the production of Passenger Car TA 350, Alvis Ltd* April 1954.
28. Clarke, *op cit.*
29. Varney, *op cit.*
30. Williams, *op cit.*
31. Clarke, *op cit.*
32. Jennifer Gilman, *op cit.*
33. Malcolm Axtell, communication with author, 2004.
34. Malcolm Axtell, *op cit.*
35. Jennifer Gilman, *op cit.*
36. Malcolm Axtell, *op cit.*
37. Jennifer Gilman, *op cit.*
38. Christopher Dowson, *op cit.*
39. Ken Jones, in conversation with author, 2004.
40. *Scheme for Production, op cit.*
41. Williams, *op cit.*
42. Pressnell, *op cit.*
43. John Sheppard, *op cit.*
44. Williams, *op cit.*
45. Pressnell, *op cit.*
46. Varney, *op cit.*
47. Atkinson, *op cit.*
48. *Daily Telegraph*, November 1955.

49. Clarke, *op cit.*
50. Turner and Curtis, *op cit.*
51. Williams, *op cit.*
52. Varney, *op cit.* There is something wrong with this story. Nixon died suddenly of a heart attack in November 1964, so the car's scrapping either took place before that date or in 1968 and another Alvis employee gave Charlie his instructions.
53. Keith Moore, letter of Nadine Fox, secretary, Alvis Owners' Club, 2002.
54. Alex Moulton, *op cit.*
55. *The Motor*, 23 November 1955.
56. Williams, *op cit.*

Chapter Seven

MINI MASTERPIECE

'I was rather excited by the whole thing.'[1]
Alec Issigonis

ALEC ISSIGONIS arrived at Longbridge in December 1955, and he was to work for the British Motor Corporation and its successors for the remainder of his professional life. The transversely engined front-wheel drive Mini which he designed for BMC bristled with such ingenuity and innovation and was so revolutionary in concept that, from a global perspective, it changed the way in which the motor industry designed its cars. But, underpriced by its manufacturer, it produced little or no profit for BMC and should therefore be judged a commercial failure.

This is a view echoed by Spen King, then involved in Rover's gas turbine car programme, who was to be responsible for the acclaimed Range Rover and subsequently, as a British Leyland executive, oversaw some of Issigonis's later work. 'I think that the Minor was a bigger success than the Mini. In the motor car industry success means making money. The Minor, bless its heart, was the money maker.'[2] It is a standpoint shared by Walter Hassan, respected Coventry Climax and Jaguar engine designer, who believed the Morris was a greater car than the Mini. He was, in particular, much impressed by the design of its independent front suspension.[3] Sir Terence Beckett, who masterminded Ford's Cortina and went on to become chairman of Ford of Britain, goes even further as far as the Mini was concerned. 'You can track the decline of BMC from that single product: it took up a huge amount of their resources, it sterilised their cash flow and it was a pretty disastrous venture.'[4]

Yet as far as the buying public was concerned, the Mini represented a stroke of genius, a motoring icon which looked like no other car, was also fun to drive and seemed to embody all the buoyancy and innovation of Britain in the 1960s. But it was the very antithesis of indigenous automobile design, which remained a bastion of orthodoxy. As Issigonis's friend, the actor, playwright and self-confessed car enthusiast, Sir Peter Ustinov, so perceptively pointed out: 'the Mini was an odd mixture of Greek and German, steeped in Turkish olive oil!'[5]

As such it was an example of that rare commodity, the classless car, to the extent that it appealed to the likes of Beatle John Lennon, Lord Hartwell, proprietor of *The Daily Telegraph* – how Issigonis must have approved – the irrepressible cockney model, Twiggy, and prima ballerina Dame Margot Fonteyn. It was gleefully embraced by the post-war generation of baby boomers who came of age in a decade which looked positively forward rather than nostalgically back. Destined to survive for 41 years, by the time that Mini production ceased in 2000, over five million had been built.

It is, therefore, like its creator, replete with contradictions. The Mini's production run was a record for a British car but the fact that it lost money for much of its life mirrored the strengths and weaknesses of the Corporation that gave it life. This was a testament forged in the likeness of its founding father, Leonard Lord, and was one to which Alec Issigonis himself readily subscribed.

Because Issigonis was given *carte blanche* by Lord, the unpalatable truism is that the Mini was over-engineered for a small car in a way in which the Minor was not. Then Alec had had to justify the design to the stern demands of Morris's technical director Vic Oak. But, as will emerge, the Mini entered the market at a price that did not begin to represent its true manufacturing cost. Tough financial targets and tight fiscal discipline, the very key to profitable mass production, were absent from the corporate psyche of a business that had been founded and run by engineers who were more preoccupied with product than profit. And a lack of planning was par for the course.

Like most other British motor moguls of the time, BMC's impulsive chairman ran his company by a combination of his considerable experience, hunch, guesswork and prejudice. It was an approach that had served him well in the relatively unsophisticated market of the pre-war years when he had been managing businesses that sold one make of car. But the increased competition that followed the sellers' market of the 1950s would be another matter.

Decisive, combative, ruthless and dictatorial, Len Lord controlled BMC with its myriad of marques and factories as his personal fiefdom. But for all his undoubted strengths, the task of directing the fortunes of Britain's largest car company virtually single-handed proved to be beyond him, because he was deficient in many crucial areas, most significantly those of finance and marketing.

When he launched the Mini in 1959 it had the virtue of being the most mechanically sophisticated small car in the world but, incredibly, was also the cheapest.

History had already provided a precedent. William Crapo Durant had, in 1908, founded the General Motors conglomerate, but in 1923 he proved himself incapable of running the business for, it should be said, wholly different reasons. It had taken the trained mind of Alfred Sloan, a graduate of the prestigious Massachusetts Institute of Technology, to bring a sense of order and discipline to Durant's rambling empire to create the blueprint for the modern corporation. At BMC Leonard Lord's successor, George Harriman, was not only cast in a similar mould, but he also lacked the strength of personality, decisiveness and flair of his predecessor.

Lord had described Austin and Morris, the constituent parts of BMC, as 'two second division teams'[6] and although he was aiming for the first division, by the time he retired in 1961 the Corporation was heading for relegation. This occurred in 1968 when it was absorbed by the Leyland Motor Corporation. Yet from a productive standpoint BMC had been thriving in the 1960s and expansion was also the keynote of the previous decade.

In 1952 the British Motor Corporation had manufactured 235,770 cars, which constituted 39 percent of British automobile output. Production was to double over the next eight years and in 1960 it would break the half million barrier for the first time and build 585,096. Although profits rose from £21 million to £32 million over the same period, the Corporation's share of the British market had dropped from 39 percent to 36, with, in particular, American-owned Ford beginning to catch up fast with 30 percent. This compared with a share of just 14 percent in 1946. The real effects of competition would not be felt until the 1960s.

Ford occupied just one British factory; its wholly integrated plant at Dagenham, Essex, was opened in 1931 while Vauxhall, which then constituted the other arm of American presence in the British motor industry, only operated from its Luton works. And while Austin possessed one manufacturing facility at Longbridge, the Nuffield Organisation, a business that had grown piecemeal over a period of some 25 years, occupied no less than 16, scattered around the Oxford area and the industrial Midlands. By 1968 BMC was wasting £2 million a year inefficiently transporting components from one factory to another.

They varied greatly in quality and efficiency. Little change had been effected at Cowley since Leonard Lord had initiated his £300,000 programme in 1934/35. But after the war he wasted little time in transforming Longbridge into one of the most modern facilities of its type in the world, so that it was capable of manufacturing 2,000 examples of Austin's top selling A40 model every week. To achieve this Lord had retained the services of talented production engineer Frank

Woollard, whom he had known at Morris Engines. Woollard, he wrote, 'regards the waste of the "unforgiving minute" with something akin to horror.'[7] For his part the latter recorded that, after the new facility's completion, 'Austin... probably employ a larger number of automatic transfer machines than any other British factory,' a commitment it shared with Renault in France.

The centrepiece of the new development was a highly automated Car Assembly Building, designed by Howard C. Crane and better known by its CAB acronym, which drew its components from throughout the site and delivered them by three conveyors concealed within a 1,000ft tunnel. Opened in July 1951, just seven months before BMC came into being, it now had a factory that would rank with any in the world and Lord would boast that the corporate initials stood for 'Bugger My Competitors.' His detractors, both inside and outside the company, waspishly countered that the letters were actually an abbreviation of 'Bertram Mills Circus.'

If the new Longbridge facility represented BMC's confident public face, the story was a less happy one as far as its senior management was concerned. There was collective apprehension in the offices of BMC when the internal telephones rang with a long, rather than an intermittent tone, which indicated that the chairman was on the line.

BMC was dominated by engineers who, like Lord, had begun their careers 'with swarf in their shoes' on the shop floor, most had never worked for any other business. 'BMC had a policy, not a deliberate policy, of tending to promote from within and very rarely outside,' recalled Ron Lucas,[8] who had joined the business in 1927 and was destined in 1965 to become its first finance director. 'They became inbred and were dominated by manufacturing.'

BMC's deputy chairman and managing director, George Harriman, was the product of such a regime, having joined the Coventry-based Morris Engines in 1923, where he had been noticed by the ambitious Lord. In those days he was known as 'Young George'; his father 'Old George' was works superintendent at the Gosford Street facility, and his entire motor industry career was due to Lord's patronage. When he moved to Cowley, Harriman went along, and when his master switched allegiance to Austin, Harriman followed suit. Lord was wont to quip, 'I shall paddle along for a few years more and then let young George take over.'[9]

As charming as Lord was abrasive, Harriman was a loyal lieutenant but he was a pliant and subservient personality in the shadow of his Lord and master. In the recollection of a former colleague 'Harriman did what he was told, that's why Len Lord liked him.'[10] Very occasionally he disobeyed. It will be recalled that Issigonis's contemporary, the talented Murray Jamieson, had in 1936 produced a trio of exquisite twin-cam racers for Lord Austin. Although Jamieson had died in

1938, Lord developed a hatred for him and all his works. During the war he asked Harriman to remove the beautifully engineered bespoke crankshafts and connecting rods from their engines, ostensibly in response to a scrap metal drive, and disable them so that they would never run again. But Harriman saved one set and hid the precious parts in his garage, where they were discovered after his death in 1973 by his widow. As a result they were reunited with one of the three cars, which ran again in 1974 for the first time since 1939.[11]

George Harriman was responsible for recruiting, in 1954, Geoffrey Rose to Longbridge as works manager. Previously, from 1951, he had been seconded from Wolseley as a temporary civil servant, assigned to the Ministry of Supply to oversee the allocation of steel, then under governmental control, to the motor industry. 'Lord and Harriman were anxious to be fair to the Morris people but as an ex-Wolseley apprentice from Nuffield going to Longbridge, it was like Daniel entering the Lions' Den.'[12]

Rose's impression of joining the Corporation was '"we're BMC, we know how to do it, we'll grind these other people into the dust." But it did become apparent that, from a production angle, stricter financial control really was very necessary. It was a formidable task running so many factories, trying to fit together a jigsaw puzzle with a lot of ill-fitting pieces. In all my contacts with Len Lord I cannot speak too highly of him. Beneath his rough, tough exterior, there was a very kind personality as well. An instance of this was his role in the implementation of the Austin Benevolent Fund. Its task was to ensure that any employee who had fallen on hard times was well looked after. Lord oversaw it with Harriman and company secretary Syd Wheeler and he was very generous in his attitude. I found George Harriman helpful but I was sorry he was such a heavy smoker. He was a smoother type than Lord. You could say that he possessed the art of letting other people have his way.'

BMC's manufacturing director, Joe Edwards, was an individual of a very different stripe, and at 12 years Lord's junior, a potential successor. Indeed, when he deputised for Harriman, who was ill with an ulcer in 1952, Lord wondered whether he had made the right choice. Tough-minded, like his chairman, and capable, Geoffrey Rose recalls: 'Edwards was not only good to me personally, he was a good production man and straight as a die. But Len Lord had the feeling that he was after the top job. In fact Joe was quite happy to serve as manufacturing director.'

Matters came to a head as the two executives were having a pre-lunch drink one day in 1956 when Lord asked Edwards, a production man, to take over corporate labour relations, so forcing his resignation. 'I was among the first people to know,' recalls Rose. 'When he told me "Geoffrey, I've packed it in," I was heartbroken.'

Edwards briefly left the motor industry and joined the then nationalised Belfast shipbuilders Harland and Woolf. But, says Rose, 'Mike Bellhouse, managing director of Pressed Steel, and Joe were close mates and he realised that Joe was far too valuable an asset to be out of the industry.' When, in October 1956, Bellhouse became deputy chairman, Edwards took over his post although it must have irked Leonard Lord that he was now based at Cowley, just across the road from the Morris works. Little wonder that Joe Edwards would later reflect that BMC's chairman 'had set back the full integration of the two companies by a decade.'[13]

There were also departures on the engineering front, some justified, others less so. Issigonis's one-time Cowley colleague, Austin's development engineer Hubert Charles, fell out with Lord and in 1946 he left Longbridge the worse for his departure. At Cowley Morris's technical director Vic Oak, who had so effectively directed Alec Issigonis's talents to bring the Morris Minor to fruition, left Cowley a year into BMC's life in 1953. But John Rix, his opposite number at Longbridge, also got his marching orders, which left a vacuum and, in consequence, Gerald Palmer, another of Issigonis's contemporaries, was appointed group chassis and body designer, dividing his time between Cowley and Longbridge.

Palmer soon found, however, that 'it was difficult to plan ahead when there could be overriding orders from Chairman Lord and his henchmen. There was no forewarning of what Lord had in mind.'[14] Palmer used his stylistic talents to good effect with the design of the Wolseley 4/44 and its MG Z Series Magnette stablemate, which enjoyed some popularity, although his Riley Pathfinder and its related Wolseley 6/90 were less successful and poor sellers. Unfortunately, *The Autocar* made some derogatory comments regarding the latter car in its road test published in its issue of 16 September 1955.

Gerald Palmer was summoned to Longbridge and was there interviewed by George Harriman, Lord's 'number one henchman, charming but still a "yes-man."' Lord had marked the offending comments in orange crayon and 44-year-old Palmer was out. Christopher Balfour, publisher of Palmer's biography, and following discussions with his subject, has written that Lord had seized on the 'minor Wolseley criticism… in order to give Issigonis a free hand which, totally in character, he was demanding as the price for his return.'[15] Having said that, *Autocar* had recorded that the Wolseley's braking 'was not in keeping with the rest of the performance' and in the factory it was known that the cost of the model's Girling system had risen to high levels. It is also worth recording that, prior to his departure, Palmer, inspired by Issigonis's experimental front-wheel drive Morris Minor, had designed what he believed to be a less costly but all-new small front-wheel drive saloon powered by a cheap-to-build V4 engine.

On his return to Cowley, Gerald Palmer was told to clear his desk there and then because Lord was due to visit the factory on the following day and did not want to see him. Reggie Hanks, 'always solid and dependable', was sympathetic, no doubt because Lord 'did a great deal to humiliate Hanks in particular and freely criticised Morris Motors and all its works on public occasions.'[16] Hanks's own departure came two weeks after Palmer's and he was to become chairman of the Western Area Board of British Railways, trains being his first love.

Gerald Palmer's place was taken by Sydney Smith, nicknamed 'Hitler' on account of his distinctive moustache and dictatorial manner, whose brief was essentially a financial one. This one-time works manager at Cowley was a strong personality who became BMC's engineering co-ordinator, even though he was not an engineer, and he therefore relied heavily on Morris's resident chief experimental engineer, Charles Griffin.

There was one sector of the Corporation's car range where Lord's relations with managers bordered on the convivial and that related to its manufacture of sports cars. One unexpected by-product of the government-directed export drive was a demand for British open two-seaters in America and the Corporation became the country's leading exporter of open two-seaters.

Donald Healey, experienced rally driver and one time technical director of Triumph, had launched his own marque in 1946, but this Riley-engined line was replaced from 1952 by the Austin-powered Healey 100 exhibited at that year's London Motor Show. Lord renamed it then and there the Austin-Healey and it became BMC's corporate sports car, despite the fact that it already owned the MG marque, which had an impressive sports and racing pedigree. Not a BMC employee, Lord would quip: 'Here comes Healey – better sew up your pockets!'[17] whenever he encountered the ambitious Cornishman.

In such circumstances MG might well have withered on the corporate vine, had it not possessed an outstanding chief executive in the shape of John Thornley, who had been appointed by Cecil Kimber, MG's creator, in 1931 and became general manager in 1952. Diplomatic, able and possessing a disarming sense of humour, Thornley succeeded in convincing Lord of the need for MG to be responsible for its own destiny, rather than being dependent on Cowley for its designs. As he later reflected: 'I must have been one of the few people not to have got on the wrong side of his tongue.'[18] In 1954 the Abingdon drawing office was reopened after 19 years and the MGA of 1955 was destined to become the world's best-selling sports car, with over 80 percent of production being exported to America.

The Corporation, however, was a notoriously unreliable supplier, as Ron Lucas, who ran its North American operations from Canada until 1965, knew to his cost. 'With BMC you never got what you wanted where you wanted it. If you wanted 150 green MG Midgets in Vancouver, you were liable to get 120 dark blue ones on the other side of the country in Halifax, Nova Scotia. They didn't realise that the St Lawrence Seaway in my day was frozen in winter and they'd flood you with cars in October.'[19]

One section of the population absent from BMC's management was the university graduate. As will have been apparent, there was a well-established discrimination against the breed within the British motor industry, although the exception was provided by Ford. At the prompting of its Corporate parent, in 1948, and, it should be said, against the wishes of its chairman, Sir Patrick Hennessy, himself a graduate, it had begun an intake which would grow in number and influence with the passing of years. By 1959 American-owned Vauxhall and Rootes had followed Ford's example, leaving BMC and Standard as the only mainstream British car makers that did not have even a modest graduate intake.[20]

BMC had its own board of directors, which was dominated by Austin executives. Longbridge became its headquarters and Lord made no attempt to duplicate the showcase CAB building at Cowley. A less desirable corporate inheritance was the Austin accounting system, which, historically, was far less rigourous and precise than Morris's. Ron Lucas, who had joined the company's accounts department in 1927 and subsequently qualified as a chartered secretary, returned to Longbridge after war service in 1947 to find that 'the number of financially qualified people there was not great.'[21]

This was no more apparent than in the costing of components. Lord Nuffield's policy was to constantly update the figure to take into account overtime and any other charges incurred. For its part Austin relied on an estimate of the part in question at the time of its introduction. Any supplementary costs were written down to corporate overheads.

Inevitably the BMC range in the first instance represented an uneasy, uneven jumble of overlapping models, cars with different engines, suspension units, chassis frames and bodies. At the time of the merger, it was producing 14 different models, nine of them Nuffield and five Austin. A policy of rationalisation therefore became essential and a collection of Longbridge-made and Nuffield components was accordingly laid out side-by-side in the basement of the BMC head office, opened in 1948 as the Austin headquarters and soon nicknamed the Kremlin on account of its architecture having something of a Muscovite flavour about it.

There each item was priced and John Thornley, who had been articled to chartered accountants Peat, Marwick and Mitchell before joining MG, recalled that 'of course, the Austin price beat the Nuffield price all the way down the line, and the Austin parts were chosen. The engineering of a lot of the Nuffield stuff was superior and the prices included every damn thing. If you costed that into every Austin part, you really were in the gravy. This, to a very great extent, contributed to the downfall of BMC.'[22]

As part of a three-year rationalisation plan all the Morris engines were therefore phased out, to be replaced by the Austin units, which did have the virtue of being of more recent design. The small 803cc power unit that had powered the Austin A30 became the BMC A Series engine that, incredibly, survived until the Mini ceased production in 2000. The A40's unit formed the basis of the B Series, although the six-cylinder C Series hailed from Morris Engines. Austin gearboxes and axles were similarly adopted. Nevertheless, BMC maintained its Cowley design facility, and Lord encouraged competition between the two engineering centres.

This modest rationalisation apart, he decided to leave the essentials of the Austin and Morris businesses intact. Each company retained its own board of directors and dealerships even though the Nuffield stable came with a quartet of marques, namely Morris, MG, Riley and Wolseley, which meant that they were all selling one against the other. The Corporation was attempting not to give ground in the face of competition by maintaining customer loyalty and, above all, keeping BMC's distributors, a powerful lobby group, happy.

In reality Lord would have been better advised to cull the line and reduce it to the Austin and Morris passenger cars and MG and Austin-Healey sports cars. At the time of the merger Wolseley was only selling in small, uneconomic numbers. The impending 1500 excepted, the best-selling Wolseley of the 1950s was Gerald Palmer's 4/44, which found just 29,845 buyers. Similarly the top-selling Riley was the 4/68, which accounted for a mere 10,940 examples.

This was the sum of progress achieved by the BMC up until the mid-1950s. The effects of the war were still being felt in the market and manufacturers could sell virtually all the cars that they could build. And, with the emphasis on production, it was, certainly as far as Longbridge was concerned, well equipped to meet demand. As Laurence Pomeroy has pointed out, in such circumstances 'engineering had been relatively unimportant, salesmanship unnecessary.'[23] In any event Lord's contempt for marketing permeated BMC. 'Build bloody good cars and they sell themselves'[24] was one of his most oft-quoted aphorisms. Alec Issigonis was in full agreement with him. 'My version of what Henry Ford said is market research is bunk. It's the engineers who decide what people want' he opined.[25]

Yet for all his apparent intransigence, BMC's chairman was sufficiently pragmatic to recognise that the seller's market could not continue indefinitely and would be replaced by a more competitive era. At the 1955 Motor Show, three years into BMC's existence, it had very little new to display although 'brighter colour schemes' were on offer. The exception was provided by its MG subsidiary, which was unveiling its newly-minted MGA sports car.

However, Citroën's sensational front-wheel drive DS saloon, announced only the previous week at the Paris event, was being seen by potential British customers for the first time. Laurence Pomeroy was ecstatic, writing in *The Motor* that it represented 'one of the biggest advances in production car design in the whole history of motoring'[26] and its 'coupling of all independent suspension with fore and aft levelling will give wholly new concepts to the terms "comfort" and "road worthiness",' adding, 'After this, automobile design can never be quite the same, and Earls Court 1955 will share with the Paris Salon the witness of the greatest single advance since the introduction of front wheel brakes.'

It was against such a euphoric response to the futuristic DS that BMC's chairman found himself cornered by Pomeroy at Earls Court, 'who suggested to Lord that it was high time he progressed from cart springs and built something a little more interesting. Lord replied "you bloody well tell us what to build and we'll build it."'[27] Then and there he commissioned from Pomeroy his ideas for a competitive European car, even if he 'put a five-cylinder two-stroke engine on the roof'. The result was what Pom named Maximin, a rear-engined four-seater, developed by ERA. But its gestation was protracted and the experimental vehicle was rapidly overhauled by Issigonis's smaller and more practical Mini.

It was not just a matter of the unadventurous mechanicals of BMC's products that required attention; the styling of its entire range, the Morris Minor excepted, was in need of a radical facelift. The body is the most expensive part of a car and styling a crucial part of the equation. Distinctive and progressive lines would attract potential buyers and meant that a model could enjoy a long production run which would accordingly reduce projected tooling costs. But anything too radical could frighten the conservative British public. The new Citroën, for all its futuristic looks, was to enjoy relatively modest British sales, which were less than half those of the Traction Avant. Just 8,668 D-Series cars were assembled at the company's Slough subsidiary in the 10 years between 1956 and 1966 and of these, about a third went for export.

It was a very different story at BMC, where the most popular Austins were the A30 and its A35 derivative, which sold some 344,000 units over a seven-year period. But by far and away BMC's most popular car, no doubt to Leonard Lord's distaste, was a Morris, Alec Issigonis's Minor no less. Its production was to increase year on year and in 1957 broke into six figures when 106,680 were made in the twelvemonth.

Although there had been some attempts at Cowley to update the design, the BMC chairman's initial response had been to completely restyle it. This decision was sprung on Cowley-based Gerald Palmer, who remembered that Lord 'arrived one day with a stack of drawings to say "Here you are. Dick Burzi and I have designed this Minor replacement at Longbridge!"'[28] In Palmer's opinion 'there seemed no attempt at a more imaginative use of space to give increased passenger accommodation. I wondered about suspension developments which we at Cowley believed were essential for world markets.'[29]

But demand for the Minor was continuing to grow. The public clearly liked its appearance so there could be no question of withdrawing it from production. Lord's response was to move the new-look Minor upmarket to the benefit of the flagging Riley and Wolseley marques. The resulting B Series-engined cars of 1957 respectively carried the One Point Five and 1500 name plates, and were, by default, successful. The latter, with over 100,000 built, was destined to be the best-selling model in the marque's 79-year history.

Yet despite Lord's modest efforts at rationalisation, what BMC really lacked were more models like the Morris Minor that could be manufactured in sufficient volumes to reap the benefits of the Corporation's enhanced production facilities. Sir Leonard needed only to cast his eye across the English Channel to see how the motor industries of Germany, France and Italy ran their businesses.

In the main Britain's continental neighbours historically built fewer, more technically advanced models that enjoyed longer production runs and were manufactured in considerably larger numbers. The success of Volkswagen's Beetle has already been chronicled and its rear-mounted engine, the cheapest location for a power unit, had a profound impact on small car design in Europe.

The Renault 4CV shared the same location and France's leading car maker built 1.1 million examples between 1947 and 1961, a decade before the Morris Minor attained the same figure. The engine of Fiat's diminutive 600 of 1955 was similarly positioned and some 890,000 were made by the time that its production ceased in 1960. Fiat's medium-sized model, the 1100, by contrast, was front-engined and sold over 1 million examples between 1953 and 1962. The power unit of the Farina-styled Peugeot 403 was similarly located and the model accounted for 1.1 million units produced in the 12 years from 1955 until 1967.

All these models, regardless of their engine locations, were driven by their rear wheels. The great exception was provided by Citroën, then the world's largest manufacturer of front-wheel drive cars. Its advanced DS of 1955 was destined to endure until 1965, by which time 1.6 million had been completed. The 2CV was to enjoy an even longer run and 3.5 million had been built when production ceased in 1990. Europe's only other significant front-wheel drive player was Saab, although production of the idiosyncratic two-stroke was modest and did not break the 10,000 cars a year barrier until 1958. (The DWK-derived Trabant, popular in East Germany, was not available in the West.)

Such developments had not escaped the perceptive eye of William Boddy, editor of the increasingly influential *Motor Sport* magazine, an avowed Volkswagen enthusiast and owner. In 1959 he reminded his readers that it had 'fought for years for a new approach to small car design by British engineers in order to combat the popularity of Continental best sellers.' They 'appeal to hundreds of thousands, even millions of motorists, because they have discarded the rigid back axle, "cart-spring" suspension, the propeller shaft and other design items which, as far as economy cars are concerned, are an unwanted legacy from the long-distant past.'[30]

It should be said that BMC was not alone in its conservative approach to design. British Ford continued to reflect its American parentage by producing cost-conscious, no-nonsense, front-engine/rear-drive value-for-money cars that were mechanically traditional in the extreme and a model of rationalisation. Ford would continue to build such vehicles until 1976 when the arrival of the Fiesta marked a switch to front-wheel drive, no less than 17 years after the Mini's appearance. It had only possessed a three-car line in the 1950s (the archaic pre-war based Popular excepted): the 100E, the Consul and its six-cylinder Zephyr stablemate. Not only did these two share commonised body components, their power units were designed with the same bore and stroke, so speeding and cheapening the production process.

The British Motor Corporation was far from being alone in the post-war years in suffering from the labour disputes that were to plague the industry with increasing intensity until the introduction by the Thatcher administration of the 1980 and 1984 Employment Acts. Prior to the war, motoring had been an essentially middle-class pursuit and employment was seasonal, with work guaranteed in the autumn, winter and spring, followed by layoffs in the summer months, prior to the annual Motor Show. The prosperity of the post-war years brought around-the-year jobs and car ownership was extended to all sectors of the community. Britain's car factories were unionised by 1945 and BMC, with its multiplicity of plants, was particularly vulnerable to strike action. When the British economy experienced a misfire in 1956, the Corporation was forced to lay off one worker in eight with no redundancy pay, and strikes were to increase in number and severity into the 1960s.

Alec Issigonis had little time for organised labour but when he arrived at Longbridge in December 1955 as the corporate assistant engineering co-ordinator, BMC was ready for a change of gear, and his appointment pointed the way forward. With Issigonis came Alex Moulton, who recalls 'he said to Leonard Lord, "I want to have a collaboration with Alex Moulton and his designs, I've been working with him at Alvis and I want to incorporate the interconnected suspension he wants to develop."'[31] As it happened Moulton had by this time left Spencer Moulton, which in 1956 was acquired by Avon. 'I had to go and present myself to Lord and Harriman to make some arrangement for this relationship. Company secretary Sydney Wheeler was also there. Lord came into the room in the Kremlin, I'd rather sensibly arrived with a big portfolio of the work that I'd done on many things, on my rubber suspension at Spencer Moulton before I'd met Issigonis, steam engines and so on. I went through this thing and Lord said, "Hm, when you've done those you'll do a lot more. OK, get on with it." It was as simple as that. He thought that I was an innovative person and said to Sydney Wheeler "make some arrangement."'

The 'arrangement' was the creation of Moulton Developments, with Alex Moulton having a majority shareholding as the owner of the intellectual property and the Austin Motor Company with a minority share of 26 percent. 'I then made a very bright remark for a young and very inexperienced man, I said, "couldn't you, Mr Wheeler, be one of our directors?" In other words, in the creation of a new thing, we were asking one of their directors to sit on our board. They funded the sponsoring of the work to be done at Bradford, with my estate I didn't want to move, and we set up the design and development operation for the suspension at the stables of The Hall. This gave BMC exclusive use of my designs and inventions that were to be exclusively manufactured by Dunlop. There was a lovely man there at Coventry called Joe Wright, who said "we'll do absolutely anything, this is a wonderful opportunity, BMC going to use rubber suspension, goodness me, you can have what you want."

That was my introduction to BMC. They respected our friendship. There were drinks at the Hyde Park Hotel at Motor Show times with George Harriman and so on. He also suggested that I went down to Monte Carlo in 1966 to see the end of the Rally although that was the year they lost!'[32]

Issigonis asked Cowley-based Doreen Schreier to become his technical assistant on 'a Tuesday and wanted to know by Friday if I could start on Monday. Money was never mentioned. But I couldn't leave my father who had had a serious heart attack. And he never did have a technical assistant.'[33] In the event she became a project engineer and moved to Longbridge in 1963.

On arrival at the Austin factory, as Laurence Pomeroy aptly described it 'Alec worked within, but not with Longbridge'[34] where he was now in charge of new small car projects. Initially based in a first-floor office in the Kremlin, soon after his arrival he telephoned John Sheppard, who had lost his job when the Alvis project came to an end, and suggested a meeting. 'He welcomed me with open arms and said "my job today is to bribe you to come," and I said "my job is to listen." This is the way he and I seemed to click.' Sheppard started work on 2 January 1956, sharing Issigonis's office. Both had drawing boards and there was also a layout table. Chairman Leonard Lord came in one day seeking Issigonis who wasn't there. 'He looked at my drawing board, and said "what have you put there today, besides dirt!"'[35]

The first project they undertook was a mid-range car designated XC9001, a 1.5-litre four-door saloon which featured Issigonis's soon to be familiar wheel-at-each corner. The single overhead camshaft four-cylinder aluminium engine was, in essence, one bank of the Alvis V8 unit. Alex Moulton was responsible for its interconnected rubber suspension, which again followed Alvis precedent. The significance of this car should not be underestimated as it marked a sea-change in the direction of BMC's products. The Citroën influence, with regard to both its looks and suspension, is immediately apparent. It is no coincidence to find that at this time Issigonis was driving a Citroën DS, BMC then taking the opportunity to try other manufacturer's cars as soon as they appeared. But on a broader canvas Leonard Lord had clearly taken to heart his recent conversation with Laurence Pomeroy.

The most significant aspect of the 9001 project was the styling, which anticipated the yet to be commissioned Mini. Its visual antecedence can be found in DO 976, Issigonis's idea for a rebodied Minor that he completed prior to his departure from Cowley, to which can be added elements of the Citroën DS. Although at the time Issigonis was pleased with the result, which he found elegant, and was pleased with the Citroën ingredient, in his later years he was wholly dismissive of this project. 'We only made one, a nasty thing. I didn't like that one and I thought it was driven at the wrong end, for it was a rear-wheel drive car.'[36] It would eventually evolve into the Austin 1800 of 1964.

Next came XC9002, which was destined to become the Morris 1100. A two-door saloon and effectively a scaled-down version of XC9001, it was intended as a replacement for the still current best-selling Morris Minor and therefore shared its dimensions. Significantly, it was powered by a transversely mounted engine and end-on gearbox in the manner of Issigonis's 1951 Minor experiment. Here in outline, if not detail, were the stylistic and mechanical essentials of the Mini.

While this front-wheel drive car clearly followed in Citroën's wheel tracks, it was the most expensive position, particularly because it required constant velocity joints to transmit power and steering forces to pull rather than push the car along. As has already been recorded, the alternative and cheaper rear position, as espoused by Volkswagen, was anathema to Issigonis. Christopher Dowson remembers[37] Alec encouraging him to 'spit at VW Beetles'; they were, of course, the opposition to the Morris Minor.

Stylistically both cars were Issigonis's work, which also constituted a shift in corporate responsibility. With Len Lord forever at his elbow, Ricardo 'Dick' Burzi, born in Buenos Aires of a French mother and later an Italian resident, had hitherto been responsible for the lines of Longbridge's products, having begun work there in the late 1920s. As will have already been apparent, the cars from Cowley reflected the talents of Alec Issigonis and, to a lesser extent, Leslie Hall. Yet both the Austin and Morris studios relied heavily on transatlantic themes for their inspiration, an influence that reached back to pre-war days. The exception had been provided in the 1950s by Gerald Palmer, a younger man, who believed that 'Italian styling was simply outstanding... Bertone, Farina, Zagato and so forth. I couldn't help being influenced by them.'[38] His MG and Wolseley saloons reflected this commitment but the remainder of the BMC range was another matter.

The catalyst for the change was no less a figure than the Duke of Edinburgh, who made his contribution just a matter of months after Leonard Lord's conversation with Laurence Pomeroy at about the time of Alec Issigonis's arrival. During a private visit to Longbridge on 8 December 1955, he found BMC's chairman in difficulties, as he invariably was when confronted with royalty. His usual response was to insult them. At one motoring event he had encountered one of his contemporaries in company with the portly figure of a royal Duke. Lord had loudly asked his associate: 'who's your fat friend?'[39] In fact he was echoing Beau Brummel's jibe in the 1830s to George, the 23-stone Prince Regent, although whether His Grace saw the joke is not recorded.

Similarly, when he acted as host to the husband of the Queen, he took the opportunity of berating him for using a Land Rover on public occasions, instead of the Champ, its Austin rival. This prompted a ticking-off from HRH. A subdued Lord then suggested a visit to view the clay models in Dick Burzi's styling studio. His royal visitor was unimpressed and told him: 'Sir Leonard, I think you ought to have another look at things because I'm not sure these are up to the foreign competition.'[40] This was in marked contrast to the telegram that his equerry sent to BMC on the following day, which spoke of the Duke being 'particularly impressed by the up-to-date ideas...' he had encountered![41]

The now-departed Gerald Palmer had already shown the way forward and the following day Lord contacted the Pinin Farina[42] studio in Turin. Although having raised its international profile by producing supremely elegant coupé bodies for the new Ferrari marque, Farina was extending its influence to the mass market and had already, in 1955, styled Peugeot's 403, which was destined for a long production run. This marked the beginning of a fruitful association between the two parties, being underpinned by an agreement made in 1958 that, for an annual fee of £100,000, Farina's services in the United Kingdon would be offered exclusively to BMC.

The corporate look was first applied to an Austin, in this instance a mechanically conventional replacement for the popular A35 line, which inherited the A40 name and that of its stylist. The body of the A40 Farina ingeniously combined the outline of an estate car with a short wheelbase and produced, by the apparent absence of a projecting boot, a 'two box' design. Although dismissed by some at Longbridge as 'a van,' progressively it anticipated today's hatchback style and although it lacked a tailgate, one would arrive in 1961. *Design* magazine was delighted. 'This is the first BMC product to have undeniable style' it opined.[43]

In retrospect it can be seen that the A40 Farina's radical styling of 1958 paved the way for the 'two box' Mini of the following year.

Farina's next offering for BMC was a wholly conventional 'three box' concept in the shape of the Wolseley 6/99, which appeared in December 1958, a four-door saloon enhanced with tail fins that inevitably dated far quicker than the A40 design. This body was mildly embellished, offered with alternative B and C Series engines, and would carry the name plates of each BMC make. The era of so-called 'badge engineering' had arrived.

The move to Longbridge presented Alec Issigonis with a problem as far as his domestic arrangements were concerned. His mother did not want to leave Oxford so for some years he lived midweek at the Albany Hotel in Birmingham and later the Worcestershire Brine Baths in Droitwich. He would then return to Linkside Avenue, on a Wednesday, Thursday or Friday, using the time to visit the Morris design facility at Cowley.

By this time the weekends in Oxford meant a visit to Alec's favoured pub, the Trout at Godstow, about a mile from his home. Stone-built and dating from the 18th century, in the 1950s its interior appeared to have changed little since then. Located on the banks of the infant Thames alongside Godstow Bridge, there was a terrace overlooking the river which increased this hostelry's appeal during the summer months.

A popular 'watering hole' with Oxford undergraduates, Issigonis was a regular there on Saturday evenings and Sunday lunchtimes, where he enjoyed the company of the Axtell and Connelly families as a member of a group of a dozen or so who regularly met there. The Trout had been bought before World War Two by one Captain Coleman, who had run it very much as a club and, when he died, his widow, 'Mum' Coleman, maintained this tradition. An unsuspecting and unwelcome visitor, arriving in the stone-flagged bar and sitting down in front of the large coal fire contained within a cast iron grate, would find it stoked up to such an extent that he was driven away by the heat…

'We used to arrive quite early, between six and half past on a Saturday evening, certainly well before seven, to enjoy some drinks and a chat and be gone by 8.30 for supper,' remembers Malcolm Axtell.[44] 'It was very special. Sometimes you saw Mrs Coleman, sometimes you didn't, she was quite a character. Her white hair was waved and she wore big glasses like an owl and long clothes rather like Queen Victoria's. She had a private sitting room and sometimes we were privileged to go in. In the summer months she sat in a little pavilion on an island on the other side of the river, walking-stick in hand, surveying the scene. She had a beagle dog called Bomber because he'd been up in bombers during the war.'

The bar at the Trout therefore became Alec's home from home. There he could enjoy a drink, smoke his cigarettes and relax among friends. In contrast to the stridency he displayed at Longbridge, when he was in a group, Axtell recalls, 'he wasn't a leader, he was quite retiring, he would comment and give an opinion. He was more of a responder. He had an active mind but he needed a lead. Alec's usual drink was Worthington E, which was a fairly strong beer, whereas most of us drank Younger's Scotch Ale Number Three. I wouldn't say he was a heavy drinker, he'd make it last. He always bought his round although I would say he was careful with his money.' The group usually returned on Sunday lunchtime, when they might be joined by Gerald Palmer or John Thornley from the world of motoring.

It could not, of course, last for ever. Mrs Coleman died, in 1961 the Trout was bought by Charringtons and Alec Issigonis and his mother soon afterwards left Oxford and moved to Edgbaston. The abiding memory he left with Jennifer Gilman 'was the size of his hands and feet!'[45] To Malcolm Axtell, 'Alec was very intense. His eyes would almost bore into you with an intensity to analyse what was happening. He wanted to know "how and why?" He wasn't a relaxed man. He was very tense and on edge as though he was always in a hurry. I remember him with great fondness and respect.'[46]

Being based at BMC's Longbridge headquarters did have its geographical advantages for Issigonis because it was only about 20 miles from The Poplars, George Dowson's farm off the A44 near Pershore. Christopher recalls[47] that for many years he 'came for lunch, usually once a week but sometimes more often. Occasionally he stayed overnight. Officially this was to test some of his experimental creations but the real reason was to savour my mother's excellent cooking, especially her roast pork. Before lunch there were always drinks in the drawing room, gin and French was Alec's tipple, together with a "Yellow Peril", his Gold Flake cigarettes. Consequently he had, among others, two nicknames "Gin-igonis" or "Pork-igonis". He was tremendous fun.'

As far as the Dowson's young family were concerned, he was 'Uncle Alec' and he became Penny's godfather. Christopher recalls a friendship that was to endure for 30 years until Issigonis's death. 'I loved him, we all did. He considered us his children. For some reason he always used to greet me "Hello, dear boy, have you shaved?" rubbing my cheek with his huge hand.' One of the gifts that Alec bequeathed, and one for which Christopher was immensely grateful, was instruction on how to use his hands. 'I've never seen anyone manipulate tools as he did, how, for instance, he used a hacksaw. The most memorable thing I remember was his ability to use tin snips. He was magic with those. Then we used to make hot air balloons and model aircraft of balsa wood, glue, tissue paper, dope and rubber bands. I remember he made a model of the Bristol Brabazon but it never flew very well. He had his own, which he nicknamed Clara, and I can remember chasing it across the fields.'

During 1956 Alec Issigonis found time to advise BRM on a suspension problem it had encountered on the 2.5-litre four-cylinder racing car. His support for the project reached back to its inception in 1947 when Raymond Mays and his friend Peter Berthon sought to produce a Formula 1 car to uphold British laurels on the motor racing circuits of the world. Its first design, a V16-engined car of 1949, proved excessively complex and never found its form in the face of much criticism from the industry and press alike.

Alec Rivers Fletcher, who was public relations officer for the Owen Organisation, which later funded the project, recalled Issigonis having 'praised and applauded their efforts which he considered were on the right lines.'[48] But in private Issigonis deprecatingly referred to Raymond Mays, a homosexual, as 'Miss Mays.'[49]

The V16 had been followed in 1955 by a simpler Type 25 four-cylinder car, although it was plagued with handling problems. Tony Brooks declined to drive for BRM in 1957 and Roy Salvadori said 'maybe, but you will have to make it handle better before I sign.'[50] It was at this point that Raymond Mays asked Issigonis and Moulton for their advice. 'They recommended rearranging the front struts and rear springs to eliminate their influence on roll stiffness, so that all roll resistance came from the roll bars,' remembered Tony Rudd, then BRM's development engineer.[51] According to Mays 'this cured the car's excessive oversteering characteristics. It began to understeer, although it still had a tendency to wander at the front under greater acceleration.'[52]

At Longbridge Issigonis's small team was in place by the autumn of 1956. Jack Daniels, who had been working at Cowley, joined them in the summer, although he continued to live in Oxford and commuted to Birmingham. He had begun working at Longbridge earlier in 1956; there was snow on the ground and he made the journey in the experimental front-wheel drive Minor that he had completed in 1952. He deemed this 'the safest car we had available at Cowley.'[53] And whether by accident or design, Daniels left it parked outside Leonard Lord's office. Chris Kingham also arrived from Alvis in the late autumn. Deeply religious, he had in any event not wished to become involved with that company's military vehicle operations.

The team were ensconced in their own self-contained facility within the factory complex on the corner of Lowhill Lane and the Bristol Road and were joined by Stan Field and Bob Robbins, who had just completed their apprenticeships and undertook detailed drawing for Jack Daniels. Kingham always did his own, and he and John Sheppard were assistant superintendents. Vic Everton was foreman of the pattern shop and transformed Sheppard's body drawing into metal. It was run by Dick Gallimore, although he was replaced by Doug Adams. Ron Dovey's responsibility was body construction. At Cowley George Cooper checked layouts.

Then fate intervened. In September 1956 Egypt nationalised the Suez Canal and in response the Arabs blew up the oil pipeline that supplied Britain with 20 percent of its oil requirements. As a result of the ill-fated British and French invasion of Egypt, the waterway was blocked, tankers had to travel around the Cape of Good Hope and petrol rose to a record high of 3s 6d per gallon. Rationing was introduced in December 1956.

Sales of large cars slumped and economical bubble cars, capable of some 75mpg, most of them of German origin, began to appear in increasing numbers on Britain's roads. As it happened, they were produced by companies, in the case of Heinkel and Messerschmitt, better known for their wartime aircraft, while BMW, which made the Italian-designed Isetta under licence, had built aero engines. Memories of the war were still raw and Sir Leonard was avowedly pro-British and anti-German. His first response was to commission an experimental bubble car from Morris, a small mid-engined vehicle intended to sell for £300. This used a two-cylinder version of the A Series, located so as not to breach the inviolate price barrier.

This initiative was destined to produce a catalytic reaction from Alec Issigonis, who recalled 'at Cowley they had an experimental department. They were making a bubble car. I said "never copy the opposition" and there and then decided on the Mini.'[54] It was March 1957 and had probably followed Lord's now celebrated remark: 'God damn these bloody awful bubble cars. We must drive them off the streets by designing a proper miniature car.'[55] Its target price was £315–£325.[56] This was, to all intents and purposes, a restatement of the Austin Seven theme; Lord had briefly contemplated reviving the model in the early post-war years and its co-designer, Stanley Edge, had even been summoned to Longbridge to discuss the matter.

Sir Leonard's angry denouncement of what he perceived to be a German invasion of British roads was empirical thinking at its worst and an extraordinary overreaction on the part of BMC's chairman, because bubble cars had only a modest and short-lived impact on the British motorist. Petrol rationing was, in any event, discontinued in May 1957, a year in which new registrations in the sub-700cc class amounted to a mere 3,308 of the 425,355 cars sold in Britain that year. The figure dropped to 2,959 in 1958, a twelvemonth in which sales in the popular 900–1000cc sector rose to 142,168. Little wonder that Morris Minor production peaked in that year.

BMC was to pay dearly for a policy born of its chairman's prejudice and it was one which chimed precisely with Issigonis's anti-German sentiments. Had Lord let XC9002, the front-wheel replacement for the Morris Minor with its transverse engine and end-on gearbox, proceed, as a relatively expensive family model it would have offered greater prospects for corporate profitability. Not only that.

When it was usurped by the smaller and narrower Mini, Issigonis was forced to replace the inline box with the ingenious, expensive and mechanically less satisfactory solution of relocating the unit in the engine's sump.

The stillborn XC9002's end-on gearbox location was subsequently independently adopted in 1964 by Fiat and then copied by the rest of the world's motor manufacturers. But the Mini's 'box-in-sump' placement was inherited by all BMC's front-wheel drive cars, to the collective detriment of its already stretched finances. And it, by contrast, was destined to become a technological dead-end.

To Alec Issigonis, his chairman's impulsive change of course represented a heaven-sent opportunity to proceed with the 'charwoman's car' he had so long espoused, even if its creation would entail redrawing the map of the motor car as defined by Emile Levassor back in 1891. That year the engine of his 3.5hp Panhard was transferred from its customary position at the rear of the vehicle to the front, to be aligned with the clutch and gearbox, with drive then conveyed to the rear wheels. Designated *système Panhard* and capable of virtually unlimited refinement, the rear-engined VW Beetle of 1938 would represent the first significant challenge to the concept, although by the 1970s its influence was in decline. *Système Issigonis* was destined to be far more enduring.

It was not front-wheel drive that made the Mini so radical, as Citroën had already shown the way forward in that regard. For instead of being positioned inline, Issigonis mounted the small car's four-cylinder engine transversely, as he had done with his experimental Minor and XC9002, to maximise the interior space and make a positive contribution to the car's road holding. Although it bristled with other technological features, this was the most influential aspect of the entire concept.

Lord's only proviso to Issigonis had been: 'you can use any engine you like so long as we have it on our present production line.'[57] Bearing in mind the size of the projected vehicle this could only be the A Series unit, although a two-cylinder version, similar to that used on the Cowley bubble car, was tried and rejected as being too crude. Bill Appleby was BMC's engine designer and Alex Moulton recalls that 'Issigonis had a fear of Bill Appleby, we always used to joke that he'd push his head up through the floorboards and say, "Alec you can't do that!"'[58]

As this was a small car, Issigonis could not use the engine with its end-on gearbox that had already been used on the larger XC9002. 'The drive shafts were too short to get enough bump and rebound and I didn't like the inaccessibility of the clutch plate which is the most usable commodity of a car. I know a woman who uses three clutch plates a year.'[59] Charles Bulmer, who in 1963 became *Motor's* technical editor, makes the point that 'he couldn't do anything else at the time because he was constrained by the front suspension. If he'd gone to MacPherson struts he would have gained a lot more space.'[60]

Instead Issigonis adopted the radical solution of placing the gearbox in the engine's sump, which was a magnesium alloy casting. But from where did this feature, which Laurence Pomeroy described as 'a stroke of genius,' originate? As Issigonis very rarely revealed his design influences this must be a matter for speculation but a strong candidate is a design that sprang from the front-wheel drive Duncan Dragonfly project to which, it will be recalled, Alex Moulton had contributed the rubber suspension.

Alan Lamburn, who had been responsible for the car's mechanicals, on his own account took the concept one step further and in 1950 designed an evolutionary concept car, also driven by its front wheels, that was the subject of an article published in *The Autocar* of 5 September 1952. Revealing his thoughts for an economy car, Lamburn envisaged it being powered by a transverse 598cc vertical twin air-cooled engine, the crankcase of which 'also forms the housing for the transmission... The pistons and transmission gears are lubricated by oil mist... The drive is transmitted through spherical rubber joints at the inner ends...'

Issigonis, with his passion for small car design, cannot have been unaware of the article, which was illustrated with drawings. Indeed, he read the piece because Lamburn, in his attempt to interest manufacturers in his idea, wrote to every car maker in the world attaching details of the design. And one of these firms was Alvis, where it landed on Alec Issigonis's desk. On 13 October 1952, in rejecting the idea, in truth a very un-Alvis concept, he informed Lamburn: 'I have followed the article published in the AUTOCAR with great interest, having myself specialised in small car design for a number of years...'[61]

Five years later, when he was beginning work on what was designated XC9003, the gearbox-in-sump became a key feature of the concept, being the lower half of an engine/transmission unit based on BMC's current 948cc A Series four. This was demanded by the fact that the width of the radiator, engine and end-on

How drive passed from the crankshaft to the three speed gearbox-in-sump of the engine for Alan Lamburn's 1950 Economy Car. (*Autocar*).

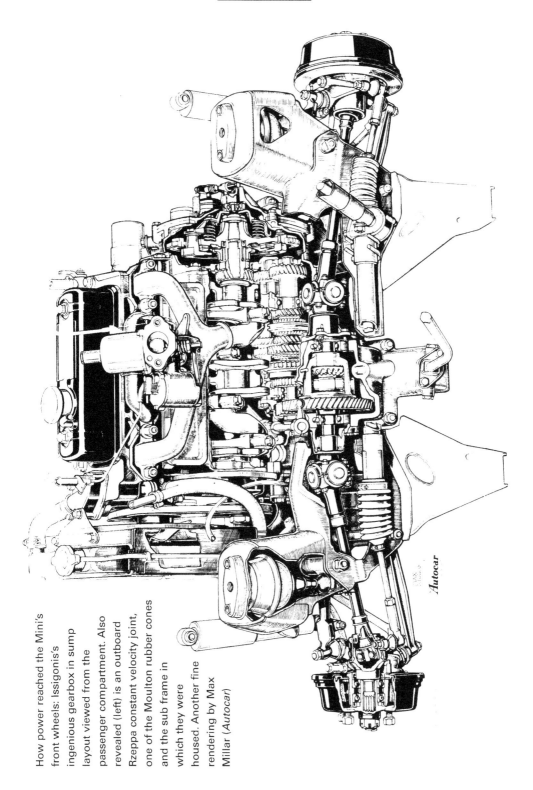

How power reached the Mini's front wheels: Issigonis's ingenious gearbox in sump layout viewed from the passenger compartment. Also revealed (left) is an outboard Rzeppa constant velocity joint, one of the Moulton rubber cones and the sub frame in which they were housed. Another fine rendering by Max Millar (*Autocar*)

Autocar

gearbox was 38in but the amount of under-bonnet space available was 20in. However, engine with gearbox in sump was only 18in. Issigonis took the precaution of patenting the combination; the application, made in conjunction with Austin, was dated 11 June 1957 but it was not published until 1960, after the Mini had entered production.

The limitation was now the matter of the constant velocity joints because, as already noted, those used on the FWD Minor were unacceptably large and the projected car was to have small wheels. Conventional joints were ruled out because they fed a straightening motion back to the driver, which immediately negated all the handling and tractive advantages of front-wheel drive.

Fortunately for Issigonis, news of the XC9003 project had reached the receptive ears of MG's chief engineer, Syd Enever, whom he had known since his days in Morris's Cowley drawing office and was another outstanding 'fag packet' intuitive engineer who could visualise complete cars. Syd put his discovery in a note which said words to the effect of 'you might be interested in this'[62] that was accompanied by a drawing of a Rzeppa constant velocity joint. To Issigonis 'as soon as I saw this joint I realised that front-wheel drive was a possibility.'[63]

A telephone enquiry revealed that this joint, patented in 1935 by the Czech Alfred Hans Rzeppa, an engineer with Ford America, was in low-volume production by its British patent owners, Unipower of Shipley, Yorkshire, and was being used for submarine conning-tower controls. Birfield, Hardy Spicer's parent company, clearly recognising the potential of front-wheel drive, had the good sense to purchase Unipower and with it came Bill Cull, formerly chief designer for Scott Motor Cycles. He was responsible for refining what was now named the Birfield constant velocity joint for use on XC9003.

The next innovation was the wheels. As he had done with the Morris Minor, Issigonis again broke new ground by using wide track 10in wheels, which visually would be in proportion with the remainder of the vehicle and not intrude into the passenger area. Theoretically larger wheels would have meant widening the car to allow them to turn on full lock and their attendant arches would have pushed the front seats back to the detriment of the occupants of the rear one.

Ten inch tyres were not in themselves new, and Issigonis himself recognised that 'bubble cars had ten inch wheels but not with such a big section [4.40in]. Dunlop co-operated immediately and understood the problem. With big wheels it would have looked terrible. If you put a big wheel against a Mini and take a picture you can see what I mean.'[64]

In his office Issigonis had a pile of five Morris Minor wheels, which he used in conjunction with four hard-backed chairs to demonstrate how successful packaging could be achieved. During a meeting attended by Dunlop's development manager, Tom French, he pointed to the Minor's 14in covers, and berated those present. 'Why the hell do you people need such huge wheels. You must squeeze them down to this size,'[65] holding his hands just a few inches apart. There was, apparently, a stunned silence and someone took a ruler and measured the proffered hand span. 'We considered eight inches as a thinking exercise,' recalled French, 'but it was never very serious because there was no room for the brakes. We looked at eleven inches as well, before deciding to make the rubber for 10in wheels.'[66]

The problem was that the existing 10in cross ply covers could not cope with the potential performance of the car and rotational speeds involved. As it happened Dunlop's sister company in Germany had been investigating tyre failures experienced by bubble cars on autobahns and Fort Dunlop was able to benefit from these developments. It acquired a Goggomobile to test the new tyres, which had 5.20x10in dimensions, although before they were ready the experimental Minis used narrow track bubble car ones.

Dunlop's involvement with XC9003 did not stop there, as it was also to make the rubber cones to be used as the suspension medium. Originally the Mini was to have been fitted with an interconnected system, as evolved on the Alvis saloon, but problems of miniaturisation proved, in the short term, to be insurmountable so individual rubber cones, of the type originally used on the TA350, were adopted.

The Mini was to have featured a dead rear axle, but its presence trespassed into the boot space so secondary rubber units were added at the rear. All independent suspension was a revolutionary concept for a cheap car and the use of rubber was equally unorthodox. Compact, light, contributing only 8lb to the weight of the car, it also had the virtue of possessing variable pitch, which meant the spring automatically stiffened as the number of passengers carried increased.

At the front the rubber cones were vertically positioned and used in conjunction with forged links of unequal length. However, the rears were horizontally mounted so as not to intrude into the body cavity and were used in conjunction with metal trumpets and trailing tubular arms. Each wheel operated with a short travel of about six inches, which produced a deflection of some 1.25in in the cones, although this required heavy loadings at their respective pivot points.

The Mini's styling, if that is the correct word, as *Automobile Engineer* later opined, was 'functional rather than graceful,'[67] a box of a car with an overall length of just 120in, although it 'grew' an extra 0.25in by the time it reached production. Its lines were effectively scaled down from XC9001 and XC9002, but managed to lose all their Citroën influences on the way. XC9003 is Issigonis pure and simple. And in designing the body, he forsook the visual influences of the sort that had been so apparent on the Morris Minor, for by this time he believed that 'styling is designing for obsolesence.'[68] 'Style,' he would declare, 'has to do with architecture, ladies' dresses and furniture. Ours is engineering.'[69]

His starting point was the 'two box' saloons of the 1920s but by the late 1930s he considered that the 'decay set in'. He cited Bugatti's universally acclaimed Type 55 open two-seater sports car, the work of Ettore's son Jean, as 'the beginning of the end. The stylist had begun to rear his ugly head.'[70] In effectively redrawing the outline of the contemporary saloon, Alec Issigonis was reverting to the theme, as he later put it, of 'the long, elegant cars of the 1920s and 1930s' which 'were all "two box" cars. The trunk was just that, a large trunk, perhaps specially shaped, and was carried on the luggage grid.'[71]

He expressed the evolution of his 'two box' concept in the Mini for a BMC film made to promote that model, illustrated with drawings. 'The three box configuration has very little aesthetic appeal,' he opined, 'because we get a thing that looks like this [draws conventionally booted saloon]. You must admit that this looks somewhat grotesque. In getting elegance back into the design this part [draws line from the top end of the roof to the base of the boot] has to be extended over the back wheel.'[72]

In Issigonis's opinion cars had become 'fashion goods,' a phrase that he repeatedly used when discussing such matters with his colleagues. He believed that 'stylists are to blame. Christian Dior would design a dress and everyone would copy it. The same thing is happening with cars. They have become fashion goods. A woman will say "we will buy that car because I like the mirror in the sun visor." Or the car will be bought for some other totally irrational reason.'

America was singled out as the guilty party. 'This preoccupation with trivial things comes from the other side of the Atlantic I am afraid. The French are not like this at all; that is why I admire their work. The Italians do it to a smaller extent. We are transatlantic, and the Germans too.'[73]

Having said that it is undeniable that the Mini is styled; there are gentle curvatures to its lines that make a subtle yet essential contribution to how it looks. Alec Issigonis emerges as an exponent, conscious or otherwise, of functionalism, a concept associated with the German Bauhaus movement of the 1920s which sought to unite the hitherto separate worlds of art and engineering to the mutual advantage of both. Its students were directed to apply their imaginations to an object while never losing sight of the purpose it should serve.

The essence of this creed was that if something was designed for a specific purpose, beauty would follow in its wake. An aircraft is a case in point. Unfortunately this approach cannot be sustained, because there are objects that, although functionally correct, are also unattractive to the eye, as in the instance of a car with aerodynamically refined 'slippery' bodywork.

However, the Citroën 2CV represented the acceptable face of functionalism and the distinguished art historian Ernst Gombrich has pointed out: 'The best works of this style are beautiful not because they happen to fit the function... but because they were designed by men of tact and taste.' Such individuals could produce an object fit for its purpose 'and yet "right" for the eye.'[74] Whether Issigonis was a man of tact is perhaps debatable, but he certainly possessed taste of a sort.

As far as the Mini was concerned, it was a shape dictated by the requirements of accommodating four people behind a transversely located engine framed within the parameters of a wheel-at-each-corner. In fact the only apparent decorative but strictly functional elements were the unusual external flanged joints turned outward for ease of manufacture, spot welded together and then covered with a U-shaped beading. Issigonis similarly made no attempt to conceal the door hinges, which convention demanded be hidden.

The car's appearance did cause some concern within BMC. One day Charles Davidson of Lucas was discussing the car's tail lights with Issigonis when 'George Harriman arrived to see the complete car for the first time. He walked round it for a bit and then said "It's very tiny isn't it, but it's good. When we get the chromium plate on it and get the styling done it's going to look quite nice." Alec said "If you do anything to that car, I'm leaving. It's finished."'[75] It was a view shared with Sergio Pininfarina, who, together with his father Pinin saw it for the first time during a behind-the-scenes visit to Longbridge. Their verdict, 'don't change a line,'[76] was unequivocal.

All of these elements were apparent in the completed Mini, with a notable exception. The first two experimental cars also lacked external boot lids, the original idea being to either allow access to be gained from the interior or through an opening back window. But one was then introduced to provide access to what *Automobile Engineer* described as a 'surprisingly commodious'[77] boot with a capacity of 5.75sqft and it could be increased when, in the pre-war traditions, the car was run with the lid in the open position. And contrary to previous published statements that the Mini was widened by 2in, it was not. John Sheppard is insistent on that!

As far as the Mini's creator was concerned, 'the thing that satisfied me most was that it looked like no other car'[78] and that particularly applied to the rest of the BMC range! It also had the virtue of appearing classless and in consequence proved to be remarkably enduring. Indeed, although variations on the theme appeared over the years, the essentials of the original lines remained until production ceased in 2000.

The interior reflected both its creators' formidable talents at utilising every inch of space to accommodate four people. 'We have deliberately made the car very small because we have found new ways of making the inside very big,' Issigonis told Laurence Pomeroy.[79] Furnishing was, predictably, rather basic. The driver sat ahead of a sparse fascia with a single centrally located speedometer graduated to 80mph, and a parcel shelf below.

The front windows were of the sliding variety, which echoed the Austin Seven saloons of the 1926–30 era, as did the floor-mounted starter button, as used on Sir Herbert's baby car until 1932. And because the window glass did not descend, and with no intrusive winding mechanism, there was room for large storage pockets, apparently able to accommodate bottles of Issigonis's favoured Gordon's gin! This also produced more elbow space while the door locks were opened by cheap and cheerful plastic-coated pull wires, also in the Seven tradition.

Development was rapid: the first experimental car, named Orange Box on account of its colour, and a red-hued companion were running by October 1957, both being disguised by A35 radiator grilles. At this point Leonard Lord, in characteristically brief and robust tones, told the car's creator to 'make the bloody thing.'[80] Geoffrey Rose recalls the investment figure 'was £10 million [the equivalent of £138 million by today's values], which was big money in those days.'[81]

To all intents and purposes the mechanical specification was seen through to production although John Sheppard remembers that weight was an ongoing Issigonis preoccupation. 'Every day I would see him, he could read a drawing straight away, he'd never speak immediately but throw a two ounce brass weight down in front of me, and say "Have you saved that for me today?". If he saw a part he thought was too heavy, he'd bang the weight up and down and ask, "why have you made so and so that thick?"'[82] Any parts that couldn't be sourced internally, Sheppard ordered from a Wilmot-Breeden catalogue he'd acquired at Alvis. 'That's why the Mini started off with stupid little slam locks. I picked them out of the book and showed them to the old man. I said "it looks a bit cheap to me," but he said "it'll do as long as it locks".'

By contrast, two modifications were effected to the car which added cost to the overall concept. Originally the engine was positioned west to east, with the carburettor facing the front. But because the drive was taken through a heavy reduction gear, it placed undue resistance on the synchromesh, which began to rapidly wear out. On the third prototype therefore the block was rotated to an east/west location and the large gear replaced by two smaller ones, making three noisy transfer cogs in all.

Jack Daniels made a point to the author[83] of underlining this as the principal reason for the change, not the often quoted reason of carburettor icing, which did indeed occur, a problem that was also eliminated by rotating the block 180 degrees. At the same time the engine's capacity was reduced to 848cc, as it was believed the original 948cc unit endowed the prototypes with a top speed of 92mph and thus made the car too fast.

As originally conceived the Mini was based on a unitary shell – it weighed just 310lb – but the second generation of prototypes was to be fitted with sub frames front and rear. These were introduced because, as Jack Daniels recalled, 'Issy had demanded the first test drive and got 100 yards before the suspension collapsed. The very high loading on the rubber units simply pushed apart the upper and lower fixings, which is why the sub frames were added as a design fix.'[84] They also had the virtue of reducing noise levels, but added to overall weight. And the rear frame, located as it was some distance from the oily engine/transmission unit, to the despair of many Mini owners, proved itself susceptible to excessive rusting.

The Mini name was to arrive late in the day and Laurence Pomeroy is often credited with having invented it, having applied *Mini-motor* to his imaginary car of 1939. 'There were lots of discussions as to what to call it,' remembered Issigonis.[85] But for much of its pre-production life the car was nicknamed Sputnik. The name was a topical one and followed Russia's launch, in October 1957, of the world's first space satellite. This coincided with the Paris Motor Show and, after visiting the event, in the evening Issigonis, Jack Daniels, Dick Burzi and John Sheppard were having a coffee in the open air at a café

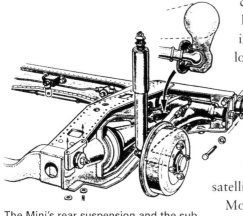

The Mini's rear suspension and the sub frame to which it was attached that, alas, succumbed to rusting. (Autocar).

on the Champs-Elysées looking up at the night sky. 'I said to Issigonis, "it's going around the world, I wonder if our little car is going around the world,"' Sheppard recalls.[86] 'When I got back to the works, I said to Jack Daniels "I think we ought to call our prototypes Sputniks, and numbers one to six were."' This followed the completion of the first two experimental cars; in all 24 prototypes would be completed before the Mini entered production.

Rose remembers that 'the work was so secret, the cell was so segregated from the rest of Longbridge, that people didn't know what was going on. My first knowledge of the Mini, which everyone called Sputnik, was when they began testing it in the evenings on the flying ground at Longbridge. My office was in the CAB 1 building and after work the prototype Mini would appear and was driven up and down.'[87] Soon afterwards both cars were transferred to Cowley because of its proximity to Chalgrove airfield, where they were tested on the overgrown perimeter track. Road-proving was the responsibility of Charles Griffin, Morris's chief designer and accomplished driver, who deserves much of the credit for imbuing the Mini with the impressive roadholding for which it became justly famous.

Alec Issigonis was still working on the designs of what he called the Sputnik during a skiing holiday in Switzerland with Antony Armstrong-Jones, later Lord Snowdon, who then drove a Morris Minor 1000 as his everyday car. He had met Issigonis in the mid-1950s through his old friend Jeremy Fry, one-time constructor of the Parsenn 500cc racer. 'He used to come skiing with me at Klosters and Davos with Alex Moulton. If I wanted him to join me, I'd send a telegram saying "windscreen wipers broken, come out at once!" Alec wore a rough three-piece tweed suit for skiing, which he loved, although he skied very badly.'[88]

Lord Snowdon has vivid recollections of his friend working on sketches of the Mini's mechanicals which, characteristically, were executed on a paper tablecloth, on that occasion in the bar of Fopps Restaurant at Davos. 'The proprietor ticked him off, it must have been about five o'clock in the morning, so we left and decided to go back to Klosters by toboggan towed behind a passing car. This was before the road had been gritted and it was lethally dangerous.'

Because of the darkness neither of them were aware of the identity of the towing vehicle but, as the sky lightened, it emerged that it was a Volkswagen Beetle, great rival to the Morris Minor and, above all, of German manufacture. When this realisation dawned, 'Alec began shouting "bugger the Germans, bugger the Germans!" he loathed them, all the way back to Klosters. When we got back to our hotel he resumed his drawing on the nearest tablecloth, saying it was a "much better quality of paper, my dear." He was great fun, very Greek in every way and it was wonderful to drive with him.'

Issigonis also enjoyed working holidays of a few days' duration in Monte Carlo with Alex Moulton and John Morris, where the design of the Mini was avidly discussed against an agreeable background, with thoughts, by all accounts, germinating on a raft off the Beach Hotel. On occasions they were joined by Alec's mother. Alex Moulton recalls[89] 'we first went there when he was at Alvis,' and Arthur Varney remembered that Issigonis 'claimed he and his friend did the journey non-stop from the Channel coast, except to change over for driving.'[90] Moulton remembers John Morris as 'a passionate Francophile and fully supportive as far as the Mini was concerned. He was a capable and profound engineer who contributed general wisdom to the process and was besotted with the Citroën 2CV! We were called The Three Musketeers and talked endlessly about engineering matters.'[91]

Later, in the mid-1960s, Ronald Barker got a flavour of this convivial dialogue when he was covering the Alpine Rally for *Autocar*. He had occasion to call in at Monte Carlo and 'while there I had a date to have lunch with Issigonis and John

Morris. They were down at the coast drinking gin and Martinis at the table, both in their bathing trunks. I don't think they had a sketch pad there but Alec said they had discussed a lot of stuff with John Morris on the design side. Right in the middle of this conversation, Morris suddenly stood up, pinched his nose and jumped feet first into the Med. We must have been about 12 feet above sea level!'[92]

This was a man whose work had recently damaged the roof of SU carburettors's experimental department in Wood Lane, Erdington. Norman Painting worked with Morris in the early 1960s and recalls[93] that the facility was 'quite small, it was only about 8ftx8ft, with only room for two engineers. Johnnie Morris was running a Jaguar XK engine with single point fuel injection system when there was an explosion which blew a panel off the roof, fortunately without great harm to himself. On one occasion he wanted to know the colour of the flames as they left the exhaust ports. To do this he needed some quartz windows but the management wouldn't pay for them. So he suggested going down to a local store and they bought a lot of mica squares of the sort used in Valor stoves. He then looked through them until the exhaust gases blew them out.' The company clearly placed research and development low on its list of priorities, preferring to rely on its long-established carburettor, and was, in due course, overtaken in the field of fuel injection of which Morris was such an early advocate. 'He ran a mechanically fuel injected Citroën DS and an Ami 6 engine converted, although not very successfully, to SU carburettors.'

Peter Knight, his successor, remembers[94] that John Morris was 'very keen on doing jobs for himself. He used to come into work in an immaculate white shirt that was soon smothered in oil. His eccentricities were well known for no other reason than he had set up an elaborately decorated tent, rather like a wigwam, in the sitting room of his home.'

David Morris, no relation, joined SU's development department in 1962 and Morris conducted the interview on the pavement because the new recruit was a Citroën Light 15 owner. The chief engineer spent most of the time with his head under its bonnet. 'He was a great one for sketching when he was talking to you. He'd draw on the workbench, wall, or even his hand although he'd then depart taking the idea with him!'[95]

When he was not talking Mini with Issigonis and Moulton, John Morris spent about six months of the year on the other side of the Atlantic with Simmonds, the American licensee of SU's fuel injection system, which it applied to the Packard-built Rolls-Royce Merlin engine then being used in tanks. Such was the individual who played a key but catalytic role in the creation of the Mini and, by 1957, XC9003 had become ADO 15.

Despite a hectic schedule Alec found time to take a skiing holiday with the

Dowson family at Arosa in the Swiss Alps in 1958. Christopher remembers[96] 'It was a fantastic holiday. I was nine years old and that was when I really got to know him. My father became terribly ill, he was confined to his bed all the time and I spent a fortnight with Alec, who acted as a surrogate father. My sister was also unwell and my mother didn't ski. I always remember him at the Hotel Seahof saying, "Christopher, go and tell your mother it's gin time." At breakfast he was very particular about how an egg should be fried. We were sitting in the dining room and they brought him the wrong egg to the table, so he jumped up and marched into the kitchen and cooked his own egg. He wanted to baste it and, this being a Swiss hotel, the staff didn't know how to cook an egg. There was no consternation from the hotel staff because he did it all with such grace and good humour. I used to have skiing lessons in the morning and then ski with him in the afternoon. Then he made a model of the Mini, this was before it had appeared, out of Meccano. He had given me a Number Five set and insisted that I brought it with me. It wasn't transverse engined but it was front-wheel drive and it had leaf springs rather than rubber ones. I've still got parts of it. We used to run it up and down the hotel corridors and chamber maids were summoned to supply olive oil to lubricate the clockwork motor!'

In the meantime the design of the full-size Mini was nearing completion at Longbridge. How would the world receive it?

Notes

1. Campbell, Making..., *op cit.*
2. Spen King, *op cit.*
3. Peter Knight, in interview with author, 2004. Knight succeeded John Morris at SU but worked at Jaguar after the war.
4. Quoted in Malcolm McKay, The dream team, *The Daily Telegraph*, 21 September 2002.
5. The Mini Man, *op cit.*
6. Quoted in Williams, Haslam, Johal, Williams, *Cars, Analysis, History, Cases*, 1994.
7. Frank Woollard, *Principles of Mass and Flow Production, op cit.* Foreword by Sir Leonard Lord, one of the few occasions on which he publicly put pen to paper.
8. Ron Lucas, interview with author, 1997.
9. Ullyett, *op cit.*
10. Quoted in Jonathan Wood, *Wheels of Misfortune, op cit.*
11. I am grateful to Philip Turner for this story.
12. Geoffrey Rose, *op cit.*
13. Graham Turner, The Leyland Papers, *op cit.*
14. Gerald Palmer, *Auto-Architect, op cit.*
15. Christopher Balfour, *Auto-Architect*, second edition, 2004.
16. Turner, *op cit.*

17. Wood, *op cit.*
18. Quoted in Wood, MG *from A to Z*, *op cit.*
19. Lucas, *op cit.*
20. I am grateful to Christopher Balfour for this information, which is contained in a letter of 26 January 1959 to him from the University of Cambridge Appointments Board. Keen to join the British motor industry, although he was interviewed by Rootes he decided instead to pursue a career in the education service.
21. Lucas, *op cit.*
22. Jon Pressnell, Mr MG, *Classic and Sportscar*, October 1989.
23. Pomeroy, *op cit.*
24. Turner, *op cit.*
25. Campbell, Making..., *op cit.* What Henry Ford actually said during a trial in 1919 when he accused the *Chicago Tribune* of libelling him, was 'History is more or less bunk. It is tradition. We want to live in the present, and the only history that is worth a tinker's dam is the history we make today.'
26. Laurence Pomeroy, The writing on the wall, *The Motor*, 26 October 1955.
27. Barney Sharratt, *Men and Motors of 'The Austin'*, 2000.
28. Skilleter, *op cit.*
29. Palmer, *op cit.*
30. William Boddy, Matters of Moment, *Motor Sport*, September 1959.
31. Alex Moulton, *op cit.*
32. Ibid.
33. Schreier, *op cit.*
34. Pomeroy, *op cit.*
35. John Sheppard, *op cit.*
36. Turner and Curtis, *op cit.*
37. Christopher Dowson, *op cit.*
38. David Knowles, *MG The Untold Story*, 1997.
39. I am grateful to Bryan Cambray, who joined *Motor Trader* in 1946 and later became its editor, for this story.
40. Sharratt, *op cit.*
41. *The Motor*, 21 December 1955.
42. From 1960 the rendering was *Pininfarina*, following a change of its founder Battista 'Pinin' Farina's surname.
43. Quoted in Wood, Wheels, *op cit.*
44. Malcolm Axtell, *op cit.*
45. Jennifer Gilman, *op cit.*
46. Malcolm Axtell, *op cit.*
47. Christopher Dowson, *op cit.*
48. Quoted in Andrew Nahum, Alec Issigonis, obituary, *The Independent*, 5 October 1988.
49. Christopher Dowson, *op cit.*
50. Tony Rudd, *It was Fun, My 50 Years of High Performance*, 2000.
51. Ibid.
52. Raymond Mays, *The BRM Story*, 1962.
53. Jack Daniels, *op cit.*
54. Hope, *op cit.*
55. Quoted in Wood, *op cit.*
56. Robson, *op cit.*
57. Campbell, Making..., *op cit.*

58. Alex Moulton, *op cit.*
59. Turner and Curtis, *op cit.*
60. Charles Bulmer, interview with author, 2003.
61. Jonathan Wood, Alec Issigonis, *Automobile Quarterly*, Volume 40, Number 1, March 2000.
62. Barker, *Alec Issigonis*, *op cit.*
63. Campbell, Making..., *op cit.*
64. Ibid.
65. Golding, *op cit.*
66. Ibid.
67. BMC ADO 15, *Automobile Engineer*, August 1959.
68. Issigonis, Elegance..., *op cit.*
69. Ibid.
70. John Sheppard, *op cit.*
71. Ibid.
72. The Mini Man, *op cit.*
73. Issigonis, Elegance, *op cit.*
74. Ernst Gombrich, *The Story of Art*, 1950.
75. Harold Nockolds, *Lucas, the first 100 years*, Volume Two, 1978.
76. D.B. Tubbs, Parties to Design, *The Motor*, 28 August 1963.
77. Automobile Engineer, *op cit.*
78. Campbell, Making..., *op cit.*
79. Pomeroy, *The Motor*, 26 August 1959.
80. Campbell, *op cit.*
81. Geoffrey Rose, *op cit.*
82. John Sheppard, *op cit.*
83. Jack Daniels, interview, *op cit.*
84. Dave Daniels, *op cit.*
85. Campbell, *op cit.*
86. Sheppard, *op cit.*
87. Geoffrey Rose, *op cit.*
88. Lord Snowdon, interview with author, 2004.
89. Alex Moulton, *op cit.*
90. Varney, *op cit.*
91. Moulton, *op cit.*
92. Ronald Barker, *op cit.*
93. Norman Painting, *op cit.*
94. Peter Knight, *op cit.*
95. David Morris, in conversation with author, 2005.
96. Christopher Dowson, *op cit.*

BMC's catalyst for change, Citroen's futuristic front-wheel drive DS with interconnected hydropneumatic suspension attracting the crowds on its launch at the 1955 Paris Salon. (*Citroën*)

John Sheppard, who began working with Alec Issigonis at Alvis and was recruited by him to join BMC. A body engineer and a key player in the Mini project, he is seen here in September 1961 at his drawing board in A Cell at Longbridge. Behind him is the office he shared with Chris Kingham. (*John Sheppard*)

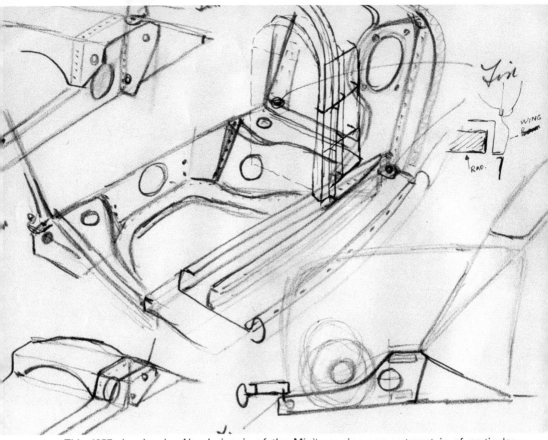

This 1957 drawing by Alec Issigonis of the Mini's engine compartment is of particular significance because it shows the structure in its original form, prior to the introduction of a front subframe required by the Moulton rubber suspension. (*Rob Golding*)

A soon to be familiar sight on Britain's roads, a 1959 Morris Mini-Minor. In September 1959 Ronald Barker and Peter Riviere, staffmen on *The Autocar*, took one of BMC's new cars on an 8,000-mile journey through Europe and North Africa. Because of a war in Tunis it had to be flown to Algeria and is here about to be loaded on board a Douglas C47 (Dakota). (*Ronald Barker*)

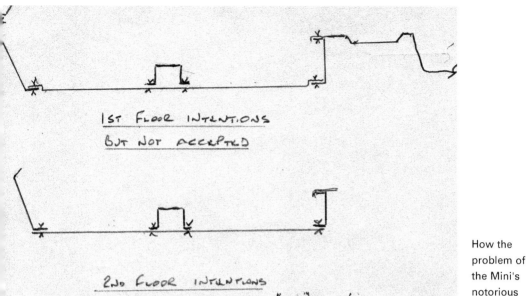

1ST FLOOR INTENTIONS
BUT NOT ACCEPTED

2ND FLOOR INTENTIONS
AS DIRECTED BY AI - "DIY" IN VOGUE
CKD KITS SUGGESTED. - ENTHUSIASTS TO BUILD
FLOOR GOES DOWN FIRST!
PROTOTYPES BUILT TO THIS CONSTRUCTION - BUT
METICULOUS SEALING APPLIED BY EXPERIMENTAL
DEPT. OBVIATED SERIOUS WATER INGRESS

AS ISSUED FOR PRODUCTION
JOINTS AT TOEBOARD & HEELBOARD
DEEMED MORE PRACTICAL - BUT
ALTHOUGH SEALER APPLIED, THIS
WAS NOT COMPLETLY SATISFACTORY
SPOT WELD HEAT CREATES DISTORTION
"GARLANDING" BETWEEN SPOTS -
SEE VIEW IN ARROW

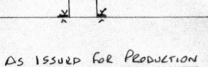

FLOOR PANEL

BEFORE WELD

TOE BOARD UNDERLAP

AFTER WELD SHOWING HEAT DISTORTION
MORE EFFICIENT & CONTROLLED SEALING INTRODUCED

How the problem of the Mini's notorious water leaks could have been avoided. This drawing, specially executed for this book by body engineer John Sheppard, shows how the original design (top) was changed by Issigonis (middle) with the final solution to the problem (bottom).

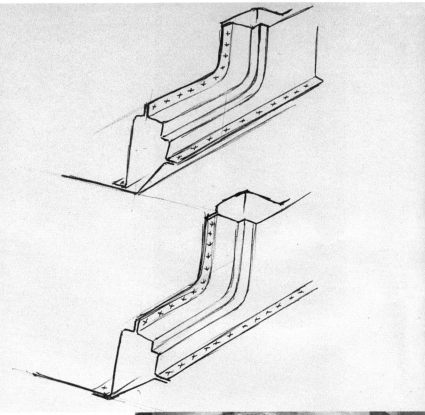

This Issigonis drawing reveals changes made to the Mini's sills demanded by modifications to the floor to counter the water leaks. The top one shows the original design in which the floor is extended to form the body's outer sill. The other reveals how the floor has been turned upwards to form an inner sill with the outer one now being a cover for it. (*Rob Golding*)

A tight squeeze but there was room in the Dakota for the Barker/Riviere Mini 667 GFC which was flown from a French airfield by Tunis Air. At the instigation of Issigonis and Laurence Pomeroy, BMC provided 68 selected motoring journalists with a Mini on an extended year-long loan. All were endowed with the same GFC Oxford registration letters and a wag suggested that this stood for Gifts for Correspondents! This example, it should be said, was returned to Longbridge. (*Ronald Barker*)

How Alec Issigonis transformed the British motoring scene in the early 1960s. The Mini belonging to the lady seeking advice from an AA patrolman can be seen behind his motorcycle. On the road a Morris Minor is followed by another Mini and Ford 100E with a further Minor about to join the traffic. Not a foreign car in sight. (*Automobile Association*)

Issigonis's Morris 1100, introduced in 1962 and Britain's best selling car for 10 years. Styled by Pininfarina, it also marked the introduction of Alex Moulton's Hydrolastic interconnected suspension. (*Author's Collection*)

12 Westbourne Gardens, Edgbaston, Birmingham, Alec Issigonis's home from 1963 until early in 1988. (Above) The double garage provided an engine shed for his model steam locomotives which departed and returned through apertures made in the outside wall. (Below) Viewed from the south, the bungalow had a pond between its two wings. The drawing room is on the right. (*Author's Collection*)

The Mini-Cooper S engine is probably the subject of this discussion at Longbridge, circa 1963. On Alec Issigonis's left is BMC's engine designer Bill Appleby, next to him is Daniel Richmond of Downton Engineering in conversation with John Cooper. Note the inevitable ashtray. (*Author's Collection*)

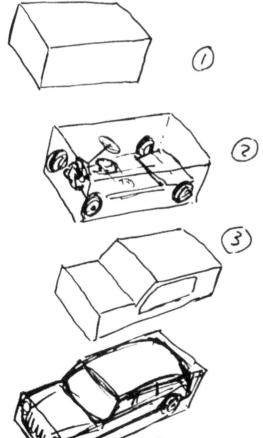

Alec Issigonis shows how the 1800's shape evolved. 1. Depicts the car's overall dimensions by the drawing of a box into which the vehicle will fit exactly. 2. The mechanical units are shown in place. 3. The body dimensions shown in rudimentary form. 4. Pininfarina now takes over to give the body form and style. (*Author's Collection*)

Sign of defiance: Alec Issigonis was a lifelong smoker, initially of Gold Flake cigarettes that he called his 'yellow perils', and also Senior Service. His companion is Gordon Wilkins of *Motor* and the photograph was taken by Edward Eves, Midland editor of *Autocar*. (*Edward Eves from Ludvigsen Library*)

The Institute of Contemporary Arts used this Issigonis rendering to publicise its exhibition of his drawings and sketches, staged in 1970. Dating from the 1960s, it may be of a stillborn open car. Note that the seat support makes a structural contribution to the sub structure. It contains Mini elements although appears to show a backbone chassis in the manner of Colin Chapman's Lotus Elan, a design which Issigonis much admired. John Sheppard, who worked with him for many years, had never seen the drawing and says that it is 'out of character for him because of cost and weight factors.' (*Paul Davies*)

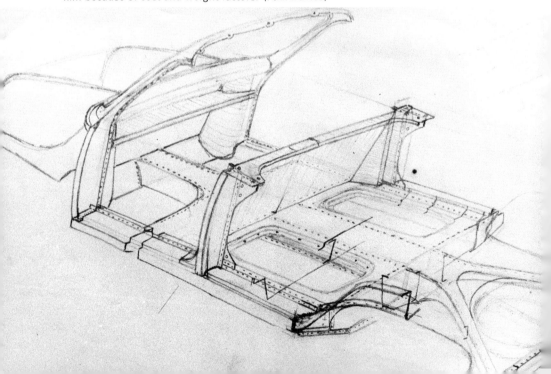

The Austin 1800's launch to the motoring press was held at the Strathgarve Hotel, Garve, Scotland in the summer of 1964. Left to right: Courtenay Edwards, motoring correspondent of the *Sunday Telegraph*, veteran motoring journalist cum rally driver Tommy Wisdom, Alec Issigonis and Alex Moulton. (*Dr Alex Moulton*)

Irrelevance: the Austin 3-litre of 1967 represented the nadir of Alec Issigonis's stewardship of BMC's technical portfolio. (*Author's Collection*)

Hot air in abundance: a balloon experiment in the hall of Issigonis's home at Westbourne Gardens, Edgbaston, circa 1969. Left to right: John Morris, Hulda Issigonis (back to camera), Alec Issigonis and vintagent Cecil Clutton. Seemingly sinking to the floor is L.T.C. 'Tom' Rolt, biographer of the Stevensons, Brunel and Telford, and brought along by Steady Barker, who took the photograph, as he had recently written a book entitled *The Balloonatics*. (*Ronald Barker*)

A study in informality. Sir Alec Issigonis photographed by Ronald Barker in the early 1970s relaxing at Westbourne Gardens with the gin and Martini that he enjoyed every evening. In the background are some of the trophies he won with the Lightweight Special. (*Ronald Barker*)

For many years Mrs Issy, Hulda Issigonis, preferred to sit on the floor rather than using a chair. However, in older age, as this photograph shows, she grew accustomed to a sofa. (*Ronald Barker*)

Alec Issigonis enjoying a convivial dinner at Motor Show time with Ronald Barker at the Hyde Park Hotel, 'my London house'. Steady makes the point that his host has started smoking before he has completed his meal! He cannot recall the date but suggests 'late 20th century.' (*Ronald Barker*)

The last production car of the Issigonis era, the Austin Maxi of 1969 created by BMC but launched in 1969, following its takeover by Leyland. An all new model, its 1800 doors excepted, with bespoke engine and gearbox, it never attained its manufacturer's expectations. (*Author's Collection*)

An artist's impression of 9X, a study in simplicity both outside and in. The lines are angular and lack the curvature so apparent in the Mini. It clearly demonstrates Issigonis's ongoing commitment to a wheel-at-each-corner. (John Bilton)

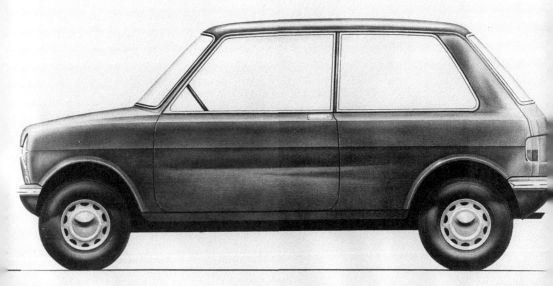

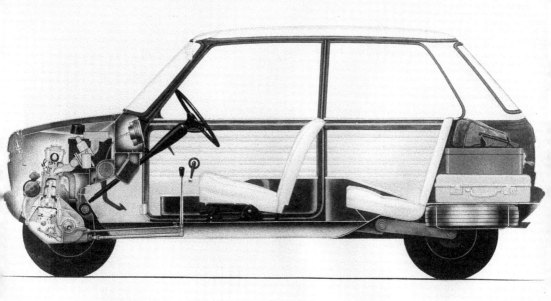

9X X-rayed, which shows the small amount of space taken up by its bespoke single overhead camshaft engine and transmission. This version is shown with wind-up windows although sliding ones featured on the second of the two built. (*John Bilton*)

The first page of a two page note by Alec Issigonis to Spen King showing a strut front suspension for the Mini in which he writes 'in our little shop we are trying to develop a new car around the existing Mini body shell –The gearless concept came as a result of this.' (*Spen King*)

John Bilton's daughter, Hannah, at the wheel of the Gearless Mini with her sister Kirsty in 1978. The simplicity of the forward/reverse control on the right will be apparent. (*John Bilton*)

Hindon Square, Edgbaston, Sir Alec Issigonis's last home, which he occupied for the last months of his life in 1988. Number 39 is the ground floor flat to the left of the entrance. (*Author*)

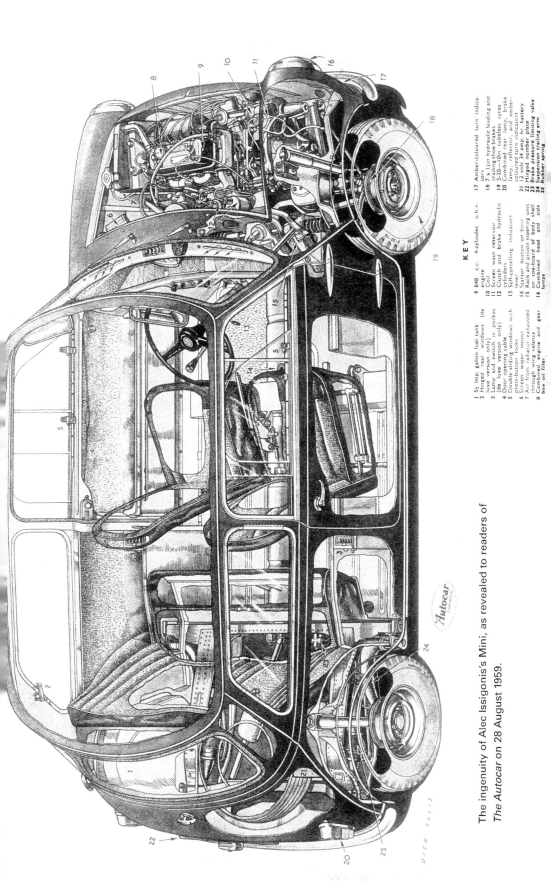

The ingenuity of Alec Issigonis's Mini, as revealed to readers of *The Autocar* on 28 August 1959.

KEY

1 5¼ Imp. gallon fuel tank
2 Hinged rear windows (de luxe version only)
3 Lamp and switch in pocket (de luxe version only)
4 Door opening cable
5 Double sliding windows with press-button locks
6 Screen wiper motor
7 Air from radiator exhausted through wing valance
8 Combined engine and gear box oil filler

9 848 c.c. 4-cylinder, o.h.v. engine
10 Coil
11 Screen wash reservoir
12 Clutch and brake hydraulic cylinders
13 Self-cancelling indicators
14 Starter button on floor
15 Rack and pinion steering unit on toe-board of body shell
16 Combined head and side lamps

17 Amber-coloured turn indicators
18 7 × 1⅛in hydraulic leading and trailing-shoe brakes
19 5·20—10in tubeless tyres
20 Combined rear lamp, brake lamp, reflector, and amber-coloured turn indicators
21 12 volt 34 amp. hr. battery
22 Hinged number plate
23 Brake pressure limiting valve
24 Suspension trailing arm
25 Rubber spring

DICK ELLIS

Alec Issigonis at Longbridge pictured by Maxwell Boyd, an accomplished photographer and motoring correspondent for *The Sunday Times*. (*National Motor Museum*)

Chapter Eight

THE MAKING
OF THE MINI

'We will never change the shape. Hope to make three or four million detail improvements.'
Alec Issigonis

ALEC ISSIGONIS wrote these words in his own copy of *The Mini Story* written by his friend Laurence Pomeroy and published in 1964. By this time the Mini had been in production for five years and, such was its sales success, that in 1965 the millionth example was completed. The Morris Minor, by contrast, had taken 12 years to attain the same figure. But the Mini was destined to suffer the same evolutionary fate, namely lack of development, initially because its creator believed that refinements were unnecessary, and latterly because of the parlous financial state of its manufacturer.

From the outset Leonard Lord was determined that the model would not want for the latest production facilities, certainly as far as the manufacture of its body was concerned, and in March 1957, when Issigonis was given the green light to proceed with the car, he also gave approval for investment in new plant. Geoffrey Rose remembers, 'Alec was very interested in how his baby was to be built. Our task was to produce the production facilities. We were told to tool up for 3,000 a week. Fisher and Ludlow at Castle Bromwich, which BMC had taken over in 1953, was then the main manufacturing unit for body panels, especially the floor pan and doors. But it was then decided to build a completely new pressings plant for the Mini because we realised the new technique for producing body panels was the transfer press, just like the transfer machines in CAB 1 for cylinder blocks. In other words it was a continuous process.'[1]

BMC was not allowed to build at Longbridge. It was then government policy that manufacturers were only able to expand in areas of high unemployment. 'Our only way to build extra factory capacity was in South Wales, across the road from the Steel Company of Wales's rolling mill at Llanelli. I went down there and chose a greenfield site, alongside the existing Morris factory which was making exhaust pipes. It was an entirely new high volume production process, receiving sheet steel in roll form and feeding it into a line of presses. What emerged at the end were completely finished doors or floors. We decided to get the best available in the world and that meant Ford expertise in America. It had a pressing plant at Chicago Heights and Llanelli was a half-scale model. The chap imported to run it was the retired press shop manager from that factory. The pressings were delivered directly by train into the Longbridge sidings and most of the rest of the body was made at Fisher and Ludlow and then came together at the West Works. Once production began engines and transmissions came from Morris's engines plant at Coventry with the front suspension and rear suspension supplied by Wolseley in Birmingham.' Rose recognises that 'in retrospect it really was not a very efficient way of building a motor car.'

About halfway through the construction of the Llanelli factory he received instructions 'that we had to double production, to 6,000 a week. This made the Mini the largest volume BMC car, comparable to the 1100, that worked up to about 5,500.'

Birmingham-based Nuffield Metal Products supplied bodies to Cowley, the Mini being assembled there until 1969 when the arrival of the Austin Maxi required that it would thereafter be solely produced at Longbridge. Peter Tothill, who in 1955 had transferred from the experimental department to production, recalls[2] that 'at the end of 1957 my boss, Leslie Ford, summoned me and said that I was to do the production engineering for a revolutionary model, ADO 15. He took me over the E Paint Shop and showed me a vacant area of concrete, saying "that's where you are going to build it."' Once assembly began about 15 Minis were being completed every hour on two shifts.

'I had to do a strip and rebuild of a prototype, number three as it happened, and during a surveillance of the drawings I picked up a dimensional error between the body and subframe attachment points. Much later I was accosted by Issigonis when he told me that I was responsible for putting the cost of the Mini up "by a whole shilling". He was not interested in my explanation, that it was the fault of the body and chassis engineers for not talking to one another. In the end he used to ignore me altogether.'

Another more serious problem later emerged in the assembly process, which related to the steering rack fouling the rear cross member of the front subframe. 'Reporting the situation to Les Ford, we realised we were in for a major confrontation. It was decided to involve Longbridge production engineering and Harold Cross came down for a demonstration that was set up for a Friday. This was the day Issigonis came to Cowley, he was still living in Oxford and returned for the weekends. Jack Daniels was there as well.

'We did a demonstration and started a discussion. Issigonis took the stance "I have designed it. It is your problem of how you put it together but you can't alter anything." Then Harold Cross, in his broad Birmingham accent, said "Mr Issigonis, you leave Leslie and myself with no alternative but to report to our respective directors on Monday that this car cannot be built at either Longbridge or Cowley."

'There was a silence for what seemed about half an hour, although it was probably only a minute. Jack Daniels fiddled with his pipe. The ball was fair and square in Issigonis's court. We were standing in a semicircle and all he did was to turn to Jack, with his back to the rest of us, and said "you'd better do what they want" and stalked off. He didn't reply to us.'[3]

In due course the pre-production problems in both factories were overcome. The Longbridge line started on 4 April 1959 and Cowley came on stream on 9 May. Jack Daniels drove a pre-production Mini to the British Grand Prix, held at Aintree on 18 July, and 'incredibly it was hardly noticed,' only generating 'amused interest.'[4]

The launch was held at the Fighting Vehicles Research and Development Establishment (FVRDE) at Chobham, Surrey, on Tuesday and Wednesday 18 and 19 August for the British and foreign press respectively. The public had to wait until Wednesday 26, which was publication day for *The Motor*. Here the hand of

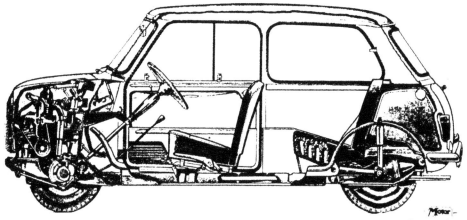

A triumph of packaging, the compactness of the transverse engine allowed Issigonis to make the Mini a genuine four-seater, despite an overall length of just 10ft.025ins. (*Autocar*)

Laurence Pomeroy is surely apparent? It wrote of a car that possessed 'a standard of road-holding and steering much more akin to a racing car than the popular conception of a family saloon.' Devotees of the magazine's *Autocar* rival had to wait a further two days to read about what it hailed as 'an outstanding and original small car,' that 'bristled with originality, yet there is nothing remotely freakish about it.'[5]

Six weeks later, readers of that magazine were able to read of the exploits of staff men Ronald Barker and Peter Riviere, who undertook an incident-filled 8,000-mile journey through Europe and North Africa in a Morris Mini-Minor. The car, fully loaded and weighing some 18.5cwt, behaved well throughout, apart from a problem with a rear suspension bracket that was soon repaired.

It had been Riviere's idea and Barker 'went up to see Issigonis, I'd met him before but never got to know him, he showed us all over the car.'[6] This paved the way for a friendship of some 25 years standing that was to endure until Issigonis's death in 1988. Barker still remembers his friend's distinctive telephone manner. 'When he rang, there'd be a little cough, and Issigonis would say, 'er, Steady,' like Morse Code.'

Alec Issigonis was on the stand at the 1959 Motor Show when he found himself in conversation with 'a famous politician... who asked me... how do you get the pipe [propeller shaft] down to the back wheels?'[7] In that interview he was tactful enough not to mention the individual's name, but it was none other than the Rt Hon Ernest Marples, one-time chartered accountant and the newly appointed Minister of Transport. He subsequently became a Mini owner and had his Cooper S converted at Longbridge to progressively incorporate a tailgate.

The cars were only initially available in varying shades of patriotic red, white and blue livery, depending on whether they were Austin or Morris versions. But the most startling element of the Mini was its price. BMC proclaimed it as: '... a real breakthrough in automobile production... and yet it *is one of the lowest priced cars in the world.*'[8] (Author's italics.) Available in two guises, the Austin version was marketed as the Se7en, in recognition of the high regard which Issigonis had for the Longbridge baby. In fact the original name, incredibly, was Newmarket, but then someone said, 'it's a long name for a big car,' and Se7en was used instead. At the time of its launch Mini was confined to the Morris variant, the Mini-Minor, drawing parallels with the Issigonis-designed Minor, still very much in production.

When the Morris began to outsell the Austin, pressure from distributors resulted in the Se7en name being discontinued, and from 1962 it was replaced by that of plain Mini. Standard cars sold in 1959 for £497, the basic price being £350, plus £147 purchase tax, although the De Luxe, enhanced with wheel trims and opening rear quarter lights, cost £537. Amazingly the standard cars were to be reduced even further in price and in October 1962 this was slashed to an all-time low of £448 with the De Luxe being cut by £2 to £535.

It should be made clear that Issigonis played no part in arriving at these figures, having little interest in or comprehension of such things. However, the Mini's pricing was to have ramifications not only for BMC but also the entire British motor industry. To give this figure some perspective, at the same 1959 Earls Court event where the Mini made its show debut, Ford announced its new impeccably costed, no-frills ultra-orthodox front-engine/rear-drive 105E Anglia, with its distinctive inclined rear window. Even in standard form it sold for £589, which was £92 more than the basic Mini, undoubtedly the most sophisticated small car in the world.

How had BMC achieved this astounding price? In the opinion of Ron Lucas, it was the product of an accounting system that hadn't changed much since Herbert Austin arrived at Longbridge in pre-World War One days. And the Corporation's lack of marketing experience, indeed its collective disdain for the subject, was reflected by the fact that the Mini was priced to occupy the position hitherto the preserve of Ford's archaic Popular, which was to cease production in 1959. It was as diametrically opposed to the Mini as it was possible to imagine, with crude Model T-inspired mechanicals dating from 1933. The cheapest four-seater British car on the market, it sold for £494. The Mini even undercut the Isetta 600 bubble car by £142 which, together with the three-wheeler Heinkel and Messerschmitt, lingered on until the mid-1960s. Their days had gone, not so much defeated by BMC's baby but by the improving economies of Britain and Germany.

'George Harriman would have decided the Mini's price and one of the key figures in the decision was Harry Williams, a cost accountant, who was very close to Syd Wheeler,' recalls Geoffrey Rose.[9] 'Both Len Lord and George Harriman thought to some extent "volume will deal with it". It's on the basis that you make cars all the week until Thursday afternoon and Friday is when all the overheads have been covered and you make the profit. Sad to say, it came down to the sheer arrogance of "we're BMC, we know what we're doing." But Alec would have been completely outside the pricing process. In some board meetings that I attended I used to have to help him through the balance sheet, through the figures.'

The final decision would, of course, have rested with BMC chairman Sir Leonard Lord. As John Thornley has observed: 'Len had the habit of being rather more right than he was wrong. Even if it was only 51 percent to 49 percent, if you pursue that line for long enough it begins to show.'[10] Nevertheless, in pricing the Mini, Lord had been faced with a dilemma. Although Issigonis had built his 'charwoman's car' its mechanical sophistication, unusual appearance and, above all front-wheel drive had a questionable reputation in the eyes of the British motorist. He therefore reasoned that, if the Mini's price was set too high, the car would not sell. As a production engineer, his principal objective was to maintain as high volumes as possible for BMC and this would have demanded the lowest price the company could bear.

Clearly the sub-£500 figure cannot have borne any real relationship to the car's true manufacturing cost and in truth most people opted for the De Luxe versions at £40 more. By 1962 they accounted for 91 percent of sales. Yet even at this price the Mini was still barely viable.

Just 14 months after the model's announcement, Leonard Lord retired as BMC's chairman, yet his arbitrary decision was to have dire consequences for BMC. Ford wasted little time in obtaining a Mini, which was scrutinised by its Product Planning department, set up in 1953 at the behest of its American parent. It was born of a recognition that a company's chief executive could no longer, by a combination of hunch and whim, be responsible for future model programmes, an approach exemplified by BMC's Leonard Lord. Ford's planning department was headed by graduate recruit Terence Beckett, an economist and engineer, who recalls that when the Mini came out it highjacked Ford's traditional marketplace slot as producer of the cheapest car on the market.

'I can remember in one month in 1960, the Mini achieved a 19 percent market penetration. That was just one model.'[11] Ford duly purchased an example, stripped it down to the spot welds and discovered BMC was losing around £30 on every car it made. 'I could see ways in which we could take cost of the Mini without in any way reducing its sales appeal.' Beckett also found that 'BMC could have priced it at £30 more and not lost any sales at all.'

When in 1963 Terence Beckett was promoted his place was taken by Frank Harris, who undertook a detailed inquiry into BMC's finances and came to the inescapable conclusion that the Corporation was heading for bankruptcy. On its completion Ford's chairman, Sir Patrick Hennessy, telephoned George Harriman to point out that BMC was underpricing its products to the extent that its profits would be seriously eroded.[12] This information was not given through any sense of altruism but purely because Ford was having to match them, to the detriment of its own profits.

This was at least the second occasion on which Ford had informed Harriman of the errors of BMC's ways. In 1960 Ford's assistant managing director, Allan Barke, a veteran of the demanding environment of the corporate purchasing department, had told him that it was not possible for BMC to be making any money on the Mini. Harriman's Delphic response to this revelation was 'the product will push the price.'[13] Here the inference was that, if sufficient numbers of people bought the car, the equation would emerge on the plus side. In truth the more people that bought the Mini the greater were the Corporation's losses.

Ford was right. Although it was widely assumed that by 1968 the Mini was making a modest profit of about £15 a car, in 1977 Colin Daniels, finance director of its successor, Leyland Cars, found that 'accounting methods at the time could not have given an accurate picture for too often cars were invoiced on the recommended sales price rather than at the price for which they were actually sold.'[14]

When tackled on the subject in 1978 Issigonis defended the price and responded that other manufacturers had 'all proved themselves wrong by doing their own front-wheel drive cars. It depends on the number you make and on the initial design.'[15] What he did not say was that while practically all other car companies adopted the Mini's transverse engine, they did not imitate its suspension and gearbox-in-sump configuration. They were steel sprung and adopted an end-on gearbox of the type pioneered by Fiat in 1964. And so, in due course, did BMC's Rover descendant, but that would not be until 1983 when the Austin Maestro became the first Longbridge-designed car to be so enhanced. Little wonder that the motor industry aphorism of 'mini cars make mini profits' was born.

It was much the same story at BMC throughout the 1960s as model after model was underpriced, a significant factor in it recording a loss in 1967. Its successors, British Leyland, Leyland Cars and BL Cars, inherited a deeply flawed accounting system and prime minster Margaret Thatcher had recourse to draw on the accountancy training of her chief whip, John Wakeham, in trying to comprehend the by then nationalised BL's figures. These she described as 'elliptical.'

One of the British motor industry's better kept secrets[16] is that even in the era of Michael Edwardes chairmanship in 1977–1982, Ford secretly loaned BL Cars its financial analysts. Their work was executed under the cover of darkness and was required to bring some sense of order to the company's still chaotic accounting procedures.

Even priced as it was, the Mini was initially a slow starter although the Queen bought one in October 1959 right at the beginning of production, and went for a short drive in Windsor Great Park in her blue Mini, accompanied by a delighted Alec Issigonis. Later a doorless Beach Car variant joined the royal stable.

The Mini was to benefit from other royal connections when Alec Issigonis's friend, Antony Armstrong-Jones, became an influential and enthusiastic owner. Indeed he was presented with a cream-coloured car as a wedding present by BMC, prior to the announcement in February 1960 of his impending marriage to the Queen's sister, Princess Margaret. Issigonis made the delivery to Clarence

House personally and his friends at the Trout at Godstow were to hear of the pleasure it gave him. 'He was thrilled to have met Princess Margaret,' remembers Jennifer Gilman.[17]

Lord Snowdon recalls that he had 'owned about three Minis. I had a marvellous one but I lent it to my secretary and she took a wrong turning down the motorway... They often went back to Longbridge and Alec was always tinkering around with them for me to make them go faster. One was lovely, racing green with a little green line around it.

'I did put a wind-up window in one and it went back to BMC but was returned with the sliding one reinstated. I said "Alec, what are you doing. I wanted a nice wind-up one." His response was that it would have been "bad for the Princess's hair." In fact he was very keen on air circulation. Everyone smoked in those days and his windows got rid of all that cigarette smoke.'[18]

Issigonis's recollection of these early days was that, 'people said "what's that thing?" The reception was bad. Then *to our horror* we discovered that rich and intelligent people bought it first.'[19] (Author's italics.) In fact demand built up very soon in 1960 although his imaginary troop of Mrs Mopps and their families appeared unimpressed by the most advanced small car in the world. If they had bought a new one, it would have probably been Ford's new, no-nonsense Anglia. In a contradictory, provocative statement of the sort he delighted in making, the Mini's creator was to later declare: 'what could be worse than a suburban housewife with money. They are so stupid – they buy Fords. Some are intelligent – they buy Minis.'[20]

In 1959, the first year of production, just 19,749 examples of BMC's new baby were completed. Any new model is likely to experience teething troubles but during the winter of 1959 and 1960 rain was found to reach the internals of the exposed distributor and this problem was cured relatively quickly. A more serious shortcoming was that Mini owners found rain water entering their cars through the floor. Mouldy, stale-smelling carpets became an undesirable by-product of ownership. Press officer Norman Milne, who was deputy to Tony Dawson, recalls driving back to Longbridge in pouring rain up the newly opened M1 in a Mini after the 1959 Motor Show. 'I had piles of press releases on board on the floor in the back that were ruined. The car had filled to the gunwales with water.'[21]

The truth, however, was that the water problem was foreseen from the day the floor was designed. Issigonis was forewarned of the problem but he chose not to address it. In later years he would claim that 'there was no rain in 1959, it was a great drought until September and the thing was just not discovered. The water problem was terrible but it only came out in production. I had to redesign the floor to solve the problem and I leapt at the chance.'[22]

The truth was rather different. John Sheppard, who laid out the original floor, 'was aware of the problem from day one. But Issigonis didn't want the floor designed in the traditional way and changed it because, he said, "my boy, these are the days of DIY, people buy kits. And the first thing they put down is the floor. I'll draw it for you."' For DIY read CKD, the abbreviation for Completely Knocked Down, which related to the kits BMC supplied to its overseas subsidiaries. 'What happened was that heat made the joint billow, there were gaps between the spot welds but there wouldn't have been any if it had been designed in the traditional way.'[23]

Peter Tothill recounts[24] that by the time the body reached the production stage 'it was well known that James Percival, the body engineering director at Fisher and Ludlow, who was a competent and forceful character, said that they could not seal certain joints in the sheet metal structure. He presented alternative methods but these were rejected.'

Despite these much publicised problems, demand for the Mini began to increase and in 1960 it emerged as BMC's most popular car, with 116,677 examples built, some 23,000 more than the Morris Minor. And thereafter production increased inexorably. The half million mark was passed in 1962 and the two millionth Mini was built in 1969. Production would not peak until 1971 when 318,475 examples were completed worldwide.

It says much for the popularity of the Mini that in 1964 The Temple Press, publisher of *Motor*, released *The Mini Story*, written by the magazine's former technical editor, Laurence Pomeroy. On paper 'Pom' was an ideal choice. He had known Issigonis since 1931 and had been able to observe the model's rapid gestation from a unique vantage point. The book is an excellent read but it has to be said that although Pomeroy was an outstanding technical journalist, that qualification did not necessarily make him a good historian. The published text followed important revisions by Issigonis; he had been supplied with a proof copy which survives. It includes the following statement, made in his own hand: 'Having established design concept available to the public – we never intended to change this image by bigger car etc such as stupid developments tend to do [sic!]'.

Charles Griffin[25] believed that an error made at the outset of Mini production was that no systemic development programme was implemented. 'Our sin, I believe, is that we sat on the Mini like eggs for too long. [Issigonis] was like a proud father, one of the worst, for saying "it's perfect, don't change anything, just build them properly."'

One of the friendships Alec Issigonis cemented during these years was with the actor, film star, playwright and car enthusiast Peter Ustinov, who in 1964 recalled their first meeting. This had probably taken place in 1957 'at a dinner... and I said to him "Why does nobody think of putting the engine across the car?" He went white as a sheet and changed the subject.' Ustinov would not hear from him again until just prior to the Mini's appearance. At that point Issigonis telephoned 'and said "now we can have lunch. I was so frightened there had been a leak." I was very flattered and since then he's always allowed me to come and try his machines before they come on to the market.'[26]

Driving the Mini before its announcement, 'I was besotted with admiration as I stepped out of it on that windswept [Chalgrove] aerodrome near Oxford. But to qualify my enjoyment of it, I did say that the gear lever felt like a brush which had been left too long in a pot of glue. Alec laughed until the tears dislodged themselves from his blue eyes and ran down the craggy cheeks. "I can't wait to tell them" he said.' To Ustinov 'the Mini had a character which is exactly like his. It has a look with its headlights of innocence at the same time of extreme sophistication and of a slight inability to grow up, a sort of Peter Pan quality.'[27]

When Issigonis spoke,[28] it was 'with the elegance of somebody from the 18th century, he chose his words very carefully and there was always a slightly moralising tone, which perhaps came from Mum.' But 'they were extremely graceful and always delivered with a look of surprise on his face.

'It has been a very valuable friendship, for me at any rate. Like anyone in the arts or the sciences, Alec is very keen to know what is going on in parallel streams of consciousness at the same time. If he's not very interested in the theatre he is interested in being entertained, and he's interested in talking.'[29] Doreen Schreier remembers[30] that 'he and Peter Ustinov got on very well because, like Issigonis, he wasn't English but a unique personality who was more English than the English. He would always call in on the rare occasions he was in the area.'

During the BMC years, which lasted until 1968, the Mini spawned a host of derivatives. The first variant, a van with a longer wheelbase, arrived in June 1960 and sold for a bargain price of £360, because no purchase tax was payable on commercial vehicles. Although ostensibly intended for small businesses, the van's price made it immensely popular with the impecunious young. Enterprising firms were soon marketing side windows and rear seats to improve the vehicle's rather austere specifications. Indeed my own introduction to Mini motoring was travelling in or driving friends' vans.

For 1961 came its first cousin, the similarly elongated Countryman estate car version which was also available with timber enhancement, echoing its Morris Minor contemporary. A Mark II version of the Mini, fitted with the interconnected Hydrolastic suspension originally intended for it, appeared for the 1965 season. It will come as no surprise to find that Issigonis responded to the utilitarian Jeep-like Moke, produced experimentally for the army in 1959 but rejected on the grounds of its lack of ground clearance and offered for public sale in 1964.

One Mini variant that the public never saw was ADO 19, the four-wheel drive Ant, an acronym of 'Alec's New Toy,' a cross-country variant like a miniature Land Rover. But that make became in-house with the creation of British Leyland and it scuppered the project. By then 24 experimental versions had been produced. Theoretically there was more potential for profitability in two up-market variants in the shape of two badge engineered Minis, namely the Riley Elf and Wolseley Hornet, which appeared for the 1962 season and sold for £694 and £672 respectively. Stylistically the work of Dick Burzi, they flew in the face of the Issigonis creed by featuring extended boots and enhanced interiors and thus weighed about 1cwt more than the originals. But the public stayed away and each was destined to sell a mere 30,000 or so examples before being discontinued in 1969. There was no MG version because of the unexpected arrival, in 1961, of the much more successful Mini-Cooper, on which more anon, a model that transformed the model's appeal in a way in which its creator had never envisaged.

In May 1963, a rival to the Mini appeared in the form of the 875cc Hillman Imp, the Rootes Group's first small car. It will be recalled that when Alec Issigonis worked for that company, B.B. Winter had taken over charge of car design and he continued to exercise his ultra-conservative approach to engineering until he eventually retired in 1959. His place was taken by Peter Ware, a veteran of the ill-fated Fedden project. Under his regime the technological pendulum swung dramatically in the opposing direction and Rootes engineers and Mini owners, Mike Parkes and Tim Fry, were responsible for the Imp, an all-new car powered by a rear-located – the cheapest place to position it – but sophisticated aluminium overhead camshaft engine.

Its appearance came as no surprise to Issigonis as he was a friend of both engineers. Parkes was the son of Alvis's chairman John Parkes, who had combined car design with a formidable ability as a racing driver. In 1958 he had taken the wheel of the Fry-Climax, built by his colleague's cousin, David, he of Freikaiserwagen fame, a stressed skin mid-engined Formula 2 car in which Alec Issigonis is have said to have had an unofficial hand. As a member of the Fry family Tim had also known Issigonis for many years. Although secrecy was paramount, every month or so during the Mini's gestation he and Alex Moulton would have supper with the Rootes duo,[31] although both parties were sworn to secrecy as far as their respective projects were concerned. As Fry later remembered it 'we all wanted to talk about cars, but we knew we couldn't say very much!'

Rootes, in any event, knew all about ADO 15 and, on one occasion, Fry 'promptly sketched a Mini suspension arm.'[32] Subsequently, they all met up at Issigonis's local pub, the Trout, prior to the Imp's introduction. The two Rootes engineers arrived in a prototype Imp and Fry could not resist handing Alec the keys. The latter's verdict, after a drive, was 'absolutely brilliant, but you've got it the wrong way around!' Issigonis was more candid when discussing the Imp with Christopher Dowson, who recalls[33] that 'he detested the Hillman Imp but he loved [sic] Mike Parkes.'

In 1962 Parkes had left Rootes to join Ferrari as a development engineer. As such, with the *Commendatore's* approval, and with Parkes by his side, Issigonis was able to drive the latest Ferrari sports racers. He had fond memories of having attained 186mph on the Modena to Bologna road at the wheel of the last front-engined Le Mans car.

Mike Parkes was also a reserve Ferrari driver, achieved great success in Formula 1 and subsequently joined in-house Lancia to oversee the development of its Stratos rally car. Tragically he was killed in a road accident in torrential rain at the wheel of a Lancia Beta on 28 August 1977 at the age of 45. At the time of his death he was engaged to be married to Christopher Dowson's sister Penny.

Ingenious as it was, the Imp, which inherited no carries-over from previous models, had the misfortune to be produced at a brand new factory at Linwood, Scotland, a combination which proved a recipe for disaster. The small Hillman's best selling year was 1964 when 69,420, about a quarter of the Mini's rate, were produced, but thereafter demand began to drop away for it proved to be a troublesome baby and early examples were accordingly plagued with reliability problems. Its reputation never recovered and, in consequence, never presented a real threat to the Mini. Indeed its failure was a factor in the American Chrysler Corporation taking an interest in Rootes in 1964, which was consolidated by an outright takeover in 1967. The Imp survived until 1976, after some 440,000 had been completed.

In the meantime the Mini range was continuing to expand. BMC had offered a De Luxe version from the very outset, which by Issigonis's standards was still fairly basic, although a Super Mini followed for the 1963 season and a Super De Luxe for the 1964 model year. But the 'rich and intelligent' who, to Issigonis's horror, had started buying the car, clearly wanted something even better. In the vanguard of this movement was the film star Peter Sellers, a self-confessed car enthusiast and then at the height of his fame. Quite what its creator thought of Sellers likening him in 1979 to being 'as clever as Inspector Clouseau. He had a suspicion that all the best things came in little boxes'[34] is not recorded but Sellers made a more serious point when he wrote that 'for thousands of us who had to get around London quickly, the arrival of the Mini was like the answer to a prayer.'

The first of Sellers's cars, completed in May 1963, was a Morris Mini-Cooper, enhanced by Hooper and outwardly distinguished by the application of canework to the lower part of the body and a better paint finish. The interior featured a walnut veneer dashboard and door cappings, electric windows and leather trimmed seats. Lord Snowdon remembers that 'Alec hated Peter Sellers's Mini, it contained so many of the things of which he disapproved that Peter, bless his heart, had added.'[35]

Others were to follow with coachbuilder Harold Radford pursuing the Sellers market with its own conversion, along with Wood and Pickett, which was also to produce an customised version for his wife Britt Ekland. Sellers's customised Mini was to spawn many imitators and these conversions were, of course, initiated by individuals.

Of much greater significance was a more potent version of the model, namely the Cooper, although if it had been left to Alec Issigonis this most successful and potentially profitable of Mini derivatives would never have been built. This underlines his disregard and indeed disinterest in corporate finances, resisting the model because it departed from his basic concept. But the astounding road-holding bequeathed to the car by its front-wheel drive meant that it had a considerable potential for use on road and race track.

It will be recalled that in its experimental 948cc form, Mini prototypes had been capable of over 90mph and the capacity of the engine was accordingly reduced for production. Thereafter Issigonis resisted the development of a faster version. An MG-badged Mini made strong marketing sense and in April 1959, four months before the model's launch, Abingdon began work on EX 220, designated a 'New Midget based on Sputnik FWD,' visually related to the as yet unannounced MGB and from which sprang the experimental ADO 34. This was dismissed by Issigonis as 'a dreadful thing,' telling Wilson McComb, editor of the in-house MG Car Club magazine, *Safety Fast*, 'you only like it because it was designed at Abingdon.'[36] In 1960 Longbridge began work on further versions and a Pininfarina-styled 1966 rendering bears a striking similarity to the Peugeot 204 Cabriolet.

The reason for his antipathy to the Mini-based concept was, according to Charles Griffin, because both Issigonis 'and I always believed that sports cars should be rear-wheel drive. Sir Alec used to say that in order to have fun in driving – an essential ingredient in a sports car – two steering systems were necessary, one of which was worked with the right foot!'[37] Nevertheless, George Harriman sanctioned production of the Mini-Cooper, against the wishes of his technical director.

The origins of his antipathy to a faster version of the Mini were rooted in the car's conception. Alex Moulton makes the point that 'Issigonis, which was very much in the character of the man, made a complete diktat that the car must have the utmost qualities of road holding which he had pioneered in the Morris Minor. I remember him saying that the Mini had so much capacity that it would be filled up with students, therefore it must always be safe handling. The origin of the car was safety.'[38]

Nevertheless, there were compelling reasons for producing what emerged as the Mini-Cooper. Because BMC could charge considerably more for the car, some £150 above the price of the mainstream model, here at last was the potential for producing that elusive machine, a profitable Mini, although whether this objective was achieved must remain open to question. It was also destined to provide the Corporation with a trio of Monte Carlo Rally wins that can only have accelerated sales of the mainstream models.

In all some 145,000 examples of all types of Mini-Cooper would be built in the 10 years between 1961 and 1971, yet it was only due to John Cooper's persistence, and his stature and diplomacy, that the Mini-Cooper was produced at all.

Back in the summer of 1959 when BMC's Competition Department, established by John Thornley at MG's Abingdon factory in 1954, began to receive its first Minis, initially the model's potential went unrecognised. Peter Browning, who was to become BMC Competitions Manager in 1967, recalled that there was 'no wild enthusiasm for the car.'[39] Indeed, shop foreman Doug Watts refused 'to borrow it to go down to the local bank because he did not wish to be seen 'in such an insignificant little car.'

Probably the first person to recognise the Mini's performance potential was Daniel Richmond of Downton Engineering Works, which took its name from its location in the village of Downton, near Salisbury, Wiltshire. His background was unusual for such a specialist, in that it was a privileged one. He was the only son of Sir Daniel Richmond, formerly of the Indian Forest Service, and his mother was the daughter of Sir James Davy, KGB. Young Daniel married the Hon. Veronica Romer, universally known as Bunty, who was the niece of the author Somerset Maugham, and their domestic arrangements were somewhat unconventional in that their bull terrier used to sleep at the bottom of the bed, inside the sheets! Ronald Barker recalls[40] that D.B. 'Bunny' Tubbs of *Motor*, noted for his erudition and wit, dubbed the couple 'Dante and Buniel,' a reference to Dante, the 13th-century Florentine poet, and Beatrice, his inspirational spouse.

In 1947, when he was only 23, Daniel Richmond took over a business which had previously specialised in agricultural engineering and switched the emphasis to such illustrious pre-war cars as Bentleys, Lagondas and Rolls-Royces. Although possessing 'some engineering training'[41] he had acquired in the aircraft industry, Richmond was a painstaking, inspirational engineer who had first encountered the BMC A Series in a Morris Minor owned by a Rolls-Royce customer. Immediately recognising it as 'streets ahead' of any other road engine, together with Hungarian refugee Janos Odor who arrived in 1958, they built up a thriving tuning and conversion business geared to the ubiquitous small four.

The work was undertaken in conditions of near-surgical cleanliness, and indeed it was rumoured that Daniel cleaned engines with gin! While he provided the business's engineering brains, finances were the responsibility of his formidable wife, who used to type all the company's correspondence on an Imperial typewriter of 1927 vintage. This was borne of necessity, because of Daniel's professed lack of interest in cash, unless it was to keep him supplied with the bottle of Mirabelle spirit that he kept readily to hand on his desk.

When the Mini, complete with its A Series engine, appeared Richmond wasted little time in improving his own car, registered UHR 850. In January 1960, just three months after the Mini's arrival, Downton announced that it would modify a customer's Mini for £39, or supply a kit for £33 which consisted of a reworked cylinder head, complete with twin carburettors and special inlet manifold.

This is to anticipate events, because the Mini was also to find its form on the racing circuits of Britain. Music teacher Christabel Carlisle, who was to make her name at the wheel of her Mini CMC 77, remembered that when the car first appeared in competition, 'it was greeted with uproarious laughter from everyone. This was reduced to quiet chuckles when the crowd noticed how fast the car went round corners and changed yet again to gaping amazement when it began to pass larger vehicles on the straight, round bends and at every conceivable point where it could squeeze by.'[42]

Such responses had not escaped the attention of John Cooper, whose mid-engined Cooper-Climax cars had won the newly introduced Formula 1 Constructors' Championship in 1959, the second occasion on which a British car had been so acclaimed, the first being Vanwall's triumph in the inaugural 1958 listing. The Cooper team, based in Surbiton, Surrey, run by the blunt, belligerent Charles and his even-tempered and personable son John, was to repeat its success in 1960.

It will be recalled that John Cooper had known Issigonis since they had both competed in hillclimbs in the early post-war years, he in the 500cc rear-engined cars that were to make the Cooper name famous and Alec in the Lightweight Special. And while it was successfully pursuing Formula 1, Cooper was continuing with its smaller racers, a line that was transformed, in 1959, into the Formula Junior series. Unlike the Coventry Climax-engined Grand Prix cars, these single-seaters were powered by front located units and the regulations stipulated that these be limited to a capacity of 1 litre and that a minimum of 1,000 had to have been manufactured.

This led John Cooper to the BMC A Series unit and the Corporation was pleased to co-operate in its development with such an acclaimed manufacturer. This was undertaken in conjunction with the Morris Engines Branch at Courthouse Green, Coventry, and its experimental engineer, Irish-born Eddie Mayer. The result was a 994cc engine, a long stroke version of the 948cc unit.

It was through this association with BMC that John Cooper was party to the latter stages of the Mini's development, a car that he considered on his first encounter to be 'unusual.' When he had to attend the Italian Grand Prix in September 1959, held just a month after the model's launch, BMC loaned him a pre-production Austin version of the Mini. While at Monza he encountered Aurelio Lampredi, creator of the 'big block' Ferrari V12 engine, then a major player in the European motor industry as head of Fiat engine design. Cooper recalled, 'He asked me, "What have you got there?" I responded "It's an Austin Se7en." He said "Can I try it?" and drove it around the inner roads of Monza where he disappeared for about half an hour. When he returned he told me, "You know John, if that car wasn't so damned ugly I'd shoot myself. That is the future motor car."'[43]

Cooper was sufficiently encouraged to arrange a meeting with George Harriman and Alec Issigonis at Longbridge and almost casually suggested: 'why not build a few of them for the boys?' Their response was to give John a car to modify, which he handed over to his chief racing mechanic 'Ginger' Devlin.

The engine was accorded some of the attention usually applied to Formula Junior units. But having got the car to go faster it was then a matter of improving the way in which it stopped! Fortunately John Cooper knew Jack Emmott, managing director of Lockheed, which was developing a disc brake for the Mini as a speculative venture to encourage manufacturers to fit them. The thinking was that, if a unit could be created for the model's diminutive 10in wheels, it could be used for anything. Cooper accordingly obtained a set of experimental discs which were fitted to the Mini's front wheels.

Once complete, he took the finished car to Longbridge, although Alec Issigonis was immediately dismissive, thought it 'a big laugh' and wasted little time in reminding John that the Mini was 'only a family car.'[44] But Harriman drove it and said 'marvellous,' even though he was sceptical about its commercial potential. Despite his apprehension they shook hands on an agreement that would see the Mini moniker united with Cooper's, a name that was familiar to most households, motoring or otherwise, in the land. There was a letter in the post the following day which confirmed that BMC could pay Cooper a royalty of £2 on every car it built.

The production versions were sold as the Austin Se7en Cooper and Morris Mini-Cooper and, as in the case of the mainstream models, the latter version consistently outsold the former, although they were both made at 'the Austin' at Longbridge. Their power units were developed by Eddie Maher and the Cooper factory, which had calculated that 55bhp would be required to give the little car a top speed of 85mph. The cars, coded ADO 50 in BMC parlance, were launched in September 1961 at the FVRDE track at Chobham, Surrey. This, it will be recalled, was the same venue where the Mini had been unveiled some two years before.

'Alec Issigonis and George Harriman hated the idea of anything being added to the cars and were insistent that the Coopers resemble the basic Minis as closely as possible,' remembered John Cooper.[45] So while they were fitted with different radiator grilles, the Morris having thicker slats than the Austin version, and roofs of a contrasting colour, a feature shared with the Super Mini announced simultaneously, most of the changes were mechanical and therefore unseen.

These included an engine with a bespoke 997cc capacity – perversely the more economically viable 998cc unit already in production was not used – remote control gear change to replace the original imprecise wand, better instrumentation, trim and front disc brakes. At £679 apiece, they cost £153 more than the standard car.

These developments brought John Cooper into closer touch with Alec Issigonis and he enjoyed some memorable lunches where they were on occasions joined by the likes of Alex Moulton or Sergio Pininfarina. Cooper recalled that on one occasion Issigonis was having an argument with Pininfarina about styling. With remarkable prescience, although displaying his self-confessed arrogance, Issigonis told his Italian friend: 'In two years time your car will be like a lady's clothes, out of date. My car will still be in fashion when I am dead.'[46]

During another lunch, which took place at a local restaurant, 'the discussion would end up with Issigonis drawing all over the table cloth and at the end of the meal saying to the waiter 'Put it on the bill.' We'd go back to the experimental department run by Jack Daniels. Issigonis had had a few pink gins by then – I hadn't, I had to drive back to London – and he would put the table cloth or a cigarette packet on the drawing board and say 'draw this for me.'

Some 10,000 Mini-Coopers were produced in the first year, and in view of its success John Cooper once again approached BMC with his ideas for a follow-up to the original. This was a car to secure homologation for Group 2 racing and 'I suggested building another Cooper using experience gained in Formula Junior engines. Harriman wanted to call it the Mini-Cooper Special and I said "No way". But 1,000 had to be built for homologation and it needed a name, so the Special became the S.'[47]

A significant role in that model's development was played by Downton Engineering's Daniel Richmond. It had not taken him long to get to work on the Mini-Cooper and in December 1961 *The Autocar* published its road test of what it described as the 'Mini-Ton-Bomb'. With its engine enlarged to 1088cc, it attained a mean average top speed of 103.5mph and 86 in third, which was about the same speed as the factory Cooper would attain flat out. The report was written by Ronald Barker. 'I'd known Daniel for years. He had a natural gift for understanding the breathing of an engine. That's where he was so good, he managed to extract so much low-speed torque, he understood about gas speeds and things like that. I'd run the odd Downton-tuned cars, like a Renault Dauphine and an A35 Austin, and I was the first to do 100mph in this Mini. We took it to MIRA and did 103. Daniel didn't know it could do it, he was amazed.'[48] *Autocar's* Stuart Bladon, who was with Barker on that occasion, recalls[49] them stopping on their return journey in Newmarket to send a telegram to Richmond giving him the good news.

As a result Ronald Barker arranged for Alec Issigonis, BMC's newly appointed technical director, to try the Downton-tuned Cooper for himself, and he had the opportunity to witness the latter's distinctive driving position. 'He moved the driving seat forward by two notches, he was tall, with his elbows up somewhere near his ears. This was the way in which he thought Nuvolari used to race, very close to the wheel.

'When he got into this thing he was like a kid. He couldn't believe his Mini could have that amount of acceleration. Within a fortnight he'd sent for Daniel Richmond, he went up every Thursday and a lot more, I think they got on extremely well.'[50] In fact Richmond was to become a close friend – he would make a significant contribution to the ongoing development of the Mini-Cooper S's engine – and Bunty became an Issigonis confidante.

Daniel accompanied Issigonis on a visit to The Poplars on the occasion of Max Dowson's birthday. Christopher was present and remembers[51] Richmond 'presenting "the birthday girl" with a magnificent box of handmade chocolates. Meanwhile Alec was standing by the door with his hands firmly behind his back. After the adulation of Daniel's chocolates had abated, it was his turn to present his birthday gift. He kissed my mother on both cheeks, I think he was slightly in love with her, said "my darling Max" and gave her the tiniest box of Weekend Assortment, explaining that he had not had time to make his!'

Daniel Richmond's input was apparent on the 1071cc Mini-Cooper S, in which he co-operated with BMC's Eddie Maher, that appeared in March 1963. This paved the way, a year later, for the definitive Cooper, the 1275 S, a project that was driven by John Cooper because the original S was too large for the 1000cc class in the European Championships and was being outclassed in the 1300cc one.

'I went back to BMC when there was a board meeting going on,' recalled Cooper. But George Harriman's reaction to his proposition was '"That's impossible!" But I'd already spoken to Eddie Mayer at Morris Engines to gauge the practicality. As I went out of the door Harriman put his arm round my neck and said "We're bloody well going to do it though." And they did.'[52]

The 1275 Cooper was to provide BMC with two of its celebrated Monte Carlo

Rally wins, in 1965 and 1967, the first success, in 1964, being with a 1071cc car. These triple triumphs represented the high point of the Mini's rallying career and, indeed, elevated Issigonis's public profile to ever greater heights. They were masterminded by Stuart Turner, a respected international rally navigator, who took over as BMC's Competitions Manager in September 1961, the very month of the Cooper's introduction. Turner was to occupy his post for close on six years, leaving BMC in 1967. But, as will emerge, one of the reasons for his departure was Alec Issigonis himself.

'I arrived at exactly the right time. The first moving-in was a fluke. Marcus Chambers, after seven years decided he wanted to leave. I've found out since that he recommended me as his replacement. I went for a coffee with John Thornley and was offered the job. We got on like a house on fire. I don't think I ever had a cross word or any form of disagreement with him.

'I have been very privileged, as well as lucky in life, to work for two great leaders. One was John Thornley, who was very much an upfront extrovert type, and the other was Walter Hayes at Ford, who was far more reflective and laid back. Once you've got their confidences the greatest thing that a boss can do for a manager is to let him get on with it. And there's support if you need it. I'm sure John Thornley fought battles with Longbridge or Cowley but he kept me out of things. He was terrific and the MG factory a paradise, there's no other word for it. One of the people there had been riding mechanic for Nuvolari when he'd won the 1933 TT. I was an enthusiast. It was heaven.'[53]

Once ensconced, Turner decided to cut down on the number of events and the variety of cars that were entered in them. 'That was partly to make it simpler and partly because we now had the Mini-Cooper. The other change I made was partly conditioned by the fact that, as a navigator, I'd had the privilege of sitting with Erik Carlsson and other Continentals and I moved the drivers from gentleman to players. That is not for a moment to denigrate the gentleman. The Morley brothers, for instance, were a great wonderful team in an Austin Healey 3000, and would have been perfect for the 96-hour Liège/Sofia/Liège event. But they wouldn't do it. They were farmers in Suffolk and it was harvest time. I brought in the Finns, it clicked and came together.'

During the 1960s BMC was to spend some £120,000 a year, the equivalent of over £1.3 million by today's values, on competitions, of which Donald Healey would receive £25,000 for racing in America. The annual programme was discussed by the BMC Competitions Committee, which met annually and was chaired by George Harriman. Alec Issigonis was also a member.

Stuart Turner therefore had the opportunity of meeting him at first hand. 'I've always been something of a hero worshipper. It was a thrill to meet Alec. He was a legend. I was not in awe of him but very pleased to be in his circle. I think I would describe his mannerisms as 'theatrical.' I had a slightly bizarre background in that my step-mother was on the stage. So from between the ages of about 12 and 16, I'd spent almost every Saturday night in a theatre. It was variety, with performers like Max Millar and Jimmy James. I was used to theatrical people and extravagant behaviour. I was at ease with Issigonis's flamboyance. Other people probably said, "Christ almighty, what's this?"[54]

'Time and again we'd sit at press lunches and I'd try and get as close as I could to him. I enjoyed his company. On such occasions a journalist would nearly always say, "Alec, how did you get this idea for the Mini?" He'd respond "well, dear boy..." and he'd get the menu and draw all over it. When he'd finished, more often than not the individual would say "could you sign that for me Alec?" not realising that's precisely what he was expecting. It was an act.'

Stuart Turner found Issigonis's attitude to rallying ambivalent. 'Although he'd built the Lightweight Special and was not averse to motorsport, he was almost neutral about competition. But one of the pleasures of my life was to stand with Alec, watching his baby under my management, win the Monte Carlo Rally which, in those days, was an event of prestige.'

That was in 1964, when Paddy Hopkirk and Henry Liddon gave BMC its first win in the event. Belfast-born Hopkirk had joined BMC in 1962 from Rootes. 'I wanted to drive the big Austin Healey 3000,' he recalls,[55] but he was soon behind the wheel of a much smaller car in the shape of the Mini. In 1962 he came third with Henry Liddon in the Tour de France rally and won the handicap category. It was this success which gave the model its international credibility and, as a result, 'the French fell in love with the car.'

In the 1964 Monte he and Liddon had started from Minsk. Western goods were in short supply in Russia and Paddy took the precaution of taking some nylons with him, which he bartered for a tin of caviar that was opened for a victory party in Alec Issigonis's room in the Hotel de Paris. 'It was so full it spilled on to the balcony. He certainly enjoyed a party, not all engineers do and he liked his food and drink. He fitted well into that posh hotel. Both he and George Harriman were very charming. In fact they seemed too nice and well mannered to be running Britain's largest car company.'

To celebrate BMC's victory in style press manager Tony Dawson had hired, at great expense, the Parrot restaurant a little further down the coast towards the Italian border. 'That was quite an evening!' remembers Hopkirk. 'Afterwards Henry Liddon and I went to Longbridge and we were given a Mini-Cooper S each, which we immediately sold. I then told Issigonis that I thought the seats were very uncomfortable but he said they would help me to stay awake!'

Stuart Turner was similarly rewarded. 'Afterwards George Harriman came to Abingdon and, totally to my surprise, took me to one side and gave me a cheque for £500. That was equivalent to the price of a car. I can remember phoning Margaret, my wife, I was nearly hyperventilating when I told her that "someone has just given me £500". That was on a salary of £1500.'[56]

Turner was able to repeat this triumph in 1965 with Timo Makinen as the victor but the 1966 event was the occasion that the winning Mini-Cooper was dismissed by the Rally's French organisers on a technicality. 'I think Harriman and Issigonis thought Christmas had come early when it happened. To put it in perspective, there was a television programme in those days called *Sunday Night at the London Palladium*. When Paddy won in 1964 they brought the car back and it went round and round on the stage with Bruce Forsyth in attendance. When we were thrown out in '66 they had all three Mini-Coopers and the audience sang *Land of Hope and Glory*. It was beneficial, no question. The world was on our side, people said "those bastard French". We nearly invaded France!'[57]

In 1967 there would be no mistake when Rauno Aaltonen in a Mini-Cooper gave BMC its hat-trick, although this was destined to be Stuart Turner's last year as Competitions Manager. 'I'd had nearly six years and I thought that was enough. I was a little bit piqued when I didn't get the job of publicity manager at Longbridge when Brian Turner left. There was that. It was 60 percent boredom, 20 percent pique and 20 percent Issigonis.[58]

'After we'd won one rally we had to go behind the Iron Curtain. I went to see him over something and then carried on to the export sales chief to let him know we were going to Eastern Europe. It didn't matter to us which rally, it could have been Poland or Hungary. I wanted to know where BMC was most likely to sell cars. And we decided where to go. Purely making conversation while we finished our coffee, I just mentioned to this salesman that we were thinking of running an Austin 1800 on rallies.

'His immediate reaction was "if you do could you mention to Alec to alter the position of the handbrake. You really would help us because the customers don't like it." You had to be an all-in wrestler on steroids to make the handbrake work. I could see Alec in his office across the grass because I'd just come from seeing him. I looked at the sales chief, pointed and said "why don't you tell him?"

'His answer was "he won't listen to sales". That illustrates the Issigonis problem, and if you won't listen to your customers… And how do you control a "genius"? They didn't. Frankly the Mini and the 1100 were pleasant cars but then it was downhill and the stuff that came afterwards [the 1800 and Maxi] should have been put in a museum of horrors.'

Stuart Turner left BMC in March 1967 to become publicity manager for Castrol. Then in 1969 he joined Ford as competitions manager and was to take that company to ever greater heights in the rallying field. He recalls that the difference between BMC and Ford was striking, certainly as far as the control of costs was concerned. 'I cannot remember any occasion at BMC when I did not get anything I wanted because of lack of money. It was never an issue. The contrast with Ford was never more graphically illustrated than when I walked into Boreham on my first day and a bloke came up to me and said 'Hello, I'm Brian Brackenbury, your financial controller.' I didn't know what a financial controller was! It's all about the bottom line and that means you survive. The other way, you don't.'[59]

The Mini-Cooper's Monte Carlo rally triumphs were applauded by Issigonis's second cousin, Bernd Pischetsrieder, then a teenager growing up in Munich. He would join BMW in 1973 and 20 years later become chairman of the company that in 1994 took over the Rover Group, as the BMC/British Leyland businesses had been renamed. Today he still 'remembers very well the Mini's victories... From thereon, for me – and for almost all my friends – the Mini-Cooper was my dream car.'[60]

Paradoxically it came to the end of the road in 1971, following Leyland's absorption in 1968 of BMC. Sir Donald Stokes told John Cooper that he was discontinuing royalty payments to outside contractors. For his part Stokes subsequently recalled 'we lost about £20 per Mini. Then people wonder why I scrapped the Cooper, but we were losing even more money on the Cooper. We were giving more money to Mr Cooper than we were making a profit.'[61] Ironically, the Mini in general and Cooper in particular had been given an unexpected fillip with the release, in July 1969, of the film *The Italian Job*.

The idea had been conceived early in 1967 by scriptwriter Troy Kennedy Martin and he had chosen the Mini because it was 'classless, very fast and represented the new Britain that did not take itself too seriously.'[62] A band of crooks led by Charlie Croker (Michael Caine) execute a plot masterminded by Mr Bridger (Noel Coward), from his prison cell in Wormwood Scrubbs, to steal $4 million of gold bullion that the Chinese have flown into Turin as a downpayment on a Fiat factory.

In this they are ably assisted by a trio of red, white and blue Cooper Ss, which career along the streets, piazzas, roofs and even the sewers of the Italian city, although the sewers part was actually filmed in Coventry! No fewer than 14 Minis were sacrificed in the making of this part of the film because their suspensions were worn out through being repeatedly driven up and down some of Turin's bumpier stairways.

Commissioned by Paramount with a budget of $3 million, which reached $3.2 million, director Michael Deeley, a car enthusiast, has recalled that the Mini's manufacturers [British Leyland] were 'completely disinterested'[63] in the project. The film company was only able to buy six Minis at trade price; the remaining cars it required were purchased from retail outlets. A further 25 standard Minis, dressed up to resemble Coopers, were also obtained from a Swiss outlet for some of the last scenes in the film when the three cars were 'pushed' – actually ejected by compressed air – from the rear of a coach to disappear over the edge of the mountain road into the valley below.

Deeley underlined British Leyland's attitude by pointedly thanking the city of Turin and Fiat for their co-operation in the credits. Head of the car company, Giovanni Agnelli, had supported the film from the outset, which opened the civic doors to Paramount. Issigonis saw the film and was 'very pleased... in particular by the role played by Noel Coward.'[64]

The Mini's suspension had already been on the British Leyland agenda when, for cost reasons, from the 1970 season the model reverted to its original dry rubber cones. And much to its creator's displeasure it also received wind-up windows and concealed door hinges. More positively, at the same time British Leyland discontinued the marque prefixes that had been applied to the Mini from its introduction and it emerged as a model name in its own right.

A new variant that also flew in the face of the Issigonis original also appeared in the form of the Clubman version with an angular front. It was the work of Roy Haynes, stylist of the Ford Cortina Mark II, who had been recruited by Joe Edwards to Pressed Steel in 1967. It survived until 1980. The same body was used for the 1275 GT, which replaced the Cooper in 1972.

The 1970s were in the main a good decade for the Mini, although production roughly halved between the peak year of 1971 and 1979, when 165,502 were completed. British personalities had moved on to other cars and the model settled down as cheap, economical transport for the masses, just the type of clientele its creator had intended. A significant feature of these years was the growth of the European market for the Mini which rose from about 20 percent of production in the mid-1960s to nudging the 50 percent figure by the early 1970s. This surge in demand was underpinned by the switchback years of recession and, from 1974, by soaring petrol prices, much to the despair of Lord Stokes. For as the economy took a downturn, 'everybody started buying the ruddy Mini again',[65] which was still only marginally profitable.

British Leyland was knocked off course by the result of the world depression of 1974. The business was nationalised in 1975 and renamed Leyland Cars. Yet another reorganisation saw Michael Edwardes appointed chairman in 1977 of what he now called BL Cars, which allowed the marque names to flourish. But by 1985 the Mini production figure had dropped by two-thirds to 49,986.

This was on account of the fact that Edwardes's Austin Metro supermini had been announced in October 1980. This was destined to be the best received Longbridge product since the introduction of the 1100, 18 years before. It had sprung from ADO 88, an intended Mini replacement, subsequently reworked in LC8 guise, and one of a number of experimental projects, many of which never attained production status.

The Mini van and its estate car versions disappeared in 1982, although changes to the survivors were relatively few throughout the decade when the emphasis was switched to special edition niche models. However, in 1986 BL had a new chairman in the shape of Graham Day, who was to rename it the Rover Group, and take its products upmarket. That year the five-millionth Mini was completed, driven off the assembly line by TV personality and car enthusiast Noel Edmonds. But by 1987 the annual production figure had dropped to 37,210.

In August 1988 the company was acquired by British Aerospace, which returned it to the private sector. There was again talk of discontinuing the Mini, which produced a characteristically robust response from Issigonis although 'propped up in bed in his 81st year.' In this 'last' interview, given to Ken Gibson of Birmingham's *Evening Mail* in 1988, and published on 4 October two days after his death, Gibson wrote that 'Sir Alec defied his frail looks.' Issigonis declared that 'it was absolutely ridiculous, the car is as popular now as it has ever been, especially in some overseas markets. What they should have been doing was to increase production to meet demand. Certain cars, like the Mini and Citroën 2CV, remain timeless.'[66] In fact Graham Day would memorably describe the Mini as 'a nice little earner,' probably for the first time in its life!

Production received a fillip in 1990 when the Mini-Cooper returned to the corporate fold, 19 years after its demise. John Cooper had, since 1985, been offering kits to Japanese customers in a box that would conveniently fit on the back seat of a Mini Mayfair. The car had generated a small but loyal following in that country and back in 1979 Ryo Murai, president of the Mini-Cooper Owner's Division of Japan, had written to 'Sir Issigonis' telling him that the number of Mini-Coopers currently in Japan 'is quite limited, so they are very precious to us.' Rover's corporate endorsement of Cooper's activities had followed the creation, in 1989, of the John Cooper Garages 30th Anniversary Mini with an engine tuned by Janspeed, a business established by Jan Odor, who had left Downton in 1962 to set up on his own account, and with a white roof echoing the original Cooper.

A cabriolet version of the Mini followed in 1993 and Issigonis did not live to see the day when, to universal surprise, in January 1994 British Aerospace announced that it was to sell Rover to BMW, which was chaired by Sir Alec's relative, Bernd Pischetsrieder, who now found himself responsible for Issigonis's ageing masterpiece. However, he soon discovered that 'the Rover management had already decided to drop the Mini by stating that it would no longer comply with European regulations.' That edict was then placed on hold because he had decided to produce a wholly new Mini (see Postscript) that was intended to enter production in 2000. 'I was always fascinated by the charisma of the Mini… With the support of John Cooper, Rover was able to implement some changes to the old Mini in order to continue in production until the new Mini was ready. It is true that many people at BMW thought that my fascination with the Mini was motivated by my family connection. But I was always convinced that the new Mini would be a great sales success and this was my only motivation.'[67]

So the car was kept in production, the idea being that the new model would follow the old off the Longbridge production line. In 1999 output dropped to a mere 11,738 cars, although in January 2000 BMW unexpectedly announced its intention to sell Rover and it did so in May, offloading the company to the Phoenix Consortium for a token £10. By this time Pischetsrieder had departed and in 2002 he was appointed to the chairmanship of Volkswagen, Europe's largest car manufacturer. But BMW decided to retain the new MINI, as the model is rendered, and it went into production a year later than scheduled in the summer of 2001 at a newly built Cowley facility.

At Longbridge production of the original Mini finally ceased on 4 October 2000 when the 5,387,862nd car was completed, 41 years after the first had been assembled in the very same factory. At the wheel was 1960s pop star, one-time Mini owner Lulu, who drove the Cooper S down the line to the theme tune of *The Italian Job*, a snub, intended or otherwise, to British Leyland, which had not only discontinued the Cooper but also distanced itself from the film. Eighty-eight-year-old Jack Daniels, who had exerted so much of his perspiration on the project, was present and expressed his sadness at seeing the model die, philosophically reflecting 'it was inevitable but it had to happen.'[68] The Mini had outlived Alec Issigonis, its creator, by 12 years and one of the great designs of world automotive history was no more.

Notes

1. Geoffrey Rose, *op cit.*
2. Peter Tothill, *op cit.*
3. Ibid.
4. Dave Daniels, *op cit.*
5. *The Autocar*, 28 August 1959.
6. Ronald Barker, *op cit.*
7. Turner and Curtis, *op cit.*
8. Quoted in Wood, *Wheels*, *op cit.*
9. Geoffrey Rose, *op cit.*
10. Pressnell, *Mr MG*, *op cit.*
11. Jonathan Wood, Archbishop to Cortina, *Thoroughbred and Classic Cars*, August 1983.
12. Jonathan Wood, *Ford Cortina Mk 1*, 1984.
13. Lord Montagu of Beaulieu and David Burgess-Wise, *Daimler Century*, 1995.
14. Quoted in Golding, *op cit.*
15. Turner and Curtis, *op cit.*
16. Private information.
17. Jennifer Gilman, *op cit.*
18. Lord Snowdon, *op cit.*
19. Campbell, *op cit.*
20. Jackson, *op cit.*
21. Turner and Curtis, *op cit.*
22. Norman Milne, interview with author, 2005.
23. John Sheppard, *op cit.*
24. Peter Tothill, *op cit.*
25. Robson, *op cit.*
26. People and Cars, Peter Ustinov, *Motor*, 14 March 1964.
27. Ustinov on Issigonis, address at funeral service, *Newslink*, December 1988.
28. The Mini Man, *op cit.*
29. People and Cars, *op cit.*
30. Doreen Schreier, *op cit.*
31. David and Peter Henshaw, *Apex, The Inside Story of the Hillman Imp*, 1988.
32. Ibid.
33. Christopher Dowson, *op cit.*
34. Golding, *op cit.* It was in fact written by Golding!
35. Lord Snowdon, *op cit.*
36. Anders Ditlev Clausager, *Sprites and Midgets*, 1991.
37. Knowles, *op cit.*
38. Alex Moulton, *op cit.*
39. Peter Browning, *The Works Minis*, 1971.
40. Ronald Barker, *op cit.*
41. Peter Garnier, Downton, *Autocar*, 27 July 1962.
42. *Mini Racing*, Christabel Carlisle, 1963.
43. Jonathan Wood, *Taking the Mini to the Max*, Automobile Quarterly, Volume 28, number 3, 1990.
44. Ibid.
45. Ibid.
46. Ibid.

47. Ibid.
48. Ronald Barker, *op cit.*
49. Stuart Bladon, in conversation with author, 2005.
50. Ronald Barker, *op cit.*
51. Christopher Dowson, *op cit.*
52. Wood, *Taking the Mini... op cit.*
53. Stuart Turner, interview with author, 2004.
54. Ibid.
55. Paddy Hopkirk, interview with author, 2005.
56. Stuart Turner, *op cit.*
57. Ibid.
58. Ibid.
59. Ibid.
60. Bernd Pischetsrieder, *op cit.*
61. John Pressnell, The Devil in Disguise? *Classic and Sportscar.*
62. *The Making of the Italian Job*, Channel 4, 1997.
63. Ibid.
64. Letter from Michael Moss, 'a personal friend' of Issigonis, *Saga* magazine, October 2001.
65. Quoted in Wood, *Wheels, op cit.*
66. *Birmingham Evening Mail*, 4 October 1988.
67. Bernd Pischetsrieder, *op cit.*
68. Last Mini Rolls Out of Longbridge, *Autocar*, 11 October 2000.

Chapter Nine

THE GOOD, THE BAD
AND THE UGLY

*'At BMC Issigonis does the basic costing in his
head.'I'm old enough now to have had enough
experience to do that' he said.'*[1]

THIS PRONOUNCEMENT was recorded by Graham Turner, that perceptive observer of Britain's motor industry, and related to the costing of the 1800 model, the statement coming from a man with a much publicised disdain for mathematics. Not only does it reveal the arrogance that had increasingly pervaded Alec Issigonis's personality, it is also indicative of the extraordinary power he wielded as BMC's technical director. It only began to be checked from 1966 onwards and followed Joe Edwards's appointment as managing director. Previously, Issigonis and George Harriman, BMC's ineffectual and vacillating chairman, had run the Corporation unbridled with, inevitably, the Mini's creator the more dominant of the two executives. By this time Alec Issigonis had emerged as that most dangerous of corporate beings: the uncontrolled 'genius'.

While the Mini's idiosyncratic appearance, ingenious mechanicals and superlative handling had chimed perfectly with Britain of the 1960s, Alec Issigonis found himself incapable of applying similar ingenuity to BMC's larger cars. With the exception of the 1100, the front-wheel drive models that followed it conspicuously lacked the flair which had made the Mini such a motoring icon.

The popularity of the 1100 and Mini ensured that BMC's production figures made impressive reading; corporate output doubled in the 10 years between 1955 and 1965. But underpricing meant that profitability was eroded to the extent that a loss was recorded in 1967 and paved the way for takeover by a thrusting Leyland Corporation, headed by Sir Donald Stokes, in the following year. And the creation of British Leyland marked the end of the Issigonis era at Longbridge.

Only four years previously, in 1964, the picture had appeared so different. Then BMC built 730,862 cars, the highest production figure ever attained during its 15-year life, and it also held a dominant 35 percent share of the British market. In international terms this made the British Motor Corporation one of Europe's largest motor manufacturers, with only Volkswagen and Fiat producing more cars. Yet in the deficit year of 1967 output had dropped by some 175,000, in part caused by a credit squeeze, but more significantly by the Corporation having lost market share to, in particular, the sure-footed operations of Ford's British subsidiary.

There were, of course, other factors. That year BMC suffered from a strike by delivery drivers which brought car production to a halt at Longbridge. Although this was not directly related to its workforce, it did expose the Corporation's vulnerability to industrial action, which increased throughout the decade. And government intervention played its part throughout these years as those in power chose to use the motor industry to regulate consumer spending. Between 1957 and 1968 hire purchase requirements on cars were changed on 11 occasions and the purchase tax rate on seven.

It was in the early 1960s that Issigonis decided to move closer to his work, a decision that was probably prompted by the fact that the Morris engineering facility, which he regularly visited on his weekly returns to Oxford, was destined for closure in 1963. As already apparent, his mother was reluctant to leave the Sollershott flat where they had lived since 1938. But then a newly-built bungalow became available in the exclusive Birmingham area of Edgbaston. Issigonis may well have of heard of the development from John Morris, who, it will be recalled, had lived in the area since 1933. Laid out by the local Calthorpe estate, the largest landowners in the city in the 18th century, Edgbaston, only a mile from the centre of Birmingham, has all the trappings of a self-contained village; leafy, secluded and exclusive. From the outset it was intended to attract prosperous owners who responded to the retention of trees which today add a sense of maturity to roads that predominantly play host to substantial architect-designed Georgian, Victorian and Edwardian houses.

In the early 1960s John Madin Design, Birmingham's leading architectural practice, had produced a master plan for the Calthorpe Estate, although Westbourne Gardens, described as 'the Beverly Hills of Edgbaston', was developed by W.H. Scrase, an orthopaedic surgeon, who lived in the first Madin-designed bungalow to be built there.

Number 12 was next to it and eventually there would be just seven bungalows. This exclusive development was located off Westbourne Road, a turning almost opposite Edgbaston's St George Church, surrounded by the parkland of Birmingham University. Issigonis could now drive down the Bristol Road to BMC's Longbridge headquarters in about 20 minutes.

Like the neighbouring bungalow, his property was U-shaped with a pond located between each wing. No doubt to his approval the frontage, executed in the 1960s style, was built in traditional brick with a flat wooden roof and was wholly devoid of decoration. Everything in the best traditions of the modernist architect, Le Corbusier, was purely functional and the property's spiritual similarity to the Oxford flat, whether by accident or design, is striking.

The northerly wing featured a double garage, with a spare bedroom behind. The front door gave access to the hall, which led into the drawing room on the southern side, which had spacious 21x15ft dimensions with an open fireplace on its western wall. Hulda occupied the adjoining back bedroom, which contained its own bathroom and dressing room. Alec's bedroom was at the north-eastern corner of the property with the kitchen, overlooking the small back garden, between the two. Set in three quarters of an acre, most of the grounds were at the front.

Although the spartan environment that had so typified the Oxford flat was perpetuated to some extent, at Westbourne Gardens Issigonis did permit himself some indulgence. He had always been fascinated by the Dowson's Victorian electric light fitting in their dining room, which came complete with pulleys and brass fittings so that it could be adjusted for height. In due course he made a similar device for his Edgbaston home.[2] A further note of opulence would be struck by the arrival of an oil painting of himself, commissioned by his mother.

The property was leasehold and tied to Issigonis remaining in BMC's employ. After its takeover by Leyland, in 1969, he purchased, for £15,154, the balance of the 99-year lease, minus, for legal reasons, three days! As such it was the first house he ever owned. Soon after his arrival, in the summer of 1964, he laid out a 00 gauge railway track in the garden. It will be recalled that he had already made sections of line and engines within the confines of his Oxford flat. The train shed was set up in the garage and he made two apertures in its northerly wall, which although now blocked are still visible, for their entry and exit. From there the track, which ran on wooden stilts, went down the side of house to the small back garden, where it followed an elongated loop to return to the garage.

Christopher Dowson helped Issigonis to lay out the track. 'When I arrived to see him he'd always encourage me to go directly into the garage to play with his steam train. We'd have a gamble as to how long it would take the trains to come back as sometimes they'd crash in the garden. He spent hours building the layout. He told me that the reason he put so much effort into it was to get away from his mother. He'd made one engine, that was from scratch, he was very proud of it, but then said "I didn't have the energy to make another one" and he was given a third.'[3]

Soon after he took up residence in Westbourne Gardens Alec Issigonis received a visit from his German relatives. Bernd Pischetsrieder, then 15 years old, was accompanied by his uncle, who, his nephew recalls, had 'always maintained contact with Alec and visited him a couple of times. The rest of the family didn't really have close contact with him. My mother sometimes referred to him as a *verschrobener Ingenieur* (eccentric engineer).'[4]

There followed a conducted tour of Longbridge, after which young Pischetsrieder 'decided that I would never join the motor industry...' In fact just five years later, in 1968, he entered Munich Technical University to read mechanical engineering, graduating as Diplom-Ingenieur in 1972. As a teenager his visit to BMC's headquarters was followed by one to Issigonis's new home. Alex Moulton recalls the occasion, Alec telling his mother, 'I've just been showing one of your relatives around Longbridge,' with the emphasis on the 'your.'[5]

Bernd viewed with delight the miniature railway laid out in the garden and he looked forward to the opportunity of playing with it. To his dismay it remained strictly out-of-bounds to the young visitor, who 'was very cross with him because I was not allowed to play with his train.' Pischetsrieder saw him 'two or three more times in the 1960s but never again. My single abiding memory was the discussion with Alec on why I couldn't play with his train!'[6] However, the visit did result in his mother making a couple of trips to her relative's Munich home and Bernd Pischetsrieder 'liked her very much.' Once there she no doubt enjoyed the opportunity of being able to speak German again.

For his own part Issigonis's holidays, albeit short ones, were now spent mainly in Monte Carlo; he had by then forsaken Switzerland. 'When I was younger I used to enjoy skiing,' he said in 1962. 'Now I can't bear the cold.'[7] He was also to go to Venice at the invitation of Lord Snowdon. 'When he came with us, I took him blindfolded to the centre of St Mark's Square. Then I took the blindfold off and said "how about that, isn't it amazing?" His response was "my dear, it's exactly like Burlington Arcade!" The only thing he really loved about Venice was going frightfully fast, cornering in a speed boat.'[8] On another occasion he took Issigonis to see the Snowdon Aviary he had designed at London Zoo in Regents Park, believing that he would respond to its functionalism. "I think he quite liked it."'[9]

At the time of his move to Edgbaston in 1963 Alec Issigonis had been BMC's technical director for a little over a year. Sir Leonard Lord had retired as BMC's chairman in December 1961 at the age of 65 and in the New Year Honours List received a barony to become Lord Lambury of Northfield, the district of Birmingham where Longbridge is located. He took his title – 'Lord Lord would have sounded bloody stupid' – from Lambury Point, near Salcombe in Devon, close to where he once had a holiday home.

Although Lord handed over the reins to his long-serving deputy, 53-year-old George Harriman, he continued to exercise an influence on him as BMC's president and his Longbridge office was left intact and unoccupied until the time of his death in September 1967. John Thornley, who served under both chairmen, was of the opinion that Harriman was 'responsible for running BMC into the ground. He tried to administer it as Lord had done – which was largely by guesswork…' But Harriman wasn't 'that lucky or that clever.'[9]

Alec Issigonis was promoted in November 1961, the month in which he celebrated his 55th birthday, although he did not join the BMC board until April 1963. He effectively took the place of the authoritarian Sydney 'Hitler' Smith, who, it should be said, had acted as a restraining influence on him in much the same way as Vic Oak had done in his Morris Minor days. Now there was only Harriman to rein in an executive who professed a dislike for committees and board meetings and lacked an appetite for administration. BMC's new technical director, who was shy by nature, much preferred the informality of small gatherings with trusted colleagues. The post, nevertheless, endowed Alec Issigonis with greater powers than any other technical director in the European motor industry. His French counterpart, Citroën's engineering maestro, André Lefebvre, had retired in 1958 having suffered a stroke, although he continued to work from home until his death in 1964.

Geoffrey Rose, who was simultaneously made BMC's deputy director of production, was apprehensive about Issigonis's promotion. 'When he was appointed technical director, in my personal opinion, it was shared by others, I thought it was one of the worst steps taken, in the sense that Alec was not a technical director. He was a brilliant innovator and designer. The post required that he be responsible for all aspects of design and be administratively responsible, that included man management and how much you are going to pay somebody. Alec wasn't interested in such things. In retrospect it was a tragic misuse of his abilities. I don't think he wanted it personally but Alec was very influenced by George Harriman and it meant he was established as a key figure at BMC with a seat on the board. I was very fond of him, but his dogmatism became even more pronounced. He was almost dismissive of anything bigger than the Mini. His attitude to the concept of big cars was, 'what do you want them for?'[10]

Issigonis was sorry to see Leonard Lord depart and Ronald Barker remembers that 'he missed him terribly. Lord was very, very direct and he got things done.

His language was absolutely amazing! Issigonis used to praise Lord but he found that Harriman was not strong enough.'[11]

Ten months after his appointment, in August 1962, BMC announced the Morris 1100, the next expression of the Mini's transverse engine, front-wheel drive concept. It similarly echoed its status by being the most technically advanced medium-sized car in the world. Unlike the Mini, which had been developed in a mere two and a half years at BMC's Longbridge headquarters, the 1100 had by comparison taken a more leisurely three and a half, mainly at Cowley. Although Alec Issigonis had overall responsibility for the project, the model's development was placed in the capable hands of Morris's chief engineer, Charles Griffin.

Birmingham-born Griffin (1918–1999), Issigonis's right hand in the years between 1960 and 1968, was an accomplished engineer, with, as far as his superior was concerned, the essential practical skills for high office. Indeed Issigonis considered him 'the best filer in the business.'[12] Receiving his technical education at Handsworth Technical College and Birmingham Central Technical College, Griffin had in 1934 begun his career with the BSA armaments business, where he served an engineering apprenticeship. In 1940 he moved across the city to Wolseley and in doing so joined the Nuffield Organisation. During wartime duties he had helped to design the wings for the Horsa glider, and after hostilities he was to develop the now forgotten Nuffield Taxi, conceived as a rival to the ubiquitous Austin cab.

Transferring to Morris's Cowley factory, he was appointed to the post of assistant chief experimental engineer with responsibility for vehicle proving. It was there that he encountered Alec Issigonis, 'it was my horrible duty to tell him when things were not right with his beloved Morris Minor – he hated me on sight!'[13] The MG TD sports car was also to benefit from Griffin's work, as did the Series II Morris Oxford, which survives to this day in India under the Hindustan name.

Promoted to the post of chief experimental engineer in 1956 and chief designer two years later, Griffin was responsible for the Wolseley 1500 and Riley One Point Five. He possessed, in every sense, a safe pair of hands. In 1960 he became Issigonis's deputy, having already shown his worth in the development of the Mini. 'We had a agreement' he later remembered with a grin, 'that if a car was good, it was down to him but if it ever went wrong, even slightly wrong, I got the blame! We realised that there had to be a personalised image which had to remain untarnished.'[14]

With Issigonis based at Longbridge, although he would return to Oxford from Wednesdays onwards, Griffin was able to develop the 1100 at Cowley without the minimalist fervour that had accompanied the Mini's development, a less desirable discipline on a more expensive model. His task was made easier by the fact that many of the problems associated with front-wheel drive had already been encountered and solved on the Mini even though only about 10 percent of parts were common to both cars.

It will be recalled that when Issigonis had arrived at Longbridge early in 1956 the second project he had begun work on was XC9002, a concept that was set aside so that he could concentrate on the development of the Mini. This first derivative of *système Issigonis* would be badged a Morris. An Austin version would have to wait until the 1964 season.

Work on the 1100, coded ADO16 in BMC's corporate parlance, began early in 1959, some six months before the Mini was launched in August of that year. It differed from its progenitor in two significant respects. Issigonis was to have styled the new car but his limitations soon made themselves apparent and later, in a rare moment of contrition, he told Ronald Barker 'I couldn't get it right.'[15] The work was therefore assigned to Pininfarina, who drew on the lines of its A40 with refinements made at Longbridge by Dick Burzi who, among other minor changes, strengthened the door pillars. The Italian styling house's input was fundamental to the model's success because the 1100 would be attracting a more affluent clientele than the Mini. While stubby lines were wholly appropriate for the BMC baby, they did not lend themselves to enlargement.

Issigonis and Charles Griffin put their heads together and supplied Farina with a sketch, as the former put it, of 'a two box car,' like the Mini 'only bigger. A wheel-at-each-corner for stability, the engine set crossways for room.'[16] This meant that the amount of front and rear overhang was strictly limited, Alec revealing that 'Sergio [Pininfarina] liked more overhang but we cured him of that.' The profile was also decided in advance and the proportions, the glass area and wing line were theirs. Pininfarina considered BMC at this time 'a paradise' because of the innovative nature of its products. With a long production run intended, he reflected, 'the more I succeeded in making the car fashionless, the longer it will last.'[17]

The model was thus endowed with timeless features that still did not look out of place in 1974 when it was discontinued. Even then the only aspects of the design which betrayed its late 1950s origins were embryo tail fins. At Cowley Alan Parker and Reg Job, the latter a veteran of the Morris Minor project, were responsible for the body engineering and Allan Webb and Bob Shirley the chassis. With an overall length of 12ft 2.75in, it was 2.75in longer than the Mini.

The second significant difference between the two cars was the suspension, because Alex Moulton was at last able to introduce his interconnected rubber system, begun on the Alvis TA350 and originally intended for the Mini. He described the essentials of his invention as being based on 'two separate, identical systems, one for the left and one for the right hand pair of wheels; there are no levelling mechanism, pumps or accumulators... the two systems are pressurised by the weight of the car.'[18] Initially some half-dozen Morris Minor 1000s were converted and Issigonis revealed that 'as Alex Moulton and I were developing the rubber springs for the Minis, we talked of practically nothing else but this coupled system which derived from it.'[19] Front and rear sub frames, similar to those used on the Mini, were perpetuated.

Charles Griffin took over the development of ADO 16 after the completion of the first Longbridge-built prototype, which was initially specified with a 948cc engine. He was appalled and appealed directly to George Harriman, telling him, 'I need your support, we've got a success on our hands if we handle it properly.'[20] He succeeded in getting the volumes increased to 6,800 a week, the engine's

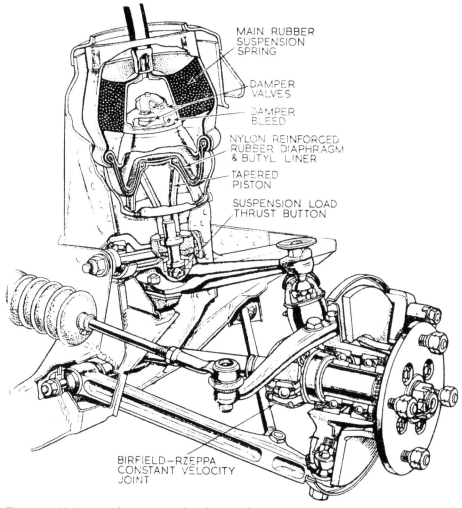

MAIN RUBBER
SUSPENSION
SPRING

DAMPER
VALVES

DAMPER
BLEED

NYLON REINFORCED
RUBBER DIAPHRAGM
& BUTYL LINER

TAPERED
PISTON

SUSPENSION LOAD
THRUST BUTTON

BIRFIELD–RZEPPA
CONSTANT VELOCITY
JOINT

The 1100's Hydrolastic front suspension. (*Autocar*)

capacity was upped to 1100cc and agreement was given to proceed with the Moulton suspension. He recalled that 'the first Hydrolastic types actually had a central fluid chamber, a "cheese" we called it, under the seats, with pipes going in all directions. It was noisy and very harsh, a cat's eye bump sounded much worse inside the cabin. The next version had displacers at each wheel.'[21]

The 1100's interior repeated the packaging triumph of the Mini although the longer wheelbase – Issigonis had increased it by about 2.5in over his original dimension – provided even greater scope. Happily it was bereft of its progenitor's starkness and possessed an A40-style speedometer and wind-up windows, the glass of which was curved and, claimed Issigonis, added a further 1.25in to the driver's elbow room. Unlike the body and mechanicals which were completed at Cowley, the interior was the work of Dick Burzi's Longbridge-based Styling Department. To the perceptive D.B. Tubbs this was the 'weakest part,' the planning 'being static not dynamic.'[22] It was during this discussion with Tubbs in 1963 that Issigonis came out with one of his more notorious aphorisms. Referring to the 1100's seats, he informed the motoring public that they 'must be uncomfortable in traffic to keep alert.'[23] As will emerge in the next chapter, this was from a man who avoided sitting on a comfortable chair in his own home, preferring an upright uncomfortable one, and his mother usually sat on the floor!

In the face of opposition from Issigonis, who had yet to be elevated to the BMC board of directors, the 1100 was fitted with front disc brakes. These he dismissed as 'fashionable; the things to have. I was not particularly in favour of them.' The suggestion had come from 'the management, even though it was the more expensive thing to do.'[24]

The fact that the A Series engine was increased in capacity to 1100cc spelt the end of the possibility of using a Lancia-inspired V4 pushrod unit which BMC had been developing since the late 1950s. It is for this reason that there is far more room under an 1100's bonnet than the Mini's. The 18 degree V-unit progressively used a toothed rubber belt to drive the central camshaft and was experimentally produced in 1100cc and 2-litre guises. Issigonis required little prompting to publicly declare that it had been 'thrown away because it didn't fit in with our design philosophy... Cars must be smaller but the "living room" must be increased. When we started work on the V4 we were using north-south engines but since we have switched to east-west in our small cars the V-4 no longer fits in with our concept because an in line engine takes up less room fitted in that way.'[25]

The Morris 1100 was announced in August 1962, to wide acclaim on account of appearance, packaging, smoothness of engine and suspension. *Autocar* was ecstatic and declared: 'the staff of this journal have never before been so unanimous about the overall qualities of a car... It is obvious that a far sighted and thorough engineering job had been done.' It found the Hydrolastic suspension 'superb' and 'although it cannot be said that the car is free from pitch under all conditions... the manner in which the car rides over really rough surfaces is quite extraordinary.'[26] It believed that the 1100 was 'fully capable of challenging the currently popular European small cars which it is destined to meet in world markets.'

Criticism was limited to the shallowness of the boot, a downside of Issigonis's wheel-at-each-corner approach, which was 'not so capacious as those of many of the car's competitors.' But its creator was later to disregard the large boot of the simultaneously introduced 'three box' Ford Cortina as 'a sales gimmick.' It emerged as the 1100's principal competitor and dominated the corporate fleet market.

BMC loaned *Autocar* two 1100s on extended test. One was driven by the wife of Maurice Smith, *Autocar's* editor, and the other went to Stuart Bladon, who remembers it as 'the most unreliable test car I'd ever had. The worst problem was that the petrol pump, a sealed unit, located at the rear, was persistently faulty, causing the engine to regularly cut out. We passed this information on to BMC but Issigonis apparently dismissed it as "nonsense". Eventually they had to change it.'[27]

Alec Issigonis was on hand to meet the press for the 1100's launch and Danish motoring correspondent Rogers Sogaard, then technical editor of the magazine *BILEN*, remembers the occasion, which was held at Worcester College, Oxford, during the summer break. Half a dozen 1100s were drawn up on the lawn and the foreign press were staying there. He 'found Issigonis relaxing at the almost around-the-clock bar and immediately understood that he was dealing with a foreign journalist whose language was far from Oxford English.'[28]

During their discussions BMC's technical director revealed that 'he had gained a lot of front-wheel drive experience, thanks to the Mini,' but during the 1100's gestation he had 'driven a Citroën D model to learn more about front-wheel drive in larger cars with active suspension and much larger wheels than those of the Mini.' Asked what he believed the limit to front-wheel drive to be, Issigonis responded: 'one of the main factors, beside suspension, is the tyres. I would say that with those we have today, 100 horse power would be the limit.' He also hinted at a larger-engined version which was destined to emerge in 1964 as the 1800.

The 1100's pricing was less draconian than the Mini's, and the public had, in any event, now got used to the concept of front-wheel drive and the 1100 sold for £661 in two-door form and £674 in four-door guise. This made it more expensive than Ford's new Cortina that was respectively priced at £639 and £659. The new impeccably costed Ford was diametrically opposed to the 1100 in practically every regard. A conventional front-engine/rear-drive lightweight saloon, it was an expression of Ford's increasingly sophisticated product planning process. In the course of the model's evolution the Cortina's steering wheel was redesigned four times because it had exceeded the planner's estimates by 1d.[29]

Unlike the Mini there was no comparable Austin version; that would have to wait until the 1964 season. Instead there was the better equipped twin-carburettored sporty MG 1100 which, costing £713, was £102 more. For once badge engineering delivered and with some 116,000 built it was destined to be one of the best-selling saloons in the history of the MG marque. Far less successful were the Riley and Wolseley variants that arrived together with the Austin version. They were destined to sell in penny numbers and Riley as a make was extinguished in 1969.

Although the 1100 made some money for BMC, viewed from his vantage point as Ford's finance director, John Barber believed that the new front-wheel drive model was, like the Mini, underpriced.[30] John Bilton, who had joined BMC as an apprentice in 1960 and in his later years as a product planner worked with Issigonis, believes 'that you could almost make a case for the selling price of the Mini. But it was less forgivable on the 1100 which was more seriously underpriced. It was quite a dramatic product and represented such a step forward over the Ford Anglia and Austin A40. It had so much going for it that for sure it should have been priced higher than it was. I suspect that might have been partly due to the difficulty of opposing sales forces. Originally launched as a Morris, and later Austin, I think it was to do with the wish of Morris people to keep the price down to A40 levels, not being an ice breaker by being a bit more pricey.'[31]

Since pre-war days Alec Issigonis had regularly attended the annual motor show initially held at Olympia, from 1937 at Earls Court and later at Birmingham's National Exhibition Centre. From the 1960s onwards he was invariably accompanied on these visits by Lord Snowdon. 'He used to tease all the other exhibitors in an appalling way. They loved it.'[32] Inevitably the German manufacturers, Mercedes-Benz and Volkswagen, were favoured targets for his jest.

Issigonis was also a familiar figure at the European shows and rarely missed the Geneva, Turin and Paris events, although he gave Frankfurt a miss. On a visit to the French show one year John Sheppard encountered yet another aspect of Issigonis's multi-faceted character. After seeing the cars during the day John and Jack Daniels decided to have a night out in the French capital and booked a table for a Bluebell Girls show at the Lido. 'Issy's response was, "Oh, I'd like to go there". But because we were on an allowance, our table was a little way back from the stage at the side. Nevertheless we changed the booking to four. We all had a meal and afterwards Issy said, "it wasn't a very good table, I know what I'm going to do now." So he climbed over the seats to be in the front row. And we saw the second show. He insisted on seeing it.'[33]

At BMC the accent was on growth and, on presenting his annual report to shareholders in September 1963, George Harriman reported that a new manufacturing facility, CAB 2, was being built at Longbridge alongside what became CAB 1, with the intention of BMC increasing production from 8,000 to 10,500 vehicles per week. Although the latter figure was never attained the public positively responded to the 1100 and, by the time that production ceased in 1974, no fewer than 2.1 million had been completed.

The model encapsulated the concept of what Harriman termed engineering excellence, its design philosophy created by Alec Issigonis and coined in 1960. At the time of the 1100's launch, he summed it up thus: 'If you don't have fancy styling there need be nothing to get out of date. I give ADO 16 [1100] 10 years and the Mini too.'[34]

The idea drew on the Citroën precedent of designing technically advanced cars which would enjoy long production runs that were refined as they progressed. The need for regular and expensive body updates, espoused by companies such as Ford, was thus obviated. That at least was the theory, but in reality Issigonis had little interest in the evolutionary part of the process, which was subject to his own whims and prejudices. To his dismay Charles Griffin watched the 1100, despite its excellence, being gradually overtaken by the opposition. The first significant changes to the model were not unveiled until 1967, a full five years after its introduction.

To implement his design policy Issigonis created what he called the 'cell' concept, as pioneered at Alvis and so successfully used on the Mini, initially for small, medium and large cars. Issigonis decreed that each cell should be headed by a practical engineer, like himself, who was all too ready to take off his coat and roll up his sleeves when the occasion arose. Despite its name, one cell occupied some 3,000sqft of floor space, tucked away from prying eyes in one of the less obtrusive areas of the Longbridge facility.

The Mini had been created in A Cell, headed by Jack Daniels, and at Issigonis's prompting, was responsible for that model's development. The next front-wheel drive car, the 1800, was, as will emerge, allocated to B Cell. Reg Job, Alan Parker, Bob Shirley and Allan Webb, answerable to Charles Griffin, were the relocated 1100 team who had arrived at Longbridge in 1962 and constituted C Cell. This small but able team concerned itself with the evolution of that model although it spent much of its time developing pot mountings to refine the sub frames for the 1100's Hydrolastic suspension. This was axed in 1968 by the incoming British Leyland management after £100,000 had been expended on tooling.[35] D Cell, which developed the Maxi, followed, while E Cell's responsibility was the slowly evolving Austin 3-litre.

Such an approach, says Spen King, 'was not the normal way of doing things. Issigonis's idea of having a team working on a complete motor car was one which no other manufacturer used. You want groups but made up of specialists on engines or transmissions so you can apply the benefits of their expertise. His way now looks ridiculous.'[36]

If the 1100 attained practically everything expected of it, the same could not, alas, be said of the 1800. Designed in B Cell, led by Chris Kingham – 'I was told to volunteer for B' – the process was to be a very 'hands-on' one. Although he ordered white coats for the whole staff, there were only three draughtsmen and four fitters, and in the event they were never used. 'It takes too much time to get them on and off.'[37]

Issigonis was to have a close involvement with its design. And it showed. In 1964 BMC's technical director, at the very height of his powers, was able to boast at the time of the 1800's launch in October that it 'was never discussed at boardroom level,'[38] and Harriman confirmed that 'it's not done by gavel and agenda.' Issigonis was also proud of the fact that he had ignored the products of rival car companies when contemplating the new model. 'I can honestly say I never specifically thought about a competitor... It was common sense not market research.' A glance at new car registrations for 1960 would have told him that a mere five percent of models occupied the 1700/1800cc sector, compared with 19.6 for the 1400/1500 one. But he could have countered that in 1958 the 800/900cc class, the one that from 1959 was dominated by the Mini, accounted for just 1.56 percent of sales.

An element of planning intruded when, five months *after* work had started on the car, George Harriman commissioned a chart which showed the 1800's place in the market and its potential competitors. This confirmed, said BMC's chairman, that 'when we came up with these final statistics we were right.'

The model was discussed informally by four of BMC's executives who met for lunches in Harriman's private dining room in the Kremlin. The quorum consisted of Harriman and Issigonis, production director Bill Davis with Sydney Wheeler present as corporate secretary.

It seems likely that the decision to expend £8 million was made at one of these gatherings, but no secretary was present to record any decisions. In consequence Issigonis could not put a precise date on when the work started although he believed it was 'about two and a half years before the launch.' (It was actually 1960, four years previously). As far as he was concerned, 'we always intended to have three basic models and, having done the Mini and 1100, I was in a sense briefed to do the 1800.' For BMC chairman George Harriman, it was a matter of deciding 'what income bracket we were aiming at and fixing the size, perfor-mance and price. This gave us the volume of production – and away we went.'[39]

As a first step Issigonis's XC9001 concept, abandoned, along with XC9002, when the Mini took centre stage, was exhumed from a static water tank at

Cowley where it had been relegated to in 1957. Transported to Longbridge on the back of a lorry and delivered to Chris Kingham's B Cell, it represented the starting point of the project, but little more, of what was to emerge as the 1800.

As a one-man think tank, the ever-creative Issigonis would then produce sketches by the score which would show the overall dimensions and how the principal components would be positioned. They were then handed over to Kingham and, as far he was concerned, the project was '100 percent problem'[40] which centred on two particular areas. Body flexing was the principal bugbear and although it was eventually solved the 1800 eventually weighed 2645lb, or nearly half as much again as a four-door Ford Cortina. A second difficulty was caused by noise being transmitted through the gear lever; eventually cables, with all their imperfections, rather than rods, were used.

Issigonis was the omnipresent figure throughout the entire process. Either he was on the spot, driving to B Cell in his dark green Downton-enhanced Mini-Cooper, or he was on the phone to Chris Kingham. 'The first call of the day, bang on 8.45, was more likely to be from Alec than from anyone else. He would say 'I was thinking about this business last night...' There would follow regular meetings in the technical director's office with Charles Griffin and engine designer Bill Appleby.

In one sense the engine proved to be the least of Kingham's worries. Using the existing BMC's B Series engine 'saved us £3 million' and it had already been enlarged to 1798cc for the MGB sports car launched in 1962. The B was originally to have been powered by the then current 1622cc unit, but because MG's chief engineer Syd Enever was designing his first monocoque, like Jack Daniels had done with the Minor, it was over-engineered to some extent and in consequence was heavier than anticipated. Had the existing 1.6-litre engine been used it would have made it slower than its MGA predecessor. Less desirably it meant the 1800 version was for a time unique to the sports car.

Therefore the MGB tail wagged the ADO 17 dog, which had originally been conceived to replace the four-cylinder 1.5-litre Farina-styled saloons. The fitment of the 1800 unit, although refined with a five-bearing crankshaft, meant that the model was enlarged to reap the benefits of the more powerful engine. Conversely, this left a gaping hole in BMC's model line between the 1100 and 1800, the slow-selling Farinas excepted. And through that gap from 1963 onwards drove Ford's 1.5-litre Cortina.

The 1800's body represented an uneasy combination of the talents of Issigonis and Pininfarina. 'I gave him a crude box with the windscreen cut off at the doors and windows fixed. He put the curves in, he called it 'motion.'[41] Farina journeyed to Longbridge every month during the 1800's evolution. 'I did the centre sections of the body and Sergio the ends... [He] did the front wings but unfortunately copied the Fiat headlights for the 1800 which were the worst feature of the car weren't they?'[42] Paradoxically, BMC would have been better off sticking with the lines of XC9001. It was much better looking, but the Citroën influence was readily apparent and Issigonis was by this time insistent that his designs should not 'copy the opposition.' As a consequence it has to be said that the 1800 looked like no other and Issigonis believed it to be 'our best car. I loved that car.'[43]

The technical director also had plenty to say about the interior. He wanted to replace the driver's panel with a simple shelf. 'If you make things ornate, people get sick of them.'[44] Charitably the end product might be described as simple, but to many it was plain stark. There was a ribbon speedometer with a parcel shelf below but not much else. Once again the packaging had much to commend it. This was a roomy five-seater, less than 10in shorter than the corporate Farina saloons and 5in shorter than the Cortina.

A pale blue prototype was completed by May 1962 and the Austin 1800 arrived two and a half years later, in October 1964, to mixed reviews. Its spaciousness and performance – it was capable of over 90 mph – and Hydrolastic suspension, particularly on poor roads, were applauded. But, said *Motor*, 'in adopting low geared steering, the 1800 has lost some liveliness of response. The rather "bus driver" control position harmonises less well with this sort of steering.' It also found that 'many drivers dislike the angle of the steering wheel; as if you sit well back from it, as the pedal position requires tall people to do, the upper part of the rim is out of reach.'[45] Alex Moulton recalls that 'we always used to say on the 1800 you operated the switches with your toes.'[46]

Ronald Barker remembers[47] that 'when the 1800 came out we borrowed one for *Autocar*, I drove it down to the Turin Show in 1964 and we went to stay at the Palace Hotel near the railway station. As we arrived I saw a black Peugeot 404 driven by Sergio Pininfarina, with Alec Issigonis, Charlie Griffin and Dick Burzi in it. It was the day before press day and Issigonis said, referring to the 1800, "I didn't know you were coming down in one of these." I said, "I suppose you flew down?" He had. My response was, "What a pity you didn't come by road, Alec, you could have found something out about your car. You've never had one of these in France have you?" He countered with "of course we have, of course we have. How did you find it?"

'I said, "well, suspension-wise for every 10 miles we went along we went a quarter of a mile up and down. It's got no pitch in it. On these long French roads, to get this sort of motion..." He wanted to know how it went and I told him that it went "satisfactorily but it's not very fast". He said "I want to have a long talk with you, can we meet over breakfast tomorrow? I'm flying back tomorrow." We had a drink or two in the bar before dinner and then we sat over breakfast for about an hour.

'Then he said "you're absolutely right. We've never had one in France. I am very bad at getting cars out properly developed. I thought that on this one that I knew all the answers and I thought we could do it on six prototypes [in fact there were only two]. It was a mistake. We should have had them in Scandinavia and everywhere else. I promise you that when I get back I'll have a couple of those cars bashing around French roads."'

Charles Bulmer on *Motor* also had first-hand experience of the Issigonis intransigence. 'I remember that I was criticising the Austin 1800 because of the poor reproduction of its radio. Issigonis's response was "that's because the sound people have told me that the principal speaker wants to be here to get good sound," he pointed to a place on top of the scuttle. Then he said, "that's where the ash tray is. Sensible people don't listen to the radio while they're motoring but they do smoke." That was his attitude.'[48]

The 1800's press launch was staged at the Strathgarve Lodge Hotel at Garve in Scotland and press officer Norman Milne recalls[49] that 16 pre-production cars, which suffered a host of problems, were used for the events that were spread over nine weeks from July to August 1964. On one of them 'I'd been with Paddy Hopkirk, who drove like a demon, and when we checked the fuel average consumption it was only 13.5mpg. In the bar afterwards I mentioned this to Issigonis, whose immediate response was "nonsense." Alex Moulton was also there and said that he had warned him from the start that the 1800 engine went rich on half throttle.'

Another problem that plagued the 1800 for the first two years of its life was engines which succumbed to very high consumption, burnt-out pistons and worn bearings. Up to 10,000 cars a year were affected and rectifying the problem was costing BMC up to £197 per power unit. Ongoing investigations even included checking the porosity of the cylinder blocks. In the end the solution proved almost laughingly simple, as Issigonis revealed in November 1968, after BMC had succumbed to takeover by Leyland. 'I found the "full" mark on the dipstick had been engraved too high up with the result that engines were being overfilled with oil.'[50]

However, this failing had little to do with the 1800's poor record sales. Had the model been successful – it sold for £809 – its potentially higher profit margins could have transformed BMC's finances. But it never attained the rash forecasts of 4,000 cars a week which, over a 10-year period, would have amounted to some 2 million cars, or about the same total as the 1100 achieved. In truth it was built at the rate of about a third of that figure and in all some 219,000 had been completed by the time production ceased in 1975. A Morris version followed in 1966 and a more expensive variant, at £10,040, the Wolseley 18/85, appeared in 1967 enhanced with much-needed power steering, a walnut fascia and leather upholstery. Yet sales only amounted to some 35,000 units over five years of manufacture.

Tantalisingly, there was an indication of what the 1800 could have looked like when in 1967 Pininfarina unveiled its own body, bereft of Issigonis influences. Named the BMC Aerodynamica Pininfarina 1800 and shown at that year's Turin Motor Show, it was a breathtakingly elegant, wind-tunnel tested concept with an abruptly curtailed tail. The lines of a new generation of European cars were to be inspired by it, of which the Citroën GS of 1970 was the first. Pininfarina was to undertake a similar exercise in 1968 on the 1100.

It is not a body Issigonis would have ever designed. Charles Bulmer recalls that 'he thought aerodynamics were rubbish, they weren't significant. As an architect he was terribly interested in how to get the most into the given volume of a car and the Mini and 1100s were masterpieces. He was interested in gaining that little extra amount of space. When he'd done all that he wrapped the body round it as closely as he possibly could. And that was it.'[51]

In many respects the 1800 represented the first demonstrable stumble for BMC and was the first indication to the public that its technical director was perhaps not quite the genius he purported to be. Some of the model's shortcomings highlighted the limitations of Issigonis's 'cell' concept and the lack of BMC's research facilities that sprang from the technical director's belief in his own abilities. Alex Moulton remembers[52] that Issigonis had 'a tremendous sensitivity to cars. He always said "I can tell what a car's going to be like when it goes over a matchstick in the yard." That was obviously a bit of an exaggeration and this was mangled by his detractors to "the only testing he did on his cars was to go into the town to buy a packet of cigarettes." One of his more supercilious comments was "you don't need a research department if you know what do."'

This chimes with Charles Bulmer's recognition that 'the thing that was peculiar about his methods was that he didn't have much of a research department. He didn't really believe in them, development departments, yes, people doing things he wanted to do, but BMC never did research and development on the sort of scale undertaken by other big manufacturers. He didn't think it was necessary. He had the ideas, he knew what was required and he didn't regard research as a profitable sort of thing to have at all. To a considerable extent he and his top henchmen, Charles Griffin and so on, were their own research departments.

'Car manufacturers usually have a department which evaluates the products of competitors in a big way. They take them to pieces, measure everything, see how all the bits and pieces were made, very often there was a cost department to analyse and see if there was anything to learn. BMC didn't have that sort of thing. Again it was down to his arrogance.'

While the 1800 had reached the public, behind the scenes another project overseen by Alec Issigonis was taking shape although, happily, this one never attained production status. Ostensibly a replacement for the Austin Healey 3000 and coded ADO 30, those who encountered this embryo sports car derisively named it 'Fireball XL5,' 'The Thing' or 'The Monster'. To George Harriman it was BMC's response to the Jaguar E-type...

The luckless Charles Griffin was accorded overall responsibility for this project and in later years was to describe it as 'a non event... I couldn't see a lot in it at the time and now I can see even less in the thing.'[53] The starting point was a special bodied Austin Healey 3000 coupé, named Firrere, built by Pininfarina in 1962, which BMC subsequently acquired. It had been designed by three students at Ulm Higher Technical School to commemorate the 10th anniversary of the *Automobile Year* annual.

The intended engine was an unusual one, being a six-cylinder 3.9-litre Rolls-Royce unit that was to be used to power the Vanden Plas R, an executive Farina-based saloon which was to enter production in 1964 and was intended to appeal to company executives. George Harriman had predicted that it would be manufactured at the rate of 200 a week, which was some three times the production rate of BMC's Farina saloons. Like so many corporate predictions this one proved to be wildly over-optimistic.

Ron Nicholls had the job of executing the concept. He recalled that Issigonis 'very much dictated the sort of thing that was required, in broad terms. In particular he was determined to have a very stiff structure. His idea was that we use the transmission tunnel as a main torsional member, boxing it in underneath and then tying it into the sills to give saloon standards of stiffness.'[54] This was driven by the fact that Fireball was to use Hydrolastic suspension. At the rear the technical director specified 1800-style trailing arms rather than the more appropriate semi-trailing arms. Alas, 'Issigonis forgot he was doing a rear-wheel drive motor car and he put trailing arms on the back. It handled like a pig,' remembered Charles Griffin.[55]

The body was a two-seater open one and there were thoughts about making it a coupé. Once a prototype was running Alec Issigonis commissioned racing driver Paul Frere to test Fireball, who later remembered that 'it was too heavy and the Hydrolastic wasn't really right for a sports car. I wasn't very enthusiastic about the thing.'[56] In its original form the engine produced about 170bhp and, in an effort to extract more power from this ioe unit, Rolls-Royce was asked to create a new twin overhead camshaft cylinder head. It then developed a more respectable 268bhp.

When Donald Healey and his son Geoffrey were shown the beast the latter recounted that they immediately recognised they were in the presence of 'a monster, consuming vast amounts of skilled labour, time and money.' Father and son were 'struck completely dumb. We could not believe that anyone could conceive that such a device could be seriously proposed as a sports car.'[57]

As will become apparent, in 1966 BMC took over Jaguar and that alliance was destined to scupper the project because Fireball had been conceived as a challenger to the E-type, which was now within the corporate corral. But, incredibly, there were thoughts about replacing the Rolls-Royce engine with a short stroke XK unit. BMC had intended to market the car in America and estimated a selling price of $4,000 to $5,000, which would have undercut the E-type, which retailed for $6,000 to $6,500. It was only when Geoffrey Rose looked into the project that he discovered that the corporate accountants had got their figures wrong. The car would cost £1,109 to manufacture, which meant a price to the US customer of $5,557, and a UK pre-tax selling price of £1,560. The complex E-type, by contrast, cost considerably less to build, at £1,083.[58] Thankfully Fireball then reached the end of the road. In the process it had absorbed about £1 million of expenditure, no small sum in the 1960s. Longbridge would have been far better off without it.

Such activities were, of course, unknown to the general public. Indeed, during the 1960s Alec Issigonis emerged as a personality in his own right, largely through the success of the Mini, and he found a particularly appreciative audience among motoring journalists. Charles Bulmer, who was technical editor of *Motor*, remembers[59] that Issigonis 'loved to be playful and outrageous if he possibly could. He always talked with a pencil in his hand. He was essentially an architect and a designer rather than a scientist, curiously enough.

'His mathematical ability was dreadful. I remember on one occasion we were talking about something in his office and he had to do a simple calculation regarding the dimensions of an engine. He thought for a long time, he usually had a slide rule in his hand, but of course you can't add on a slide rule, so he picked up the telephone and asked his secretary, "send so and so in from the design office and get him to bring his calculator with him." And it was a very, very simple sum. I'd done it in my head in a few seconds and told him the answer but he didn't believe it.

'It wasn't easy to sway his opinion. The trouble was, it's all part of the arrogance, he didn't study carefully what other people were doing. He was fully confident that his own ideas were better. That's not a good thing, there's got to be a balance, you really need to keep your eyes and ears open to what the rest of the world is doing because you might suddenly find that there is something there you need to adopt. Cars only advance by engineers standing on the shoulders of their predecessors. He was part of BMC's problem.' For his part Issigonis would counter: 'people say, well, let's get hold of a Peugeot and see how someone else does it. And I say, don't be stupid, if I had a Peugeot I should be even more confused than I am now. We *must* be able to resolve our own problems.'[60]

Issigonis did, nevertheless, provide good copy and the articles were invariably accompanied by drawings and sketches which he could produce with great rapidity in the twinkling of his mischievous eye. Lionel Burrell was working on the now defunct *New Motoring* magazine in the 1960s and accompanied journalist Courtenay Edwards to such an interview. Burrell recalls that 'we saw Issigonis in his office. There was an easel with paper on it and as he spoke he illustrated what he was saying with drawings done in blue Pentel. But they always seemed to come back to the Mini! Then at the end of our talk, having signed them, we were presented with them. It was rather like a musical hall act.'[61]

Peter Tothill remembers[62] that, as far as BMC was concerned, 'you never saw a drawing with Issigonis's name on it. There certainly wasn't one on the Mini ones because I looked. He used to go about with a 4B, a very soft pencil. He'd look at what someone had done and go over it. He was a very good freehand artist, brilliant at sketching.'

It is a measure of the acclaim that Issigonis was accorded at this time that his drawings were compared with those of Leonardo da Vinci. The resemblance can only be superficial because Leonardo's were magnificent works of art in their own right, and, above all, the expression of the wide-ranging mind, the work of a true genius who remains an object of wonder some 400 years after his death.

Issigonis did encounter da Vinci's work at first hand in 1960 when he was in Turin to attend the opening of the city's motor museum. John Sheppard remembers the occasion.[63] 'Sergio Pininfarina suggested that we might like to see the da Vinci exhibition there so Issy and Dick Burzi and Jack Daniels and I went. We spent quite a lot of time there because of the displays of drawings and working models. Wonderful. But we hadn't been there for many minutes when Issy turned to me and said "there's nothing new here. We're going." And they did.'

In 1970 the Institute of Contemporary Arts was to stage a display of Alec Issigonis's drawings and sketches, the exhibition having been initiated by Lord Snowdon. He recalls that the 'ICA were amazed to have someone of Alec's background'[64] and he was delighted to see that the display included some of the sketches he had witnessed taking shape on the table clothes of Davos and Klosters some 13 years before.

For his part Issigonis readily dismissed the da Vinci comparison. 'It is only right in so far as they are freely sketched and not really done for any kind of publication...' Some of the 'doodles' at the ICA exhibition 'had no relevance whatsoever to anybody else. Only other people thought it was a good idea to exhibit them. I didn't think they were worth exhibiting. They have very little artistic merit. When I draw a tree the branches look like connecting rods.'[65]

The foibles of BMC's technical director were witnessed first hand at Longbridge by Doreen Schreier,[66] who had moved to Longbridge in 1963 to become Charles Griffin's technical assistant and secretary. As such she shared an office with Issigonis's secretary, Sue Hankey. 'He used to ask the office "go-fer" Frank Lester to "find me the bhp on such-a-such a car as quickly as you can." Frank would come back with the information to which Sir Alec would say, "what about the rpm?" Off Frank would go again. He did it for sheer devilment.' But a note of paranoia was apparent in the Issigonis psyche as "he used to drink Malvern Water because at one stage he thought he was being poisoned…

'He never had any money and would not discuss money so everyone who worked with him was never well paid. Yet he hardly ever claimed any expenses for himself. He was always asking his "boys in the shop" to get his blue Pentels for him and they would buy them 12 at a time. Members of his staff would also have to get cigarettes for him and his mother and they were never recompensed although he would pay for their visits to London at motor show time. My husband Eric was a member of his group and when they were in Oxford, Issigonis would often suggest that they lunched at the Randolph Hotel. Once seated he would disregard the menu and order bacon and eggs. But he hardly ever paid. Eric did.'

1965 was destined to be a turning point for BMC, certainly at director level, as the recognition dawned that, financially, all was not well within the business. Paradoxically it was the year in which George Harriman received a knighthood for 'services to export.' For although the Corporation had produced a record number of cars in 1964, its pre-tax profits of £21.1 million were not much more than those it had recorded in 1958 when it had made some 280,000 fewer vehicles. Even Laurence Pomeroy, who in 1955 had played such an influential role in the switch to front-wheel drive, 10 years later cautioned on the 'lower profitability' that had resulted. Then he reported BMC had been making an average profit of £40 a car: that figure halved in 1965.

Attention had begun to be focussed on the manufacturing costs of the Mini. In truth the car's ingenious mechanicals were far too sophisticated for what had been priced as a cheap car, even though the Citroën two-cylinder 2CV had shown the way forward.

Production engineer Peter Tothill was summoned to a meeting at Longbridge to discuss the matter. 'They'd come to realise the massive cost penalty being incurred by the Mini. A cost comparison was done between it, the A40 and the Minor and all the bits were laid out to see if any parts could be commonised. If, for instance, we used the same sun visor we'd save a half penny a visor. The trouble was the Mini was over-engineered, there was so much cost built into the car with, for example, a penalty of £20 to £25 on the sub frames and suspension.

Because it worked at a ratio of 5 to 1 you've got forged arms instead of pressings and ball and roller bearings for the pivots.'[67]

Later it emerged that the Mini's 10in wheels also carried a cost penalty. John Bilton recalls that 'when researching wheels and tyres I found the 12in wheel was cheaper than the 10in one. It was larger but the tyre was lighter, fundamentally you've got less material. Later 12in wheels were used very effectively on the 1100 and the Hillman Imp. Philosophically you can't argue with it but proportionally it would actually have made very little difference to the Mini's interior space. The bit you had given away would have been more than compensated for by using a standard product.'[68] It was for this reason that 12in wheels were introduced to the Mini, the 1275 GT being the first recipient in 1974, and they were extended to the rest of the line 10 years later.

'The gearbox was yet another expensive feature, namely the very high cost of the aluminium casting that was necessary to create the unique sump. The good news was that it would eventually be carried over to the 1100 and Issigonis, with his forward thinking, knew that he would get more mileage out of the transmission casing. That was a logical bit of planning.'[69]

On the corporate front Sir George Harriman was running the business in much the same authoritarian manner in which Leonard Lord had presided over proceedings. A.E. Smith, the Nuffield Organisation's company secretary, used to attend BMC board meetings and expressed his concerns about how they were run to Peter Tothill. 'I remember him saying to me that Harriman's approach was "absolutely extraordinary". There was an agenda and against every item he used to say "I'm going to defer the decision on that one". When the minutes came out they'd all been taken.'[70]

It says much for the paucity of fiscal talent at Longbridge, coupled with the fact that BMC always tended to promote from within, that Ron Lucas, who since 1947 had been running the Corporation's North American activities from Canada, was brought back to Britain with the title of deputy managing director, finance. 'Sydney Wheeler, who'd been very close to Len Lord, was due for retirement [on 13 April 1965]… I wasn't enthusiastic,' he remembered.[71] 'We had a lovely home at Oakville, Ontario, my daughter was at university… we'd been there for 18 years.' However, his time in the New World meant that he was distanced from the more introspective aspects of the Longbridge culture, which weighed in his favour.

When Lucas attended his first BMC board meeting, chaired by George Harriman, he was alarmed at what he found. 'I could never understand his management style.' For in addition to technical director Alec Issigonis, 'he had three deputy managing directors, production, sales and finance… But he never talked to Bill Davis, Lester Suffield and myself together. Board meetings were designed to convey as little as possible to anyone.'

The chairman of Britain's largest car company 'used to go away in a corner and brood without ever having discussed anything with any of us. If he ever did come to a decision that was the exception rather than the rule. And he vacillated. Things were quite different in Leonard Lord's day. Although a man of impulse, he was a broad thinker, a very tough nut. Harriman never had the guts to fire anyone.

'Issigonis influenced Harriman entirely, he would never talk to us but go and have a natter with Issigonis. Alec had a phobia, he hated styling, he had a contempt for what he called fashion goods, interior trim, that sort of thing. As far as he was concerned, if you've got to have somewhere to sit, it didn't really matter what it was on.'[72]

With such a rigid doctrine emanating from the technical director, Lucas was to witness battles between Issigonis and Lester Suffield, who had been promoted to the post of sales director at the time of his own appointment. 'He was constantly being fought tooth and nail by Suffield who used to say "don't give me that rubbish Alec, I want something I can sell." But he wasn't tough enough and Issigonis had Harriman in his pocket.'

When it came to his all-important financial brief, 'I came off the boat wet behind the ears and I couldn't even understand the board papers. They'd been produced like that since about 1910 or thereabouts. The basis of all pricing has to be volume, the number of vehicles you produce, and if you've got a heavy element of fixed overheads, then the more cars you produce spreads those overheads. I don't know why, but BMC based all its costs on the output of one million cars a year but they never made a million, the best ever was 730,000.' As such, each vehicle was accorded an unrealistically low overhead, which greatly distorted the financial picture. 'We had the facilities to make a million but never did, largely through strikes.'

Such disputes were to become an increasing issue at BMC during the 1960s. To Ron Lucas 'labour relations were the fundamental root problem.' Disruptions to production were bad enough but BMC's management, because it did not have a sufficient grasp of its manufacturing costs, tended to lay all its financial ills at the door of unions. Above all, said Lucas, 'strikes concealed the other problems. Profit margins were hairline thin, three strikes in a row and that was it.' It is a view shared by Geoffrey Rose. 'It would be wrong to underestimate the impact of strikes, but I don't really think they were the real reason for BMC's problems.'[73]

As Ron Lucas looked around the boardroom table he reflected on his fellow directors, both executive and non-executive. One of them, he recalled, never said a word! 'Bill Davis and I were close colleagues. I joined Austin in 1927 and he'd been apprenticed at the Austin and never been anywhere else, he was soaked in the Longbridge philosophy. Lester Suffield was not an innovator, he just wanted to keep the status quo with no fuss. Peter Davies, who was responsible for the service side, was newish [appointed in 1962] and was probably the brightest of the directors.'

As far as the non executives were concerned 'Alec Laybourn was a protégé of Ernest Payton, Austin's chairman who had also been chairman of the Legal and General Insurance Company.' He had died in 1945 and Laybourn, a director of C.T. Bowring insurance, had joined the board in 1957. 'Then there was Robin Stormonth-Darling, a stock broker. Nice chap. He was the uncle of Major Herring, VC, an associate of Herbert Austin,' who had been deputy chairman to Leonard Lord and retired in 1959. 'And what should be more natural than Robin take over, which he did.'[74]

With his financial brief Lucas began to reorganise the way in which the information was prepared. 'One of the first things I did was to present the financial facts in a way in which people could understand. It became obvious to me when I'd been there for a short time that there was something quite fundamentally wrong. But I should never have allowed myself to be diverted into discussions with Pressed Steel [it merged with BMC in September 1965] and I spent hours with Bill Lyons discussing the Jaguar absorption,' an event which was to come to fruition in 1966.

While the latter dialogue was underway Ron Lucas looked to Rover, which was of a similar size to Jaguar and also reliant on Pressed Steel for its body supply. 'I said to Harriman, "once we've digested Jaguar, let's look to Rover, a cracking good company. They've got Land Rover which would take you through any recession." As ever, Sir George prevaricated and in December 1966 news broke of Rover's projected merger with expanding truck manufacturer Leyland Motors, which was confirmed in March 1967. In 1960 it had acquired an ailing Standard-Triumph, taken its products upmarket and transformed it into a profitable business. Leyland's chairman, Sir Donald Stokes, who had made his name as a tenacious truck salesman, now had BMC in his sights.

The merger with Pressed Steel brought in its wake significant managerial repercussions for BMC because Joe Edwards came back into the corporate hierarchy. Lucas regarded him as 'tough, like Lord.' In fact one of the first people to greet Edwards at Longbridge was the ennobled Lord Lambury. 'There is only one man in this office today whose hand I want to shake. I should never have done what I did,'[75] he told Edwards, but the latter was unimpressed. While he continued to run Pressed Steel Edwards also joined the BMC board as deputy managing director and, in June 1966, he replaced George Harriman as managing director. Harriman became executive chairman. This action had been taken, said *BMC World*, 'in view of the extended responsibilities arising from the growth of the group.'[76] Geoffrey Rose is of the opinion that from about this time Harriman was a sick man, the long years of cigarette smoking having taken their toll on his health.

Edwards had already found a ready ally in Ron Lucas and they set about introducing changes that were tailored to ensure BMC's survival by sidelining the empirical thinking that had been such a feature of the Harriman/Issigonis alliance. In May the Corporation was reorganised into four new divisions: home sales, export sales, engineering and manufacturing, with associated improvements to book keeping, following advice from Cooper Brothers, its accountants. Lucas was assigned the task of implementing the plan. Although Alec Issigonis still remained supreme on car development, a product planning team on the Ford model was introduced for commercial vehicles at the end of 1965 although it was two years before the idea was duplicated on cars.

Geoffrey Rose joined the board in the new post of director of planning. His team was to grow to 28 strong and their brief was to analyse prices and market sectors, matters that had previously been decided by Harriman and Issigonis on an ad hoc basis over lunch. An accountant – how the technical director resented his presence – was brought into the engineering division to begin to evaluate the cost of components, again in emulation of the Ford system although still a world away from it.

BMC also began a policy of graduate recruitment, over 15 years since the first of them had begun to trickle into Ford. It even began to recruit externally. 'The sort of people we want are able to train for the top in many professions. Production, Mechanical, Electrical Engineers, Physicists, Chemists and Mathematicians, Economics and Arts graduates,' declared the corporate advertisement.[77] It was titled 'We're looking for people to get ideas like this off the drawing board' and reproduced a drawing by Alec Issigonis of how he envisaged 'the small car of 1984'. Interestingly, this illustration reappeared over 30 years later in the motoring section of the *Daily Telegraph* of 8 March 1997. Incorrectly dated 'the early 1970s', it professed to show Issigonis's thoughts for a Mini in the year 2000…

Most of BMC's new graduates were destined for an embryo market research department of 30, where they accounted for 75 percent of the team. As soon as they began to produce reports, their findings flew in the face of one of Alec Issigonis's most sacredly held tenets: it appeared that the motoring public was beginning to become more fashion conscious. And the arrogance that stemmed from BMC's technical director and permeated much of the organisation was reflected by its findings. BMC would have 'to move away from the approach that our customers are anonymous people who have the opportunity to purchase our goods.'[78]

Edwards and Lucas estimated that they had 18 months for these changes to take effect. But a further expansion in BMC's corporate status occurred in July 1966 when what was promoted as a merger between the Corporation and Jaguar to create British Motor (Holdings) was announced. In truth it was a takeover of

Jaguar by BMC, for which it paid £17.4 million. From the product standpoint it was a good match. BMC's strength was Alec Issigonis's small and medium-sized front-wheel drive saloons, a market sector not occupied by Jaguar, which specialised in lower-volume higher-cost sports saloons and sports cars. Indeed, the E-type of 1961 was often spoken of in the same context as the Mini as an indicator of the vibrancy of Britain's motor industry.

BMC's Austin Healey and MG sports cars were also unaffected because they were far cheaper than the Jaguars but, as already mentioned, it did give Longbridge the opportunity to cancel the potentially calamitous corporate sports car 'Fireball XL5'. A further casualty was another of George Harriman's pet projects, namely the Rolls-Royce-engined Vanden Princess R executive saloon, which had turned into a slow-selling liability and was destined to find a mere 6,555 customers over a four-year period.

The world-famous Jaguar company had been founded and was still being run by Sir William Lyons, who was also responsible for styling his own cars. Sadly, he had no one to inherit the business, his son John having been killed in a car crash in 1955. Aged 66 in 1966, Sir William's mind had been concentrated by BMC's takeover the previous year of Pressed Steel, which supplied Jaguar's bodies. Joe Edwards recalled a meeting held in his office above the Jaguar showrooms in Piccadilly when Lyons broached the idea of a merger. 'He said we had the whole of the body capacity which was his lifeline.'[79] An agreement was reached with BMC which, above all, left Sir William in charge of his beloved business.

Soon after the announcement, William Heynes, Jaguar's accomplished chief engineer, attended a meeting at Longbridge chaired by Alec Issigonis, now, theoretically, his superior. It will be recalled that the two had once worked together at Rootes in the 1934–36 era and they had, of course, since met at motor shows and other motor industry functions. But Heynes was far from impressed by his one-time colleague's performance as an executive. His recollection of the meeting was one of exasperation, as a result of the ramblings of BMC's technical director and his inability to stick to the subject under discussion.[80]

For his part Lyons was to bitterly regret the alliance. He had to a great extent taken George Harriman and BMC on trust and, very unwisely, not taken the advice of professional auditors to investigate the Corporation's financial health, what today would be described as 'due diligence'. For all Lyons's stylistic and administrative strengths he was parsimonious by nature and his daughters believed[81] that he was therefore reluctant to spend money on professional fees. In reality Sir William would only have needed to have consulted back numbers of *The Economist* magazine, where he would have found BMC's deficiencies analysed with a high degree of clarity and objectivity.

Just three months after the Jaguar takeover, at the 1966 Motor Show, Ford replaced its fast-selling Cortina with a Mark II version which was to prove to be as successful as its predecessor. This was in marked contrast to BMC, which had nothing new to display at Earls Court, an absence which prompted an indignant letter to *Autocar* by a reader, E.G. Rawlings of New Barnet, Hertfordshire, who was sufficiently incensed to record his dismay 'at the lack of any new models from BMC this year and perhaps even more so by the meagre non-existent improvements to the existing range... The 1100 might be a good car but it still has a foot-operated dip switch, the crash bottom gear, the lorry driver steering position... after four years!'[82]

In reality BMC engineers had in part been diverted to pursuing projects about which they were unenthusiastic. One had been 'Fireball XL5' and, as will emerge, the Austin 3-litre and Maxi. What they should have been doing, according to engineering director Charles Griffin, 'was to have developed the 1100, we were mad keen to consolidate that.'[83]

Mr Rawlings and his like had to wait a further 12 months for significant revisions to the 1100 when it belatedly appeared in Mark II form powered by a 1300cc engine and all synchromesh gearbox, the latter a feature of the Ford Cortina since its inception and a refinement long resisted by Issigonis ever since the model's introduction. Then he declared, 'I don't like synchromesh on bottom gear... I have driven most of the small Continental cars which have synchromesh on bottom gear, and engaging bottom when the car was stationary was almost impossible.'[84] It was also in 1967 that at long last work started on an 1100 replacement, coded ADO 22.

At the same 1967 Show BMC unveiled a model that can only have further undermined the Corporation's now faltering public face. The Austin 3-litre, visually and so obviously related to the 1800 by the use of its doors, was an inelegant, unrealistically priced rear-wheel drive saloon that was intended to replace the ageing six-cylinder Farina-styled Austin Westminster.

Jeff Daniels, then assistant editor of *Car* magazine, records that on its unveiling at Longbridge, the event was compèred by Raymond Baxter, 'who built up the tension superbly and then the car was driven in. There was a scattering of polite applause which died away to an embarrassed silence.'[85]

Although Alec Issigonis, as technical director, had overall responsibility for this big Austin, its instigator had been chairman George Harriman. The finished product, he told Anne Hope, motoring correspondent of the then IPC-owned *Sun*, was 'the executive car of the future.'[86]

Coded ADO 61, its shape had been finalised four years previously, in 1963, and was another project for which Charles Griffin had little enthusiasm. Overall development was the responsibility of an equally apprehensive Ron Nicholls, who recalled[87] that 'the project was totally against the Issigonis philosophy of what a car should be. It was not conceived from an ideological or engineering standpoint – it was simply seen as a replacement for a vehicle then in the market place.'

The technical director's principal contribution was 'insisting on self-levelling. The first car had a leaf sprung rear and we replaced the rear shackles with a combined damper and levelling unit. It was pretty unrealistic but we went ahead. It was so inefficient we never got it to work.' Nicholls was switched to other duties and a 12-month hiatus then ensued, something that befell many BMC projects at this time, but was reactivated with Hydrolastic suspension. 'Pitch frequencies were very low, comparable with the Citroën DS, and the advantage of interconnected Hydrolastic was that it made a vehicle which handled exceptionally well for its size.'

This was the first occasion that Alex Moulton's system had been applied to a production rear-drive BMC model. At the front double wishbone suspension straddled the units. Trailing arms, of the type used on the front-wheel drive models, were employed at the rear, drive being transmitted via exposed drive shafts. The rear self-levelling system was pressurised by an engine-driven pump.

Gone was the customary Issigonis wheel-at-each-corner approach. There was a capacious 17cuft flat floored boot, and twin headlamps which looked as though they had been added as an afterthought. Under the bonnet was a revised version of the C Series engine which produced *less* power than its predecessor and was also extended to the maligned MGC sports car. The Austin was offered with the option of automatic transmission and most cars were so equipped.

Much of the interior was related to an upmarket version of the 1800; the seats and door cappings were thus courtesy of the Wolseley 18/85. In truth there was more room in the 1800 because of the 3-litre's intrusive transmission tunnel. Priced at £1,418, the new Austin was to be a thirsty tank of a car which returned a consumption of some 15mpg. Although intended to sell at the rate of 10,000 per annum, it staggered into production in mildly uprated form at Cowley in 1968 and by the time its manufacture ceased in April 1971, a mere 9,992 had been completed.

None of these ill-conceived, poorly executed projects should be allowed to cloud Alec Issigonis's extraordinary achievements during his career with Morris Motors and BMC. In 1966 he was awarded the Leverhulme Medal by the Royal Society for his contribution to car design, which specifically related to the Morris Minor and the Mini.

On this and on subsequent occasions when he was in receipt of an honour he was accompanied to London by Christopher Dowson. 'Alec always took a suite at the Hyde Park Hotel, he called it his London house, and a room with a bar and barman. When the Royal Society awarded him its medal, the presentation was followed by a very official invitation to a party afterwards which stated "medals to be worn". He'd been presented with this medal which was suspended on a long ribbon that went over his head.

'For the party he had it dangling down in front of him, rather than being attached to a point above his breast pocket where everyone else had theirs. We suddenly realised the mistake so he and I went into the gents and he said to me, "you're going to have to sort me out Christopher." So I found a safety pin, fortunately I had one in my pocket. I pulled the medal up to a point where everyone else had theirs and pinned the ribbon to the back of his trousers. But then he couldn't bend over... Talk about eccentric!'[88]

Then in 1967 the Society accorded Alec Issigonis a fellowship, its greatest honour. He viewed the FRS initials with immense pride. 'I had to write my name in a book in which the first signature was that of King Charles the Second. And I thought to myself, my word. An ironmonger among the academicians.'[89] He is, to date, the only member of the British motor industry to have been so honoured.

This fellowship was far from being the first accolade he had been accorded. A CBE had arrived with the Queen's birthday honours in 1964 and the same year he was made an RDI (Royal Designer for Industry). Then in 1962 came an approach from an unexpected quarter in the shape of a letter from Dr D.H.A. Leggett, vice-chancellor of the Battersea College of Technology, successor to Battersea Polytechnic which Issigonis had attended, without great distinction, in 1925–28. Its offer of an honorary fellowship was duly accepted.

The College was to evolve into the University of Surrey with a campus at Guildford, from where it would be wholly based by 1970. In 1966 it had offered Issigonis an honorary degree, and he replied that he was 'deeply honoured... and very proud,'[90] and the installation ceremony was held there on 22 October when Professor J.M. Zarek, head of the department of mechanical engineering, spoke of him as 'the greatest car designer of our time.' Later in 1968 came an honorary doctorate from the same source and although he could now be addressed as Dr Issigonis he chose not to be. Ironically this was the year in which BMC fell prey to Leyland.

The end had come in January 1968 when BMC 'merged' with the Leyland Motor Corporation and effectively brought the entire indigenous motor industry within a single organisation. Like the creation of the British Motor Corporation 16 years before, it was nothing more than a takeover, but this time it was BMC who was the junior partner. The alliance had the blessing of Harold Wilson's Labour Government, which had viewed BMC's deteriorating financial performance with some alarm. Indeed Anthony Wedgwood Benn, Wilson's minister of technology, recognised that 'poor old Harriman wasn't up to the job'[91] and although Sir George initially became chairman of the newly created

British Leyland Motor Corporation, he stepped down in September 1968 to become president and died in 1973 at the age of 65.

Harriman's replacement as chairman was Sir Donald Stokes, whose high profile sales and marketing background was thought to provide precisely those ingredients that BMC had so conspicuously lacked. A victim of the takeover was Joe Edwards, who left the company in April 1968. Had he taken over from Leonard Lord as BMC's chairman in 1961 the story might have been a very different one.

In the meantime ADO 14, the last of Issigonis's cars, which was to emerge in 1969 as the Austin Maxi, was reaching the final stages of its evolution. Its announcement had been delayed by the completion of a £20 million factory at Longbridge, which was required to manufacture the model's wholly new E Series overhead camshaft engine and five-speed gearbox. Unfortunately the start of work had been held up by the granting of planning permission. Ian Elliott, then a BMC apprentice and later to be a member of its publicity staff, recalls that 'There were all sorts of things wrong with the Maxi engine which Stan Johnson [BMC's senior engine designer] had to sort out.'[92]

Elliott still retains vivid memories of a three-week period in the summer of 1966 when the partially completed Cofton Hackett facility was being used to store unsold 1800s. 'We'd been told to move hundreds of them from a nearby airfield where they were exposed to the elements. It was hard work, the 1800's steering was heavy, there was no power assistance, and the sun was baking down through the glass roof.' Both building and car were unhappy memorials to the six-year tenure of BMC's technical director; one Issigonis folly was being stored inside another.

Notes

1. Graham Turner, The Mini Comes of Age, *Observer Magazine*, October 1964.
2. Christopher Dowson, *op cit.*
3. Ibid.
4. Bernd Pischetsrieder, *op cit.*
5. Alex Moulton, *op cit.*
6. Bernd Pischetsrieder, *op cit.*
7. Peters, *op cit.*
8. Lord Snowdon, *op cit.*
9. Jon Pressnell, *Mr MG*, *op cit.*
10. Geoffrey Rose, *op cit.*
11. Ronald Barker, *op cit.*
12. Turner, *op cit.*
13. Robson, *op cit.*
14. Ibid.
15. Ronald Barker, *op cit.*
16. Tubbs, *op cit.*
17. Ibid.
18. Alex Moulton, *Automobile Engineer*, *op cit.*
19. Joseph Lowrey, Why is the ADO 16?, *The Motor*, 15 August 1962.
20. Sharratt, *op cit.*
21. Robson, *op cit.*
22. Tubbs, *op cit.*
23. Ibid.
24. Lowrey, *op cit.*
25. BMC's V4, *Small Car*, 1963.
26. *The Autocar*, 17 August 1962.
27. Stuart Bladon, *op cit.*
28. Sogaard, *op cit.*
29. Wood, quoted in Wheels, *op cit.*
30. Ibid.
31. John Bilton, interview with author, 2003. Bilton won a Nuffield Scholarship to Southampton University in 1963, where he took a BSc in mechanical engineering, an award that was not open to his counterparts at Austin.
32. Lord Snowdon, *op cit.*
33. John Sheppard, *op cit.*
34. Tubbs, *op cit.*
35. Allan Webb, interview with author.
36. Spen King, *op cit.*
37. Turner, *op cit.*
38. Ibid.
39. Ibid.
40. Ibid.
41. Ibid.
42. Turner and Curtis, *op cit.*
43. Ibid.
44. Graham Turner, *op cit.*
45. *Motor*, 17 October 1964.
46. Alex Moulton, *op cit.*

47. Ronald Barker, *op cit.*
48. Charles Bulmer, *op cit.*
49. Norman Milne, *op cit.*
50. Secret of a dipstick that blew up a car, *Sunday Telegraph*, 10 November 1968.
51. Charles Bulmer, *op cit.*
52. Alex Moulton, *op cit.*
53. Jon Pressnell, Fireball!, *Classic and Sportscar*, April 1992.
54. Ibid.
55. Ibid.
56. Ibid.
57. Geoffrey Healey, *Austin Healey The Story of the Big Healeys*, 1977.
58. Pressnell, *op cit.*
59. Charles Bulmer, *op cit.*
60. Bardsley, *op cit.*
61. Lionel Burrell, in conversation with author, 2005.
62. Peter Tothill, *op cit.*
63. Lord Snowdon, *op cit.*
64. John Sheppard, *op cit.*
65. Jackson, *op cit.*
66. Doreen Schreier, *op cit.*
67. Peter Tothill, *op cit.*
68. John Bilton, *op cit.*
69. Ibid.
70. Peter Tothill, *op cit.*
71. Ron Lucas, *op cit.*
72. Ibid.
73. Geoffrey Rose, *op cit.*
74. Ron Lucas, *op cit.*
75. Graham Turner, *The Leyland Papers, op cit.*
76. *BMC World*, June 1966.
77. Jonathan Wood, Alec Issigonis, *op cit.*
78. Graham Turner, *Business in Britain*, 1969.
79. Ken Clayton, *Jaguar rebirth of a Legend*, 1988.
80. I am grateful to Philip Porter, co-author of *Sir William Lyons, the official biography*, who was able to hear an account of this meeting from William Heynes.
81. Philip Porter and Paul Skilleter, *Sir William Lyons*, 2001.
82. *Autocar*, Correspondence, 18 November 1966.
83. Charles Griffin, *op cit.*
84. Lowrey, *op cit.*
85. Jeff Daniels, *British Leyland The Truth about the Cars*, 1980.
86. Anne Hope, in conversation with author, 2005.
87. Jon Pressnell, It's no barge! *Classic and Sportscar,* January 1994.
88. Christopher Dowson, *op cit.*
89. Guild of Motoring Writers, Newsletter, October 1988.
90. Letter from Alec Issigonis to Surrey University, 16 May 1966.
91. Tony Benn, interview with author, 1995.
92. Ian Elliott, in conversation with author, 2004.

Chapter Ten

THE CRANKY INVENTOR

'I am the last of the Bugattis, a man who designs whole cars. Now committees do the work.'[1]
Alec Issigonis

THE QUOTATION cited above was made in 1979 and Issigonis was referring to 9X, the last car for which he was wholly responsible. The designs had been completed in 1968 and this all-new Mini replacement was powered by a new engine of his own design. Sadly for its creator it was never to enter production as the formation in 1968 of British Leyland marked the end of Alec Issigonis's influence at Longbridge. In any event the Mini was still selling strongly and what financial resources that were available were channelled to produce a car to challenge the Ford Cortina and to create a replacement for the best-selling 1100/1300 family.

The company was also plagued by an escalation of the labour disputes that had been all too apparent in the BMC years, which grew in severity and frequency. Soon the Corporation was being criticised for producing some of the worst built and designed cars in the world.

But, following the completion of 9X, Charles Bulmer feels that Alec Issigonis had 'shot his bolt technically because he'd had these ideas which had been put into practice. Then they became rather fixed in the way in which ideas tend to as people get older. There were no wonderful new ones clamouring to replace those that he'd done.'[2]

In addition to 9X, Issigonis was also allocated a number of research projects which, like the stillborn Mini replacement, never came to fruition. Although Sir Alec, as he became in 1969, officially retired in 1971 at the age of 65 he did, nevertheless, continue to work, first at the factory and then from his home. Regular weekday meetings were still being held at his Edgbaston bungalow up until the late 1970s. It was now the turn of Christopher Dowson to visit him, rather than vice versa, and, he believes, 'that he never got over the isolation he felt during the Stokes era.'[3]

Sir Donald Stokes had brought with him the team who had transformed Triumph's fortunes although the architect of its revival, his former colleague, Stanley Markland, had by then departed. George Turnbull, its general manager, was now based at Longbridge to run the renamed Austin Morris Division of British Leyland while his chief engineer, Harry Webster, was to take over Alec Issigonis's title and his office.

While there was widespread dismay at the arrival of Donald Stokes and the Leyland management, Geoffrey Rose's attitude was rather different. 'Personally I had a warm regard for him. Donald Stokes and I had known each other since we were both apprentices and secretaries of the graduate section of the Institution of Automobile Engineers in our respective areas. We used to meet. I have to say in my book Stokes was heavily leaned on by Harold Wilson and Tony Benn, sweethearted by them. They told him "you are the top man in the industry. We must have a British motor industry, the boss of BMC is dying and we must bring Leyland and BMC together."

'But the two companies were oil and water. Although Leyland had a degree of volume car production at Standard-Triumph their main business was in heavy trucks at 150 a week, BMC was producing cars in volume at a rate of 7,000 a week. It was very different and I'm sure it was very bewildering for Stokes.'[4]

The British Leyland board was, inevitably, dominated by Sir Donald's appointees, but one of the few survivors of the BMC regime was Ron Lucas, who became a director, and the Corporation's London-based corporate treasurer. Another was Robin Stormonth-Darling, while Sir William Lyons shared the deputy chairmanship with Lewis Whyte, chairman of the London and Manchester Assurance Company. 'He was supposed to be the chap who knew all about the city,' recalled Lucas.[5] 'A non-executive, Lewis seemed to me to have a chip on his shoulder because he hadn't quite made top grades. Stokes had the ability to surround himself with some tough people.' One, who became deputy managing director, was Jack Plane, 'extraordinary chap, South African, I could never quite understand what he was doing on the main board.' Engineering input came from another deputy managing director, Dr Albert Fogg, the first director of the Motor Industry Research Association. Fogg, says Lucas, 'was so jealous of Alec Issigonis and Alec had nothing but contempt for Bertie Fogg.'

'Donald [Stokes] was very cute' and Lucas rated George Farmer of Rover 'who ran a very good shop,' as he did finance director John Barber. 'I worked closely with him, he had all the right ideas… As a thinker and an ability to see problems and as an analyst he was first class. But I don't think he was a very good picker of people.' For his part Barber was soon at odds with Harry Webster, who, unlike his high-profile predecessor, did not have a seat on the board. 'I don't think that Alec had much time for him,' said Lucas with commendable understatement. Issigonis's opinion of Donald Stokes was similarly robust and he invariably dismissed the British Leyland hierarchy as 'that lot.'[6]

For his part Webster recalled that the Mini's creator would 'rarely be seen in the drawing office, and he rarely gave his draughtsman instructions directly, he'd go round after everyone else had gone and scribble instructions over the drawings. He was a loner, too much of a loner. A strange man with a flair for brilliant originality.'[7]

Ron Lucas's forthright views nevertheless highlight the tensions that Lord Stokes, as he became in 1969, had to reconcile in the running of British Leyland. In later years he conceded to the author that 'I wasn't, none of us, were trained to run a company of 190,000,'[8] and his problems were compounded by the fact that the BMC management it inherited was 'much worse than we could have imagined.' He was not alone in this opinion. Geoffrey Rose 'talked to Harry Webster about it. They were very concerned about what they found, it was a shock to them. Poor old Alec's attitude was that, once you've produced a vehicle it would run for 10 years and you haven't got to do anything about updating.'[9]

To Stokes Issigonis was 'a brilliant innovator but innovators aren't always good as chief engineers and putting models into production.' He correctly believed that BMC's technical director had been given too much rein and 'when he decided on something *it couldn't be changed*. He had some odd ideas as well as some brilliant ones, but as far as the individual aspects of a car were concerned he was completely dogmatic.'[10] John Barber disagreed. 'Stokes was a bit stupid with Issigonis because he didn't encourage him when he still had a lot in him. He tended to push him aside and treat him as a cranky inventor rather than a serious person.'[11] But Spen King believes that, as far as Issigonis was concerned, 'British Leyland, from a human and engineering point of view, was an anathema to him.'[12]

Yet to the outside world he was at the very height of his fame and, immediately after the takeover, in January 1968, he went to Russia to give his opinion on a front-wheel drive People's Car. Geoffrey Rose was asked by George Harriman to be his 'minder.'[13] The conversation took place in Leonard Lord's old office, which he then occupied, and 'it was one of the moments that I could see how sick Harriman was.

'We went to Moscow, the small party included Jack Daniels, and we had the VIP treatment from the word go. We all wore fur caps, it was -30C. They wanted Alec to see drawings of their car which in the end was never put into production because they tied up with Fiat instead. We were there for about five days.' Out of an office environment it was a good opportunity for Rose to talk with Issigonis. 'He had a mischievous sense of humour although you had to penetrate a little outer wall. If you were accepted, he'd open up.

'The Russians would start the vodka going at the breakfast conference, the number of wilted aspidistras in that hotel... and Alec was soon drawing front-wheel drive designs on the tablecloths. They were good engineers but he was Leonardo da Vinci to them. One evening when we were in Moscow we were taken to the ballet, not in the Bolshoi but in the Kremlin itself, and I know Alec was very moved by that. He had a rapport with ballet.'

Demotion was in the offing and it came in two stages, the first on 27 February, and *BMC World* reported that Issigonis had 'asked to be relieved of executive responsibilities for the operational and administrative aspects of the Corporation's engineering function.'[14] He would continue as technical director to answer to managing director George Turnbull and 'would report to the board on long-term vehicle research projects.' His executive responsibilities would be taken over by Charles Griffin, who occupied the new post of director of engineering, and his deputy Stanley Dews, who had recently joined BMC from Ford. For his part Griffin was to become disillusioned with the new regime, believing himself to be under employed, although he was responsible for ADO 88, a Mini replacement which evolved into the Mini Metro of 1980. He retired in 1978.

In May 1968 Harry Webster became technical director of British Leyland's Austin Morris division and Issigonis was appointed director of research and development. The end was witnessed by stylist Sid Goble. 'Issy had been away and when he came back he found Webster installed in his office. He came to Dick Burzi almost in tears. The great man had been humiliated. He no longer had an office and didn't know what to do about it. Dick had a room where he kept his old styling models so he cleared those out and put Issigonis in there.'[15] Subsequently Issigonis's role became more formalised: he was allocated a budget, an experimental workshop, run by Eric Schreier, and given a number of projects to undertake. Eric's wife, Doreen, became his unofficial secretary.

In April 1969 came the last production model of the BMC/Issigonis era in the shape of the Austin Maxi, the long awaited 1.5-litre car. Work had started on the project, designated ADO 14, in 1965 and, the 1800 doors apart, insisted upon by George Harriman, this was a wholly new model with, progressively, a five-door hatchback body, which followed in the wake of the acclaimed Renault 16 of 1965.

There was a new overhead camshaft engine and five-speed gearbox, while the Hydrolastic suspension was regarded as being the best of any BMC car. It was suggested that its spacious interior made it suitable for camping. On paper at least the specification appeared a promising one. Sadly the finished product, overseen by Eric Bareham, did not meet expectations, which further undermined Issigonis's authority in the eyes of the incoming British Leyland team. In Geoffrey Rose's recollection 'I got the impression that Alec wasn't particularly interested in the Maxi. It wasn't his baby.'[16]

While BMC's technical director had, characteristically, wanted the smallest possible package, the Maxi had gradually grown in size, with the nose coming to a modest but visually unsettling peak. The interior offered the Issigonis characteristically bleak prospect which brought the response from Stokes that it was 'ridiculously stark, like a hen coop.'[17] Mechanically the 1.5-litre E Series engine seemed reluctant to rev and the actuation of the cable gear change felt vague and imprecise.

John Barber was dismayed by the Maxi. 'Maybe we should have taken the decision and scrapped it. But they'd [BMC] invested a lot of money in the Cofton Hackett engine plant, so we soldiered on, made some improvements, but the car wasn't any good.'[18]

The front end was tidied up and efforts were made to improve its mechanicals but the model received a decidedly lukewarm reception on its announcement. Questioned about the quality of the gear change on the *Today* programme, Donald Stokes chided the reporter with the riposte that he was 'better at asking questions than changing gear.'

Work was soon underway on radical improvements and in 1973 the Maxi 1750 appeared with an enlarged engine, even though this brought it into 1800 territory. A considerably better and more responsive car than the original, with a much enhanced interior and a gear lever with rod actuation, the Maxi remained in production until 1981, by which time 472,098 had been completed. However, a six-cylinder derivative only attracted some 21,000 buyers.

Harry Webster was, in the meantime, overseeing the creation of the wholly conventional Morris Marina of 1971, which was based on the running gear of the Morris Minor. In fact work on a rear-wheel drive, conventionally sprung B Series engined car had begun in BMC days. Charles Griffin, concerned by the high manufacturing costs of the front-wheel drive range, and unbeknown to Alec Issigonis, had moved Allan Webb from C Cell to unofficially work on the vehicle. It was accordingly not allocated a project number.[19]

Because of this preliminary work, Griffin was able to promise the incoming British Leyland regime that the Marina could be in production in two rather than the more usual four or five years. Issigonis's cryptic comment on seeing the finished product was 'that's not a car. Anyone could make that.'[20] Nevertheless, the funds required to produce it were substantial. A total of £47 million was invested in the project, of which about half, some £23 million, was needed to modernise BMC's outdated Cowley factory that British Leyland had inherited.

Next came the replacement for the successful Issigonis-designed 1100/1300 that was still selling strongly in Britain at over 100,000 units a year in 1972, a full 10 years after its announcement. Following a six-year gestation, ADO 67 emerged in 1973 in the dumpy form of the Austin Allegro, British Leyland's 'Car for Europe,' a model that was manifestly inferior to the one it replaced. Styled in-house by a young Harris Mann, it perpetuated the Issigonis front-wheel drive theme. Moulton's suspension was retained, although the interconnected Hydragas system also took over the function of shock absorbers. More compact than Hydrolastic, it had the advantage of not requiring a rear sub frame, a cross tube taking its place.

Spen King recalls, 'the Allegro was a much worse car than the 1100. I can remember going to the styling studio and seeing it as a clay for the first time. I shut my eyes; it was just the look of it.'[21] Destined to sell on the home market at about a third of the rate of the 1100, the Allegro's failure to attract buyers in sufficient quantities marks the demonstrable start of the decline in Britain's indigenous motor industry as a volume producer of cars. A total of 642,350 were manufactured before production ceased in 1982. Ray Horrocks, who ran Longbridge during the Michael Edwardes era, dismissed it as looking 'like an egg [and] was expensive to make...'[22]

In 1974, the year after the Allegro's arrival, British Leyland became a victim of the world depression triggered by the oil price rise of the previous year. In December the British Government guaranteed its capital and the business was nationalised in 1975. Coincidentally, the very same month Citroën, for so long the inspiration for Alec Issigonis's design philosophy, also succumbed to the recession and was taken over by Peugeot, once sarcastically dismissed by BMC's technical director as 'a wise little firm.'[23] Citroën would have to learn, said veteran French motoring journalist, Edouard Seidler, 'cost control, which has always been one of its weakest points, marketing or more generally modern management techniques.'[24] Such deficiencies could have been BMC's epitaph.

With the Mini continuing to sell strongly throughout the 1970s, Alec Issigonis's unique contribution to the British motor industry was reflected in a knighthood that was announced in the Queen's birthday honours on 13 June 1969. The ceremony at Buckingham Palace took place on 27 August and Issigonis was accompanied by Christopher Dowson, who recalls[25] 'it was either on this or the previous occasion that Alec wore morning dress but he also had on yellow socks. At the investiture the Queen said to him: "I see that you're setting a new fashion Alec!"'

Lord Snowdon remembers him 'as a great Anglophile. He was absolutely mad about the Queen. I got him to come and have dinner at Buckingham Palace once. He always used to drink Dry Martinis. I must have told her. Beforehand she got him a large Dry Martini and he never forgot it. A wonderful lady.'[26]

The same week that his knighthood was announced the two millionth Mini was completed on 19 June. Driven off the production line of CAB 1 by George Turnbull, with the newly ennobled Sir Alec as his passenger, the snowberry white car was used by the *Daily Mirror* as a prize in a competition for its women readers. It was the first occasion on which a British car had attained such a productive record and *Austin Morris World* recorded that the figure was made up of 1,271,157 Austin and Morris saloons, 114,904 Coopers and Cooper Ss, 94,518 Mini Mokes, 198,518 Estate cars, 58,918 Wolseley Hornet and Riley Elfs and 339,985 vans and pickups. Current weekly rates of Mini production, including overseas production, amounted to 'nearly 7,000' units.[27]

The Mini clearly still had plenty of life in it – as already noted production would not peak until 1971 – but Sir Alec had by this time designed a replacement. This sprang from his realisation by the mid-1960s that 'the Mini was unnecessarily large and also too expensive to become a best-seller in Europe…'[28] Despite his outward intransigence, its creator was all too aware of its shortcomings and, significantly, of the cost disciplines involved in small car design. In particular, he recognised that the 'A series [engine] was very expensive to make.'[29]

Knowing that he had a capable deputy in Charles Griffin, and with the 1800 seen into production, Issigonis asked his chairman George Harriman 'if he could be relieved of all other responsibilities for BMC engineering.'[30] This was late in 1966. He was, in truth, returning to his first love and what he envisaged was even smaller than the Mini.

This is a project that had begun in the previous year when Innocenti, BMC's Italian licensee, asked Longbridge to produce a smaller version of Issigonis's baby, the work being undertaken by Jack Daniels and ex-MG development engineer Dave Seymour. Issigonis designed a new slimmer and lighter power unit, his concept being interpreted by Stan Johnson, who had not allowed his profound deafness to prevent him from becoming Longbridge's leading engine designer. He was assisted by Fred Eysenck and the new power unit was accorded the 9X coding.

The new engine's slimmer lines saved four inches of room inside the car and the Mini's 80in wheelbase could therefore be reduced to 76. The outcome was the so-called Mini-Mini, and John Sheppard was given the task of scaling down the familiar lines. Although two, or possibly three, were built experimentally the idea was stillborn. Issigonis, however, had other plans for the 9X engine.

But the creation of the Mini-Mini, and the car that followed it, marked Issigonis's ending of his friendship, both personally and professionally, with Alex Moulton, because, instead of Hydrolastic suspension, it featured steel springs all round with MacPherson struts at the front and coils and dampers at the rear. This obviated the need for subframes.

John Bilton says that at this time 'Issigonis's thinking became more and more simplified, he became utterly convinced of the need to go down simpler routes and throw away the complexities of the Mini's suspension. That, at a stroke, took away the rubber cones, the high loads and the complex wishbones.'[31] He also chose to simplify the transmission, and this new approach would also manifest itself in the Gearless Mini, of which more anon. But Issigonis also applied himself to the way in which 9X was to be manufactured.

'He actually uttered these words to me: "I have researched the machine tool industry and enormous savings can be made by buying standardised machine tools that would only operate at 90 degrees." All the manufacturing operations that were required to make the engine's block, crankcase and cylinder head were driven by three axis spindles but all at 90 degrees to each other and they only went vertically and horizontally. He designed the power unit to be made only with those. None of those fancy angles. That illustrates the extent to which his simplification was coming through.'

Alex Moulton believes that Issigonis was 'under the pressure of costs which came from the Ford influence, when Ford people were coming in. He said, putting the blame on me a bit, "you don't need Hydrolastic, you can use ordinary coil springs." 9X had coil springs and struts. It wouldn't have survived, it had no character at all, compared with the real Mini.'[32] For his part Moulton maintained his connection with Longbridge and got on well with Harry Webster, an association which Issigonis also resented.

Ronald Barker recalls: 'what Issigonis said was "when the Mini came out the suspension was absolutely terrific. Fairly soon afterwards the Renault 4 showed what could be done with simple, cheap metal springs." That was why he wanted to get away from rubber and Hydrolastic suspension.'[33] But there was rather more to it than that. Alex Moulton, because of his involvement in the Mini's conception and his responsibility for its suspension, had in the public mind became closely associated with the car and that was something Issigonis was to resent. Barker believes that he wished 'to take all the credit for himself and get Moulton out of it. I really think he could be that bitter.'[34]

Publicly Issigonis chose to distance himself from Moulton's suspension. 'I regret I ever did it. It was a novelty at the time but in retrospect I would have used coil springs,' he declared in 1979.[35] 'The creep of the rubber is far greater than that of a coil spring. The things drops after 10 months and on an old car the drop is well below the six-inch ground clearance.'

John Bilton remembers having 'many conversations around the table with Issigonis on the subject which centred on the rapid deterioration of the Mini rear sub frame demanded by the rubber suspension. He said he was "appalled at the rate at which they had to replace them". In the early 1970s Mini production was running at about 7,000 cars a week worldwide and British Leyland was buying that number of sub frames, mainly from Sankey. But they were also purchasing an additional 4,000 weekly for replacement on relatively young cars. That made a total of 11,000 rear sub frames a week and the same ailment afflicted the 1100.'[36]

On 9X sub frames were therefore dispensed with because there was no rubber and interconnection, which made a significant contribution to reducing the number of parts. There were Ford-style MacPherson struts at the front while at the rear were trailing arms and short transverse torsion bars in the manner of the Renault 4. All suspension loadings could therefore be fed into the body structure. Initial experiments had been carried out on a standard Mini, *sans* front sub frame, with MacPherson struts, courtesy of a Hillman Imp.

John Sheppard was charged with managing the six-strong team responsible for 9X. 'For a time I was on my own and Issy left me to ponder the construction for the small car. He insisted it was to be 120in long although the Mini was actually 120.25in, and I made it 120.'[37] But thanks to the new engine there was 3.5in more legroom and 0.75in extra rear headroom.

Interpreting Issigonis's lines, Pininfarina, in its last major commission for Longbridge, was responsible for the styling and produced a wooden mock-up of 9X which was dispatched to Longbridge. This had a hinging rear window, à la Hillman Imp, but 'I said to Issy, if we're going to have hinges we might as well have something worth lifting up and who wants to post parcels through a window when people have luggage.'[38] The result was a hatchback, a progressive feature for the day and well before they became an obligatory fitment on small cars. Fiat's 127 so-enhanced supermini appeared in 1971 while Volkswagen's best-selling Golf would not arrive until three years after that.

Two experimental 9Xs were built in 1968 although they were 2.5in wider than the Pininfarina mock-up. Made by Doug Adams, the first was finished in red and differed from the second blue example by being fitted with winding windows. This was eventually 'burnt,' motor industry parlance for destroyed. But Issigonis managed to save the second 9X, which used the more familiar Mini-style sliding windows, and it survives in the collection of the British Motor Industry Heritage Trust at Gaydon, Warwickshire.

According to a Design Study on 9X completed in August 1968 and produced by BMC's recently formed car product planning department, the 'new 750-1000cc Mini,'[39] was aimed foursquare at the European market because Continental car makers were 'eroding away British penetration in traditional markets, including the United Kingdom.' Being an Issigonis concept, weight was a key element and 9X was intended to turn the scales at 1120lb, which was 162lb less than the Mini, which then weighed 1398lb.

It has to be said that stylistically the body lacks the curvaceous individuality that made the Mini so appealing. Its prominent circular headlamp units bequeathed their shapes to the contours of the front wings and these were extended throughout the car. On 9X the lights were slightly recessed and thus secondary to the hatchback's more brutal angularity, which is accentuated by an almost flat front to the bonnet. The doors were wider than the Mini's so it was possible for the driver to stick his head out if the need arose.

The single overhead camshaft power unit was completely new, with a maximum design capacity of 1000cc, the plan being to initially offer it in 750 and 950cc forms, increasing to 850 and 998cc two years after its introduction. Issigonis had by this time developed a high regard for the small capacity six 'I have done enough work to know that a small straight six can be absolutely fabulous, as quiet and unobtrusive as a V12.'[40] A projected six-cylinder version of the 9X engine, of 1200 and 1500cc, was developed. These would have powered 10X, a four-door version of the design, intended as a successor to the 1100.

There was a flat Heron type head and the combustion chambers were in the pistons, with two valves per cylinder actuated by a single overhead camshaft driven by a toothed neoprene belt, the Fiat 124 Coupe of 1966 having made that feature a production reality. However, detonation problems during development caused the Heron to be changed to a shallow bowl, which permitted a 10:1 compresion ratio.

There were also thoughts of a 'double ohc head' although 'with hemispherical chambers' for an S version which would have retained the Mini-Cooper's competitiveness. It was calculated that the 850cc unit would produce a respectable 48bhp, which compared with the Mini's 37, and the 998cc units 57bhp, as opposed to 40.

The transversely located engine differed radically in construction from the A Series in having a cast iron block, Austin Seven-style, sandwiched between the aluminium 'head and sump which contained the all-synchromesh gearbox, a concession to fashion, no less! The alternator, integral with the flywheel, was an unconventional aspect of the design, still popular on motorcycle engines, with echoes of the device that had been a feature of the Model T Ford of the 1908–27

The lubrication system of 9X's single overhead camshaft engine. (*John Bilton*)

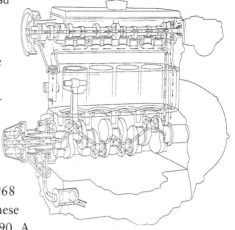

era. The combined unit took up less space than the Mini's, which left more room for the car's occupants.

The number of engine and transmission components were '40 percent less than the current Mini,'[41] there were for instance only two, rather than three, transfer gears between the engine and gearbox. In 1968 it took 120 minutes to assemble these units; the 9X's was anticipated to take 90. A production rate of a hitherto unprecedented 360,000 cars per annum was envisaged, which was some 120,000 more than that of the Mini.

The projected investment figure for 9X, less manufacturing facilities, was an enticing £10 million, the same figure that in 1957 was allotted to the Mini. But the car was a completely new one and sales of its progenitor were still increasing.

Spen King, who replaced the departed Harry Webster as British Leyland's director of product development in 1974, recalls driving one of the 9X prototypes. 'I thought it was marvellous, the steering geometry was all up the creek but it would have been terribly easy to put right. Issigonis wasn't very interested in that sort of thing. It went beautifully, was short and small and not bad looking.'[42]

Unfortunately for Issigonis, the completion of 9X's design coincided with the eclipse of his own career and Donald Stokes and George Turnbull decided instead to concentrate on producing a car that was intended to take on the Ford Cortina. Bilton says that 'it broke his heart not being able to put 9X into production.'[43] although its existence remained unknown to the public until October 1978. Then he was permitted to reveal most details of the car to his friend, Philip Turner, Midland Editor of *Motor*.

Issigonis had been assisted in the design of 9X's cylinder head by his great friend Daniel Richmond but, like Issigonis, his influence would be curtailed by the incoming Leyland management. To Charles Bulmer, 'he was a brilliant engine man, far better than anyone they had at Longbridge in getting power and economy, but not in the sense of design.'[44] In 1970 Downton Engineering had over 60 employees, a turnover in excess of £250,000 and was exporting over 30 percent of its work.[45] Its proprietor was running a Ferrari and his taste for Krug champagne was such that the landlord of his local pub, the Bull, always kept a bottle on ice for him. His other watering hole, the Bat and Ball, which he irreverently referred to as the Truncheon and Testicle, was down the A338 in the nearby village of Breamore. There Löwenbrau lager was his favourite tipple. Paddy Hopkirk recalls[46] a visit to Richmond, 'a gentleman, not the usual rough-talking type,' ostensibly to go fishing at Downton which developed into a session with 'Danny on the Krug…'

It all came to an end when Harry Webster, Issigonis's successor as technical director, informed Richmond that 'he knew him as the man who was responsible for all the Cooper S warranty claims, and then told him his services were no longer required.'[47] This was the model that had given BMC its trio of Monte Carlo Rally wins but, inevitably, its potent power unit placed undue stress on the model's running gear.

Richmond began to lose interest in his business, although Downton did produce tuned versions of the Marina and Allegro. He began to spend more time at Beehive Cottage, a 16th-century thatched residence he owned in Devon close to the River Torr. There he was able to pursue his passion for fly fishing and contributed articles to *The Field* on the subject. He owned the fishing rights on one bank and subsequently acquired those on the opposing one. He told his fishing companion, the medic-cum racing driver 'Doc' David Blackridge, that his consultancy fee for developing the MG 1300 cylinder head had paid for it.[48]

By this time he had left Bunty and had a new lady friend, although all parties were to be overtaken by tragedy. Ronald Barker recalls[49] that 'in 1974 he went into hospital for an operation for piles, which he'd suffered from for years, had a heart attack and then a second fatal one. He was 47.' Bunty had, in the meantime, been carrying on with the business, but made it clear that 'when the dog died' she would go and indeed when this happened, in July 1977, she committed suicide, leaving instructions that Richmond's Mini, on which Downton's 1960s reputation had largely been built, be either destroyed by fire or go to a museum. Happily, it went to British Motor Heritage.

The Design Study for 9X makes reference to 'an automatic option being developed,' its engine being coded 9XP, and that would manifest itself as the Gearless Mini – the name was Issigonis's – and it can be viewed as an extension of his simplification philosophy. It was a project on which he began work in the early 1970s and it would not be until 1980 that it was finally laid to rest. Like the 9X prototype, he was able to retain one of the experimental cars, a green example with duly modified bonnet, completed in 1975.

'We must not call it an automatic transmission,' he told Charles Bulmer, 'because people associate them with poor economy, low performance and high cost.'[50] An automatic Mini, ingeniously but conventionally refined by Automotive Products, had gone on sale in 1966, although sales had not been good. Issigonis's solution was far simpler and took the form of a lightweight car 'with an enlarged engine, modified for maximum low speed torque – the ultimate in simple automatics or, if you like, the simplest CVT [Constant Variable Transmission].'[51] The modified Mini was powered by an A Series engine enlarged to 1375cc but with a kerb weight reduced to 1304lb, which was 175lb less than the production 1275.

Issigonis delighted in showing its potential to favoured visitors to Longbridge by staging an impromptu sprint meeting, accompanied by tyres squealing aplenty, between the Gearless and a standard Mini around the factory's roads. Such escapades delighted the occupants of the Kremlin but the security staff were less amused. The Gearless was always the victor and the results were sufficiently encouraging for it to be pursued.

Using a 9X engine of 1500cc as its starting point, he transformed it from a small, high revving unit to a low revving high torque one. Once this first experimental gearless car was completed it was loaned to Charles Bulmer, who had in 1967 become editor of *Motor* but left in 1973 to join British Leyland as its London-based manager of advanced product planning. 'I had a legitimate interest in everything he was doing.'[52] He returned a creditable 42mpg during a daily commute between his Camberley home and London office and longer cross country journeys.

Lord Snowdon was another temporary recipient of the Gearless Mini. 'He sent it down for me, the eternal guinea pig, to try out. It wasn't very fast. I said "make it go faster Alec." His response was "it's quite fast enough for you, you're not a very good driver!"'[53]

In the summer of 1976 Peter Stubbs, then an executive engineer with Leyland's Solihull-based Advanced Engineering department, began what was destined to be an intermittent involvement with the project that was to last for over four years. His diary entry for 9 June of that year records his first meeting with Sir Alec at his Edgbaston home. 'First it was with Charles Griffin and then alone. He was quite lively, full of humour, slightly impish and right on the ball. He repeatedly spoke of his desire to simplify manufacturing and was horrified by the amount of money that had been spent on retooling to convert the E Series engine to the O Series. But this enthusiasm was at times replaced by depression.'[54]

As far as the project was concerned, 'it took me about a half an hour to see that the Gearless Mini wasn't going to work, before we'd even decided on a budget for it. But I was prepared to go through the motions. I knew you couldn't put a car on the market that didn't have the ability to start fully laden on a 1 in 6 gradient, and didn't have ability to crawl down hills fairly slowly in slippery conditions. Sir Alec did not see these as difficulties, he believed customers wouldn't mind.

'We perceived these as disadvantages. But they were not disadvantages that he wished to be told about. He was dogmatic but that was part of his charm. Frankly, I very quickly discovered that there was no point in mentioning them. Those things were told to Charles Griffin.'

In 1977 Stubbs again met Issigonis on 10 March to discuss the project, then on 8 April, 25 July and 1 September. But as time passed Stubbs could see that 'Alec was failing by this time. He was elderly and not very well. A relative, a beautiful old lady with no English at all, came from abroad to look after him. There was a full-size drawing board in his drawing room and he had a chaise longue, a bed kind of arrangement, that he had to rest on nearby so he could leap up and add a few lines.'[55]

In the spring of 1978 John Bilton, then product planning manager of the power train section, recalls that the project gained an added impetus.[56] 'There was little incentive to make another version of the Mini because the Metro programme was already underway. But the thought was that we might be able to do one which could perhaps be read across into Metro with a Maxi engine using the gearless concept.

'So Issigonis was re-approached in his consultancy role and I worked with him for six months. But the original gearless car had succeeded because it was very light. We spent this time trying to prove that something that worked experimentally at 10cwt would do the same in production form at 14. It was very difficult and was done under Ray Horrocks's jurisdiction, who'd taken over at Austin Morris. We'd see him every few months or so and he'd ask, "how's it going?" Our response was, "we've got to find a way of shedding four cwt." Perspex windows, aluminium doors, bonnet and bumpers were all tried.'

Bilton had in the meantime obtained, 'an interesting vehicle,' an automatic version of the Honda's Civic supermini, the Hondamatic, which like the Gearless Mini used a torque converter but had two gears, low and drive. 'The engine ran backwards which saved an intermediate gear. It had two speeds, low and drive, but this was anathema to Alec. He'd made up his mind for the car to be one geared, or gearless, and he refused to countenance the introduction of a lower gear.'[57] On a broader canvas Spen King and BL chairman Michael Edwardes both drove the automatic Civic, which much impressed them and, believes Bilton, it represented the first link in a chain of events that lead to BL's liaison with Honda being forged in 1979.

'Issigonis was living most of the time at home. But he still came into his office at Longbridge and there were one or two keen engineers who helped him during this period, one of whom was Stan Johnson, an absolute Issigonis devotee and, incidentally, of the three-cylinder engine concept,' recalls Bilton. There had been thoughts of developing such a unit for the Mini but 'Issigonis was not keen, he told me that it 'sounds as if you've left one plug lead off!'[58]

Two white Mini Clubmen, straight off the line, were adapted for what Peter Stubbs termed the FTM (Future Transmission Mini) because there was marginally more room under their bonnets to install an E Series 1.5-litre Maxi engine, the intention being to obtain more torque than the 9X unit was capable of producing. Even then some modifications were required. Subsequent developments of the theme were undertaken on two Allegros to avoid the expense of altering the Mini's engine compartment. What was now termed the FTA (Future Transmission Allegro) used the French Verto two-speed transmission although, diplomatically, Issigonis was not told about this development. 1980 saw the official ending of the project and Stubbs has the distinction of being the last engineer to have worked directly with Sir Alec Issigonis. In December 1980 he joined Land Rover as chief transmissions engineer.

The Gearless Mini was far from being the only project to occupy Issigonis's later years. One related to hydrostatic drive, work that was executed in conjunction with the National Engineering Laboratory at East Kilbride. The NEL had been investigating the possibility of applying the system to very un-Mini like vehicles in the shape of tractors and bulldozers, the idea being that the engine pumped oil to pressurise hydraulic motors on each wheel. Issigonis designed a four-wheel drive Mini to these ends, executed by Bob Shirley, a veteran of the 1100 project, with two oil pumps; working together they gave the highest gear, applying one pump gave the lowest. These were available in all four speeds with the option of either two or four-wheel drive.

'But what we discovered after years of work was that, try as we might, we could not get the efficiency of either pump or motor above 80 percent, which gave an overall efficiency of over 64 percent,' Sir Alec recalled.[59] In addition you also have losses in the pipe line, so the thing would hardly go up hill.' Because of the high pressures involved it used to leave behind a trail of oil.

Issigonis also applied the hydrostatic principle to drive the blades of a petrol-engined motor mower, which his gardener used to cut the grass at Westbourne Gardens. John Sheppard recalls that, like the hydrostatic Mini, it also leaked oil. 'It couldn't contain the enormous pressures and it killed most of his grass.'[60]

Steam had held a lifelong fascination for Issigonis and Spen King recalls 'being rung up by Dennis Poore of Norton Villiers who said that he'd been talking to Alec about a steam motor bike!'[61] Issigonis had known Poore since his hillclimbing days, when the latter invariably drove an ex-Nuvolari 3.8-litre Alfa Romeo. In mid-1969 there had been press speculation that Issigonis was intending to leave British Leyland, to become technical supremo of Norton Villiers, of which Poore was chairman. There he was to 'have a completely free hand in designing new machines.'[62] In the event Issigonis stayed where he was but he did advise the motorcycle company on the potential of hydrostatic drive.

The steam-powered motorcycle was, of course, a flight of fancy, but on the face of it a steam-powered Mini appeared to offer greater potential and an experimental car was completed. After all steam cars had been on the road in the days before World War One and, although quiet in operation, they were limited by the need to constantly replenish water and the time lag necessary to get up steam. It was the virtually instantaneous starting which gave the noisier petrol engine an edge and, in truth, sounded the death knell for steam.

Issigonis drove the steam-powered Mini, executed by Eric Bareham, to the Dowsons for one of his favourite roast pork lunches. There was no indication from its external appearance that there was anything special under the bonnet and he handed to keys to Christopher, suggesting that he 'went down the [three quarter mile long] drive. I opened the door and sat in the Mini; it was covered in Dynotape instructions all over the place! I put the key into the ignition whereupon there was a red flashing light. The instruction beneath it said to wait until it stopped flashing. I suppose that was about three minutes...'[63]

There was no clutch pedal, just an accelerator and brake and a gear lever which indicated F, N and R (forward, neutral and reverse). When Christopher selected F, 'it went like hell. I still had not realised that I was under steam power and I remember being puzzled by the absolute silence of the thing, apart from tyre noise. Soon after lunch I was back in the driving seat again. My duty was to convey Alec back to his house in Edgbaston, he was rather the worse for wear after maybe one too many Dry Martinis...'

Unfortunately, after two years work, this project also came to nought when it proved impossible to produce an efficient steam-power unit because of thermal losses in the boiler and engine. The experiments were undertaken after the rift with Alex Moulton, who, with immense frustration, had to view the proceedings from a distance.

It will be recalled that Moulton had built a steam car at the age of 14 and later 'set up Steam Power, a little company developing steam engines, although I decided they had no commercial future and from 1959 onwards concentrated instead on bicycles. Issigonis had always been fascinated by steam but when he had withdrawn and was working on the steam Mini he didn't consult me one tiny little bit. Wasn't that silly? I had this great well of modern knowledge on the subject. There was a lot wrong with his figures and terrible mistakes were being made.'[64]

In retrospect Issigonis said that he 'never had much faith in either of these projects, but they at least kept me busy and interested. My own opinion is that this type of research is done for prestige reasons by all manufacturers, so we had to join the stream. But my preoccupation has always been to build something that will go into production in the very near future.'[65]

He was similarly dismissive of the gas turbine programme that British Leyland inherited from Rover. He obtained a small petrol unit from George Clarke, whom he had known at Alvis, his department now being part of Rover Gas Turbines. It was a starter unit for a large aircraft engine and a Mini was duly converted by John Sheppard. The unit, located at the rear of the vehicle, still drove the front wheels. Issigonis's feeling was that the hiatus between opening the throttle and the engine response time was insuperable. 'When overtaking on the road, a time lag of even half a second can seem like a quarter of an hour.'[66]

Then he was asked for his opinion on the viability of the Wankel engine, the German NSU company having given the concept a fillip with its acclaimed Ro80 saloon in 1968. After studying the drawings, he advised against it, correctly as it transpired, when despite early promise, the problem of wear in the rotor tips proved, at that stage, to be impossible to overcome.

Issigonis kept abreast of international developments with regular visits to motor shows. As already mentioned he always made a point of attending the Geneva event, which was usually held during the first week of March. On one occasion in the early 1970s he was accompanied by Christopher Dowson, who acted as 'a sort of valet.'[67] They flew from Elmdon Airport in a Piper Aztec with Tom French of Dunlop, who had played such a key role in developing the 10in tyres for the Mini, as the other passenger.

Issigonis had arranged for a party to be held in the cocktail bar of the Hotel les Burges, one of the most expensive establishments of its type in the Swiss capital. However, 'Alec never allowed his bosses to pay for that sort of thing,' remembers Christopher, 'he paid for them out of his own pocket.' Dowson's role was to stage-manage the event. A pianist was present and played extracts from *The Merry Widow*, which was Issigonis's favourite piece of music. Guests came from the motoring press, industry and the world of motor racing and included John Bolster of *Autosport*, Robert Braunschweig of the Swiss *Automobil Revue*, *The Daily Telegraph's* John Langley, Patrick Menham of the *Daily Mirror*, Jack Brabham, Sergio Pininfarina, Enzo Ferrari, Stirling Moss, Rudy Uhlenhaut and, of course, the locally-domiciled Peter Ustinov.

Alec handed Christopher a 'huge wad of Swiss Francs over an inch thick and the first round of drinks came to about £500.' At a late stage in the proceedings Issigonis took to the stage to lambast his old enemy, the Volkswagen Beetle. It was, he said, 'like driving a submarine down the Hagley Road [Edgbaston].' During their stay in Geneva, Dowson recalls 'Alec eating Eggs Florentine, a spinach and poached egg dish, one of his favourite meals, every night.'

Sir Alec's 65th birthday had fallen in November 1971 and he officially 'retired' from British Leyland in the following month. To coincide with his birthday, *The Sunday Times Magazine* published a profile by Judith Jackson, the paper's motoring correspondent, illustrated with photographs of him and his mother by his friend, Lord Snowdon. The meeting did not begin altogether propitiously when Miss Jackson arrived clad in the latest Mary Quant trouser suit. Issigonis's response to her attire was 'My dear, what have you got on, you look like a Bulgarian soldier.'[68] As she reflected 'later I discovered that he enjoys being rude and quotable remarks pepper his conversation.'

His retirement was marked by a lunch held in his honour by British Leyland at Longbridge on 21 December, hosted by George Turnbull. Then he was presented with a Number 10 Meccano set, complete with steam producer and electric power train, something, apparently, 'he always wanted'. Although, ostensibly, he was stepping down from work, Turnbull revealed that while British Leyland's executives normally retired at 65, 'we have bent the rules because we do not believe that Sir Alec's extraordinary talents have waned or dried up,' and predicted that 'new and original concepts still flow from his mind and we want to ensure that these are the exclusive property of British Leyland.'[69] He accordingly became advanced design consultant, continued to work at Longbridge until the late 1970s and thereafter spent an increasing amount of time at his home.

In 1973 Sir Alec had been diagnosed with Menière's Disease, which was to progressively affect his hearing and balance although he was able to continue work. He had an operation although his condition did not much improve. These later years were overshadowed to a great extent by increasing loneliness. His mother had died on 15 September 1972 in her 86th year and her estate was valued at £6,346 gross, £6,062 net. In accordance with her will, made on 13 January 1969, this passed to her son. Had he predeceased her, it would have gone to Vera Griffin, the wife of Charles Griffin, with whom she had established a firm friendship, and Dr Barnado's Homes.

In his later years, following his mother's death, Issigonis was looked after by Ralph Pape and his wife Peggy although they did not live in. He had met Ralph during the years he had stayed at the Albany Hotel, Birmingham, and their titles of butler and housekeeper belied the fact that they were close friends who devoted themselves to his care. Following his mother's death Issigonis took down an oil portrait of himself she had commissioned.

'When his mother died it knocked him absolutely sideways. He drank far too much gin, he really did,' recalls Christopher Dowson. 'Ralph Pape was an absolute godsend. Then there were visits from the likes of me, my father died in 1979, and his other friends.'[70] One of these was John Morris, who had retired in the mid-1960s and Alec Issigonis and his mother had been witnesses to the will he made in 1972. Ronald Barker remembers him[71] as 'one of those larger than life very entertaining characters. Issigonis once took me along to his place for drinks. It was extraordinary, all mahogany and deep burgundy coloured drapes, rather like a decadent London opera house. It was Victorian really and very old fashioned.

'Following Mrs Issy's death, Morris used to go around every evening, have a few gin and Martinis and do what he could to reduce his loneliness.' Then, on 27 April 1976, John Morris died at the age of 75 although the circumstances of his demise were totally in keeping with such an eccentric personality. Ronald Barker takes up the story. 'Issigonis rang me and said "have you heard about John, John Morris? He was around here yesterday evening. We were discussing how much horsepower a man develops and I said 'well, John it's not difficult to calculate, all you use is a staircase, what I haven't here, it's a bungalow, and a stopwatch and you need to know your weight. What you do is stand at the bottom of your stairs with your stop watch, time yourself and off you go." He said "my dear, when his cleaner lady arrived in the morning he was slumped at the bottom of the stairs with a stop watch in his hand. Now he's in hospital."' Morris was to die soon afterwards.

So a friend of some 40 years standing had gone, as had Daniel Richmond, and Issigonis never spoke to Alex Moulton again. Indeed he believes that the egocentricity that had always been part of Issigonis's personality became markedly more pronounced as he got older. However, Barker was able to keep the latter informed with news of his one-time friend. 'I used to go up to see him at Edgbaston on my Yamaha two-stroke motorcycle, spend a few hours there and then ride home.'[72]

There were regular visits from Issigonis's doctor, solicitor, hairdresser and gardener and occasional ones from Peter Ustinov. One day Christopher Dowson called in at Westbourne Gardens after hillclimbing in Lancashire. 'I parked my Brabham BT 15 racing car and trailer outside his house. He was ever so pleased to see me but he immediately asked me to move it. "I won't have cotton reels", he was referring to wide racing tyres, "on my drive". So I took it off to the nearby Botanical Gardens, came back and went into the drawing room. It was a long room. The fireplace was at the far end with a big sofa and couple of arm chairs. But Alec never sat at that end of the room. Then there was a big table and chair to the side of it and an extremely uncomfortable sit-up-and-beg chair. Alec always sat on that, by the door. I didn't realise there was someone else in the room but there was, at the other end by the fireplace. It was Peter Ustinov, sitting there reading a book. But Alec never introduced me. I was furious with him.'[73]

In his conversations with Dowson over the years, Alec Issigonis rarely had a good word to say about other passenger car designers. His disdain for the Beetle can be taken as read and 'he didn't have much time for Mercedes-Benz either, because they were, to him, so heavy and cumbersome. But Alec admired and had got on with the other "dear boy", as he called him, Colin Chapman. Almost on his instructions I bought a Lotus Elan. He was very impressed by the design.'

Just about every other car designer of the day met with his utter disdain, usually because their products were, as he put it, 'merely fashion goods'. There was the inevitable anomaly to this creed, however: 'Alec adored Sergio Farina and Pinin too,' Christopher added, and 'if they didn't produce "fashion goods" who on earth did!'

Dowson was also not in any doubt about Sir Alec's strident opinions on immigration, which he describes as being 'controversial' and 'verged on racialism. Although a foreigner himself, he had very strong views about "sending blacks home" and ridding England of them. By this means the population would be stabilised. I think he was horrified at the parts of Birmingham where you rarely see a white face.'

In 1975 Sir Alec received his last accolade, an honorary Doctorate of Technology, awarded by the Council for National Academic Awards. Two years later, in 1977, he wrote a revealing article on style for *Autocar*, the opening paragraph of which provocatively began 'Cars of Today are so boring.' It contains many of his well-voiced prejudices but he did record his admiration for the Jaguar XJ6 saloon. 'It looks like no other car and is elegant. Of course it was designed by one man, Bill Lyons, not a committee of stylists, therefore it has cohesion.'[74]

The Citroën 2CV came in for its customary acclaim but perhaps more surprising was his admiration for Panther's Bugatti Royale-inspired De Ville. It is not difficult to see why. It reproduced his favoured 1920s styling, accordingly lacked a boot, having a trunk in its place, and was mounted on a separate chassis with its wheels firmly planted at each corner. He also thought the Morgan came closest to his ideal sports car. Otherwise they were 'filled with radios and tape recorders' and had 'winding windows'. His ideal sports car wouldn't have a heater. 'What's wrong with a hot water bottle to keep your feet on?'

Thereafter practically all of Alec Issigonis's time was spent in the seclusion of his Edgbaston home, which he 'deprecatingly' referred to as 'the bungalow.' Crosswords, a lifelong preoccupation, for which he used his familiar blue Pentels, were part of his daily routine. And he enjoyed reading Raymond Chandler thrillers and books which chronicled events in that idyllic, unreal but enticing England created by P.G Wodehouse. Favoured guests sometimes accompanied him to lunch at a nearby Italian restaurant.

In 1979 journalist Christy Campbell visited Sir Alec to write an article to commemorate the impending 20th anniversary of the Mini's introduction for *Thoroughbred and Classic Cars*. Campbell arrived on election day (3 May) and Issigonis went off to the polling station, by Mini. Once there he may have cast his vote for Jill Knight, the Conservative candidate for Edgbaston, on the day that brought Margaret Thatcher to 10 Downing Street. But was he a supporter of the Conservative party? On the face of it one might suppose that Issigonis, with his veneration of the Establishment and his attitudes which could be identified with the British upper middle classes, was politically right of centre. But at least one member of his Longbridge office believed him to be 'one of us.' And she was a socialist.

At Westbourne Gardens Campbell noted 'the spaciously ordered drawing room with a table at one end strewn with sketches and plans, and his study dominated by the world's largest Meccano set he received as a retirement present.'[75] An open fire was burning in the grate of the former and above the mantelpiece was a silver scale model of the Mini, inscribed 'The launching of the Sputnik 26 August 1959. Best wishes Alex and Douglas.' There was another of Nicholas Cugnot's steam-powered artillery tractor of 1769 which, with its single driven front wheel, might be considered the world's first front-wheel drive vehicle. Campbell took the opportunity of looking at Issigonis's bookshelves. 'I noticed nesting ingloriously between Harry Ricardo's autobiography and Setright's *The Designers*, a good edition of *The Wind in the Willows*. Mr Toad in cap, goggles and gauntlets blinking triumphantly through the spine.'

For the same anniversary *Autocar* sent Anne Hope to interview him and while much of the content covered familiar territory, his words were regularly punctuated by 'boring.'[76] He had just been photographed for the front cover of the *Radio Times*. They went to lunch in the Gearless Mini. 'Mark my words, within 10 years the barbaric gear lever will have disappeared,' prophesied Sir Alec. He did not use his seat belt. 'I never wear a safety belt. It is much easier to drive without having an accident.' He also 'never had a car with a radio. I like concentrating on the job of driving. I never smoke when I drive either.'

Later, when Anne availed herself of the Issigonis loo, she recalled that its walls were decorated by two posters, one of the General Motors proving ground and the other of the 'car' which accompanied the American astronauts on their successful moon landing. The latter, perhaps the ultimate in functional vehicles, had been sent to him and inscribed by his friend Sergio Pininfarina.[77]

Later, in 1979, Lord Snowdon again visited Issigonis at Westbourne Gardens to photograph him for British *Vogue*. On that occasion he was accompanied by his son, Viscount Linley, who 'acted as my father's assistant.'[78] A keen classic car enthusiast, in 1988 he bought a Morris Minor, 'which looked beautiful,' and was mechanically uprated with a 1300 Series 3 engine and disc brakes.

When he met Issigonis 'he said he didn't like cars any more and had given his Number 10 Meccano set away.' (It went to Charlie Lane, one of his mechanics). But there was an opportunity to view the 9X prototype 'which I liked very much.

It was a hatchback which predated the Golf didn't it? The house seemed a bit stark inside and Alec prepared my father his favourite dish which was Steak Tartare.

'I can remember him saying that he did not like the Aston Martin DB5 which he described as "an old British lorry."' This had resonances of Ettore Bugatti's denunciation of Bentley as 'manufacturers of the fastest lorries in Europe,' an opinion which Issigonis would have shared.

Charles Griffin and Dick Burzi visited, as did Issigonis's cousin, Mark Ransome, and one day Jeremy Fry arrived, complete with a Morris Minor courtesy of the Bath-based Morris Minor Centre. When Courtenay Edwards, motoring correspondent for *The Sunday Telegraph*, who had known him for many years, arrived he found him unwell. However, 'Alec was able to enjoy his gin and French ("fairly dry if you don't mind"). "The doctor told me not to stop drinking because it helps the circulation of the blood" he explained with a twinkle.'[79] But in 1986 his medic said otherwise and there was no more alcohol.

Sadly, 'towards the end of his life he was ever so lonely,' remembers Charles Bulmer.[80] 'Fewer and fewer people went to see him. He was terribly grateful if you did go. He was not really mobile and quite isolated, having fallen from a position of such power and strength when everyone wanted to see and talk to him. I think he felt it very badly.'

On one of his sorties to Westbourne Gardens in the mid-1980s Ronald Barker, by then a columnist for *Car* magazine, was accompanied by its editor, Steve Cropley. He recalls 'we took a steak-and-kidney pie baked in Cirencester, which was about the only thing he liked to eat at that stage. We talked without much insight about the early days of the Mini (a story about racing early prototypes along a path near the Longbridge offices which was actually a footpath) and he also told the well known one about letting four inches into the Morris Minor to widen it. But he was a very old man, and didn't have much energy, so we left pretty soon. He didn't much care what other people thought, it seemed to me, but he was very glad to see Steady, who was a face from his salad days, I guess.'[81]

Some time after this visit Barker, in his monthly contribution to *Car*, made some complimentary comments about Fiat's Dante Giacosa, words to which Issigonis took exception. 'I took this to be my final rejection from the dwindling circle,' he remembered and it was not until early in 1988, 'that he rang as though there had been no bad feeling between us.'[82]

Sir Alec had been housebound since 1984 and was reliant on full-time nursing care. John Sheppard had been a regular visitor since Issigonis's retirement. 'I used to go and see him about once every five weeks, generally on a Sunday morning for a drink and a chat to keep him up to date with all the gossip at Longbridge. Later he had four nurses looking after him, two each day and two at night. One

Sunday I went to see him and saw that he'd bought a television. He wouldn't have one but the two nurses wanted to watch it in the evenings when he was asleep. He hardly watched it but told me that there was a TV programme he did enjoy. I thought it would be a motoring one but his favourite was Basil Brush!'[83]

It was the increasing cost of this support that forced Issigonis, in 1987, to sell Westbourne Gardens, his home for 24 years. Placed on the market in September by estate agents Shaw Gilbert and Froggat, it was marketed as a 'detached bungalow... the home of Sir Alec Issigonis, designer of the world famous Mini.' Offers of 'around £150,000' were invited.

It was bought by Birmingham solicitor Gurmail Sidhu and his father, who recalls that although Sir Alec was quite lucid, he was 'bedridden with a nurse in attendance.'[84] Contracts were exchanged in February 1988. Issigonis left in March but the Sidhu family did not move in until a few months later because there was much work to be done on the property. Sidhu extended it in the mid-1990s, filling in the gap between the two wings, and in the summer of 2004 a second storey was added to a building which today bears little resemblance to the bungalow that Alec Issigonis once occupied.

He had moved into a ground-floor flat at 39 Hindon Square, Edgbaston, only a short distance from his former home. In the same month of March news broke that British Aerospace was intending to buy the Rover Group and this came to fruition in August. After 13 years of nationalisation, the much slimmed-down BMC descendant had returned to the private sector. Sir Alec was delighted. In an interview given to the *Birmingham Post*, he declared: 'I think it's good if, for no other reason, that the group remains in British hands. It is vital that we keep a British car manufacturer that is capable of designing and turning out mass produced cars.'[85]

He now required constant nursing on 12 hour shifts and when Ronald Barker saw him 'he sat up in a chair besides his bed, head propped between pillows, the voice rather crackly, but the mind in the frail body as incisive as ever.'[86]

John Sheppard, who visited during the first half of September, also found him very frail and later, on the 29th, his long time colleague, Jack Daniels, went to see him and his son Dave recalls how distressed his father was following the visit. 'He did not get upset very often but he was on that occasion.'[87] Just three days later, on Sunday 2 October 1988, Sir Alec Issigonis died at the age of 81, just seven weeks from his 82nd birthday.

The funeral was held close by at St George Church, Edgbaston, on Tuesday 11 October 1988, almost in sight of Westbourne Gardens. The address, essayed in his customary humorous but perceptive style by Peter Ustinov, was read by Sir Alec's solicitor, Timothy Smith of Lee Crowder and Co. of Edgbaston. Ustinov had written of Issigonis being 'both intensely human and one of man's best friends,' then he drew parallels between him and the Mini. It was the design which pleased him above all and it reflected 'his own twinkling personality. His eyes, of a surprisingly intense deep blue, were recalled in the wide-eyed innocence of the Mini's headlights... childish but hugely sophisticated. The Mini was not only a triumph of engineering but an enduring personality as was Sir Alec with his exquisitely caustic tongue and infectious merriment.'[88]

John Bilton was one of the mourners and recalls that there were some 70 attendees and about eight members of his family for whom 'we all signed an attendance book.'[89] Paddy Hopkirk felt 'very sad at the funeral, I was very fond of him and I was sorry that, not being married, he had no children there.'[90]

Just over four weeks later, on 4 November, a memorial service was held in his honour at Birmingham Cathedral when the address was given by Lord Snowdon. Ian Elliott, one time BL press officer, recalls[91] that 'Sir Alec's death caught everyone napping and the organisation of the memorial service was a very hurried affair. My old PR colleague at Austin Rover, Pam Wearing, had the job of pulling it all together and I took time out from my marketing activities to help her out. The main thing was to fill the Cathedral, which we managed quite well. The Bank of England, then alongside St Phillip's, kindly provided post-event refreshments for our VIP party which included Lord Snowdon, Austin Rover managing director Les Wharton and Tony Dawson.

'We decided to put three cars on show outside, in a low key sort of way. One of my ex-apprentice friends, Viv Rowe of Sign Specialists in Birmingham, made up some appropriate plates for two 'Number one' cars, the first Morris Minor and Mini. A new Mini was taken off the line that week which, by a strange coincidence, happened to be 5,100,001.'

In his address Lord Snowdon spoke of Alec Issigonis as 'a true engineer, designer and perfectionist. His genius, for he was a genius, lay in his inventive brain concentrating on pure function and essential truth in engineering design. He hated styling and unnecessary fol-de-rols.'[92]

In his will, dated 24 November 1988, Sir Alec left an estate valued at £112,028 gross, £99,563 net. This was to be shared equally between his cousin, May Ransome, of Topsham, Devon, and her two children, Sally and Mark, and he left his own Mini to Ralph Pape, who had been so supportive in his later years.

The last words on this remarkable life should go to Spen King, a former colleague, distinguished engineer and contemporary of the creator of the Morris Minor and the Mini. 'Alec Issigonis's greatest strength was that he was a superb architect who saw things as a whole. He was a Minimalist who wanted to break new ground if he possibly could. He was lucky to have achieved what he did. Most people don't.'[93]

Notes

1. Hope, *op cit*.
2. Charles Bulmer, *op cit*.
3. Christopher Dowson, *op cit*.
4. Geoffrey Rose, *op cit*.
5. Ron Lucas, *op cit*.
6. John Sheppard, *op cit*.
7. Harry Webster, Harry's Game, *Classic and Sportscar*, November 1990.
8. Wood, Wheels, *op cit*.
9. Geoffrey Rose, *op cit*.
10. Wood, Wheels, *op cit*.
11. Ibid.
12. Spen King, *op cit*.
13. Geoffrey Rose, *op cit*.
14. *BMC World*, March 1968.
15. Sharratt, *op cit*.
16. Geoffrey Rose, *op cit*.
17. Quoted in Wood, *op cit*.
18. Ibid.
19. Allan Webb, *op cit*.
20. Sharratt, *op cit*.
21. Spen King, *op cit*.
22. Quoted in Wood, *op cit*.
23. Motor, 1962, *op cit*.
24. Edouard Seidler, Lessons from France, *Autocar*, 28 December 1974.
25. Christopher Dowson, *op cit*.
26. Lord Snowdon, *op cit*.
27. *Austin Morris World*, July 1969. The Mini Moke figures appear overly optimistic, only 14,518 examples were made in Britain before production was transferred in 1968 to Australia.
28. Charles Bulmer, Alec Issigonis's Gearless Mini, *Car Design & Technology*, June 1992.
29. Hope, *op cit*. The A Series engine then cost £74 to manufacture, the comparative 9X was £68.
30. Philip Turner, The Mini that Might Have Been, *Motor*, 21 October 1978.
31. John Bilton, *op cit*.
32. Alex Moulton, *op cit*.
33. Ronald Barker, *op cit*.
34. Ibid.
35. Campbell, *op cit*.
36. John Sheppard, *op cit*.
37. Ibid.
38. John Bilton, *op cit*.
39. BLMC Volume Passenger Car Division, *Proposal for a new 750-1000cc Mini, Small Car Future Projects (Design Study)*, 9 August 1968.
40. Ronald Barker, *Alec Issigonis op cit*.
41. Design Study, *op cit*.
42. Spen King, *op cit*.
43. John Bilton, *op cit*.
44. Charles Bulmer, *op cit*.
45. *Mini The Racing Story*, John Baggott, 1999.

46. Paddy Hopkirk, *op cit.*

47. Quoted in Baggott, *op cit.* Richmond had told 'Ginger' Devlin, John Cooper's racing mechanic, of his conversation.

48. Ronald Barker, *op cit.*

49. Baggott, *op cit.*

50. Charles Bulmer, Alec Issigonis's Gearless Mini, *op cit.*

51. Ibid.

52. Charles Bulmer, *op cit.*

53. Lord Snowdon, *op cit.*

54. Peter Stubbs, *op cit.*

55. Ibid.

56. John Bilton, interview, *op cit.*

57. Ibid.

58. Ibid.

59. Turner and Curtis, *op cit.*

60. John Sheppard, *op cit.*

61. Spen King, interview, *op cit.*

62. *Motor Cycle*, I am grateful to Mick Woollett, author of *Norton, The Complete Illustrated History*, for drawing my attention to this story. Issigonis's association with Norton Villiers was, he believes, 'at best a consultancy rather than a full-time job.'

63. Christopher Dowson, *op cit.*

64. Alex Moulton, *op cit.*

65. Turner and Curtis, *op cit.*

66. Ibid.

67. Christopher Dowson, *op cit.*

68. Jackson, *op cit.*

69. *Birmingham Post*, 22 December 1971.

70. Christopher Dowson, *op cit.*

71. Ronald Barker, *op cit.*

72. Ibid.

73. Christopher Dowson, *op cit.*

74. Issigonis, Elegance, *op cit.*

75. Campbell, Making, *op cit.*

76. Hope, *op cit.*

77. Anne Hope, in conversation with author, 2004.

78. Viscount Linley, interview with author, 2004.

79. Guild Newsletter, *op cit.*

80. Charles Bulmer, *op cit.*

81. Steve Cropley, communication to author, 2005.

82. Ronald Barker, Issigonis, *Car* magazine, December 1988.

83. John Sheppard, *op cit.*

84. Gurmail Sidhu, in conversation with author, 2004.

85. *Birmingham Post*, 4 October 1988.

86. Ronald Barker, *op cit.*

87. Dave Daniels, in conversation with author, 2005.

88. Ustinov, *op cit.*

89. John Bilton, *op cit.*

90. Paddy Hopkirk, *op cit.*

91. Ian Elliott, communication to author, 2005.

92. Lord Snowdon's address, courtesy Ian Elliott.

93. Spen King, *op cit.*

Postscript

THE ISSIGONIS
INHERITANCE

'I feel very, very proud that so many people have copied me.'[1]

Alec Issigonis

THE TECHNOLOGICAL impact of the Mini's innovative transverse-engine/front-wheel drive mechanicals spread throughout the world's motor industry and by 1984 every major manufacturer of small and medium-sized cars had followed in Alec Issigonis's wheel tracks. But while most car makers adopted the Mini's transverse engine location, few imitated the gearbox-in-sump arrangement, although exceptions were provided by the Peugeot 204 of 1965 and the 1970 Datsun Cherry.

An all-important refinement to the configuration had come in November 1964 when Fiat introduced its Autobianchi Primula model and it subsequently extended the essentials of the engine/gearbox unit to the 128 of 1969 which was its first front-wheel drive model. For while Fiat's engineering czar, Dante Giacosa, 'admired the constructional simplicity of the Mini's coachwork. I was against the high manufacturing costs of the mechanicals.'[2]

As a result when the Autobianchi was being designed he specified an end-on gearbox in the manner Issigonis had adopted for his experimental front-wheel drive Minor of 1951. Coincidentally, it had been described in a patent filed by front-wheel drive pioneer, Walter Christie, back in 1908!

When this inevitably resulted in an experimental car with an unacceptably wide track, Giacosa insisted that the combined unit be shortened. The stalemate was broken by Fiat engineer Ettore Cordiano, who was able to dispense with the clutch's bulky thrust bearing and lever by hydraulically actuating the unit via a rod placed inside the gearbox driveshaft.

This meant that the cost of the combined engine/gearbox used transversely was not much more than when applied to the conventional north/south position. 'I remember the thrill I got when I was told that the problem had been solved,' Giacosa recalled.[3] How this solution must have irked Issigonis, for not only was his solution more expensive, its sump-located gearbox was also the subject of increasing numbers of warranty claims, the motorways of Europe exposing its mechanical shortcomings. Fiat's solution side-stepped, as it were, that problem and today it is used on the overwhelming majority of front-wheel drive cars. But a downside of the arrangement was unequal length drive shafts which produced 'wind-up' on hard acceleration.

Nonetheless, in 1974 Volkswagen adopted the Fiat approach with its Golf, as different in concept to the rear-engined air-cooled Beetle as can be imagined. Nonetheless Issigonis would have had the satisfaction of seeing VW eventually forsake its rear engine and switch to 'his' transverse unit and front-wheel drive layout for a model that was destined to become Europe's best-selling car. When Ford launched its first front-wheel drive model, the Fiesta supermini in 1976, it provided an element of refinement by introducing an additional jackshaft to permit the fitment of equal length drive shafts.

Although America remained the traditional home of the front-engine/rear-drive configuration, a downturn in the world economy in the late 1970s saw the mighty General Motors switch to the Issigonis theme with its X-car line of 1979 and it became the first manufacturer to transversely locate a V6 engine. This was supplementary to its rear drive cars which are still produced, albeit in smaller numbers. Opel, GM's European subsidiary, had introduced the front-wheel drive Kadett in 1979. Similarly Chrysler's K Cars of 1981 saw input from its Japanese Mitsubishi subsidiary which had produced its first fwd car, the Colt Mirage, in 1978.

Neighbouring Honda had back in 1966 launched its front-wheel drive Mini-like N360 although power came from a sophisticated but unrelated 354–598cc two-cylinder engine of motorcycle ancestry. Yet it was not until 1984 that market leader Toyota introduced the Carina, which was its first front-wheel drive model.

Paradoxically all of these companies survive but, as will have been apparent BMC, which pioneered the configuration, succumbed to takeover in 1968 and, after a succession of restructuring and slimming down, ceased trading in 2005. It has paid the price for innovation in the same way in which Panhard, which created the front-engine rear-drive configuration in 1891, succumbed to oblivion. Similarly Essex popularised the cheap saloon body in 1926 and is no more, while Lancia, which in 1950 gave the world the V6 engine, was subsequently absorbed by Fiat.

Between 1994 and 2000 BMC's now defunct descendant, the Rover Group, was owned by BMW which, coincidentally, was headed by Alec Issigonis's relative, Dr Bernd Pischetsrieder. As will have been apparent he initiated a revival of the Mini which appeared in 2001. But while the shape of the new MINI bears some relationship to the original, the space saving attributes and scrupulous attention to weight-saving, so intrinsic to Alec Issigonis's design philosophy, are noticeably absent.

To Alex Moulton it is 'absurdly overweight, really nearer to the 1800, although the shape is evocative of an extremely famous car. I am sure Issigonis would have been shocked.'[4] Lord Snowdon agrees. 'I can't bear the new one. It's huge. Alec would turn in his grave. And it's styling. He loathed anything to do with styling.'[5]

However, Spen King is one of many satisfied MINI owners, for the model has proved to be a great sales success. While Britain remains its most popular market, its reputation is growing throughout the world. Overseas sales are headed by America, followed by Germany, Italy, China, Japan and France. Demand has resulted in BMW being the fourth most productive car company in Britain behind the Big Three from Japan. In 2004 a total of 193,455 MINIs left the Cowley factory, which is built at a site close to where Alec Issigonis created the Morris Minor.

To Dr Pischetsrieder 'Alec was a true petrol head and always enthused about his own ideas. Unfortunately I do think that the times of single-minded geniuses in our industry are over. Alec wouldn't be a good manager in today's industry as he was anything but a team player. Nevertheless, he left a lasting impact on our industry as the one who invented the modern front-wheel drive car.'[6]

Notes

1. Anne Hope, *op cit.*

2. Dante Giacosa, *Forty Years of Design with Fiat*, 1979.

3. Ibid.

4. Alex Moulton, *op cit.*

5. Lord Snowdon, *op cit.*

6. Bernd Pischetsrieder, *op cit.*

End of the beginning. The date is 1 September 1947, the occasion the Brighton Speed Trials, the car the Lightweight Special, Issigonis is at the wheel and his friend Laurence Pomeroy is sitting astride the tail. Alec has written in blue Pentel on the back of this photograph 'with Pom on the return run.' *(Christopher Dowson)*

SELECT BIBLIOGRAPHY

Books on Alec Issigonis and his cars

Baggott, John, *Mini The Racing Story*, Crowood, 1999.

Barker, Ronald, Alec Issigonis, in *Automobile Design: Great Designers and their Work*, David and Charles, 1970.

A.D. Clausager, Gillian Bardsley, Jack Daniels, *The Development of the Mini*, British Motor Industry Heritage Trust, 1993.

Golding, Rob, *Mini,* Osprey, 1979, 1984 and 1994.

Nahum, Andrew, *Alec Issigonis*, The Design Council, 1988, new edition, *Issigonis and the Mini*, Icon Books, 2004.

Pomeroy, Laurence, *The Mini Story*, 1964.

Pressnell, John, *The Mini*, Shire Publications, 1994.

Sharratt, Barney, *Men and Motors of 'The Austin,'* Haynes, 2000.

Skilleter, Paul, *Morris Minor*, Osprey, 1981, 1989 and 2005.

Ullyett, Kenneth, *The Book of the Mini*, Max Parrish, 1964.

Williams, John Price, *Alvis: The Post War Cars*, Motor Racing Publications, 1993.

Related books

Bolster, John, *Specials,* Foulis, 1949.

Palmer, Gerald, *Auto-Architect*, Magna Press, 1997, second edition, 2004.

Platt, Maurice, *An Addiction to Automobiles*, Frederick Warne.

Reynolds, John, *Citroën Daring to be Different*, Haynes, 2004.

Thomas, Sir Miles, *Out on a Wing*, Michael Joseph.

Turner, Graham, *Business in Britain*, Eyre and Spottiswoode, 1969.

Turner, Graham, *The Leyland Papers*, Eyre and Spottiswoode, 1971.

Wood, Jonathan, *The Austin Seven*, Shire Publications, 2002.

Wood, Jonathan, *The Ford Cortina Mk 1*, Osprey, 1984.

Wood, Jonathan, *Wheels of Misfortune*, Sidgwick and Jackson, 1988.

Woollard, Frank, *Principles of Mass and Flow Production,* Iliffe, 1954.

Magazines, newspapers and periodicals

The Autocar (now *Autocar*)
Automobile Engineer
Car
Classic and Sportscar
The Motor (Motor)
Motor Sport
Thoroughbred and Classic Cars
Birmingham Post
Birmingham Evening Mail
Oxford Times
Proceedings, Institution of Automobile Engineers
Proceedings, Institution of Mechanical Engineers (Automobile Division)

INDEX

ND - #0249 - 270225 - C0 - 234/156/21 - PB - 9781780910970 - Gloss Lamination